Jonathan Williams

The History of Radnorshire

Jonathan Williams

The History of Radnorshire

Reprint of the original, first published in 1859.

1st Edition 2023 | ISBN: 978-3-37513-689-5

Verlag (Publisher): Salzwasser Verlag GmbH, Zeilweg 44, 60439 Frankfurt, Deutschland
Vertretungsberechtigt (Authorized to represent): E. Roepke, Zeilweg 44, 60439 Frankfurt, Deutschland
Druck (Print): Books on Demand GmbH, In de Tarpen 42, 22848 Norderstedt, Deutschland

THE HISTORY

OF

RADNORSHIRE.

BY THE LATE
REV. JONATHAN WILLIAMS, M.A.,
AUTHOR OF A "HISTORY OF LEOMINSTER," ETC.

Reprinted from the "Archæologia Cambrensis."

TENBY:
R. MASON, HIGH STREET.
1859.

Mynachty.

CONTENTS.

Introductory Notice	1
Prospectus	4
Dedication	7
Preface	8
CHAPTER I.—Section 1, Situation, Boundaries, &c.	11
Section 2, Name, Etymology, &c.	15
CHAPTER II.—Section 1, Origin of the Inhabitants, &c.	20
Section 2, Character of the Silures, &c.	26
Section 3, Ancient Divisions	28
Section 4, Tommenau, &c.	31
Section 5, Fortifications, Camps, &c.	36
Section 6, Roman Stations and Roads	41
Note on Roman Stations and Roads	57
Section 7, Offa's Dyke	58
Section 8, Castles	61
CHAPTER III.—Civil History, Lords Marchers, &c.	69
List of the Lords President of the Court and Council of the Marches	74
CHAPTER IV.—Titles of Honour	75
List of Sheriffs	79
List of Members of Parliament for County	82
Supplemental Lists of Sheriffs and Members of Parliament	83
CHAPTER V.—Hundreds, Parishes, and Cantref Moelynaidd	85
List of Stewards of Cantref Moelynaidd	94
List of Manors, &c.	100
Forests, &c.	101
List of Crown Lands, &c.	102
Extracts from Domesday	104
CHAPTER VI.—Parochial Antiquities, Hundred of Radnor	106
Parish of Cascob	106
Parish of Colfa	110
Parish of Gladestry	112
Parish of Discoed	115
Parish of Llanfihangel-Nant-Melin	115
Parish of New Radnor	119
List of Bailiffs, Recorders, &c., of New Radnor	128
List of Members of Parliament of New Radnor	132
Parish of Old Radnor	138
Parish of Presteigne	144
Hundred of Knighton	161
Parish of Bugaildu	162
Parish of Cnwclas, Castle and Borough	164
Parish of Knighton	171
Parish of Llanbadarn-Fynydd	185
Parish of Llanano	189
Parish of Llanbister	192
Parish of Llanddewi-ystrad-Ennau	195
Lordship of Stanage	202
Hundred of Pain's Castle	206

CONTENTS.

Parish of Bettws Clyro	209
Parish of Boughrood	209
Parish of Clasbury	211
Parish of Clyro	214
Parish of Bryngwin	217
Parish of Llanbedr Pain's Castle	219
Parish of Llanddewi Fach	220
Parish of Llandeilo Graban	221
Parish of Llanstephan	222
Parish of Llowes	223
Parish of Michaelchurch (Llanfihangel-ar-Arrwy)	226
Parish of Newchurch	226
Hundred of Rhayader	228
Parish of Monachlog, or Abbey Cwmhir	230
Parish of Cwmddauddwr, or Llansaintfraid	234
Parish of St. Harmon	237
Parish of Llanfihangel Fach, or Helygen	241
Parish of Llanhir	242
Parish of Nantmel	243
Parish of Rhayader	247
Hundred of Cefn-y-llys	260
Parish of Blaiddfâ	261
Parish of Cefn-y-llys	264
Parish of Llanbadarn-fawr	268
Parish of Llandegla	269
Parish of Llan-y-drindod	271
Parish of Llangunllo	274
Parish of Llanfihangel-rhyd-Ieithon	279
Parish of Pilleth	281
Parish of Whitton	284
Hundred of Colwyn	284
Parish of Aberedw	285
Parish of Bettws Diserth	289
Parish of Clascwm	289
Parish of Crugina	293
Parish of Diserth	294
Parish of Llanbadarn-y-Garreg	295
Parish of Llanelwedd	296
Parish of Llanfaredd	301
Parish of Llansantfraid	301
Parish of Rulen, or Rhiwlyn	305
Addition to the Account of Castles	306

APPENDIX.

No. I.—Ministers' Accounts, Radnorshire, in the Augmentation Office	309
No. II.—Comitatus Radenore et Brecknock	312
No. III.—Grant of Charles I.	314
Editor's Note	315

HISTORY OF RADNORSHIRE.

INTRODUCTORY NOTICE.

THIS valuable work was compiled by its learned author in the early portion of the present century; and, as we learn from the prospectus with which it is headed, was intended to be given to the world in his lifetime. The manuscript, after his decease, became the property of his daughter; and, through the kindness of that Lady and her Husband, John Jones, Esq., of Cefnfaes, near Rhayader, late High Sheriff of the county of Radnor, it has been entrusted to the Cambrian Archæological Association for publication.

In undertaking the delicate task of editing a posthumous manuscript, we have endeavoured to reconcile the reputation of the author, arising from his extensive researches, with the requirements of modern science. Had Mr. Williams lived till the middle of this century, he would most probably have been among the foremost of the archæologists and naturalists of Wales; he would have profited by the advantages of general science, and by the local discoveries made since that period, and various portions of his work would have been arranged in a different manner. We think, therefore, that we are acting as archæological disciples should do towards one of their masters, by omitting, or at least postponing, some inconsiderable portions of his work, which are now rendered superfluous by the greater amount of scientific and historical knowledge which we have inherited, or otherwise obtained. Thus a general History of Wales and Siluria; an Historical Account of the Lords Marchers; an Account of the Geography, the Geology, and the Agriculture of Radnorshire, may, we think, be either left unpublished, or deferred till the rest of the manuscript is printed; because we possess other more elaborate and more accurate works on the same subjects, written since the time of Mr. Williams, and the authority of which we are confident—judging from the admirable spirit of candour and careful research pervading his pages—he would himself have hastened to admit. The portions, here alluded to, form but a small part of the whole, and the great body of the work is so valuable to the local antiquary, so interesting to the Association, and the archæological world generally, that we congratulate all our members on the opportunity thus afforded of becoming acquainted with its contents.

If, as Editors, we appear to be too diffuse, we must plead for excuse our sense of the responsibility lying upon us to be as careful of our author's thoughts and labours as of our own. We shall omit nothing except what we have mentioned above, but shall print the MS. *verbatim;* and we shall trust to the antiquaries of Radnorshire, and to other members of the Association, for aid in supplying notes and observations, to illustrate, to amplify, and, if need be, to correct the text. We shall hope, indeed, as the work proceeds,—for we intend to go on printing it in consecutive numbers of the *Archæologia Cambrensis*,—to receive numerous communications, whether of observation or of illustration, from gentlemen connected with that county; and we shall endeavour to embody all such additional matter in a running Commentary, or else in a Supplement.

The MS. is a large one, consisting of 659 closely written folio pages, the calligraphy distinct, the arrangement clear and methodical; and its publication in our pages will extend over a considerable interval of time.

The Association is under a great obligation to the owners of this document for the very kind and confidential manner in which it has been communicated.

PROSPECTUS.

It is proposed to publish a general History of the County of Radnor. To conduct an undertaking, of this extensive and multifarious nature, to a desired state of completion, much expense must be incurred, and great application exerted. A subscription, therefore, is solicited, as necessary to the support of the projected work, of which the following sketch, or prospectus, is respectfully submitted to the consideration of the public, and especially of the gentry and clergy of Radnorshire.

Besides adverting to those objects of inquiry, which constitute the subjects of every topographical work,—besides a personal application to original authorities existing in public libraries, and, where he may be permitted, in private collections also,—the author's researches will extend to an exact survey of every parish in the county. Throughout this progress, he will feel grateful to those respectable and intelligent persons, resident on the spot, who shall communicate to him the knowledge of interesting objects, memorable occurrences, the names and short biographical memoirs of eminent natives, the genealogies of families, the transmission of property, the sight of ancient coins and weapons, the account of curious manners and customs, and the perusal of authentic manuscripts and memorials. He trusts that the gentry of his native county will, on this occasion, evince a becoming spirit of liberality, and allow free access to those stores of original authorities which they may possess, without the least tincture of absurd jealousy, or mistaken apprehension, of thereby disclosing secrets, that may be attended with unpleasant consequences. The impartial administration of the laws of their country opposes a sufficient bar to any such fears. He likewise respectfully addresses himself to his brethren, the parochial clergy, whose local knowledge of their respective districts, as well as intimate acquaintance with their own parish registers, renders them peculiarly qualified to communicate valuable and useful information; particularly the antiquities of their churches, the pedigrees of the principal families, armorial blazonings, catalogues of incumbents, curious epitaphs and inscriptions, &c.,—such communications the author will always receive with gratitude.

The struggles which the ancient inhabitants of this district maintained for the preservation of its independence, in opposition to its several invaders, will be faithfully recorded; whilst the errors into which English antiquaries and historians have fallen, respecting the primæval colonization of Britain, the genius of the Druidical system, the scientific attainments of its professors, and the campaigns of the celebrated *Caradoc*, or *Caractacus*, the renowned sovereign of the kingdom of *Siluria*, of which the territory, now called Radnorshire, once formed a considerable part, will be corrected and rectified.

An attempt will likewise be made to throw new light on the original designation and use of *Tommenau, Carnau,* and *Cromlechau*, with which this county abounds; its camps, also, and its castles, will be enumerated and described, and the different æras of their construction, as well as the names of their proprietors, ascertained.

The nature of the close and peculiar connexion, in which this county stands related to the sovereign of this United Kingdom, whereby it has been dignified with the appellation of the " Royal county of Radnor," will be developed and explained, and the patrimonial inheritances of the crown of Great Britain, which it contains, enumerated and described.

To a more complete description than what is to be found in any book of a similar nature of the vast power and authority of the Lords Marchers, and of the nature and extent of the jurisdiction of those dread magistrates, to whom the inhabitants of this district were long subject, will be joined an original account of the extent, privileges, and powers of the paramount manor or lordship of *Cantref Moelienydd*. This dissertation will close with a description of the peculiar constitution of the court of great session, together with the boundaries, customs, privileges and liberties of the capital borough, and of its several contributories.

The state of the agriculture of the county, that principal and most respectable branch of human industry, will be regarded with peculiar attention; the number and efficacy of its medicinal waters will be minutely detailed and described; the seats of its gentry, together with the paintings with which they are severally adorned, will not fail to receive a due tribute of respect; and, under the cheering influence of encouragement, elegant engravings of those seats, and of the picturesque natural scenery with which they are surrounded, will embellish the work.

A new and correct map of the county, taken from actual survey, will be prefixed to the title-page. The entire text of Domesday, so far as it relates to any part of it, will be incorporated with the work. The late returns of population, and charitable donations, will be subjoined to the account of every parish. A catalogue of the *reguli*, or chieftains, of this district, of the lords president of the Marches, of the stewards of *Cantref Moelienydd*, of the lords lieutenant of the county, members of parliament, sheriffs, magistrates, &c., will be transmitted from the earliest periods down to the present times.

With respect to the limits of such an undertaking, it is impossible, on the outset of the plan, to speak with precision. Neither the number of engravings, nor the quantity of letter-press, are at present reducible to accurate calculation. Were the author to call into requisition the amplifying powers which some of his predecessors, in this walk of literature, have exercised, two volumes quarto, containing four or five hundred pages each, might easily start into existence. But he wishes it to be understood, that in the use of the materials committed to him, his great objects will be selection and compression; that the bulk of this work will never be purposely swelled by prolix and insignificant narrative; that none but subjects which derive an importance from their antiquity, their picturesque beauty, or their connexion with historical facts, will be treated of in detail; and that every care will be taken to avoid unnecessary expense. As a conjecture, rather than an assertion, it may be stated, that one volume quarto, of between six and seven hundred pages, will probably complete the work, which will be handsomely printed, on fine royal paper, and delivered to subscribers at £3. 3s., or, with proof impressions of the plates, at £3. 13s. 6d.

A list of the names of the subscribers will be prefixed to the work, and subscriptions will be received by Messrs. Longman, Hurst, and Co., London, and by all the booksellers in the county of Radnor, and in the adjoining counties.

The printing of the work will commence as soon as 300 copies, or as many as will cover the expenses, are subscribed for.

July 16, 1818.

DEDICATION.

To the King's most excellent Majesty.

SIRE,

Nothing could have so highly exalted your royal character and virtues in the estimation of Europe,—nothing could have so firmly enthroned your royal person and government in the hearts of your subjects, as the promptitude and zeal which your Majesty has upon all occasions displayed in aiding and promoting the cause of literature, and in encouraging and patronizing works of utility and information.

Having at much labour and expense collected and digested valuable matter for composing a topographical history of my native county, viz., Radnor; and having at length brought my undertaking to a desired state of maturity, I feel anxious that the appearance of my book before the eye of the public, should be, in one respect at least, commensurate with the dignified nature of its subject, and possess that respectability which the description of a county long distinguished by the honourable appellation "Royal," containing parcel of the ancient patrimony of your crown, and connected with your Majesty in a very peculiar manner, so justly deserves.

The attainment of this object of my hopes and of my ambition, depends upon your Majesty's gracious favour and condescension. The prefixing of your royal name to the list of subscribers to the history of a "royal" county, would be not only an appropriate ornament and decoration, but also confer upon the work itself that importance and dignity which would be its best recommendation and surest protection. I therefore humbly petition your Majesty, that your Majesty will be graciously pleased to take my request into your royal consideration, and to allow me the permission to make this particular use of your Majesty's royal name upon this occasion; an honour which will be as gratefully remembered, as it is now earnestly desired, by,

Sire,

Your Majesty's most loyal and dutiful subject,

JONATHAN WILLIAMS.

Leominster.

PREFACE.

In the first contemplation of this work, the author was not unaware of the many and great difficulties which he should have to encounter. The attempt is entirely new; no regular account of any one part of it having ever before been submitted to the public. Besides, Radnorshire, on a general and transient view, appears little calculated, either to afford encouragement to the arduous prosecution, or to furnish materials for the successful completion, of an undertaking of this extensive and multifarious nature. Diminutive in size and population, inferior in the arts of industry and cultivation, devoid of busy towns, flourishing manufactures, and magnificent structures; of an aspect if not immediately repulsive and forbidding, yet generally sterile and uninviting; and involved in great penury of information; it seems to possess few attractions to interest the antiquary and historian, to kindle the flame of curiosity, and to repay the labour of research. This opinion, however, was found, on further consideration, to admit, like all other generalities, of considerable modifications. For a district which formed a part of the ancient and renowned kingdom of *Siluria*,—the seat of Druidical rites,—the site of Roman garrisons and encampments,—the scene of much hazardous conflict for national liberty and independence, in opposition to the lawless and insatiable ambition of Romans, Saxons, Danes, and Normans respectively,— and which abounds in Silurian vestiges, religious and military,—must necessarily contain and embrace materials, that only want to be developed, in order to be known; and to be known, in order to be felt interesting. To the celebrity which it possessed in ancient times, may be added the just claims to public notice and distinction, founded on the consideration of its present state and circumstances. For seldom can we behold a more diversified and undulating line of surface; such an assemblage of picturesque, if not magnificent scenery; so much sinuosity of valley, and verdure of mountain; such a variety of meandering and fertilizing streams, and so many medicinal springs of approved efficacy and virtue. These, together with the rapidity of its agricultural improvements, the simplicity of manners that still adheres to many of its inhabitants, as well as its close connexion with the imperial crown of this United Kingdom,—the peculiar constitution of its supreme court of judicature,— the incorporation of its capital borough,—and the customs and privileges of the several contributories,—supply a fund of information, not only gratifying to the man of research and curiosity, but also subservient to historical purposes.

Such is the general outline of the following work. The materials of which it is composed have been derived from various sources,—from public libraries and from private collections,—from the usual printed authorities, and the obliging communications of the gentlemen and clergy of the county—particularly the manuscript collections of Percival Lewis, Esq., of Downton Hall, near New Radnor, embracing a valuable mass of original information relative to the most essential parts of the subject, which that gentleman contributed with a politeness and liberality peculiarly flattering. Considerable aid has been received from consulting the *History of Brecknockshire*, published by the late Mr. Theophilus Jones, a work which reflects the greatest credit on the perseverance and abilities of the author. To these and other like authorities, references will be made in the course of the work, either in the subjoined notes, or in the appendix. The topographical division required and obtained the extension of the author's researches to an exact survey of every parish in the county; and, in all instances, wherein it was neccessary to collect the particulars on the spot, adequate pains have been taken to give a complete and accurate detail. The state of the agriculture of the county has been drawn up partly from a publication of

Mr. W. Davies, and partly from oral information. In recording the skill and ingenuity with which the Silurian generals selected their encampments, the author has profited by the perusal of manuscripts left by the late General Harvey, who, for his health, resided some time at Llandrindod, and amused himself with examining the military positions of the neighbourhood. In short, there are few sources from which endeavours have not been used to glean such hints as bear upon the subject. The numerous contributors are requested to accept this general acknowledgment of their assistances in the composition; whilst it is humbly hoped the candid critic will exercise his accustomed lenity towards the unavoidable imperfection of a work undertaken under considerable disadvantages, and embracing and involving subjects of great variety and importance.

CHAPTER I.

GEOGRAPHICAL STATE AND CIRCUMSTANCES, VIZ., SITUATION, BOUNDARIES, EXTENT, NAME AND ETYMOLOGY.

Section 1.—Situation, Boundaries and Extent.

RADNORSHIRE is an inland county, situated in that part of Great Britain called South Wales, and in the dioceses of St. David's and Hereford, and in the province of Canterbury; and lying between 51° 57' and 52° 22' north latitude, and between 2° 46' and 3° 3' longitude west of London.

It is bounded by the county of Salop on the north-east, of Hereford on the south-east, of Brecknock on the south and south-west, of Cardigan on the north-west, and by Montgomeryshire on the north.

The boundary line between the counties of Radnor and Hereford commences at a spot on the left side of the river Wye, opposite to the town of Hay, in Brecknockshire, keeping the course of that river to a place called Rhydspence, where it takes a western direction by Cwmyrafar and Caehiggin to Pant and Cwmyreithin, and northwards to Little Hill, where it turns abruptly to the east as far as Wern; it there crosses the Kington road, and takes an eastern direction for a mile; it then descends southwardly to the old mill, then by Pentiley, Gwernybwch, and Pentre-yr-drain, in a northern direction to Huntington Hill, where it again turns eastwardly between Lanybala and Yat, and New Shop to Pentwyr Castle, by Huntington Park to Rabbar, across Gladestry brook and the road to Kington, leaving Lanyfelyn Hill on the left. It ascends by Great Rabbar, Hargest Hill to Cwmgwillim, thence by Bwlch, between Janter Hill and Whetstone to Rhiwbach, and crosses the Radnor road at Stanner Rocks, which it skirts to the right, and at Lower Harpton crosses Offa's Dyke and the river Somergill; it then passes between Knyll and Byrfâ Bank, which it skirts, passing on to the north through Radnor Wood; and, penetrating through the middle of Radnor Wood, it then turns eastwardly through Cwmrosser Green to a place called Folly; it then descends a little way to the south, by Corton and Wignall's Mill, along the line of the Somergill to Cwm and Broad Heath, where it takes the course of the Lug on its left side to the town of Presteigne, where it crosses that river, and ascends by Boultibrook Mill to Stocking, Cooke's House, Old Warren, by Carter's Lane, where it turns to a place called the Cefn, passing by Hill House, Oak Hill, Black Venn, in a straight line to Black Venn; and, leaving Brampton Brian to the right, it turns to Hearts-ease, where it crosses the turnpike road to Knighton, and so by the turnpike gate it passes on to the river Teame, the line of which it keeps to the town of Knighton, where it crosses the river, and insulates a small tract of land forming the eastern boundary of that borough.

The said river Teame constitutes the boundary line which divides the county of Radnor from Shropshire to a place called Hendrèf, where a stream named Ruthyn Rhiwgantyn separates it from Montgomeryshire. The boundary line then takes a direction to the west to a place called Rhiwdan Llwynglas, leaving Gwain-gellu-felyn considerably to the right; thence passing on to a place named Ambo-benwyn, *alias* Crugain Terfyn, dividing the parishes of Llanbadarnfynydd and Llandinam, near to the beacon called Garn-Vaonce; it then proceeds to a spring called Ffynon trinant, and Esthop, and to the head of the spring leading to the brook Dulâs, then to a huge stone upon the mountains, on which Gwynne, the son of Llewelyn, was slain, dividing the parishes of Llangurig and St. Harmon, where a house or building formerly stood; then crossing the mountains to Cefn Eliwd, where it takes a southern direction to Cefn-Cennarth, where it turns to the west and crosses the river Wye at a place called Safan-y-coed. It then ascends to the head of a small brook named Nant-y-dernol, in a northerly direction; afterwards, taking a small circuit, it arrives at the head spring of the river Talog, which separates the counties of Radnor and Caerdigan. It crosses this river at Tynrhôs, and then descends southwardly to the head of a small stream called Claerwen, and follows the course of the said river, which forms the boundary line between the said two counties, until it discharges itself into the river Elan.

The boundary line between the counties of Radnor and Brecknock is the said river Elan, until it comes to a place called Glyn, about a mile to the south of the town of Rhayader, where it forms a junction with the Wye. From the point of this junction the separation of the two counties is continued by the river Wye, till it arrives at Glasbury Bridge, where the boundary line crosses the Wye into Brecknockshire, at a place called Ffrwd-fawr, and passes to Llwynaubach, about half a mile distant from that river, towards the south; it then turns both westwardly and eastwardly, and takes a circuit around Glasbury church-yard to the left; thence it crosses the turnpike road to the town of Brecon, and passes through the Sconces into the river Wye, which it recrosses, and follows the line of its course to the spot opposite to the town or bridge of Hay, where it commenced.[1]

---

[1] Radnorshire lies between 52° 5' and 52° 25' north latitude, and 3° 3' and 3° 35' west longitude. The Ordnance survey made since the time of the Rev. Jonathan Williams enables us to give the following corrected account of the limits of Radnorshire:—The boundary line between the counties of Radnor and Hereford commences at a spot on the left or west side of the river Wye, opposite to the town of Hay in Brecknockshire, and proceeds along the course of that river to the ferry just above Rhydspence; thence by Cwmrhefr or Cwm 'r afar, Crowther's Pool and Caeau to the Red Lane; by Michaelchurch, Wern, Burnt-Bridge, Pentyle, Gwernybwch, Disgwylfa, Huntingdon Castle and Rabbar; then across Gladestry brook and the road to Kington, leaving Glanfelin Hill on the left; thence by Great Rabbar, Hargest Hill, Cwmgwilim, Bwlch and Rhiwbach; then across the Radnor road and skirting Stannar rocks on the right. At Lower Harpton the line crosses Offa's Dyke and the river Somergill, passing between Knill and Byrfâ Bank, which it skirts; thence through Radnor Wood, Rosser's Wood, by a place called the Folly, Corton and Wegnall's Mill, and along the line of the Somergill to Cwm, Broadheath and Rosser's Bridge; ascending the Lug on its left side to Presteign, it crosses that river and proceeds by Boultibrook Mill to Stocking, Old Warren, Reeves' Hill and Cefn, leaving Brampton Brian on the right; then to Hearts-ease, where it crosses the turnpike

A small part of Herefordshire, called Lytton Hill, in the parish of Cascob, near the town of Presteign, is insulated by the county of Radnor.[2]

The extent of Radnorshire from the junction of the rivers Hendwell and Lug on the east, to the opposite border road to Knighton, and by the turnpike gate on to the river Teame, which line it keeps to Knighton, where it crosses the river, and insulates a small tract of land, forming the eastern boundary of that borough. The river Teame constitutes the boundary line which divides the county of Radnor from Shropshire to a place called Cefn-Bedw. The line then proceeds onward by Castell Bryn Amlwg, or Castell Cefn Fron, to the junction of Nantrhydyfedw and Nant-Rhyddwr. The former brook divides Radnorshire and Montgomeryshire. Afterwards the line passes by some tumuli and intrenchments to Camnant Bridge, following the course of that brook; thence across Llyndwr Hill to Crugyn Terfyn, dividing the parishes of Llanbadarn Fynydd and Llandinam, to a spring called Ffynnon Trinant; thence it follows the line of the river Tylwch to where the Llanidloes road crosses it; then striking off by Cefn-Aelwyd to a huge stone upon the mountains on which Gwynne the son of Llewelyn was slain, and where a cottage still stands, called Lluest Llewelyn. From Wain Cilgwyn the line extends itself to where Nantfach empties itself into the Wye; thence down the Wye to the mouth of Dernol brook, which it ascends, and, taking a small circuit, arrives at the spring of the brook Talog, which separates the counties of Radnor and Cardigan. Afterwards, down the Talog into the river Elan to Abergwngy, and upwards along the Gwngy brook to Llyngwngy. It then descends, enclosing some disputed ground, to Llynfigen-felin, and thence along Nant-y-figen to the Claerwen, where Cardiganshire ends. The boundary line leaves the Wye about a mile to the west of Glasbury bridge, and passing through the great meadows called the Sconces, it crosses the Brecon turnpike road; from thence it passes round Glasbury church-yard, and runs eastwardly. The boundary then turns abruptly to the north, and afterwards to the east, and then again to the north. It then runs between two farms called Llwynau bach and Ffordd-fawr, recrossing the Brecon turnpike road, and rejoins the Wye at a bend some distance above Llowes Church.   J. J.

[2] By the statute 7th and 8th Victoria, c. 61, the detached portion of Radnorshire, on the south-east side of the river Wye, has been annexed to Brecknockshire for all purposes; in consequence of which the river Wye is now the boundary of the county of Radnor from its junction with the Elan, near Rhayader, to the town of Hay, and the repairs of Glasbury bridge, which formerly fell on the county of Radnor, are now done at the joint expense of the counties of Radnor and Brecknock. The detached portion of Herefordshire, in the parish of Cascob, has by the same Act become part of Radnorshire.   W.

Ty-yn-y-rhôs on the west, is about 29 miles in length; and from Rhiwthyn Rhiwgantyn brook on the north, to Rhyd Helyg, or Sally Ford, on the south, is about 26 miles in breadth. Various, however, and differing from each other, are the estimated contents of its area. One gentleman lays it down so low as 385 square miles; another raises it to 447 ditto; a third to 455, and a fourth to 510 ditto. Perhaps a middle statement between the two greatest extremes approximates nearest to the truth. Its circumference, according to some calculations, exceeds 90 miles, encompassing a territory of 310,000 acres.[3]

Section 2.—Its Name and Etymology.

The signification of the name, as well British as English, which designates this district, is enveloped in such obscurity as hitherto to baffle the ingenuity and elude the researches of modern antiquaries. At a period so remote from its original imposition, the reader will be content with such information as a subject so necessarily obscure and difficult will admit, and will judiciously exercise his discretion with respect to the preference which the various conjectures that have been formed upon it deserve. In doing this, he will previously reflect that this is the only county in the Principality to which the British word *Maes* is prefixed, and that there must have existed some reason for this peculiarity.

The late Mr. Theophilus Jones, who is universally acknowledged to have been deeply skilled in British history and antiquities, was of opinion that this county received its name, *Maesyfedd*, from a chieftain called *Hyfaidd*.[4] Mr. Jones' usual acuteness appears in the mind of the author to have failed him in this particular. For, surely, a district occupied by the *Silures*, and tra-

---

[3] The Rev. Walter Davies in his Report of the Agriculture of Wales, published in 1811, estimated Radnorshire to contain 86,000 acres of tillage land, 40,000 acres of meadow and pasture, and 200,000 acres of waste; total, 326,000 acres.

[4] History of Breconshire, i. p. 69.

versed by Roman legions, must have possessed a name many centuries prior to the existence of a chieftain, whose father, *Caradoc Fraich-frâs*, was the contemporary only of the renowned Arthur. Besides, if Mr. Jones' conjecture be correct, this county would have been denominated *Sir Hyvaidd*, and not *Sir Faesyfed*; as *Brecknockshire*, if his statement be received, is called *Sir Frycheiniog*, from *Brychyn*, its chieftain. But there exist strong grounds for doubting the justness of Mr. Jones' derivation, even of the appellative *Brycheiniog*, as a reference to the appendix will evince. This opportunity is favourable for expressing an unqualified disapprobation of the too general practice of deducing the British appellations of large and extensive districts from the names of their respective chieftains,— a mode of interpretation which has given rise to innumerable fictions, and peopled countries with persons who never had existence. When an author finds himself at a loss to develope the etymon of the name of a district or country, he indolently supplies his inability, or his ignorance, by the introduction of some imaginary and fabulous hero, on whom is conferred an appellation corresponding in sound: thus, *Geoffrey of Monmouth*, unable to explain the signification of the name *Britain*, falsely imputes its origin to *Brutus*, a Trojan, the supposed discoverer and colonizer of the island. To ascribe the British names of places to chieftains is a practice pregnant of a thousand errors, and has occasioned inextricable confusion in history. Among the ancient Britons a reversed order universally and unexceptionably prevailed; and to the territory the chieftain was beholden for his name, and not the territory to the chieftain. The Welsh, indeed, as they degenerated from the virtues, so were they less tenacious of the customs, of their ancestors, adopted the presumptuous practice of their arrogant invaders, who, in order to establish a property in the lands, the possession of which they had violently wrested from the natives, called them after their own names. Thus *Ewias Harold*, *Ewias Lacy*, and *Tre-faldwin*, were imitated by *Powis Fadoc*, *Powis Wenwynyn*, and *Tir-raulph*. Different was the mode observed by the ancient Britons; their names of places are exceedingly significative, appropriate and impressive; they describe some peculiar and distinguishing feature of the situation, which is, at the same time, pleasing to the eye and soothing to the mind; and it is rather by paying due attention to these characteristics, than by having recourse to the creation of imaginary persons, that the true etymology of the ancient names of places and districts in Britain is to be obtained.

Let this rule be applied to the derivation of *Maesyfed*, or *Maes y Fed;* for on the mode of its orthography depends its signification. That there existed a chieftain of the name of *Hyfaidd*, who resided at *Maesyfed*, is an authenticated point of history. But probability preponderates in favour of the presumption that he received his name from the place, rather than the place from him. If the former manner of writing the name, viz., *Maesyfed*, be preferred, it becomes susceptible of a twofold etymology. First, *Maesyfed* signifies a " field that drinks or absorbs wet or moisture." This interpretation corresponds with the quality of the soil that characterizes the district which lies above and below the town of New Radnor, where the river Somergill is completely absorbed for a considerable space, and emerges from its subterraneous course, and reappears, on encountering, at the distance of about a mile or more, a different and more tenacious soil. Secondly, the word *Maesyfed* implies " a moist or damp field." This signification accords with the nature of the soil of the middle, or interior, parts of this county, which, principally consisting of clay, is retentive of wet or moisture.

If the latter mode of spelling the name be adopted, it is necessary to attend to a striking peculiarity in the British language, which requires the Æolic digamma *F* to be pronounced as the consonant *V*, and substitutes the letter *V* in the place of *B*, as *Ved* instead of *Bed.* Now *Bed* is a contraction of *Bedw*, consequently, *Maes-y-Fed*, or *Maes-y-Fedw*, or *Bedw*, signifies a field of birch, a species of tree with which the district of Old Radnor, and indeed the whole county, even to this day, abounds, and of which it had anciently large and extensive forests. This tree was holden in great estimation by three most respectable parties, viz., the British Druids, Bards, and Ladies.[5] The latter expressed their acceptance of a lover's addresses and vows by presenting him with a garland composed of the twigs and leaves of this delicate tree. On the contrary, a wreath of hazel modestly typified the rejection of his suit. Nor was this elegant and beautiful tree less propitious to the inspiration of poetry, than of love. For thus Dafydd ab Gwillim, the Ovid of Wales, describes himself:—

> "Bodlon wyw 'ir ganiadaeth
> Bedwlwyn o'r coed mwyn ai maeth."
>
> 'Mid groves of birch, well pleased I sing
> The tuneful verse the muses bring.

And it is a well known fact that the British Druids formed the letters of their alphabet in resemblance of its buds and sprays.[6] So many, and so varied, were the inducements which our Radnorian ancestors had for planting and cultivating the waving birch. Accordingly, in no part of Great Britain doth this delicate tree so frequently occur as in this county. About two miles west of the church of Old Radnor, is a grove of wood, called *Cae-bedw*, and near the church of Llanvihangel Nantmelan, another of the same name,—a circumstance that affords no small confirmation of the etymology now offered, which appears further entitled to respect from the consideration of analogy. *Maes-y-fedw* is by this derivation assimilated with neighbouring places, such as *Pengwern*, *Treffawydd*, and *Celyn*, the ancient names of *Shrewsbury*, *Hereford*, and *Clun*, which were so denominated from the particular species of trees which once grew in the immediate vicinage of each, respectively; the first signifying the "Ridge of Alders," the second, the "Town of Beech-trees," and the third, "Holly."

[5] Owen's Welsh Dictionary, "Bedwen Collen." Davies' Celtic Researches, p. 250.   [6] *Ibid.* p. 271.

The Saxon, or English, name of this county is Radnor. Many and frequent have been the attempts to assign to this appellation a rational and appropriate etymology. All have hitherto proved uncertain and dissatisfactory. The first reflection that occurs, is the great difference of its two names; *Radnor* bearing no assimilation with Maesyfed, or Maes-y-fed. Our inability to ascertain the true meaning of the former is the more vexatious from the circumstance of its comparatively recent imposition; for Domesday Book is the first authentic document in which the name *Radenore* is recorded. Leaving the senseless derivation proposed by Camden, (who makes the word Radnor to spring from Rhayader, and the equally unappropriate signification, viz., "Red Hills," for there are none of that description in the county, on the contrary, the hills contiguous to the town of Radnor have their summits clothed with verdure,) to the oblivion in which they deserve to be ingulphed, the author submits, with diffidence, a new and unnoticed conjecture. *Rade* is the Saxon word for road, and *Nore*, in the same language, signifies narrow. Hence the appellation *Radenore*, when applied to the town, means the town in the narrow road, or pass, or defile; when used to designate the county, it signifies the county of narrow roads, passes, or defiles. This etymology of the word Radnor has, at least, the merit of being characteristic of the county to which it is applied. For this county, more especially on its English frontier, abounds more in defiles than any other county in the Principality of Wales.

Still the name Radnor is susceptible of another, and very different signification, deduced from the rank and condition of the people by whom this part of the district was inhabited. In the Saxon and Norman languages, certain freeholders of lands, *liberi tenentes*, were denominated *Radehenistri*, who ploughed and harrowed, or reaped and mowed, at the manor of the lord. There were also certain men called *Rad-knights*, who held their lands by serving their lords on horseback. Now Radnor may be an abbreviation or corruption of one or other of these two words, and Radnor men, in the reign of Edward the Confessor, may have holden their lands, of that king, by the conditions here specified. This mode of tenure was also called Socage, the servile part of which was commuted by paying a small rent to the lord of the soil.

CHAPTER II.

THE ORIGIN OF ITS PRIMITIVE INHABITANTS; THEIR CHARACTER, RELIGION, GOVERNMENT, POPULATION, &c.; THE NAMES OF THE ANCIENT DIVISIONS OF THE DISTRICT; ITS ANTIQUITIES; ITS TOMMENAU, CARNAU, AND CROMLECHAU; ITS FORTIFICATIONS AND ENCAMPMENTS; ITS ROMAN PROVINCE, STATIONS, AND ROADS; ITS SAXON AND NORMAN VESTIGES; OFFA'S DYKE; ITS CASTLES AND MILITARY WEAPONS; ITS RELIGIOUS EDIFICES, ABBEYS, CELLS AND CHURCHES.

Section 1.—The Origin of its Primitive Inhabitants.

The primitive inhabitants of this district were called, in the British language, *Essylwyr*, and by the Romans, *Silures*. They were a tribe of the *Britanni*, or *Britons*, and identified with them in their origin, and in their other characteristics. The question then that offers itself is, whence did the ancient Britons migrate into Britain? The generality of English antiquaries espouse the conjecture of *Tacitus*, the Roman historian, who supposes that they came hither from Gaul, and, like him, rest their argument on the contiguity of the two countries, Gaul and Britain. But if contiguity of situation be admitted as an argument for determining the sources of the population of countries, why is the obvious and popular notion of *Ireland* having been peopled from Britain, discarded from the creed of every sensible and judicious antiquary? The conjecture that the original colony of *Britain* migrated from *Gaul* or *Spain*, seems to be founded on the erroneous notion that all ancient migrations were effected on land alone, and that the continent, having been first filled, emptied its superfluity upon the bare islands. We are warranted, as well by the authority of the Roman historian, as by an appeal to universally received matter of fact, that the reverse was the general mode of peopling the regions of the earth; " Nec terra olim," says he, " sed classibus advehebantur, qui mutare sedes quærebant." " Emigrants removed by sea, not by land." And it is well ascertained that many parts of the continent of *Asia*, and of *Europe*, received their primitive colonization from the contiguous and adjacent islands.

And the reason is obvious. Islands acquired civilization and refinement much earlier than continents. They presented fewer obstacles to improvement, and are less subject to the domination of foreign invaders, and to those violent and retrograde revolutions which impede and retard the progress of national melioration. Commerce and navigation are objects to which islanders are necessarily attached; and navigation and commerce promote and assist the arts of civilization and improvement. Accordingly, in every age of the world, the inhabitants of islands have excelled the people of the continent in the spirit of liberty, in the science of legislation, and in the cultivation of the fine arts. Such was *Crete;* its inhabitants had obtained a considerable degree of civilization and refinement, when the people of *Greece* remained in a state of profound ignorance and barbarity. And such was the case with Britain in the time of *Julius Cæsar*. This ambitious invader attests its superiority, and affirms " that the druidical institution originated in Britain, and passed from thence into Gaul; so that whosoever aspired to be complete adepts in this mystical science, were wont to resort to *Britain*." This decisive testimony justifies the inference that those historians and antiquaries, who assert that *Britain* was indebted for her institutions to the neighbouring continent, have misrepresented this subject. The reverse was the fact. The neighbouring continent received its institutions, and the improvement of them, from *Britain*. This obligation the Gallic Druids always had the grace to acknowledge. It was reserved to English writers alone to assert the contrary.

The attempt of a modern "Inquirer into the origin of the

inhabitants of the British Islands," to identify the *Britanni* of *Britain* with the *Britones* of *Gaul*, and thereby to prove that the first settlers of the former country came from the latter, seems to be one of those stratagems, with which the framers of hypothetical assumptions endeavour to support their airy speculations. For no such people as the latter existed in Gaul at the period alluded to. In justice to this correspondent of the Antiquarian Society of London, it is to be added, that the error appears not to have been wilfully committed, but to have been occasioned by a corrupted text of Pliny, which escaped the "Inquirer's" observation. The true reading is *Brixones*, not *Britones*. This instance of inadvertence and misquotation, however involuntary, suggests a lesson of caution against drawing premature conclusions from unsubstantiated premises.

The reason why modern writers are so generally inclined to ascribe a Gallic origin to the first population of Britain seems to have resulted from the accidental circumstance of the Romans having transferred some of the names of the petty states of Gaul into this island, and imposed Gallic appellations on British tribes; whence, it has been hastily concluded, that those people of Britain, who bore Gallic names, were descended from those Gallic tribes which were designated by those names; and, consequently, that the original population of Britain arrived from Gaul. To omit the illogical process of this deduction, from particulars to universals, let it suffice to observe that, of all historical blunders, this is the grossest. It has induced modern historians to ascribe the population of countries to people who never beheld those countries. The question is, not what names the ignorant Romans chose arbitrarily, and often without appropriate meaning, to affix, but how Britons were designated by Britons. This identity of Roman names doth not necessarily imply the identity of the two people; nor were the *Senones* of Britain derived from the *Senones* of Gaul.

Upon the whole, the argument of *Tacitus*, derived from contiguity of situation, and a supposed similarity of feature, may as well be adduced to prove that the population of *Gaul* and *Spain* was received from *Britain*, as that this island was colonized from those countries. The studious care with which the Britons have preserved genealogical descents, would certainly have operated in a case of this national and important concern; and the remembrance of a Gallic, or of an Iberian, extraction, some document or tradition would assuredly have perpetuated. But, as nothing of either is known to have existed, or to have been transmitted, there is every reason to justify the rejection of an hypothesis which, as it was deemed by its first framer to be conjectural, remains to this day unsupported and unconfirmed by his followers.

But, though no national testimony can be adduced to support the supposition of a Gallic origin, yet there doth exist at this day, through the whole of the Principality of Wales, an historical tradition, handed down from time immemorial, asserting that the discoverers and first colonizers of Britain were emigrants from *Asia*. Let us see what kind of evidence may be adduced in support of this tradition.

In proof of an Asiatic colonization of Britain, we have,—1. Presumptions. 2. Arguments. The striking resemblance of names, opinions and practices, that subsisted among the ancient inhabitants of these two distant countries, affords presumptions; and the testimony of British Bards and of the Triades, furnishes arguments.[7]

1. From the circumstance of a striking resemblance between the two people, we derive presumptions in favour of the tradition, which ascribes the first population of Britain to a tribe of emigrants from Asia. In their plan of education, which committed nothing to writing, but to the memory alone, and dispensed instruction through the

---

[7] Hu Gadarn is said to have brought the race of the Cymry to the Island of Britain from the land of Haf, which is called Deffrobani, and they came from the place where Constantinople now is. Prydain the son of Aedd Mawr first established government and laws in the Island of Britain.—*Historical Triads*, 4; *Davies' Celtic Researches*, p. 154.

medium of oral poetry,—in their literary and philosphical attainments, for what the Magi were in Persia, the same were the Druids in Britain,—in their forms of government, which were sacerdotal, and founded on the influence of opinion,—in their religious practices, for, with both people, the sun and fire were emblems of the Deity,—in the construction of their sepulchral tumuli, or tommenau, or barrows,—in their use of military chariots,—in the names of distinguished leaders, viz., *Husheng* and *Phridun*, in Asia, and *Huysgwn* and *Prydain*, in Britain,—and in various other subordinate particulars,—may be discerned in the people of *Asia Minor*, and in the earliest inhabitants of *Britain*, a surprising coincidence and similarity, which it is difficult to account for by the intervention of any casual or fortuitous contingencies. So exact an identity of thinking and of acting, by two people so far removed from each other, in the same epoch of time, cannot be satisfactorily explained, but on the supposition of the latter people having been connected with the former, and deriving their origin and their institutions from them.

Hitherto we have adduced only presumptions in favour of an Asiatic colonization of Britain. We will now state our arguments, as furnished by the testimony of British Bards and the Triads.

2. The aggregate amount of the information derived from these authoritative sources is this:—"That the original colony which migrated to Britain was conducted hither by a leader named *Huysgwn*,"—identified with *Husheng*, an appellation extremely familiar, and common to celebrated natives of *Asia;*—"that the first settlers of Britain came hither after a long and devious voyage by sea,"—which account agrees with the character of a voyage from the coasts of Asia, but militates against the commonly received but erroneous notion of a short run from the shores of *Gaul;*—"that they came from the Summer-country,"—that is, from Asia;—"that they anciently inhabited *Deffro-banu*,"—a word undoubtedly substituted by the negligence of a transcriber in the place

of *Dyffryn-banu*, or *Dyffryn-albanu*, that is, the deep vales or glens of Albania, a country situated between the Euxine and Caspian Seas;—"that they were natives of a country in Asia;"—and, lastly, "that they came to Britain from a city called *Gaf-is*,"—that is, the lower *Káf*, or the lower Caucasus, a mountain stretching between the Caspian and Euxine Seas. Cities, towns, and even people, were anciently denominated from the neighbouring mountains, rivers, &c. Caucasus being both originally, and at the present time, pronounced *Káf*, and being divided into higher and lower, is certainly identified with *Gáf-is*, that is, the lower Caucasus, the British language having the power to convert the initial letter *K* into *G*.

Here then is a climax of evidence, consisting of strong presumptions and conclusive arguments, mutually supporting and corroborating each other, and confirming the credibility of an existing tradition, which ascribes to the original colonizers of Britain an Asiatic origin and extraction. The only difficulty attending its reception, that remains to be removed, arises from the consideration of the distance which separates the two countries, and the hazard which must have attended such an enterprize in times of comparative inexperience of nautical affairs. The force of this objection will be considerably diminished, if not entirely removed, by recollecting that the art of navigation had made a wonderful progress in the early ages of the world,—that sea-voyages of considerable length and difficulty had been performed in a period equally remote,—that the Atlantic Ocean had been navigated by Phœnician ships seventeen centuries anterior to the Christian æra,—that the merchants of Asia trafficked in British tin as early as the days of Moses,—that the maritime skill and experience by which the first settlers of Britain were distinguished, whom Thaliessin calls "warlike adventurers on the sea," rendered them qualified for the enterprize,—that the population of Britain could not have been effected at so early a period as it may be proved it was, had the emigrants journeyed by land,—

and, lastly, that their voyage to Britain was not performed at one run, but had its several resting-places, such as *Tan-is*, in lower Egypt; *Algiers*, in Africa; *Gadir*, in Spain; *Lisbon*, in Portugal, &c. When these ascertained particulars are duly weighed and considered, not only the reluctance to submit to the attested antiquity of our island will be relaxed, but also the alleged difficulty of navigating vessels from the coasts of Asia, to the shores of Britain, in so remote a period as is contended for, will appear much abated and diminished.

Whilst time hath drawn its oblivious veil over the four proud empires of the world, and almost effaced the remembrance of them from the countries, in which they once triumphantly flourished, there exist at present in this island a people, whom neither the revolution of almost 3000 years, nor the most destructive invasions, nor bloody wars, nor repeated massacres, have been able to extinguish; still continuing to speak the same language, and to retain many of the customs which distinguished their Asiatic progenitors;—a spectacle worthy of the contemplation of the philosopher and antiquary, as unexampled in the page of history as it is unparalleled by any nation now subsisting,—that only excepted, whose preservation constitutes a peculiar object of the regard of Divine Providence, and is made subservient to the accomplishment of His wise and majestic decrees.

Section 2.—Character, Religion, Government, Population, &c., of of the Silures.

The character which Tacitus, the Roman historian, has transmitted of these people, redounds greatly to their credit. He ranks them among the *validissimas gentes*, the most robust and valiant nations, and represents them as not only inured to hardship and war, but so implacably averse to, and impatient under, a foreign yoke, that they were neither to be won by courtesy, nor restrained by force. Their long and obstinate resistance to the Romans proves them to have been animated by an unconquerable spirit, and ardent love of freedom and independence.

The form of government established among the Silures resembled that which prevailed among the other tribes of Britain; at first hierarchical, and preserving peace and concord, and preventing aggression and outrage, not by the dread of punishment, but by the influence of opinion. At a subsequent period it assumed a monarchical form. For the district or kingdom of Siluria, which comprehended, in addition to what has since been called Radnorshire, the present counties of Hereford, Monmouth, Glamorgan and Brecknock, was governed by its own independent regulus, or chieftain, who, in conjunction with the other reguli of the island, was invested with the power of electing, in seasons of public danger, a supreme sovereign, on whom was conferred the title of " Brenhin Prydain oll," or the king of all Britain. To the Druids were committed the superintendence of religious ceremonies, the decision of controversies, and the education of youth. The jurisdiction of the Silures was simple, and their laws plain and few. Their courts of justice were holden by the Druids, and by the princes or reguli, in the open air, and on an eminence crowned with a cairn, that all might see and hear their judges, and their decisions. One of these courts was erected in the territories of every state, perhaps of every clan, or tribe. The Arch-Druid held a grand assize once in every year, at a fixed time and place. Their court stood upon an even fair spot of ground, piled with stones to a considerable height, and of an elliptical form, opening directly to the west. No laws could be either enacted or repealed, without the consent of King, Nobles and Druids, expressed in a general convention.

Their religion was partly patriarchal, and consisted in the acknowledgment of One infinite, eternal, omnipotent and self-existing Being, whom they denominated *Duw*. The worship of the true God was preserved inviolate by the British Druids, under every adverse circumstance of their country, whatever indulgences, in condescension to the wishes and commands of their proud and intolerant conquerors, might have been conceded to the vulgar.

They neither erected temples nor carved images. Their acts of devotion were performed in the face of the sun, being taught to consider that grand luminary, for its great benefits to mankind, as a proper representative of the deity; and were either on the tops of mountains, or on open plains, whereon were erected for the purpose plain and unchiselled stones or altars. On every one of these was kindled a large fire; which, from the beneficial influence of light and heat, in producing and maturing the fruits of the earth, the surrounding votaries were instructed to regard as an emblem of the deity; "for," observed the Druid, "as God fills all space, so does heat pervade all things."

The amount of the population of the district under consideration, during the remote period in which it constituted a part of ancient *Siluria*, it is impossible at this day to ascertain. Undoubtedly, it participated in the prolific increase which characterized all the other districts of the island in ancient times. To this increase the division of the great landed properties, and the equal distribution of inheritances, effected and secured by the law or custom of *gavelkind*, must have greatly contributed; and hence Boadicea was enabled to bring into the field an army of 300,000 fighting men.

Section 3.—The Ancient Divisions of this District.

These have been different at different times. Long prior, as well as subsequent, to the Roman invasion of Britain, it constituted a part of the renowned kingdom of *Essyllwg*, a word which signifies an open country abounding in prospects, and was denominated by the Romans *Siluria*. From the time of their departure from Britain to the reign of Athelstan, the Saxon king of England; this district, together with a part of Montgomeryshire, a part of Shropshire, a part of Herefordshire, and a part of Gloucestershire, was included in that territory, which went under the denomination of *Ffer-llys*, corruptly written *Fferregs* and *Ffernex*. Ffer-llys is a compound word, signifying a country "copious in grass," which Virgil would have Latinized by the word "herbosa," and perhaps Homer would have rendered into his sonorous tongue by the epithet λεχεποίη. This etymology strikingly accords with the character and quality of the soil of that country, which lies between the rivers Wye and Severn, agreeably to the old distich,—

"Blessed is the Eye
Betwixt the Severn and the Wye."

And with the more detailed and beautiful description given of it in the Shaksperean language of *Lear*, a British sovereign,—

"With shadowy forests, and with champaigns rich'd,
With plenteous rivers, and with wide-skirted meads."

The abundant fruitfulness and enchanting amenity of this extensive district, confirm the propriety and justness of its ancient appellation, *Ffer-llys*, as well as of the derivation now for the first time given of that appellation. At this time Hereford, the capital town of the territory, was called *Fferley*. This, among other proofs that may be adduced, the following distich evinces, extracted from the monkish hymn, or elegy, sung in the church of Hereford, at the celebration of the funeral of Ethelbert, a Saxon prince, who was assassinated by Offa, king of *Mercia*, when he came invited to treat with him concerning the espousals of his daughter:—

A.D. 750.

"Corpus tandem est delatum,
In *Fferleiâ* tumulatum."

The princely corpse from thence at length convey'd,
With funeral pomp in *Fferley's* church was laid.

Hence may be perceived the absurdity of the derivation ascribed to the word *Ffer-llys* by English antiquaries, unacquainted with the British language, viz., the "country of Fern," because some ignorant copyist erroneously transcribed it *Ffernlys*; and, hence, it may be inferred that the city now called Hereford had not received that name at this period; nor, indeed, was it so denominated until a considerable time after.

A.D. 880. In the reign of Roderic the Great, Prince of Wales, about the year 880, the district under consideration belonged to the principality of Powis, or Mathrafal, which formed the third grand division of Wales, conferred by the afore-mentioned prince upon his third and youngest son, Merfyn. By virtue of this partition it consisted of three cantrefs, and ten cwmwds. The cantrefs were,—1. Moelienydd; 2. Elfel; 3. Y Clawdd. Moelienydd comprehended four cwmwds, viz., —1. Cerri; 2. Swydd y grè; 3. Rhiwyrallt; 4. Glyn yr Eithon. The cantref of Elfel contained three cwmwds, viz.,—1. Uwch mynydd; 2. Is mynydd; 3. Llech Ddyfnog. The cantref of Y Clawdd comprehended three cwmwds, viz.,—1. Dyffryn Tafediad; 2. Swydd Wynogion; 3. Penwyllt.

A.D. 1060. About the latter end of the reign of Edward the Confessor it is supposed that a certain part of this district first assumed the name of Radenore; the other divisions retained their British or Welsh appellations.

During the reign of the first kings of England of the Norman race, this district was distinguished as forming a part of the Marches of Wales, a word that seems to be derived from *mears*, boundaries. This tract, lying contiguous to Offa's Dyke, became on each side a disputed frontier, varying as the success of war between England and Wales preponderated. It was at different times granted by the kings of the former country to their nobles, who hence acquired the names of Lords Marchers, and who instituted a peculiar species of government.

At the complete and final incorporation and union of Wales with England, in the twenty-seventh year of the reign of King Henry the Eighth, this district, then distinguished as a part of the Marches of Wales, was formed into a distinct and independent county, comprehending fifty-two parishes, which are arranged in six hundreds, and including one capital borough, four contributory boroughs, and four market-towns.

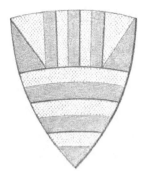

Arms of the Borough of New Radnor.

Section 4.—Its Tommenau, Carnau, and Cromlechau.

A tommen, tumulus, or barrow, is a mound of earth thrown up in a conical form. If there was no other evidence of the scientific attainments of the British Druids, the construction of tommenau, or barrows, affords a convincing proof. They are all raised upon an outline struck with geometrical exactness from a centre, and as true as if it was drawn with a large pair of compasses. Many of them reach to the height of about thirty feet; the circumference measures nearly as many yards, and they are deeply ditched and moated round.

It is probable that the tommenau, or barrows, were applied by the Silures, or Britons, to various and different uses. First, and principally, in them were deposited the remains of the illustrious dead, and also of warriors slain in battle in defence of their country. Secondly, they were used as a temporary resort and defence against the sudden inroads of their enemies, the circular form of them enabling the few to repel the many. Hence they are generally situated in the vicinity of a mansion, or church, or village, and constitute the fortifications of those places. Sometimes they are placed on the tops of high hills, where they are seen at a great distance, probably for this reason,—being thus exposed to the sight of every one, they brought to their remembrance the venerated hero there interred, and stimulated the spectators to revenge his death. Taken collectively, they exhibit a complete system of vigilatory communicating points. Lastly, they are supposed to have been the scenes of some druidical rites, and also used as places of local assemblies.

On the side of the road leading from New Radnor to Walton are three barrows, one of them of a considerable magnitude. In the parish of Llanfihangel-Nant-melan are also three barrows, forming a triangle almost equilateral, the longest side being about a mile. The one barrow is situated above Blaenedw, on the brow of the Forest of Radnor; it is deeply moated round, and also defended by other trenches cut on the side of the hill. From it is seen a most extensive, diversified and picturesque view of the country to the south and west. The name of an adjacent farm-house being Gwern-yr-Arglwydd, that is, the Lord's Orls, affords a presumption that in this tommen was interred the corpse of one of the *reguli*, or chieftains, of the district. One is near the church, adjacent to the turnpike road; and the third about half a mile distant to the east, on the brow of a steep precipice, large, and deeply moated round. The position of these three barrows is such as would fulfil most of the purposes obtained by the establishment of telegraphic posts.

In the parish of Llanddewi-ystrad-ennau, on the bank of the river Ieithon, is a very considerable tommen, or barrow, called Bedd y Grê, that is, the grave of the equerry. But as Bedd is not a Celtic word, its present orthography is susceptible of doubt; and it has been suggested that the original writing was Budd-y-Grè, which signifies the race of victory, thereby denoting that the enemy sustained a repulse in his attack on this barrow and the adjoining camp, which is British.

Agreeably to the plan adopted and executed by Roderic the Great, Prince of Wales, of dividing his kingdom into three principalities, a cwmwd, or habitation, of this district, assumed the name of Swydd-y-grè, that is, the office and jurisdiction of Grè, who is supposed by some to have been a chieftain, slain in combating the invaders and despoilers of his country on the very spot on which the barrow, or tumulus, that bears his name is constructed. The circumstance of the tommen being not of a sepulchral, but of a military, nature, favours either supposition, and, in conjunction with other similar works, proves that the neighbourhood has been the scene of much conflict. The right interpretation, however, seems to be this. Grè is an abbreviation of Greorion. Now Greorion are those tenants of the prince who held lands under him upon the condition of entertaining the keepers of those live stock and cattle which were to be slaughtered for the use and provision of the prince's family, or attendants, whilst he resided in their manor, on his royal progress through his dominions. For which purpose the prince had a manor-house in every cantref. And each manor was obliged to provide for his retinue, as long as he resided in it, and whilst he travelled through it. The manor of Swydd-y-grè was of this sort.

On the common, in the parish of Llandrindod, are several tommenau, or tumuli, five of which are placed at a very small distance from each other, a proof that in ancient times there had been upon this spot a dreadful carnage. These five have been opened, and were found to contain human bones, pieces of half-burnt charcoal, and spear-heads, called celts, &c., covered with a heap of loose stones.

On the right bank of the river Wye, near the town of Rhayader, and in front of the church of Llansaintfread Cwmdauddwr, stands a tommen, or barrow, of very considerable magnitude, deeply ditched or moated round. It has long been supposed that the bones of St. Fraid, who flourished in the seventh century, and to whom the church was dedicated, were deposited in this tumulus. But on removing some of its materials a few years ago, for the repair of the adjacent road, or for laying a foundation for the contiguous cottages, a silver coin, about the size of a crown-piece, of most exquisite workmanship, and in excellent condition, was found, on which was inscribed in *relievo* the word "Serais." Now Serais is a city in Palestine, which, after sustaining a long and bloody siege, was captured by the army of the Crusaders. Hence it is conjectured that this silver piece was a medal cast in commemoration of this signal victory, and that the person inhumed in this receptacle was not a saintly hermit, who devoted his days and nights to prayer and fasting, but a military hero, whose bravery in fighting against the Saracenic infidels of the Holy Land, and whose interpidity in mounting the breach of the stormed Serais, were remunerated with this medal, but whose name, after diligent inquiry, seems at this distance of time to be irrecoverable. It is not improbable that, as the saint and the hero were engaged in the same cause, —viz., in promoting the Christian faith,—the one by the spiritual, and the other by the temporal, sword, so after their deaths the ashes of both were mingled together in this sacred repository. Close to the bridge of Rhayader is another barrow of much inferior dimensions, having at its top a circular hollow, whence it is supposed the hoary Druid harangued and instructed the surrounding populace, and who, at a small adjoining eminence, called Bryn, or the Tribunal, expounded to them the law. About the half of a mile east of the town of Rhayader is another barrow, in a field called Cefn Ceidio, that is, the Ridge of Ceidio, a saint who lived in the sixth century, and whose bones, it is supposed, lie there inhumed.

The numerous valleys in which the rivers of this county, viz., the Ieithon, Edwy, Teme and Lug, flow, are studded with these artificial mounds of earth, demonstrating at once the strenuous opposition which their respective invaders encountered, and the slaughter that preceded the submisssion of the natives. Every inch of ground therein seems to have been obstinately disputed. Nor are these memorials of the courage of the inhabitants confined to the low grounds; they also crown the summits of the hills. On an highly elevated ridge of hills, in the parish of Aberedwy, stand eminently in view three tumuli, or barrows. These are not placed in a straight or direct alignment with each other, but at the angles of an equilateral triangle, each side of which measures about a hundred paces. They are all deeply ditched, or moated round, forming conspicuous objects at a great distance, and commanding a most extensive and diversified prospect. Their number and their position completely overthrow the hastily formed conjecture of those tourists who have erroneously pronounced all such works of the ancient Britons—rude, indeed, if compared to the modern improvements in the art of war, but constructed on truly geometrical and military principles—to be nothing more than beacons, or specula, erected for vigilatory and exploratory purposes only; a sentence that accords as little with a discriminating judgment as it does with the circumstances of the situation of the country, where every hill presents a natural watch tower.

To prevent, therefore, the recurrence of these and the like misconceptions, it may not be amiss briefly to notice the characteristics by which these artificial mounds of earth are distinguished, and by which their original designation and use may be ascertained. Those barrows, then, which, constructed in the simplest manner, form merely a circular protuberance of inferior dimensions, without either a fosse or a rampart, were appropriated to sepulchral purposes, and used as places of interment; whilst such as indicate a more laborious and complete finish, and are surrounded with a high *agger* and a deep ditch, served as military fortifications, and, indeed, seem upon the whole admirably adapted to the operations of a defensive campaign. Of these several uses, however, the appointment was arbitrary; and no tommen, or barrow, was applied to one particular purpose exclusively. The Britons were a people of too free a turn of thinking, and too little controlled in acting, to be enchained to a system, and they designated the same tumulus to many and various uses,—now as an exploratory speculum, and now as a military post,—but made all of them indiscriminately repositories of the dead. This latter was a political arrangement, and seemed calculated to produce a beneficial effect. For the knowledge that a brave defender of his country's independence was inhumed in such a tumulus, or barrow, served to stimulate the survivors to imitate his valour, to revenge his death upon the enemy, and to preserve his sepulchre from pollution. No duty was of more imperious obligation among the Britons than that of guarding from hostile insult the sleeping *manes* of their respected forefathers.

Section 5.—Its Fortifications and Encampments.

Whoever looks at the Silurian encampments of this district with a mind divested of prejudice, and with the discriminating eye of a soldier, will soon have just cause to doubt the accuracy of those writers whose practice upon all occasions is to decry the skill and ingenuity of the ancient inhabitants of this island in general, and to expose the rudeness and imbecility of their fortifications in particular. A very different opinion of the latter, however, has been entertained and expressed by military officers in the British army, of acknowledged merit and eminence in their profession, who, after a strict examination of these works, have not hesitated to declare in strong terms their approbation,—that it is impossible to excel the judgment with which these fortified posts have been selected, and that the smallest change of their respective positions would not prove so well calculated to produce the desired effects of a defensive system, to retard the progress of an invading enemy, and to facilitate and keep open communications with the besieged. They go on further, and add that, by the plan of Caractacus, all his dominions were distributed into spaces comprehended by equilateral triangles, and that fortified encampments were placed at each of the angles—all three within the view of each other, and capable of giving and receiving mutual succour and support,—and that an invading force, by successfully carrying one of these fortified angles, could make no progress, nor remain secure, in a country previously exhausted of supplies, unless he also carried all the three. If this were the case, if such be the character and disposition of Silurian encampments,—the truth of which may be verified or disproved by actual examination, —it is more easy to account for the long opposition which Caractacus, with an inferior and undisciplined force, was enabled to make against the conquerors of the world, aided by several of his own countrymen, than to justify the unmilitary conjecture whereby some have attempted to confine the operations of nine years to a short line, supposed to have commenced at Malvern, and to terminate, alas! at Coxwall,—a space of ground comprehending little more than thirty-five miles,—a conjecture which, if realized, would have left the resources of his kingdom almost untouched, and rendered his various and triangular positions unserviceable and useless.

Nor is the configuration of each distinct and separate encampment less scientific than is the disposition of the whole judicious. It has been a subject of dispute with military people whether is most eligible, on the principles of a defensive system of operations, a square camp like that of the Romans, or the elliptical camp of the Silures, or Britons. The preference has been awarded to the latter. It requires fewer men for its defence; the eye of the commander embraces the greater part of its circumference; and the point of attack, whether made in front, or in flank, is more speedily succoured, and more easily repelled. Whereas a square camp has four sides to defend; it must present a distinct front on each side; the commander can take a view of only one side at a time; and by a false attack on the flanks, the rear and front are liable to be forced.

That the kingdom of Siluria was anciently distributed into triangular districts studded with camps, is an assertion founded not on testimony alone; the result of a personal examination will likewise evince its truth; nay, the inspection of a common map of the territory will suffice. Even this small district of it presents examples of this singular and truly military arrangement of its defensive fortifications. Burfâ Bank, Newcastle, and Cwm, or Wapley, secure its north-eastern frontier, while its south-eastern boundary is guarded by the several camps of

Brilley, Huntington, and Leonhales. The Silurian camp of Burfâ, which is within the limits of this county, and Bradnor, a Roman intrenchment, about a mile west of the town of Kington, and on the Welsh side of Offa's Dyke, occupy the opposite sides of a valley watered by a river called Hindwell, and stand as if opposed to each other. Burfâ is situated on the south-eastern extremity of the Vale of Radnor, on the summit of a conical or pyramidical eminence, as the monosyllable *Bur* signifies, and is defended by a triple ditch. The sides of the hill are steep and almost inaccessible. It stands within view of the other two intrenched angles, Newcastle and Cwm, and corresponds in all respects with the camps occupied by Caractacus, the Silurian commander, whose system of defence, as described by Tacitus, consisted partly in fixing the positions of his encampments on the banks of the rivers opposed to the line of march of the Romans. Its form is elliptical, its area contains about three acres, and it commands a very diversified and picturesque view of the adjacent country. Newcastle camp is situated about three miles and a half west of the town of Presteign, almost adjoining the turnpike road leading to the town of New Radnor. It is quite perfect, and is circular in form. Its diameter measures about 220 yards, and its circumference about 660 yards.

At a place called Gaer, in the parish of Llanddewi-ystrad-ennau, is a camp of superior style and strength. This fortification occupies the summit of a high hill impending over the Vale of Ieithon, of an oval form, defended by two parallel intrenchments, and almost inaccessible on the side of the river Ieithon. Various have been the conjectures formed respecting the original occupancy and property of this distinguished military post. From its elliptical form, many have been induced to adjudge its original construction to the Silures, who generally preferred positions of that particular shape and figure. In this opinion we are inclined to coincide, adding that, from its name, Gaer, and from other circumstances, it appears to have been possessed and occupied by the

Romans, if not as a military station, yet as an exploratory position; and that, in a subsequent period, it was garrisoned both by the defenders and invaders of this district, in alternate succession, is a fact not only extremely probable, but altogether certain; as well from the circumstance of this neighbourhood having been the scene of many bloody engagements between the native Welsh and Normans, as from the natural and artificial strength of this post, not to be slighted or overlooked with impunity by either party. On a hill opposite is the large mound, or tommen, of earth, inclosed by a small moat, noticed above.

In the lordship of Stanage, on the declivity of a hill, and near its summit, is a small camp of a circular form, and, consequently, of British construction. Its area has been planted with trees by Charles Rogers, Esq., the proprietor. Its particular designation is unknown. It might have served as a place of retreat to the discomfited Britons flying from Coxwall Knoll, or as an exploratory post. In the same lordship, on the right bank of the river Teme, in a low situation, is a large barrow, or tumulus, deeply moated round, and closely connected on the east side with a level area, resembling in figure a parallelogram, and surrounded with an agger. The original designation of the whole it is by no means difficult to explain. It belonged to the lord, or regulus, of the district. On the elevated mound stood his palace; the apartments of his domestics occupied the area below; and on each side of the valley, which this fortification was intended to protect, were placed the scattered habitations of his vassals, all of whom were within the hearing of the sound of his horn, when danger approached, and the alarm was given.

There are many other Silurian intrenchments in the northern division of the county; especially one in the parish of Bugaildu, called Crug-y-Buddair, that is, the Mount of Ambuscade; contiguous to which is an ancient Silurian fortification, accompanied with considerable remains of building. Immemorial tradition ascribes remote antiquity to this dilapidated relic, and records it to have been the occasional residence of Uthyr Pendragon, the father of the renowned Prince Arthur. Traditionary reports contain some truth, mingled with much falsehood. There is, however, reason to believe that this place belonged, if not to the celebrated hero above named, who was a Silurian, yet to some noted chieftain of the district, of a more recent era, whose name and whose actions are equally forgotten. At the foot of Crug-y-Buddair is a field, still called the "Bloody Field," in which it is said a battle was fought; but neither the year, or the occasion, can now be ascertained.

We pass on to record some of the principal encampments that fortify the line of the river Arrow, on the south-eastern frontier of this district. Here we discern three of considerable magnitude and respectability; the one being dignified with the appellation Gaer, or Caer, the usual designation of military stations. This camp, which is British, occupies the summit of a high and commanding eminence, from which a most beautiful prospect extends to several adjoining counties, both Welsh and English. The inclosed area is a large corn-field, containing about thirty-one acres. It is situated in the parish of Michael-church, and, under the denomination of Upper and Lower Gaer, includes outposts which guard the fords of the river Arrow, the valley of which is here studded with numerous tumuli, or barrows, which denote that this spot has been the scene of much conflict and carnage. At a short distance to the south is a military work of the Britons, denominated Pencastle Camp, and situated in the parish of Llanbedr. This is a camp of considerable magnitude and strength, and calculated to serve the purposes for which it was constructed. The third camp, forming the west angle of this triangular position, is situated about a quarter of a mile to the north-east of the village of Clâscwm, on a farm called Wern, on a commanding eminence, judiciously selected to guard the defile leading to the village, as also to check the progress of an enemy advancing through the narrow vale, in which flows a rivulet called Clâs, which unites and empties itself into the river Arrow, in the neighbouring parish of Colfâ. It consisted of a double intrenchment, encircling three-fourths of the summit on which the camp is situated. Being partly open to the south and south-west, the natural difficulty of access from those points, and the little apprehension of an enemy approaching from that quarter, rendered the addition of an intrenched work on that side unnecessary. It is called Clâs-gwyr; the dingle leading to the foot of the eminence is denominated Cwm Twarch. No traces of building are at present discernible. These three camps were undoubtedly occupied by the Silures, and used by them as military posts of defence against the Romans invading this territory from the side of Herefordshire.

This part of the county is rendered very interesting by a number of artificial mounds, fortified posts, cromlechau, and other vestiges of antiquity, all which will be described in the historical account of the several parishes in which they are respectively situated. The security of the remaining portion of the district to the south and south-west seems to have been consigned by the Silures to the natural fortification of the Wye and of its precipitous banks, especially on the south side, whilst the river Teme, in conjunction with the positions of Caer-Caradoc and Cnwc-las, which latter was originally a camp, subsequently a castle, protected its north-eastern quarter.

Section 6.—*Roman Stations and Roads.*

Having thus noticed the antiquities of this district which are Silurian, or British, our next inquiry will be devoted to the consideration of those that are reputed Roman. On a subject that has been exposed to much controversy it may afford some gratification to the reader to have the ancient and modern names of the stations, which the Romans established within the territory of the Silures, presented at once to his view, together with their relative distances, expressed in Roman and English miles; whereby he will be better enabled to exercise his judgment with respect to the justness of the arrangement that has been made of their respective situations.

A Table showing the names of the Roman Stations in Siluria, together with their Relative Distances in Roman and English Miles.[8]

		R.M.	E.M.
1.	Mariduno, from Caermarthen		
2.	Leucarum, to Lougher, near Swansea	15	22½
3.	Nidum, to Neath	15	22½
4.	Bovium, to Boverton, near Cowbridge	15	22½
5.	Iscam. Leg. II. Aug., to Caerleon	27	40½
6.	Burrium, to Uske	9	13½
7.	Gobannium, to Abergavenny	12	18
8.	Magna, to Kenchester	22	33
9.	Bravonium, to Brandon	24	36
10.	From Isca to Venta, Caerwent	9	13½
11.	From Gobannium to Blestium, Monmouth	11	16½
12.	From Gobannium to Ariconium, Rosehill, or Bolitre	11	16½
13.	From Ariconium to Clevum, Gloucester	15	22½
14.	From Bravonium to Viroconium, Wroxeter	27	40½

It is supposed upon good grounds that many more stations of considerable note were occupied by the Romans within the district of the Silures; but these are all that the Itinerary of Antoninus has enumerated. Some of these, as it appears from the column of English miles, are erroneously placed, and misinterpreted, as will be proved hereafter.

Of the stations above-named, four, viz., Venta, Gobannium, Ariconium, and Magna, are declared to have been cities, and Isca and Blestium towns. The justness of this distribution, though supported by the authority of Richard of Cirencester, is very disputable; because the acknowledged celebrity of Isca (Caerleon), the residence of a Roman legion, and the seat of an archbishopric, entitled it to a precedency above all the others, and secured to it an undeniable claim, not only to be classed among the cities of Britain, but also to have been, as it really was, the metropolis of the kingdom of Siluria.

---

[8] We print this table exactly as it stands in the MS.—ED. ARCH. CAMB.

Whilst Magna, which contained only one Roman cohort, generally consisting of between two and three hundred men, seems to have been undeservedly raised into the honourable distinction of a British city.

But whatever might have been, in ancient times, the rank and dignity of the Roman station Magna, whether of a city or a town, it must forego all pretensions for having occupied the site assigned to it by Mr. Horsley and his followers. This declaration will, no doubt, be received with a degree of astonishment, and treated as presumptuous, by those who implicitly subscribe to this learned antiquary's sentiments, and deem his opinions little less than oracular. But notwithstanding the imposing and prepossessing name of Horsley, and the numerous retinue of his able and ingenious supporters, we despair not of being able to convince every impartial and unprejudiced inquirer of the inadmissibility of his arrangement of Roman stations within the district of the Silures, and that the placing of Ariconium at Rosehill, Magna at Kenchester, and Bravonium at Brandon, not only militates against every rule that ought to guide researches of this nature, but is in fact erroneous and unfounded.

In the first place, the liberties which this learned antiquary has taken with the admeasurement of the Itinerary, and the violence with which he has altered the distances between the stations therein enumerated, making them either longer or shorter, as it suited the convenience of his hypothesis, must tend to vitiate the whole fabric of his arrangements. To accede to his representation of a work which was intended to serve as an authorized standard to the nation, is to allow a strange and unaccountable variation in computing the distances of the several stations, and that the Itinerary admeasurement signifies one thing in one province, and another thing in another province. Nor is this all. The proportion between the Itinerary and the English admeasurement not only varies in the same province, but even in the same district. Nay, to complete the absurdity, it is added that the distances between certain stations, as expressed in the Itinerary, do not differ from the present English admeasurement; whilst between other stations in the same district, not only the Roman and English standards vary considerably, but also require a reversed mode of computation; two Itinerary miles making in some instances three English ones, and in others two English being equal to three Itinerary miles. What faith is due to so many and such gross contradictions? Or what confidence can be placed in such uncertainties? And what commentator, using such bold and unwarrantable liberties with his author, distorting the text, and perverting its natural and obvious meaning, can hope to be received with any kind of complacency or approbation?

If the Itinerary admeasurement possess that uncertain and varying signification, and require those emendations which Mr. Horsley has discovered and recommended, why was not this necessity pointed out by its original framers? Why has it escaped the notice of its various editors for the space of sixteen centuries? And why was the detection of the error reserved for Mr. Horsley? The imperial surveyors observe total silence with regard to a point, which, whilst it involves their own integrity and correctness, is of too great importance to be concealed from the public. The Romans were too wise a people to affix several quantities to the same measure, which could not have failed to produce embarrassment and confusion; nor durst the authors of the Itinerary have presented to their emperor a topographical survey of his British dominions fraught with inaccuracy and error, and which admitted so many and so various contradictions in its computation of the several distances of the stations.

This brief exposition of Mr. Horsley's attempt to affix a double and uncertain signification to the admeasurement expressed in the Itinerary of the Emperor Antoninus, must shake the stability of the topographical arrangement of Roman stations within the territory of the Silures, by which this antiquary is distinguished. A more minute examination of the justness of his position of Ariconium and Magna respectively will produce a stronger conviction of his erroneous adjudication.

For, unless actuated by the disposition so often ascribed to him by competent judges, viz., "of seeing every object, in his antiquarian researches, with Roman eyes," how could he, with the least colour of probability, fix the site of Ariconium at Rosehill, or, agreeably to Sir Richard Hoare's emendation, at Bolitre, near Ross? a position which strongly militates against the admeasurement expressed in the Itinerary. The distance from Clevum to Ariconium is fifteen Roman miles, equal to twenty-two miles and a half English. But Rosehill, or Bolitre, is but twelve miles from Gloucester. Consequently, there is a deficiency of ten miles and a half, and therefore Rosehill, or Bolitre, cannot be the site of Ariconium. Besides, there is not the least assimilation of sound between the words Rosehill, or Bolitre, and Ariconium. This Roman station is, by every author that has written of it, represented to have been situated in that division of Siluria which was called by its ancient inhabitants Erenwc. Now, the territory around Ross composed no part of this ancient and noted division; consequently Rosehill, or Bolitre, both which places are contiguous to Ross, cannot be the site of the Roman station Ariconium.

If, then, the arrangement of Mr. Horsley, in placing Ariconium at Rosehill, and of Sir Richard Hoare at Bolitre, be unsupportable, the opinion of the former, respecting the site of Magna, will be found not less unfounded. He has fixed this Roman station at Kenchester, a position that likewise militates against the admeasurement expressed in the Itinerary. For the distance from Gobannium to Magna is twenty-two Roman miles, equal to thirty-three English. But the distance from Abergavenny to Kenchester is but eighteen miles, consequently there is a deficiency of fifteen miles. Therefore Kenchester cannot be the site of Magna. Besides there doth not exist the least assimilation, or coincidence, of enunciation between the words Magna and Kenchester.

If, then, we have satisfactorily refuted the notion of

Rosehill, or Bolitre, being the site of Ariconium, and of Kenchester being that of Magna, where shall we fix these two stations? Let this be the subject of our next inquiry.

With respect to the former, viz., Ariconium, where can it be so properly and truly fixed as in its ancient and native seat, Kenchester, of which it is the original and rightful proprietor; and comes clad in the armour of truth to demand a reversal of its sentence, and to reclaim possession of the inheritance from which it had been unjustly ejected; and this is the sum of the evidence with which it substantiates its claim.

It has been before observed that a division of Siluria was called Erenwc. This division comprehended the site of what is now called Hereford, and a considerable extent of the adjacent country, especially that which stretches towards the south and west. Now, the appellation Erenwc is the true and undoubted root of Ariconium, in which word is perceptible a Latin termination, and, in the preceding syllables, a coincidence of sound with the original. This was the invariable practice of the Romans in giving names to their military stations. They forbore to obliterate the ancient and original names, as did their barbarous and desolating successors, the Saxons. They only clothed them in a Roman dress, affixing a Latin termination, but retaining sometimes a syllable, or sometimes more, of their pristine enunciation. The recollection of this important circumstance should inseparably accompany every attempt to investigate the site of Roman stations in Britain. The neglect of taking this useful and sure guide hath occasioned numerous errors, and every deviation from this maxim hath been punished by a proportionable absurdity. Kenchester is universally admitted to have been the site of a Roman station. It is situated in that division of the county of Hereford which was anciently called Erenwc, and the only site of a Roman station within that division. But Ariconium was a Roman station, and also situated in Erenwc. Kenchester, therefore, must be the site of Ariconium. Will the conclusiveness of this syllogism suffice, and spare the trouble of referring to other proofs, such as the coincidence of the two words Ariconium and Kenchester, one syllable at least of the former being preserved in the latter, which was used anciently to be written Conchester; and also the perfect accordance of the distance between Clevum and Ariconium, with the number of miles from Gloucester to Kenchester.

Considerable advantages will result from the restoration of the site of Ariconium to its ancient and original patrimony, Kenchester. It will be a means of terminating the long-agitated controversy respecting the origin and etymology of Hereford. To dream that this city rose from the ruins of Magna, is the extreme of absurdity. But many authors of the first respectability have not hesitated to assert that Hereford derived its name and its existence from Ariconium. This idea, which, at its first formation, was perhaps only conjectural, is now completely realized; and the sole objection that opposed its general admissibility removed, by placing Ariconium not at Rosehill, or Bolitre, but at Kenchester, a situation so conveniently contiguous to Hereford, whither the spoliations, torn from the parent, might easily have been floated down the river Wye for the accommodation and ornament of the daughter; whereas such an operation from Bolitre or Rosehill must have proved, in those days, if not impracticable, at least difficult. Lastly, with respect to Brandon being the site of the Roman station Bravonium, whoever has seen this camp will readily conclude that no Roman station was ever placed there. Its relative distance from other acknowledged stations is also irreconcilable with the Itinerary admeasurement.

A second advantage following the replacing of Ariconium at Kenchester is this:—it becomes the clue, or the stepping-stone, that helps us to ascertain, and fix, the true site of the Roman station, Magna. And, indeed, this was the reason that induced us to enter upon the preceding detail. The same attention to the relative distances expressed in the Itinerary, and the same regard for the coincidence of names, which have hitherto so successfully conducted our researches, will likewise assist us in fixing the true situation of this much-contested station.

With respect to the adjudication of Camden, who placed it at Old Radnor, a personal inspection of this vicinity has put us in perfect unison with Mr. Horsley, who says, "that there never has been a Roman station there, nor any military way leading to it." But though we are necessitated to abandon the pretensions of Old Radnor, yet we need not travel beyond the limits of this county for the attainment of this long-desired object. It is reasonable to suppose that the prudent and cautious Romans would adopt and execute proper means of securing the line of the river Ieithon, as they did that of the other rivers within the kingdom of Siluria, along the course of which they penetrated into the country, and on the right banks of which they established their stations. This stream, indeed, if compared to the Wye, is not entitled to particular consideration. But, viewed as the boundary which terminated the Roman conquests in this district, the Ieithon became an object of no small importance in the estimation of a military people, intent upon the security of their acquisitions, and constantly occupied in devising means to increase them. To have left this frontier unfortified, and by this neglect to have exposed the interior country to the incursions of its fierce inhabitants, would have been a deviation from their accustomed policy, as strange as it was culpable.

These suggestions suffice to convince us that the line of the Ieithon was fortified by the Romans; and, in fact, we find this to have been the case. In the parish of Llanfihangel Heligon, on the right bank of this river, and partly overhanging it, and near to the mansion-house of John Williams, Esq., of Cwm, is a military station, universally acknowledged to be Roman. There exist strong reasons for believing that this station is the real site of the identical Magna of Mr. Horsley, or rather Magos, agreeably to the mode of writing the word used by Camden, and the respectable authors of the *Ancient*

Universal History. The reasons which confirm this belief are the following:—

1. The distance from this station to Gobannium (Abergavenny) exactly accords with the admeasurement expressed in the Itinerary, viz., twenty-two Roman miles, which, being brought to a conformity with the English standard, amount to thirty-three miles of our computation.

2. The relative distance of this station from other relative stations is in complete unison with the Itinerary admeasurement. We have already seen its perfect accordance with that of Gobannium, or Abergavenny. If the true site of Bravonium be fixed, it preserves its due distance with that station also. Now, that Brandon is not the site of Bravonium, appears incontrovertibly evident by many cogent reasons. There is a place on an eminence adjoining to the river Lug, about three miles east from the town of Leominster, in Herefordshire, which, from great quantities of Roman coins and other ancient relics, as well as from its contiguity to several British camps, seems entitled to be considered a Roman station, though never before publicly noticed as such. It is usually called by the common people Blackardun, from the blackness of its soil. This word is supposed to be derived from the British Bwlchgaerdun, as its situation is at the head of an important pass.

3. The coincidence of its name with Magna, or Magos, affords a considerable argument in its favour. For the present name, that was given to Sir Richard Hoare by Mr. Williams, a gentleman little conversant in ancient history, or in the knowledge of Roman antiquities, viz., Castell Gollen, is founded on no authority whatever, and was then for the first time imposed, and merely from the circumstance of a few hazel trees growing on its sides. Prior to this time it was always distinguished by the name Gaer, thereby denoting its Roman construction and quality. But it appears from tradition, as well as from other sources of information, that its original and primitive appellation was Gaer-fagu. And it is a singular event, that as a small and obscure hamlet, called Farley, near

H

the Clee Hill, in Shropshire, is the only spot that now retains the ancient name of the country lying between the Severn and the Wye, viz., Ffer-llys, so there exists at present nothing but a ruinated mansion-house, situated about a mile and a half towards the north-east from this station, that preserves the memory of its primitive appellation. This mansion-house is called Caer-fagu, and entirely constructed of stone, thereby forming a singular phenomenon in this vicinity. It bears marks of remote antiquity, and indicates fallen grandeur. It commands an important pass called Bwlch-trawspren, and was embosomed till lately with groves of oak, as that name signifies. From many vestiges of buildings, and other relics, which have been discovered, extending themselves in this direction, there is strong reason for supposing that this mansion-house was an appendage to the station, perhaps its citadel, where the præfect of the Pacensian cohort held his proconsular tribunal, or court, issued his edicts, and received the homage and tribute of the pacified Silures. Its name, Caer-fagu, which, by the peculiarity of the British language, has converted the letter M into F, assimilates itself with Magos, or Magna; and as it signifies the populous city, it consequently corresponds with the Latin appellation Magna Castra.

Sir Richard Hoare, in his splendid edition of *Giraldus Cambrensis*, thus describes this Roman station:—" Its square form is perfect, and encircled by a wall. It appears to have had many out-buildings, as without the area of the camp there are great irregularities in the ground. Numerous fragments of Roman brick and pottery are dispersed about all the adjoining fields. The south-east side of the camp hangs over the river Ieithon." It is much to be regretted that a writer so well qualified to do justice to this neglected station had not afforded himself more time, and taken greater pains to examine and investigate its name, and its other numerous appendages. He might then have added that this station in all its parts is the least mutilated of any belonging to the Romans in Britain; that it constitutes a square of one hundred and twenty yards, and that its wall is built of hammered or rough-hewn stone; that within it may be traced the remains of partition walls, and that the prætorium, or the site of the tent of the commander-in-chief, is very visible; that it is situated on the north-west bank of the river Ieithon, with an elevated area, commanding a fine view of the adjacent country; that the entrance into it on the north-west side, being the quarter whence the greatest danger was apprehended to arise, was guarded by a double trench and rampart; that on the south-east side the buttresses of the bridge, which preserved the communication with the country in that direction, remain to this day; and that besides bricks and pottery, Roman coins also of the Empress Faustina, and human bones, have been thrown up. With these, and many more interesting particulars, the learned antiquary might have furnished his commentary, and entertained and instructed the public. But it did not at the time enter into his conception that he was treading upon the much-disputed station Magos, or Magna, which, in deference to the overbearing authority of Horsley, and in acquiescence with his great name, he erroneously supposed to have left many miles in his rear, viz., at Kenchester.

Many remains of ancient camps and fortifications, as well British as Roman, abound in this vicinity, more especially in the adjoining parishes of Llanydrindod and Disserth, which not only testify that this part of the district hath been the scene of military action in remote periods, but also demonstrate the obstinate resistance made by its inhabitants to the Roman arms. For, from the vestiges of many small camps, not fewer than eighteen in number, in the same direction, extending upwards of a mile and a half over the commons of Llanydrindod and Howey, placed irregularly, some at the distance of sixteen paces, others at three or four hundred, along the line of march which the Romans are known to have used, all of a square form, with obtuse angles from each other, it appears evident that every yard of ground was warmly disputed, and that the invaders durst not advance into the country without the precaution of throwing up, at almost every step, camps for their defence and security, which in some places deviate from the line of march only for the manifest purpose of gaining the high ground. They measure generally from twenty to thirty yards within the agger, and have an entrance on each side, and opposite to each entrance a mound. The agger is formed of earth, and a few stones, about five or six yards thick, and two feet high, and surrounded by a small trench, except at the entrances. The cultivation of the country, and the growth of trees, opposed and frustrated the endeavours to ascertain how far the continuance of these *castra minora* extended. Probably they reached much farther, as well on the north-east towards Caer-fagu, as on the south-west towards Llechrhyd, than can now be traced.

Some persons are inclined to dispute the original designation and use which the preceding statement ascribes to these inferior encampments, and to suppose them to have been merely *castra æstiva*, summer camps. If this had been their sole use and application, where existed the necessity of constructing so many in number, so small in size, and placing them at so short a distance from each other as only sixteen or eighteen paces? If they had all been occupied at once, they would have contained more than three legions of soldiers, a number far exceeding the Roman contingent that was ever at any one time quartered in this part of Britain. Others think that these camps were the habitations, or residences, of the workmen employed in constructing the military road. But this conjecture is as untenable as the other, and for the same reason; because the construction of so many receptacles for the accommodation of the roadmakers, at so small a distance from each other, was an unnecessary and a superfluous labour. Could not a numerous company of workmen walk the space of sixteen paces to the scene of their labour, without being under the necessity of forming, every successive day, a new and fortified encampment? Probability, therefore, predominates in favour of the first supposition, which ascribes the existence of these numerous camps to the violent and pertinacious resistance which the Romans experienced in this part of Siluria. This supposition is further confirmed by the existence of several tommenau, or barrows, contiguous to these camps, indicating that at an æra long prior to the introduction of Christianity into this part of the island, there had been a dreadful mortality, or carnage, of its inhabitants. Now, to what æra in our national history can this carnage be assigned with greater congruity than to that which the noble achievements of Caractacus so illustriously signalized? That the scene of some of the exploits of this intrepid and renowned commander lay on this very common, is rendered very probable by the circumstance of its proximity to the site of his last sad conflict at Caer-Caradoc, on the north-eastern frontier of this county, and lying almost in a direct line from this place. In short, when we recall to our recollection the many reverses and defeats which the Romans sustained from the vigorous and repeated attacks made by the indignant Silures, when we take into consideration the irregular collocation of these temporary encampments, which bespeaks not choice but compulsion, and indicates the alarm that had seized the minds of their constructors, together with the numerous places of sepulture, that is, tommenau, or barrows, with which this common is studded, we cannot but allow to it as strong a claim for having been the scene of at least some of these exploits as any situation in the ancient kingdom of Siluria whatsoever. That a great battle was fought here in very ancient times the numerous barrows evince; nor doth it seem less probable that these small square fortifications, raised on situations not in immediate contact with water, a convenience invariably regarded by the Romans, are the result of the hasty and compulsive effort of an invading enemy to secure himself from impetuous attack, and avert sudden surprize.

It doth not appear that there exist in the district under consideration any more stations of Roman construction, unless that distinction be allowed to one of a superior style, which is situated upon the bank of the Ieithon, in the parish of Llanddewi-ystrad-ennau. This fortification has been already in part described, and various conjectures are formed respecting the original occupancy of this distinguished military post. Its elliptical form, and its situation on a high and almost inaccessible eminence, indicate a Silurian or British construction; but it is to be remembered that the Romans, like a wise people, were not obstinately tenacious of their own military system, but often changed their tactics as occasion and circumstances required, and adapted the configurations of their encampments and stations to the nature and external appearance of the ground selected for that purpose. Hence their camps were of different forms, generally, indeed, squarish with round angles, and often oblong, or inclining to a parallelogram. The site of their stations is to be traced on the northern banks of rivers, and fronting the south. Whereas, the form of British or Silurian encampments is round or elliptical, and their situation is an high eminence and difficult of access. That this fortified post was originally Silurian, we do not adventure to deny; but many reasons concur to induce us to suppose that it was also possessed and occupied by the Romans, such as the discovery of Roman coins; the existence of a Roman road, called in the British language Ystrad; the usual application of its name Caer, or Gaer, to signify a Roman fort or garrison; and, lastly, the circumstance of its being the link which preserved the line of communication between Caer-fagu, or Magos, on the one hand, and Caer-sws, in the parish of Llandinam, Montgomeryshire, on the other.

Access was had to every Roman station in Britain by the formation of Roman roads. Accordingly we find these modes of communication issuing from the station of Caer-fagu, or Magos, on the Ieithon, intersecting the county in various directions, and facilitating and preserving an intercourse, not only with its different parts, but with the more distant divisions of Siluria. On this subject Sir Richard Hoare has committed himself greatly.

For in his map of the Roman roads in Wales he has drawn a straight line from this station on the Ieithon to Kenchester, on the Wye, through a most hilly part of the county, presenting obstacles which the Romans exerted all their care and skill to avoid. A laborious investigation of the relative situation and circumstances of the district under consideration has obtained, we trust, a more successful result.

In the first place, this station communicated with the adjacent country by means of a bridge built over the Ieithon, on its south-eastern side. From this bridge the road took a north-western direction, and proceeded by Cae-bach, through the fishpond of Llanerchidirion, crossed the commons in a straight line, entered upon the cultivated lands, passed through the fold-yard of a farm-house called Rhewl,[9] in the parish of Disserth, and arrived at Llechrhyd, on the bank of the river Wye. Here the Romans constructed a fort, or castellum, of a regular and square form, for securing the passage over that river. Having crossed the Wye, and having previously detached a branch to communicate with the towns of Builth and Hay, it traversed the county of Brecon, and arrived at Maridunum, or Caermarthen. This branch, commencing at Llechrhyd, passed by Llanelwedd, and proceeded in a straight line to Colwyn Castle. Leaving Clascwm Church a little on the left, it passed on in a line parallel to the river Arrow, till it came to Newchurch; it then ascended Brilley Hill, by a place called Gwryl-fâch-ar-rhewl, that is, the watch-tower on the road; and, having crossed that eminence with a gentle and easy sweep, it proceeded in as straight a direction as possible through Bolingham, Elsdun, Lyonshale, Noke, Milton, &c., to Mortimer's Cross, where it formed a junction with the two roads that came from North and South Wales. This course is rather circuitous; but it has the recommendation of avoiding the impassable hills which impede the route pointed out by Sir Richard Hoare.

[9] *Yr Heol*, the Street Road.—ED. ARCH. CAMB.

The third road from this station was that which passed by the church of Llanbadarnfawr, and proceeded, not along the new turnpike-road, but along the old narrow way leading to the fingerpost on the Pen-y-bont road, the direction of which it kept for a few yards. It then crossed over the cultivated fields on the left of that road, and, having taken a line parallel to the river Clewedoc, passed through the opening of the hills, and arrived at a place near to Abbey Cwm-hir; whence it proceeded through Bwlch-y-sarnau, that is, the Defile of the Causeway, to Caer-sws, in Montgomeryshire, on the bank of the Severn, whence there was a Roman communication with Deva, that is, Caer-leon-gawr, or Chester. This road secured an intercourse between the Silures and Ordovices, the latter of whom inhabited North Wales, and were friends and allies. A branch of it striking across the country by Sarn Hel,[1] and communicating with Lantwardine and Caer-Caradoc, proceeded to the Severn and Viroconium, or Wroxeter. Nor was the communication with the south less free and open. For a Roman road, commencing at Caerleon-upon-the-Usk, in Monmouthshire, proceeded to Gobannium, or Abergavenny; and, passing through a very interesting country in the north-west direction, abounding in military positions, and giving an idea of the *"montes ardui & locorum difficultates"* of Tacitus, crossed the Wye at the town of Hay; thence it proceeded through the parishes of Clyro and Llanstephan, at Ty-yn-y-rhewl, and soon afterwards fell into the road first mentioned, that led from Caerfagu, or Magos, on the Ieithon.

In the vicinity of these several roads have been discovered coins, bricks, cinders, fragments of pottery, and other relics, which distinguish the residences of the Roman people in Britain; whilst in their formation a uniform regularity of line remains everywhere conspicuous.

[1] *Sarn Helen?*—ED. ARCH. CAMB.

NOTE ON THE ROMAN STATIONS AND ROADS.

REMARKS ON THE SITES OF ARICONIUM AND MAGNA CASTRA.

THE publication, in the Journal of the Cambrian Archæological Association of a paper, compiled many years ago, intended as a "History of Radnorshire," offers a subject which has been formerly one of much controversy, although now considered closed by the almost unanimous consent of modern antiquaries; and, had the learned author lived in the present day, it may not be too much to say that he, probably, would have joined in the concordat.

Diverse as have been the statements of older authors respecting the sites of the Roman stations of Ariconium and Magna Castra, there is good reason to adopt the opinion which now generally prevails, that they were situate within the confines of the county of Hereford, the former at Bury Hill, in the vicinity of the town of Ross, and the latter at Kenchester, about five miles west of the city of Hereford; and the proof is readily adduced.

The opponents of this theory have not denied that the Roman stations of Glevum and Gobannium were respectively situated at Gloucester and Abergavenny; and, taking this as a postulate, no very difficult problem is involved.

According to the Itinerary of Antoninus, the distance from Glevum to Ariconium was fifteen miles, and from Gobannium to Magna, twenty-two miles; and the same figures are quoted by the author of the "History of Radnorshire;" but his arguments in favour of the positions which he advocates appear to be based upon the supposition that the Roman mile was equal to one mile and a half English, although he admits that there is great uncertainty in the exact distance of the miles in the Itinerary, being in some cases more than one mile, and in many instances less, so that, he contends, little faith can be placed upon such contradictions.

In the absence of proof to the contrary, there seems no reason why the miles in the Itinerary may not be taken at the acknowledged length of one thousand paces, or five thousand feet, and the chief difficulty is removed. Now the writer states that the distance from Glevum to Ariconium was fifteen miles; but, as he calculated the Roman mile at one and a half English, Ariconium, he says, must have been twenty-two miles and a half from Glevum; whereas the *supposed* site (and which, it is contended, is the *exact* one) is only about twelve miles from Gloucester.

The same line of argument is pursued with respect to Magna, which the author admits to have been twenty-two miles from Gobannium; whereas he states that the distance from Kenchester to Abergavenny is only eighteen miles, instead of thirty-three.

The theory which is now generally adopted, as already stated, of the sites of these respective stations, is therefore borne out by the writer himself, whose error appears in not following the standard measure of the Roman mile, which clears up the difficulty raised against Bury Hill and Kenchester.

Should anyone gainsay the conclusion, it may be proper to sum up these remarks by putting the question as a very simple mathematical problem. Given two points, viz., Glevum at Gloucester, and Gobannium at Abergavenny, as admitted, what other places, at the distances quoted, correspond with Ariconium and Magna? Or, in another way, what Roman stations in like manner lay claim to Bury Hill and Kenchester, which present undoubted evidence of having been occupied by an imperial people? J. DAVIES.

Section 7.—*Offa's Dyke.*

The description of this astonishing, but useless, labour, participating neither in the character of a camp, nor of a castle, naturally takes its place, as does the era of its construction, between the conclusion of the account of the one class of antiquities and the commencement of that of the other. It is called, in the Welsh language, Clawdd Offa, and, in English, Offa's Dyke, because it was constructed in the reign and by the order of Offa, the eleventh king of that part, or division, of the Saxon Heptarchy called Mercia, who was a most formidable enemy of Wales, and a violent abridger of the ancient limits of that Principality. It extends about one hundred miles in length, from Basingwerk, in Flintshire, to Chepstow, in Monmouthshire, and enters this county, on its north-eastern frontier, from the county of Salop. Skirting the west side of the town of Knighton, or Tref-y-Clawdd, it passes along the ridge of Frith Hill, leaving Jenkin Allis to the east; thence along Reeves' Hill, in a straight line from north to south, by

A.D. 750.

Penllan and Gilfach, towards the west, having Norton village on the east, and Whitton and Lytton on the west; it then crosses the river Lug, at its junction with a mill stream, by a yew tree, to Maestrayloe and Discoed, leaving Beggar's Bush on the west, and also Ebnol Chapel, together with the Four Stones near the river Hindwell; it then continues its course, by Newcastle Camp, to Evenjobb Hill, and Bareland, and Burfâ Bank, and Lower Harpton, and Morgel Hill, where it assumes an eastern direction along the ridge of Rushock Hill, Sheepwalks, Kennel, and Golden Bank, near Eyewood; thence to Kinsham, and, crossing the Arrow at Lord's Mill, it runs in a parallel line with that river to Downfield; thence through Lyonshall Park, Heath and Pen-rhôs; it then crosses the turnpike road, and stretches on to Holme's Marsh, by the village on the east, whence the vestiges of it disappear.

In many of the places above mentioned, the remains of the Dyke are very visible, and form a monument of the unperishable nature of works constructed of earth. The sharpness of the contour of this Dyke is astonishing, and appears almost as fresh as if cut yesterday, excepting the edges, which are clothed with a fine verdure. The castles of this district, which were once deemed impregnable, and frowned terror into their neighbourhood, and the stone walls that environed and fortified the town of New Radnor, have all crumbled into dust, and scarcely left a fragment to ascertain their site, while this Dyke, composed entirely of earth, remains to this day, in every place where the plough has not intruded, an undecaying monument of the labour of past ages.

On the original policy and intention of constructing this embankment, various writers have expressed various opinions. Some of the English historians have espoused the conjecture that the intention of it was to protect the kingdom of Mercia from the incursions of the Welsh. But how weak a barrier must a mud wall present to a ferocious and an intrepid people, whose animosity to the

Mercians was inveterate, and whose indignation was kindled into fury by the rapacious and unprincipled invaders of their country! If, on the contrary, the Welsh were a spiritless and pusillanimous enemy, as, from the appearance of so weak a fortification, some modern wits have been led to infer, where could be the occasion for a protecting barrier at all? The true account of the matter seems to be this: after a violent contest of twenty years' continuance with the Mercian Offa, at the head of the whole Saxon Heptarchy, in which both parties experienced many reverses and defeats, a peace was concluded betwixt the hostile nations, and a new boundary line fixed, which the subjects of both concurred in forming. And, in order to induce the Welsh to submit quietly and peaceably to surrender the territories of which the fortune of war had despoiled them, their enemies engaged that this line should be the utmost limit—the *ne plus ultra*— of their encroachments, and confirmed this assurance by causing the bank to be thrown up on the east, as well as on the west, side of the trench, testifying thereby that the Dyke was hence to serve as a perpetual boundary, which neither of them should be permitted to transgress. This treaty, like all others of a similar nature, was observed with good faith no longer than the moment when the parties saw it convenient to violate its conditions.

By virtue of this line of demarcation, the town of Kington, the parish of Huntington, and a considerable portion of the adjacent territory, were included in Wales. The Dyke extended no farther than the river Wye, which afterwards constituted the boundary.

[*Note.*—We print this section without any commentary, and refer the reader to the articles on Offa's Dyke which are in the pages of this volume of the *Archæologia Cambrensis*. The author's observations are of interest, chiefly as showing that he was aware of the Dyke being a line of territorial demarcation.—ED. ARCH. CAMB.]

Section 8.—*Castles.*

The Silures, in common with the Britons, constructed no castles from principle, and not from incapacity. They disdained to shelter themselves behind walls, and always evinced a strong aversion to confinement of any kind. Personally brave and intrepid, yet impatient of continued exertions, they preferred the immediate decision of the field, to the prolonged fluctuations of a siege. In this respect, they were imitated by the Welsh : and few, or no, castles were constructed in any part of Wales, prior to the invasion of the Romans, Saxons, and Normans.

The principal castles contained in this district, were the following :—1. New Radnor. 2. Payne's Castle. 3. Boughrhyd. 4. Colwen, or Maud's Castle. 5. Aberedwy. 6. Knighton. 7. Cnwclas. 8. Cefn-y-llys. 9. Cwmaron. 10. Moelienydd. 11. Duybod, or Tibboeth. 12. Rhayader.

In a field on the south side of the church-yard of Pencraig, or Old Radnor, from which it is separated by the road, is to be seen a circular piece of ground, surrounded by a deep moat, and called the Court-yard. Foundations of buildings have occasionally been dug up in this place, which seem to favour the general supposition of there having been a round tower constructed on this site, intended as well for defence as for imprisonment, agreeable to the practice of the Silures and Britons, who, on circular mounds of earth erected round towers, capable of containing twenty or thirty men. The name affords sanction to the conjecture that there was holden a court of judicature, under the authority either of the Princes of Wales, to whom this part of the district once belonged, or of the ancient reguli of the district, or of the Lords of Radnor, or of the Lords Marchers; and perhaps under the control of all these four powers successively. Its contiguity to the church must have given additional solemnity to the administration of justice. The outward circular apartment was the audience hall and court of judicature; the oblong building was the chief's own retirement; around this principal building were others of various forms and dimensions.

1. *New Radnor Castle.*—It does not appear that any castles were constructed within this district before the Saxons had gotten a permanent footing in the eastern frontier of it. This event happened in the year 1064, and was the consequence of Earl Harold's second irruption into South Wales; for his first had proved eminently unsuccessful, when that ill-fated and divided country was destitute of a head, or governor. This calamity, together with pieces of all-subduing gold scattered among the needy chieftains, was the means of facilitating the enterprize, and promoting the usurpations, of this ambitious and unprincipled peer, who seized the possession of the vale of Radnor; and, for its security, erected the castle of New Radnor, and garrisoned it with troops. Harold excelled in the art of war, and evinced his military judgment by selecting this advantageous situation for constructing a fortress, which should awe and bridle the adjacent country. It was built on an eminence, which, whilst it had an entire command of the town below, defended the opening of a narrow pass, or defile, that led into it between two hills from the west. This castle appears, from the delineation given of it in Speed's map, a copy of which is annexed, to have been a fortress of considerable strength, and to have consisted of an inner keep, and a base-court with semicircular towers at the flanks, or angles. The intrenchments that surrounded it are at this time almost entire. The outer ward, called Baili glâs, or the green court, is still distinct from the inner one, or keep, and preserves its original form. The walls of the town had, it is said, four gates, obtending the four cardinal points of the compass: parts of them are still remaining. Their site, together with the moat, is very visible, especially on the west and south sides of the town. They rested upon rows of small Gothic arches. Near the western extremity of the parish, and about a mile from the town of New Radnor, is an intrenched dyke, which was continued from one ex-

A.D. 1064.

tremity of the narrow vale to the other, and evidently constructed as an outwork for the purpose of guarding the defile, and securing the castle from a sudden *coup de main.*

No other castles were constructed within this district till subsequently to the year 1108, when the rapacious Normans, having undertaken its conquest, endeavoured to secure their lawless encroachments by bridling the country, and domineering over the natives by means of garrisoned fortresses.

A.D. 1130.   2. *Payne's Castle* was built about the year 1130, by Payne, a Norman follower of the conqueror of England, from whom it received its name. Its original extent, splendour and magnificence are unknown, there being neither history nor tradition left to assist the researches of the author, who spared no pains to collect the desired information of its history. His efforts totally failed in the quarter to which he was recommended. The remains of this castle exhibit at present a very inconsiderable and mean appearance. Its site is, indeed, discernible; and a few loose fragments of its external walls show that there formerly existed a building upon the spot.[1]

3. *Boughrhyd Castle* stood on the bank of the river Wye, and was built by Eineon Clyd, Lord of Elfael. On the site of it is recently erected a very elegant mansion and seat, by the late proprietor, Francis Foulke, Esq.

4. *Colwen Castle,* or *Maud's Castle,* is situated about four miles west of Payne's Castle, and stands on the Forest Farm, in the parish of Llansaintfread. It was built in the reign of King John, about the year 1216, by William de Braos, Lord of Brecknock, in honour of his

---

[1] Payne had a son, named Thomas, who left an only daughter and heiress, named Alice. She having married Henry, the third Earl of Lancaster, conveyed to that family this and all her other Welsh estates, which devolved to her from William de Londres, and Richard Seward, to whom she was related. He terminated his life in the Crusades.

wife, whose name was Maud de Saint Valeri, whence it received the name of Maud's Castle. Its other appellation was Colwen.

However celebrated may have been its ancient fame, and whoever were its possessors, few or none are the vestiges which bespeak its pristine splendour. There still exist, indeed, a deep moat, and a green grass plat, to point out the site on which this once frowning fortress stood, but its walls compose the materials with which a farm-house and out-buildings have been constructed.

5. On a narrow ridge contiguous to the junction of the rivers Edw and Wye, and about four hundred yards from the church, once stood the "Castle of Aberedw." At what time this fortress was constructed, and by what person, are points equally unknown. It is now in ruins. At a little distance is an elevated mount of earth, on which was constructed the keep, or tower. This castle did certainly belong to Llewelyn, the last Prince of Wales. There is also a cave, cut in the rock, about six feet square, having a very small entrance, called Llewelyn's Cave. It is said that this unfortunate prince was used to secrete himself in this cave, and thereby foil the pursuit of his enemies.

There was also in this neighbourhood another castle, or fortification, that belonged to this prince, the ruins of which are to be seen at a place called Llechrhyd, adjoining the road leading from Buallt to Rhayader, and at the distance of two miles from the former town, and contiguous to the river Wye. Its regular and square form has induced some persons to ascribe its construction to the Romans, who used it for the purpose of securing a passage over that river. It is certain that it did belong to Llewelyn, who, in his last effort to save his country's independence, made it a post for preserving a communication with Cefn-y-bedd, on the bank of the Irfon, in Brecknockshire, and for facilitating his retreat into North Wales.

6. *Knighton Castle.*—This town was anciently forti-

fied with a castle. The mount on which the keep stood is to be seen on the west end of the town; no other vestige of it remains; nor does there exist any clue to direct us through the labyrinth of obscurity in which it is involved, or introduce us to the knowledge of the person by whom, or of the time when, it was constructed. Probably, as the assailants of this part of the district came from the county of Salop, the castle of Knighton owes its origin to the family of the Arundels, or of the Fitz-Warrens, of Clun. There subsists to this day a close connection betwixt these two towns.

A.D. 1242. 7. *Cnwclâs Castle* has long been so completely destroyed, as not to preserve the smallest vestige.

8. *Cefn-y-llys Castle* stood on a bank of the river Ieithon, and was almost surrounded by that river, excepting one narrow isthmus which communicates with the country. Strong by nature, and fortified by art, this fortress, before the invention and use of gunpowder and artillery, must have been impregnable; it being inaccessible on all sides, its north side only excepted, on which is a narrow defile, which a hundred men might defend against a thousand. Here was holden that tremendous court of justice, or rather of injustice, called the Lords Marchers' Court. From this appropriated use of the place, and from the etymology of the name, which signifies the "Ridge or Bank of the Court," Mr. Malkin is induced to think that there never existed a castle at Cefn-y-llys. This opinion militates against the concurring testimonies of tradition, and of printed authorities. Nor does the etymology of the name controvert in the least the general allegation that there has been a castle at Cefn-y-llys; for, by the Lords Marchers, courts of justice were holden in castles; so that there appears no foundation for Mr. Malkin's singular opinion. The castle of Cefn-y-llys was built by a Lord Marcher, viz., by Ralph Mortimer, Earl of Wigmore, and Lord of Moelienydd, in the year 1242, and continued in the possession of his family, with

A.D. 1242.

the exception of occasional interruptions by the Welsh Princes, and attainder for high treason and rebellion, till the reign of Henry VI., when Edmund, the last Earl of March, of the name of Mortimer, died. It then devolved to Richard, Earl of Cambridge, who married his only sister and heiress, and upon his attainder, and finally upon the accession of his eldest son to the throne, by the title of Edward IV., it became again vested in the Crown.

In a place called the Castle Garden was dug up, some years ago, a silver thumb ring. Many have supposed it to be the signet ring of one of the Princes of South Wales, who resided at Cefn-y-llys. The author ascribes it to a much earlier age. This curious relic is now in the possession of Mrs. Edwards, of Greenfields.

The same noble persons who constructed the castle of Cefn-y-llys, built also the

9. *Castle of Cwmaron*, on the bank of a river of that name. The site and moat are still visible, but not a fragment of the superstructure remains. The

10. *Castle of Moelienydd* is said to have been originally constructed by the Earl of Chester, after a sudden and successful irruption into Cantref Moelienydd. It was afterwards taken and destroyed by the natives, headed by their regulus, or lord.

11. *Duybod*, or *Tibboeth Castle*, is situated on a steep hill, called Crogen, on which, it is said, the refractory inhabitants endeavouring to recover the possessions of their forefathers,—in other words, exciting rebellion,—suffered execution. This hill impends over the river Ieithon, in the parish of Llanano, and is about nine miles to the north-west of the town of Knighton. The existing remains of this mutilated fortress consist only of a confused heap of thick walls, and fragments of walls. The site, however, and a piece of the keep may be traced; the whole being surrounded by a deep moat. The obscurity of its history, excepting only its final demolition by Llewelyn ab Gruffudd, Prince of Wales, in the year

1260, is to be regretted. Neither record nor tradition respecting it exists. Perhaps it derived its name from a nobleman called Tibetot, a justiciary of South Wales, in the reign of Edward I., who is said to have possessed property in this vicinity. The situation of this castle is remarkably wild and elevated; it commands an extensive prospect, and the frowning aspect of its ruins may be discerned at a great distance. Naturally strong, and inaccessible on all sides but one, which was well defended by intrenchments that still remain visible, it might bid defiance to the most violent and repeated assaults.

12. *Rhayader Castle* was constructed in the year 1178, by Rhys ab Gruffudd, Prince of South Wales, for the purpose of checking and repelling the incursions of the Normans, who, having established themselves on the maritime coasts of Cardiganshire, and extending their encroachments into the interior, carried on a kind of desultory and murderous warfare against this vicinity. It stood on a nook of the river Wye, on the west and north-west sides of the town, at the extremity of a small common called Maesbach. Of the superstructure, no vestige at present remains; but the original foundation may be traced. The only entrance which preserves a communication with the castle, is a narrow space on the north-east, between two deep trenches cut out of an exceedingly hard and solid rock; the one of which leads to the river towards the north, the other inclines more to the east. Along the south foundation runs a foss, about sixteen feet deep and twelve wide, until it communicates with a steep precipice, at the summit of which flows a spring of excellent water, formerly used by the garrison, and the bottom of which precipice is level with the bed of the river. These three trenches form the three sides of a quadrangle. At the bottom of the precipice was a barrow, or tommen, surrounded by a moat, where was erected the castle mill. The other tommen, or mount, on the opposite bank of the river, in a straight line from the castle, and excavated at top, has been noticed before,

and is introduced here merely for the purpose of subjoining a different conjecture of the original design of its formation; it being, in the opinion of some, nothing more than a mound of earth thrown up by the republican forces of the Protectorate, for the purpose of erecting a battery of cannon to demolish the walls of the castle. The tower, or citadel, stood in a direct line between the castle and the prison, now a Presbyterian meeting-house, overlooking the river, and guarding its ford. The adjacent mount still retains the name of Tower Hill.

Many other castles formerly existed within the district under consideration. These, in general, were of inferior note, and little deserve historic remembrance. There remains, however, one, which impartiality requires us to endeavour to rescue from oblivion. It was the opinion of Camden, that Vortigern terminated his life among the fastnesses contiguous to the town of Rhaiadrgwy, or Rhayader. This opinion, controverted by many, the result of the author's researches, during his progress through the county, seems in some measure to confirm. It is certain that Vortigern, who was Lord of Erging and Ewias, in Herefordshire, possessed large property in the lordship of Moelienydd, if he was not also its regulus. His Silurian, or British, name was Gwytherin. Now, there is a spot of ground in the lordship of Gwrthreinion, so called, it is supposed, after his name, within the cantref of Moelienydd, and in the parish of Llanbister, designated by the appellation of Nant Castell Gwytherin, or the Dingle of the Castle of Vortigern. This dingle is very lonesome and retired, and is situated near a place called Arthur's Marsh, not far from the source of the Prill, Nant Caermenin. In its neighbourhood is a row of stones, or cairn, called Croes y Noddfa, that is, the Cross of Refuge. Combining all these circumstances together, we derive a strong probability that this solitary spot constituted the last retreat of this traitorous and wretched king.

CHAPTER III.

CIVIL HISTORY.

WALES, at the time of its conquest by King Edward I., consisted, partly, of Lordships Marchers, some of which were kept by the King of England in his own hands, and others granted to English lords, to hold of the Kings of England *in capite;* and, partly, of lands which the Kings of England had conquered, and kept in their own hands, as the counties of Caermarthen, Cardigan, and Flint; and, partly, òf the territory possessed by the last Prince thereof, viz., Llewelyn ab Gruffudd, a little before his death, comprehending the couhties of Merioneth, Caernarvon, and Anglesey. The Marches were the borders, in which this county, with others, was included. They were neither part of the realm of England; so that when William Rufus granted the lordships of Moelynaidd and Elfael to Roger Mortimer, he disposed of property that was not his own; nor were these Marches governed by English laws, but constituted what is deemed a solecism in political administration, an *imperium in imperio.*

With respect to the power and jurisdiction of the Lords Marchers, they had in their several seigniories all royal rights; and this enjoyment of royal rights consisted in the following particulars:—

I.—All writs within the seigniory ran in the name of the lords, and were *contra pacem* of the lord.

II.—The Lord Marcher had judgment of life and limb in all capital and criminal cases; and to this was the power of pardoning all offences.

III.—The Lord Marcher had the power of constituting boroughs.

IV.—He had the power of appointing justices of *oyer* and *terminer*.

V.—He had a right to hold plea of all actions, real, and personal, and mixed, within his seigniory.

VI.—The king's writ could not run into the Marches, for they were no parcel of the realm of England; nor could the king *intromittere* into any of those liberties for the execution of justice.

These two last heads may be reduced into one, viz., an unlimited exempt jurisdiction in all causes arising within the seigniory; in consequence of which the Lords Marchers had each of them their own chancery for original writs.

Notwithstanding this exclusive jurisdiction, there were two

sorts of causes wherein the king's courts held plea, though they arose within the Marches. The first took in all controversies when the Lord Marcher was a party, either in respect to the lordship itself, or the boundaries of it. The second comprehended all such causes wherein it was necessary to write to the bishop, as *quare impedits*, and all issues of marriage and bastardy. In these cases, an appeal was open to the king and his privy council.

The courts of the Lords Marchers, which were generally holden in their castles, consisted of a justiciary, chancellor, seneschal, mareschal, chamberlain, and constable, all of their own appointment, and held their authority *durante bene placito*.

Radnor was at first a royal demesne, and consequently an honour, but subsequently granted to the Lords Marchers. Moelynaidd was a Lordship Marcher, holden originally by Hugh Mortimer under the King of England *in capite*, and afterwards, when a descendant of that family was raised to the throne, it became a royal inheritance. The other Lordship Marcher in this district was Elfael, which descended to William de Braos, Lord of Brecknock and Buallt, by marriage with Bertha, granddaughter of Bernard de Newmarche. Roger Clifford, of Clifford Castle, the Earls of Shrewsbury and Montgomery, were also Lords Marchers. The clashing rights of so many petty sovereigns bordering upon each other, produced infinite tumults and disorders. Their several castles were points of attraction as receptacles of felons, criminals, and outlaws, the disaffected and factions subjects of the Welsh Princes, and desperate adventurers, who fled thither to escape the sword of justice, and who were made useful in serving the violent and oppressive purposes of the lords. These neighbouring tyrants sometimes confederated together, and acted in unison, in extending their mutual encroachments, despoiling and destroying the Welsh natives: sometimes they quarrelled about the division of the spoil, involving all their respective tenants, who also were their vassals, in the devastating effects of those bloody frays: sometimes they directed their allied arms against the Princes of Wales, or erected the standard of rebellion against the sovereigns of England: or seduced the martial natives to spend their useless valour on the sands of Ascalon, and in the fields of Cressy. So great, indeed, was their power, which had often made the Kings of England tremble upon their throne, that even Edward I., after having accomplished the conquest of Wales, made no attempt to innovate or intrench upon their jurisdiction; and, though a new form of government was imposed upon the country, yet the inhabitants of the Marches were left to all the rigour of their former severities.

By the famous statute of Rhuddlan, 12 Edward I., Wales was divided into eight counties,—viz., Glamorgan, Caermarthen, Pembroke, Cardigan, Merioneth, Flint, Caernarvon, and Anglesey. The government and jurisdiction of these counties were framed, in all respects, upon the English plan. The justices were constituted by like commission with the justices in England, and invested with all jurisdiction as full and extensive, as well in bank, as in their circuits. The sheriffs had the same power in their towns and county courts, and the office corresponded in all respects with the English sheriffalty. They had their chancery and exchequer answerable to the English, and the methods of proceeding in all actions, real and personal, were the same, without any variation, as the methods of proceeding in England, These courts, in short, were sisters of the courts of England. and in all respects their equals. The judges in Wales were equal with those in England; nor could the former receive any record sent by the latter. Writs of error must come out of Wales into parliament. In the eyes of the law, Wales was considered as an independent kingdom, ruled and ordered by its own laws and customs. Hence the courts of Westminster assumed no jurisdiction over it; they could not direct processes to the officers of the Welsh courts; they did not hold Wales to be subject to, or placed within, their jurisdiction; and hereupon is grounded the maxim, *Quod breve regis non currit in Walliam.* The king's writs runs not into Wales in all cases whatsoever. And, lastly, the king's courts at Westminster exercised no jurisdiction in these eight shires of Wales, either concurrent or superintendant; but the king's justices there were equal in dignity and power with the justices of England, and absolutely independent of them.

Edward I. allowed but two justices of assize for the whole Principality, one for the northern, and the other for the southern, division. The shires being divided into seigniories, had their courts baron, and courts leet; and the corporate towns had their courts of record. Out of all these courts, and also the sheriff's court and quarter sessions, matters were removable to the great sessions, and not elsewhere, by writ of *corpus cum causâ, certiorari, recordare,* false judgment, or error. To ingratiate himself with his new subjects, he allowed them, through a mistaken policy, to enjoy their liberties, and to hold their estates under ancient tenures, and to bequeath them under the operation of gavel-kind. This intermixture of Welsh and English tenure was the source of vexatious litigation.

By the 29 Elizabeth, all Wales and the Marches were committed to the government of a lord-lieutenant, who had the authority to appoint deputy-lieutenants. She also added the puisne judges.

Of the Welsh jurisprudence of Edward I., the defects were immediately experienced. It possessed no control over those petty tyrants of Wales, the Lords Marchers, who were too powerful to be corrected by the ordinary course of justice. Their rapacity knew no bounds, and the venality and corruption of the judges were infamous. Hence it was often found necessary to have recourse to an extraordinary jurisdiction by the king himself, who, when the matter was of sufficient importance, held plea originally, and heard the cause sometimes in parliament, and sometimes by persons specially commissioned to try that particular cause. The causes which called for this extraordinary cognizance were generally the riots and tumults occasioned by these overgrown lords, together with disputes about jurisdiction, which were generally attended with great disorders. These weighty causes, after trials in parliament grew out of use, came to be determined by the king in council, or by such particular persons as he assigned for that purpose. And hence arose the establishment of a new court of law, called

The Council and President of the Marches of Wales.

Edward IV., King of England, perceived, with regret, when he was Earl of Wigmore, and Lord of Moelynaidd, the outrages committed in the Marches. Gratitude for services he received from the Welsh in the battle of Mortimer's Cross, and compassion for their sufferings, prompted him to digest and execute a plan which should put a check to these desultory enormities. With this view he instituted a court, which was holden in the castle of Ludlow, in the county of Salop, in the centre, as it were, of the Marches of Wales, with all the power, dignity, and splendour of of royalty. The superior members of this court were,—a lord president, a vice-president, a chief justice, and council, among which were the chief justice of Chester, with three other then-existing justices of Wales, representing its three principalities, and many of the nobility resident in the several counties bordering upon the Marches. Subordinate officers were,—a clerk of the council, clerk of the signet, keeper of the castle, gentleman porter, serjeants-at-arms, messengers, and a variety of others.

This court was erected, not by Act of Parliament, but by the king's sole authority. And the end, originally proposed by the institution, was to keep the Lords Marchers in order, and to exercise, as king's vicegerents, his sovereign jurisdiction over these sturdy subjects. And thus having gotten some footing in criminal matters, they began presently to enlarge their bounds, and thrust themselves into all civil causes. They therefore soon superseded the necessity of appealing to the king and privy council, to whom little or none of the Welsh business was henceforth delegated. Most causes, some, perhaps, of the highest consequence only excepted, were submitted to the cognizance of the President and Council of the Marches. The judges allowed them to hold plea in all actions at common law, as debt and trespass upon the case, under £50, in all causes of equity, and in all criminal causes. So great was the extent of business in this court, that more causes were dispatched in a term than in any court in England—above twenty causes have been moved in an afternoon. Perhaps, in addition to the reputed equity of its decisions, the inferiority of the established fees contributed to increase the multiplicity of its business. For all the motions and pleadings in one cause, in one term, the retained counsel received a fee of but five shillings. The superior members of this court were allowed six shillings and eightpence per day, and diet for themselves and servants.

As all human institutions in process of time degenerate from the original rectitude of their proceedings, so it befel this celebrated court; which, though at its first outset, and for some time after, public justice was administered impartially, fell at length into the commission of those corruptions and abuses which its establishment was intended to correct. The preamble to the Act of Parliament enacted for its dissolution, in the first year of the reign of William and Mary, stated that " the powers of the Lord President had been much abused, and that the institution had become a great grievance to the subject. Among these grievances were the malpractices of the attorneys and inferior officers of the court,. whereby," as the record stated, " justice had lacked due execution, and the inhabitants had been sundry ways most grievously vexed and molested, as also by long delays of suits, and new exactions of fees, greatly impoverished, so that the court which in the beginning was erected for the ease and relief of the inhabitants, was become to them, through such abuses, most grievous and intolerable." The grievances alluded to may be specified under the following heads: this court adopted the practice of the Star Chamber, whereby the members of it became the sole judges of the law, the fact, and the penalty; informations were allowed to be received instead of indictments, in order to multiply fines and pecuniary penalties; and a set of harpies, under the denomination of promoters and relators, equally hated by the good and bad, were encouraged, who by hunting out obsolete penalties, taking out writs of *capias*, and using other oppressive devices, continually harassed the subject, alarming the quieter sort of people by processes from London, and robbing the poorer by forced compositions.

A List of the Lords President of the Court and Council of the Marches, from the commencement of its Institution to its Dissolution.

A.D.
1469. John Carpenter, Bishop of Worcester
1482. Edward, Prince of Wales
1502. William Smith, Bishop of Lincoln
1513. Geoffrey Blythe, Bishop of Lichfield and Coventry
1525. John Vesey, Bishop of Exeter
1535. Rowland Lee, Bishop of Lichfield and Coventry
1543. Richard Sampson, Bishop of Chester
1549. John Dudley, Earl of Warwick
1551. Sir William Herbert, Knight of the Garter
1553. Nicholas Heath, Archbishop of York, and Chancellor of England
Thomas Young, Archbishop of York
1555. Sir William Herbert, Knight, re-appointed
1556. Gilbert Browne, Bishop of Bath and Wells

A.D.
1559. Sir John Williams, Lord Williams of Thame, Oxon
1560. Sir Philip Sidney, Knight
1577. John Whitgift, Archbishop of Canterbury
1580. Sir Philip Sidney, Knight, re-appointed
1587. Henry, Earl of Pembroke
1602. Edward, Lord Zouch
1610. Ralph, Lord Eure
1610. William, Lord Compton, Earl of Northampton—(Council, member of, Thomas Harley, Esq., of Brampton Bryan Castle)
1669. Prince Rupert
Richard, Lord Vaughan, Earl of Carbery
1673. Henry, Marquis of Worcester
1684. Henry Somerset, Duke of Bedford
Sir John Bridgman, Knight
1688. Charles, Earl of Macclesfield

It is probable that the use of this court had been superseded, long prior to its dissolution, by the operation of the statute of 27 Henry VIII., cap. 26. From that time Wales became part of the realm of England, governed by the laws and statutes of England, administered by the king's justices, after the same form and fashion as is used in the shires of England. Out of the extent of the Marches were erected five new counties, Radnor, Brecknock, Monmouth, Montgomery, and Denbigh. Monmouth was afterwards annexed to England. In consequence of this statute, Wales is incorporated with England, and made part of the realm.

CHAPTER IV.

TITLES OF HONOUR; A LIST AND SOME ACCOUNT OF THE NORMAN LORDS OF THIS DISTRICT; EARLS OF RADNOR; NAMES OF THE SHERIFFS; A LIST OF THE KNIGHTS OF THE SHIRE.

In ancient times, the Lords or Earls of Fferllys, that is, the country lying between the Severn and the Wye, were also Lords of Moelynaidd. This latter title, together with the patrimony annexed, was retained by the descendants of the ancient Reguli of the district, not only long after the arbitrary and unjust cession which William Rufus, King of England, made of it to Ralph de Mortemer, Lord of Wigmore, but almost to the period of the final subjugation of Wales by Edward I. So long did this district persevere in its resistance to Norman encroachments; its last lord of British extraction, viz., Cadwallon ab Maelgon ab Cadwallon, having paid the debt of nature in the year 1234. The title of Lord of Moelynaidd, claimed, indeed, before, and nominally assumed, was then actually devolved upon, and the territory possessed by, the elder branches of the house of Wigmore, with whom they remained, with the occasional interruptions caused by treason and rebellion, till the time in which Edward, Duke of York, Earl of Marche, and Lord of Moelynaidd, grandson of the only surviving heiress of the house of Mortimer, having finally triumphed over the Lancastrian party, ascended the throne of England, under the title of Edward IV. Here follows a list of the Lords of Moelynaidd of the house of Wigmore:—

1087.—Ralph de Mortemer. According to *Domesday Book*, he possessed Pilleth, Norton.

1109.—Robert de Mortemer.

1154.—Hugh de Mortemer. He took Rhys ab Hywell prisoner, and slew in battle Meyric ab Madoc ab Riryd, and Meredudd ab Madoc ab Idnerth.

1171.—Reginald de Mortemer, who married Gwladus ddu, the only surviving child and heiress of Llewelyn ab Iorwerth, Prince of North Wales, and in her right was entitled to succeed to the throne of the Principality.

1263.—Roger Mortimer, Lord of Wigmore, and by right of inheritance Prince of Wales. He married Mawd, daughter of William de Braos, Earl or Lord of Brecknock, Buallt, Pain's Castle, Huntington, Radnor, &c. In the year 1242 this Roger built the castles of Cnwclas and Cefn-y-llys, and also the church of Presteigne. He likewise confirmed to Abbey Cwmhîr the grants of the lands with which Cadwallon, Lord of Moelynaidd, its founder, had endowed it; and, in order to ingratiate himself with the natives, and to overawe their refractory disposition, resided occasionally in his castle of Cwmaron, in which he is even said to have been born. In right of his wife he became possessed of Buallt, Pain's Castle, and Radnor, in the plain of which latter place, a little below the town, he, together with Hugh de Saye, Chief Justiciary of Wales, received a signal defeat from Prince Rhys.

1281.—Edmund Mortimer, Lord of Wigmore. He was wounded in the battle of Buallt by the soldiers of the last Prince of Wales, and died soon after of his wounds in the castle of Wigmore.

1320.—Roger Mortimer, Lord of Wigmore. His immense estates were all confiscated, and Cantref Moelynaidd became a royal property.

1357.—Roger Mortimer. This young nobleman was of the king's body-guard in the battle of Cressy. Edward III., in the 29th year of his reign, restored him to the Earldom of Marche and Wigmore, and Lordship of Moelynaidd, and to all his grandfather's inheritances, honours, and estates, both in England and Wales. He possessed Radnor, Werthrynion, Cwmydauddwr, Cefn-y-llys, Pilleth, and Cnwclas, all in this district, and was one of the council of nine appointed to direct the business of the kingdom, during the minority of Richard II., King of England. —(1377.)

Edmund Mortimer, Earl of Marche and Wigmore, and Lord of Moelynaidd, married Philippa, daughter and heiress of Lionel, Duke of Clarence, second son of King Edward III., in whose right he was Earl of Ulster in Ireland, and had issue Roger and Edmund. King Richard II. announced Roger to be his successor; the parliament declared him heir to the crown,—(1397,) and the Duke of Gloucester, his uncle, proposed to give him immediate possession of the throne of England. This project he modestly declined. He was soon after made Lord-Lieutenant of Ireland, where he was slain in a skirmish by the natives. Edmund was killed in the battle of Pilleth, by Owen Glyndwrdwy.—(1402). His nephew, a youth, and heir to the crown, was also taken prisoner by the Welsh chieftain, whom Henry IV., through jealousy of his just claims, detained in honourable custody at Windsor, and allowed not his name to be once mentioned in parliament.

Roger Mortimer, Earl of Marche, Ulster, and Wigmore, Lord of Trim, Clare, and Connaught in Ireland, and Lord of Moelynaidd in the Marches of Wales, married Eleanor, daughter and heiress of Thomas Holland, Earl of Kent, by whom he had issue Roger and Edmund.

Edmund, son of the above named Roger, was the last Earl of Marche and Lord of Moelynaidd of the house of Mortimer. He died without issue,—(1425). But his sister Anne, who had espoused Richard Plantagenet, Earl of Cambridge, transmitted her brother's immense estates, as well as claim to the crown, to her son Richard Plantagenet, Duke of York. He was slain in the battle of Wakefield,—(1460,) and succeeded by his son Edward, Duke of York, Earl of Marche, and Lord of Moelynaidd, who, in the following year, renewed the claim made by his father to the throne of England, achieved a decisive victory at Mortimer's Cross, in Herefordshire, principally by the assistance of his Welsh partizans, and was soon after proclaimed king, under the title of Edward IV.—(1461). His daughter Elizabeth was married to King Henry VII., and thereby became the mother of King Henry VIII.

We learn from *Domesday Book* that Radnor was selected by William I., the conqueror of England, to be his royal demesne, and from that circumstance obtained the distinguished title of *Honour*. How far it descended among the posterity of that monarch, or whether it was conferred on the person of Hugh Lasne, who, according to the same authority, claimed it under a promise said to have been made him by William Fitz Osborn, the great and first Earl of Hereford of the Norman race, is equally uncertain. It is, however, well known that, during some of the baronial wars, the town and castle of Radnor were possessed by Richard, Duke of Cornwall, and King of the Romans.—(1100).

It is, therefore, probable that Richard at that time united the Lordship of Radnor with the Dukedom of Cornwall, an alliance subsisting in the remotest period. Long, however, before the time of Richard, there existed Lords of Radnor, if not among the branches of the royal family of England, yet among the descendants of those who accompanied the Conqueror in his expedition. For Philip, *alias* Peter, de Braos, having espoused Bertha, daughter of Milo, Earl of Hereford, and grand-daughter of Bernard de Newmarche, the conqueror of the three cantrefs of Brecknockshire, was, in his wife's right, Lord of Brecknock, Buallt, and Radnor. He had issue William, Giles, and Reginald.

1. William de Braos was a Lord Marcher of immense estates, and consequently possessed great influence and power over the affairs of Wales. Devoid of principle, he joined and deserted the barons in their wars against King John, as his interest preponderated, and once mortgaged the castles of Brecknock, Hay, and Radnor to that monarch. Having invited some Welsh chieftains to an entertainment holden in his castle of Aber-

L

gavenny, he violated the sacred laws of hospitality, and caused them to be assassinated. He possessed, besides vast property in Brecknockshire, Monmouthshire, and Sussex, the castles of Colwyn, Pain's Castle, and Radnor, in this district, and the castle of Huntington, in Herefordshire. He married Eva, daughter of William Marshall, Earl of Pembroke, who had for her dower the Lordships of Abergavenny, Kington, Radnor, Knighton, &c. He endeavoured to atone for his numerous iniquities by bequeathing the tithes of the parish of Llanfihangel-nant-moelyn, in this county, to the Knights of St. John in Jerusalem; but the King of England, provoked at his atrocities, compelled him to flee into Ireland, and thence into France, where it is said he perished in great want and misery.

2. His brother Giles was consecrated Bishop of Hereford in the year 1200: a great warrior, and who had an active part in procuring the *Magna Charta*. Through his intercession, Pain's Castle, Elfael, Clun, and Knighton, were restored to Walter Fychan, son of Eineon Clyd, Lord of Elfael, who was murdered by the Normans, as he was returning from the splendid entertainment given by his father-in-law, Prince Rhys, in the castle of Aberteifi, in Cardiganshire. At his death, Giles left his large possessions to his younger brother Reginald,—(1215,) who married Gwladus ddu, daughter of Llewelyn ab Iorwerth, Prince of North Wales. This noble lady, surviving her husband, was espoused by Reginald Mortimer, Lord of Moelynaidd, who, in right of his wife, carried out of the family of de Braos a very considerable property in addition to his own. From this period, the Lords of Moelynaidd became Lords of Radnor.

1275.—Humphrey de Bohun, Earl of Hereford, espoused a daughter and co-heiress of William de Braos, in the reign of Edward I. He joined Roger de Mortimer against King Edward II.—(1321.)

1361.—Died, William de Bohun, Earl of Northampton, &c., who, by espousing the widow of Lord Edmund Mortimer, was Lord of Moelynaidd and Radnor.

1399.—Edmund Stafford, Earl of Buckingham, married a Bohun, who carried the Radnor property into that family.

1460.—The Bohun property was divided into two shares; one remained in the house of York, and the other was distributed among the Buckingham family.

Earls of Radnor.

The first Earl of Radnor was John Robarts, Lord Robarts of

Truro, in the county of Cornwall. He was created in the year 1679, and was succeeded by his grandson Charles Robarts, in the year 1685, who, dying in 1723, was succeeded by his nephew Henry. He died in the year 1741, and the last Earl of Radnor of this name and family was his cousin, John Robarts. The title being extinct in the year 1757, was restored in the person of William Pleydell Bouverie, who was created Earl of Radnor September 28, 1765, and, in default of issue, the title of Earl of Radnor was to descend to the heirs male of his father. His lordship married, January 14, 1748, Harriet, only daughter and heir of Sir Mark Stuart Pleydell, Bart., who left his estate to his lordship, directing each person enjoying the same to use the name of Pleydell Bouverie. By this lady, he had issue Jacob, who, on his father's death, on January 28, 1776, succeeded to the title, and was the second Earl of Radnor of that name. He was born March 4, 1750, and married, January 23, 1777, Anne, daughter and co-heir of Anthony Duncombe, Lord Feversham, by whom he had issue William, Viscount Folkstone, who, born May 11, 1779, married, October 3, 1800, Catherine Pelham Clinton, only child of Henry, Earl of Lincoln, eldest son of the second Duke of Newcastle, by whom he has several children.

The family of Bouverie is of ancient and honourable extraction in the Low Countries. The first of this name that settled in England was Lawrence des Bouveries, whose grandson William was created a baronet by Queen Anne, February 19, 1714, whose second son, Sir Jacob, having succeeded to the baronetage, changed his name by Act of Parliament from Des Bouveries to Bouverie, and was by George II., June 29, 1747, created Lord Longford, Baron Longford, and Viscount Folkstone. He married Mary, daughter and heir of Bartholomew Clarke, Esq., of Northamptonshire, by whom he had William Pleydell, the first Earl of Radnor of that name.

A List of Sheriffs.

HENRY VIII.

A.D.
1544. John Baker, Presteigne
1545. James Vaughan, Hargest
1546. John Bradshaw, Presteigne

EDWARD VI.

1547. Richard Blick, New Radnor
1548. Peter Lloyd, Boultibrook
1549. Rhys Gwillim, Aberedw
1550. Sir Adam Milton, Salop
1551. Thomas Lewis, Harpton
1552. James Price, Monachtu

MARY.

A.D.
1553. Griffith Jones, Trewern
1554. Edward Price, Knighton
1555. Sir Adam Milton, Salop
1556. John Bradshaw, Presteigne
1557. Peter Lloyd, Boultibrook

ELIZABETH.

1558. John Bradshaw, Presteigne
1559. Stephen Price, Pilleth
1560. Evan Lewis, Gladestry
1561. John Knill, Knill

HISTORY OF RADNORSHIRE.

A.D.
1562. Sir Robert Whitney, Whitney
1563. Morgan Meredith, Llynwent
1564. John Price, Monachtu
1565. Evan Lewis, Gladestry
1566. Robert Vaughan, Winforton
1567. Griffith Jones, Llowes
1568. John Bradshaw, Presteigne
1569. Edward Price, Knighton
1570. Lewis Lloyd, Boultibrook
1571. Robert Vaughan, Presteigne
1572. David Lloyd Meredith, Nantmel
1573. William Lewis, Nash
1574. James Price, Monachtu
1575. Edward Price, Knighton
1576. John Price, Monachtu
1577. John Price, Pilleth
1578. Evan Lewis, Gladestry
1579. Hugh Lloyd, Bettws
1580. Roger Vaughan, Clyro
1581. Lewis Lloyd, Boultibrook
1582. Rhys Lewis, Gladestry
1583. Thomas Wigmore, Shobdon
1584. Evan Lewis, Gladestry
1585. Morgan Meredith, Llynwent
1586. Thomas Hankey, Ludlow
1587. Lewis Lloyd, Boultibrook
1588. John Weaver, Stepleton
1589. John Bradshaw, Presteigne
1590. Edward Price, Knighton
1591. Hugh Lloyd, Bettws
1592. Evan Lewis, Gladestry
1593. Peter Lloyd, Stocking
1594. Thomas Price, Knighton
1595. Humphrey Cornewall, Stanage
1596. Edmund Vinsalley, Presteigne
1597. Clement Price, Coedgwgan
1598. Thomas Wigmore, Shobdon
1599. James Price, Monachtu
1600. Richard Fowler, Abbey Cwmhir
1601. James Price, Pilleth
1602. Lewis Lloyd, Boultibrook

JAMES I.

1603. Edward Winston, Presteigne
1604. John Bradshaw, Presteigne
1605. Humphrey Cornewall, Berrington
1606. Evan Vaughan, Bugaildu
1607. John Townshend, Ludlow
1608. — Whitney, Whitney
1609. Sir Robert Harley, Brampton
1610. John Vaughan, Kinnersley
1611. Hugh Lewis,
1612. Thomas Powell, Cwmydauddwr
1613. James Price, Pilleth
1614. John Lloyd, Bettws
1615. Richard Fowler, Abbey Cwmhir
1616. Robert Whitney, Whitney
1617. Richard Jones, Trewern
1618. Ezekiel Beestone, Walton

A.D.
1619. Samuel Parker, Ludlow
1620. Hugh Lewis, Harpton
1621. Humphrey Cornewall, Brampton
1622. Allen Currard, Presteigne
1623. Thomas Rhys, Disserth
1624. John Read, Presteigne

CHARLES I.

1625. Humphrey Walcot, Walcot
1626. Richard Fowler,
1627. Evan Vaughan, Bugaildu
1628. Robert Weaver, Aylmstry
1629. Griffith Jones, Presteigne
1630. William Vaughan, Llowes
1631. John Maddocks,
1632. James Philipps, Llan
1633. Roderic Gwynne, Llanelwedd
1634. Richard Rodd, Rodd
1635. Nicholas Meredith, Presteigne
1636. Morgan Vaughan, Bugaildu
1637. Morris Lewis, Stones
1638. Evan Davies, Llanddewi
1639. Brian Crowther, Knighton
1640. Robert Williams, Caebalfa
1641. John Powell, Stanage
1642. William Latchard, Bettws
1643. Hugh Lloyd, Caerfagu
1644. Hugh Lloyd, Caerfagu
1645. Brian Crowther, Knighton
1646. Thomas Weaver, Aylmstry
1647. Robert Martin, New Radnor
1648. Robert Martin, Jun., New Radnor

INTERREGNUM.

1649. Henry Williams, Caebalfa
1650. Nicholas Taylor, Presteigne
1651. John Danzey, Gladestry
1652. John Will,

OLIVER CROMWELL.

1653. John Walsham, Knill
1654. Samuel Powell, Stanage
1655. Richard Fowler, Abbey Cwmhir
1656. John Davies, Monachtu
1657. James Price, Pilleth

RICHARD CROMWELL.

1658. Thomas Lewis, Harpton
1659. Thomas Lewis, Harpton

CHARLES II.

1660. Evan Davies, Llanddewi
1661. John Walcot, Walcot
1662. — Lewis, Hindwell
1663. Henry Williams, Caebalfa
1664. Thomas Eaglestone, Presteigne
1665. Nicholas Taylor, Heath
1666. Robert Martin, New Radnor
1667. Andrew Philipps, Llanddewi

A.D.
1668. Ezekiel Beestone, Walton
1669. Roger Stephens, Knowle
1670. John Walsham, Knill
1671. John Richards, Evanjobb
1672. Edward Davies, Llanddewi
1673. James Lloyd, Kington
1674. William Whitcombe, London
1675. William Probert, Llanddewi
1676. Robert Cuttler, Farrington
1677. Richard Vaughan, Monmouth
1678. Hugh Powell, Cwmellan
1679. Thomas Vaughan, Bugaildu
1680. Henry Probert, Llowes
1681. Henry Mathews, Lantwardine
1682. Evan Powell, Llanbister
1683. Thomas Lewis, Harpton
1684. John Davies, Coedglasson

JAMES II.

1685. Samuel Powell, Stanage
1686. Henry Davies, Graig
1687. William Taylor, Norton
1688. Nicholas Taylor, Heath

WILLIAM III.

1689. Richard Vaughan, Clyro
1690. John Fowler, Bron-y-dre
1691. William Probert, Llanddewi
1692. Thomas Vaughan, Bugaildu
1693. Hugh Lewis, Hindwell
1694. Robert Cuttler, Street
1695. Thomas Lewis, Nantgwyllt
1696. William Fowler, Grainge
1697. Thomas Lewis, Harpton
1698. Thomas Williams, Caebalfa
1699. Walter Davies, Ludlow
1700. Edward Price, Boultibrook
1701. John Waddeley, Hereford

ANNE.

1702. John Read, Montgomery
1703. — Price, Presteigne
1704. Morgan Vaughan, Bugaildu
1705. David Morgan, Coedglasson
1706. Edward Howarth, Caebalfa
1707. Adam Price, Boultibrook
1708. Hugh Gough, Knighton
1709. William Chase, London
1710. Charles Hanmer, Llanddewi
1711. Charles Walcot, Walcot
1712. Jonas Stephens, Bessbrook
1713. Roger Tonman, Vron

GEORGE I.

1714. Walter Price, Cefnbwll
1715. Edward Fowler, Abbey Cwmhîr
1716. John Clarke, Blaiddfa
1717. John Miles, Evanjobb
1718. Marmaduke Gwynne, Garth

A.D.
1719. Hugh Powell, Cwmellan
1720. Fletcher Powell, Dowaton
1721. Nicholas Taylor, Heath
1722. Charles Hanmer, Llanddewi
1723. Giles Whitehall, Moor
1724. Hugh Morgan, Bettws
1725. Folliot Powell, Stanage
1726. Edward Burton, Vronlâs
1727. Edward Shipman, Bugaildu

GEORGE II.

1728. Henry Williams, Skynlâs
1729. Harford Jones, Kington
1730. John Tyler, Dilwyn
1731. Stephen Harris, Bessbrook
1732. Thomas Holland, Llangunllo
1733. Thomas Gronous, London
1734. Matthew Davies, Presteigne
1735. John Clarke, Blaiddfa
1736. John Williams, Skreen
1737. John Jones, Trevannon
1738. Sir Robert Cornewall, Berrington
1739. Henry Howarth, Caebalfa
1740. Mansel Powell, Yerdisley
1741. Edward Price, Boultibrook
1742. Thomas Hughes, Gladestry
1743. Peter Rickards, Evanjobb
1744. William Wynter, Brecon
1745. William Ball, Kington
1746. Henry Williams, Skylâs
1747. John Patteshall, Puddlestone
1748. John Warter, Kington
1749. Morgan Evans, Llanbarrhyd
1750. Hugh Gough, Knighton
1751. Francis Walker, Vernyhall
1752. Thomas Vaughan, Bugaildu
1753. Richard Lloyd, Llanbadarn fynydd
1754. John Bishop, Gladestry
1755. William Go—, Kingwood
1756. John Lewis, Presteigne
1757. John Evans, Cwmydauddwr
1758. Daniel Davies, Llanbadarn fawr
1759. David Stephens, Nantmel
1760. John Daykins, Llanbister

GEORGE III.

1761. John Evans, Llanbarrhyd
1762. Evan Vaughan, Llwynmadoc
1763. James Williams, Trawley
1764. James Broom, Ewithington
1765. Sir Hans Fowler, Abbey Cwmhîr
1766. Samuel Bevan, Newchurch
1767. Sir John Meredith, Brecon
1768. John Trumper, Michaelchurch
1769. James Watkins, Clifford
1770. Marmaduke Gwynne, Garth
1771. Charles Gore, Ty-fannor
1772. William Whitcombe, Clyro
1773. Bernard Holland, Llanbister

A.D.
1774. Walter Wilkins, Maeslough
1775. John Griffiths, Kington
1776. Richard Davies, Llanstephen
1777. William Powell, Llanwrthwl
1778. Harford Jones, Presteigne
1779. Jonathan Field, Llanbadarn fynydd
1780. Thomas Cook, Ludlow
1781. Jonathan Bowen, Knighton
1782. Thomas Bevan, Skynlâs
1783. Thomas Price, Clascwm

A.D.
1784. Buthe Shelley, Michaelchurch
1785. James Price, Clyro
1786. Bridgwater Meredith, Clyro
1787. John Price, Penybont
1788. Bell Lloyd, Boultibrook
1789. Thomas Duppa,
1790. Francis Garbett, Knill
1797. Percival Lewis, Downton
1803. M. H. T. Gwynne, Llanelwedd

A List of Members of Parliament for the County of Radnor.

CHARLES II.
A.D.
1660. Sir Richard Lloyd
1661. Sir Richard Lloyd
1678. Rowland Gwynne, Esq.
1681. Rowland Gwynne, Esq.

JAMES II.
1685. Richard Williams, Esq.
1688. Sir Rowland Gwynne

WILLIAM III.
1690. John Jefferies, Esq.
1695. John Jefferies, Esq.
1698. Thomas Harley, Esq.
1701. Thomas Harley, Esq.

ANNE.
1702. Thomas Harley, Esq.
1705. Thomas Harley, Esq.
1708. Thomas Harley, Esq.
1710. Thomas Harley, Esq.
1713. Thomas Harley, Esq.

GEORGE I.
A.D.
1714. Sir Richard Fowler.
1722. Sir Humphrey Howarth

GEORGE II.
1727. Sir Humphrey Howarth
1734. Sir Humphrey Howarth
1741. Sir Humphrey Howarth
1747. Sir Humphrey Howarth
1754. Sir Humphrey Howarth

GEORGE III.
1761. Lord Caernarvon
1768. Chase Price, Esq.
1774. Chase Price, Esq.
1780. Thomas Johnes, Esq.
1784. Thomas Johnes, Esq.
1790. Thomas Johnes, Esq.
1796. Walter Wilkins, Esq.
1802. Walter Wilkins, Esq.
1807. Walter Wilkins, Esq.
1812. Walter Wilkins, Esq.
1818. Walter Wilkins, Esq.

HISTORY OF RADNORSHIRE.

Supplemental List of Radnorshire Sheriffs to supply deficiencies in previous List.—By JOHN JONES, *Esq., of Cefnfaes.*

A.D.
1791. Thomas Jones, Esq., Pencerrig
1792. John Lewis, Esq., Harpton Court
1793. William Symonds, Esq., M.D., Hereford
1794. Richard Price, Esq., Knighton
1795. Francis Fowke, Esq., Llanstephan
1796. John Pritchard, Esq., Dolyfelin
1797. Percival Lewis, Esq., Downton
1798. John Benn Walsh, Esq., Cefnllys
1799. John Bodenham, Esq., Grove
1800. James Lloyd Harris, Esq., Kington
1801. Hugh Powell Evans, Esq., Noyadd
1802. John Sherburne, Esq., Llandrindod
1803. Marmaduke Thos. Howell Gwynne, Esq., Llanelwedd
1804. Thomas Frankland Lewis, Esq., Harpton
1805. Charles Rogers, Esq., Stanage
1806. Thomas Stephens, Esq., Kinnerton
1807. Edward Burton, Esq., Llanbister
1808. Thomas Thomas, Esq., Pencerrig
1809. John Whittaker, Esq., Cascob
1810. Geo. Crawford Ricketts, Esq., Cwm
1811. John Cheesement Severn, Esq., Michaelchurch
1812. Thomas Grove, Junr., Esq., Cwmelan
1813. Daniel Reid, Esq., Cornel
1814. Charles Humphreys Price, Esq., Knighton
1815. William Davies, Esq., Caebalfa
1816. Sir Harford Jones Brydges, Bart., Boultibrooke
1817. Penry Powell, Esq., Penllan
1818. Hugh Stephens, Esq., Cascob
1819. Morgan John Evans, Esq., Llwynbarried
1820. James Crummer, Esq., Howey Hall
1821. Robert Peel, Esq., Cwmelan
1822. Peter Rd. Mynors, Esq., Evancoed
1823. John Hugh Powell, Esq., Cliro
1824. Hugh Vaughan, Esq., Llwynmadoc
1825. Sir John Benn Walsh, Bart., Cefnlleece

A.D.
1826. James Watt, Esq., Doldowlod
1827. Samuel Beavan, Esq., Glascomb
1828. David Thomas, Esq., Wellfield
1829. John Morris, Esq., Kington
1830. Robert Bell Price, Esq., Downfield
1831. Thomas Duppa, Esq., Longueville
1832. Thomas Evans, Esq., Llwynbarried
1833. Walter Wilkins, Esq., Maesllwch
1834. Guy Parsons, Esq., Presteigne
1835. Thomas Williams, Esq., Crossfoot
1836. James William Morgan, Esq., Glasbury
1837. Hans Busk, Esq., Nantmel
1838. Sir John Dutton Colt, Bart., Llanyre
1839. Henry Lingen, Esq., Penlanole
1840. Edw. Rogers, Esq., Stanage Park
1841. Edward Breeze, Esq., Knighton
1842. David Oliver, Esq., Rhydoldog
1843. Edward David Thomas, Esq., Wellfield
1844. David James, Esq., Presteigne
1845. James Davies, Esq., Moor Court
1846. Thomas Prickard, Esq., Dderw
1847. Henry Miles, Esq., Downfield
1848. John Edwards, Esq., Brampton Brian
1849. Edward Myddleton Evans, Esq., Llwynbarried
1850. Edward Morgan Stephens, Esq., Llanauno
1851. Aspinall Phillips, Esq., Abbey Cwm Hir
1852. Sir Harford James Jones Brydges, Bart., Boultibrooke
1853. Jonathan Field, Esq., Esgyrdrainllwyn
1854. John Jones, Esq., Cefnfaes
1855. John Abraham Whittaker, Esq., Newcastle Court
1856. Robert Baskerville Mynors, Esq., Evancoed
1857. Francis Evelyn, Esq., Corton

List of Members returned for the County and Borough of Radnor from the Union with Scotland.—By J. JONES, *Esq.*

Session.	Radnor County.	Radnor Boroughs.
1707.	Thomas Harley, Esq.	Robert Harley, Esq.
1708.	Thomas Harley, Esq.	Robert Harley, Esq.
1710.	Thomas Harley, Esq.	Robert Harley, Esq.
		Edward Lord Harley
1715.	Sir Richard Fowler, Bart.	Thomas Lewis, Esq.
1722.	Sir Humphrey Howarth, Knight	Thomas Lewis, Esq.
1727.	Sir Humphrey Howarth, Knight	Thomas Lewis, Esq.

M

1734. Sir Humphrey Howarth, Knight	Thomas Lewis, Esq.
1741. Sir Humphrey Howarth, Knight	Thomas Lewis, Esq.
1747. Sir Humphrey Howarth, Knight	Thomas Lewis, Esq.
1754. Sir Humphrey Howarth, Knight. On his death a new writ ordered, February 19, 1755, and Howell Gwynne, Junr., Esq., Lord-Lieutenant of the County, was returned	Thomas Lewis, Esq.
1762. James, Marquis of Caernarvon, only son of the Duke of Chandos	Edward Lewis, Esq. Thomas Lewis, Esq. A double return. Mr. Edward Lewis did not defend his seat, and his name was erased from the return.
1768. Chase Price, Esq.	John Lewis, Esq., of Harpton Court Edward Lewis, Esq., of Downton Edward Lewis, Esq., petitioned, and the House declared that he was duly elected
1774. Chase Price, Esq., on his death a new writ was issued in July, 1777, and Thomas Johnes, Senr., Esq., Lord-Lieutenant of Glamorganshire, was elected. On his death a new writ was ordered in June, 1780; and Thomas Johnes, Esq., son of the late member was elected. He was made Receiver-General of the Customs of Wales, and was re-elected May, 1781.	John Lewis, Esq., of Harpton Court Edward Lewis, Esq. Edward Lewis, Esq., petitioned, and was declared duly elected
1780. Thomas Johnes, Eqs.	Edward Lewis, Esq., of Downton John Lewis, Esq., of Harpton Court Edward Lewis, Esq., petitioned, and was declared duly elected
1784. Thomas Johnes, Esq.	Edward Lewis, Esq.
1790. Thomas Johnes, Esq.	David Murray, Esq., brother to Lord Elibank. Upon his death a new writ was issued in May, 1794, and George Viscount Malden, eldest son of the Earl of Essex, was elected
1796. Walter Wilkins, Esq.	George Viscount Malden. On his succeeding his father as Earl of Essex, a new writ was ordered March, 1799, and Richard Price, Esq., was elected
1801. Walter Wilkins, Esq.	Richard Price, Esq.
1802. Walter Wilkins, Esq.	Richard Price, Esq.
1806. Walter Wilkins, Esq.	Richard Price, Esq.
1807. Walter Wilkins, Esq.	Richard Price, Esq.
1812. Walter Wilkins, Esq.	Richard Price, Esq.
1818. Walter Wilkins, Esq.	Richard Price, Esq.
1820. Walter Wilkins, Esq.	Richard Price, Esq.
1826. Walter Wilkins, Esq.	Richard Price, Esq.
1828. On death of W. Wilkins, Thomas Frankland Lewis was returned.	
1830. Thomas Frankland Lewis, Esq.	Richard Price, Esq.
1832. Right Hon. Thos. Frankland Lewis.	Richard Price, Esq.
1834. Right Hon. Thos. Frankland Lewis resigned on being appointed Chief Commissioner of the New Poor Law, and was succeeded by Walter Wil-	

	kins, Esq., grandson of Walter Wilkins, the former member.
1835. Walter Wilkins, Esq.	Richard Price, Esq.
1837. Walter Wilkins, Esq.	Richard Price, Esq.
1840. On the death of Walter Wilkins, Esq., Sir John Benn Walsh Bart., succeeded.	
1841. Sir John Benn Walsh, Bart.	Richard Price, Esq.
1847. Sir John Benn Walsh, Bart.	Right Hon. Sir Thomas Frankland Lewis, Bart.
1852. Sir John Benn Walsh, Bart.	Right Hon. Sir T. F. Lewis, Bart.
1855.	Right Hon. Sir T. F. Lewis, Bart., died, who was succeeded by his son Sir George Cornewall Lewis, Bart., and, on his being appointed Chancellor of the Exchequer, was again returned.
1857. Sir John Benn Walsh, Bart.	Right Hon. Sir George Cornewall Lewis, Bart.

CHAPTER V.

HUNDREDS; PARISHES; MARKET TOWNS.

CANTREF MOELYNAIDD, EXTENT AND PRIVILEGES OF; STEWARDS OF; CROWN LANDS AND GRANTS; BOROUGHS AND FORESTS; MANORS.

Radnorshire contains six hundreds, and fifty-two parishes, including one capital borough, viz., New Radnor; with four auxiliary boroughs, viz., Knighton, Cnwclâs, Cefn-y-llys, and Rhayader; and four market towns, viz., Presteigne, Radnor, Rhayader, and Knighton.

I.—Radnor hundred contains eight parishes, including one capital borough and two market towns,—1. Cascob; 2. Colfa; 3. Discoed; 4. Gladestry; 5. Llanfihangel Nant Moelyn; 6. New Radnor; 7. Old Radnor; 8. Presteigne.

II.—Pain's Castle hundred contains thirteen parishes, —1. Bettws Clyro; 2. Boughrood; 3. Bryngwyn; 4. Clâsbury; 5. Clyro; 6. Llanbedr; 7. Llanddewi fâch; 8. Llandeilo Graban; 9. Llanstephan; 10. Llowes; 11. Michaelchurch; 12. Newchurch; 13. Pains Castle.

III.—Knighton hundred contains nine parishes, including two contributory boroughs and one market town, —1. Bugaildu; 2. Heyop; 3. Knighton; 4. Llananno;

5. Llanbadarn fynydd; 6. Llanbister; 7. Llanddewi ystrad ennau; 8. Cnwclâs; 9. Stanage.

IV.—Cefn-y-llys hundred contains nine parishes, including one contributory borough,—1. Blaiddfâ; 2. Cefn-y-llys; 3. Llanbadarn fawr; 4. Llandegla; 5 Llanfihangel rhyd Ieithon; 6. Llangunllo; 7. Llan-y-drindod; 8. Pilleth; 9. Whitton.

V.—Colwyn hundred contains ten parishes,—1. Abereddw; 2. Bettws Dyserth; 3. Clas Cwm; 4. Cregrina; 5. Diserth; 6. Llanbadarn-y-carreg; 7. Llanelwedd; 8. Llanfaredd; 9. Llansantfraidd; 10. Rhulen.

VI.—Rhaiadrgwy hundred contains six parishes, including one contributory borough and one market town,—1. Cwmdauddwr; 2. Llan Hîr; 3. Llanfihangel Helygen; 4. Nantmel; 5. Rhaiadrgwy; 6. Sant Harmon.

The amount of the population of this district during the Saxon heptarchy, or when subject to the dominion of the Lords Marchers, is a point of as much uncertainty as it was in the time of the Silures. The wars which the inhabitants of this district, in common with the rest of their countrymen, so long maintained for national freedom and independence, and the contests which raged among themselves, must have tended to diminish their numbers, and to impoverish and devastate their country. The oppressions of the Lords Marchers, and the unexampled severities and cruelties of the edicts of Henry IV., enforced with peculiar rigour on this district, likewise contributed to produce the same deleterious effects. That torpid spirit of indifference which these desolating and exterminating calamities never fail to introduce, has extended and diffused its baneful influence to a recent period, manifesting its paralyzing genius by the stagnation of agricultural pursuits, a suspension of commercial activity, and a necessitous migration. In proportion as the spirit of the people has revived by the consciousness of being subject to equal and protecting laws, by the assurance of domestic tranquillity, by the security of life and property, and by the encouragement holden to laborious industry, so have their numbers increased, their comforts enlarged, and their prosperity augmented. And it appears, from an inspection of the parliamentary census, that the population of the county of Radnor has for some years been in a progressive state of increase,—that in the year 1801 it amounted to the number of 19,700; in 1811 to 21,600; thus receiving in the course of ten years an accession of almost 2000 persons.

Cantref Moelynaidd; Extent and Privileges; Stewards; Boroughs; mode of making Burgesses.

In the historical description of the county of Radnor, Cantref Moelynaidd constitutes a prominent and principal figure. We have therefore devoted a whole section to the consideration of this important article. This ancient and extensive territory was possessed and governed by its successive *reguli,* or chieftains, the Lords of Fferr-llys and Moelynaidd, some of whom were Kings of all Britain, many Dukes and Earls of Cornwall, and all of noble blood and regal descent. A bar was put to this long chain of succession by William II., the red-haired King of England, who was very liberal of what had cost him nothing, and bestowed upon his favourites a property that was not his own, and which he had not the courage himself to seize and usurp. By virtue of a grant of unparalleled injustice, this extensive lordship, or manor paramount, of Cantref Moelynaidd, was conferred, by this arbitrary monarch, on Ralph de Mortimer, a relative and follower of the illegitimate conqueror of England, on the terms of military or feudal tenure; the Lord of Wigmore holding *in capite* under the king, and the inhabitants under his lordship, who covenanted to bridle the country with castles, and to maintain in each a certain contingency of soldiers ready for the royal service. The conquest of the territory, however, was not so easy to be accomplished, as the signing and sealing of the grant. This nobleman and his successors found it a work of danger and difficulty. They met with a violent opposition from the native princes, who struggled long and hard for independence, and did not finally submit, after many reverses of fortune, till the entire conquest of Wales was effected by King Edward I., who confirmed the grant of Moelynaidd to Roger Mortimer, Earl of Wigmore. During the minority of Edward III., this extensive lordship, or manor paramount, was by the treason of its lord, the paramour of Queen Isabella, and chief minister of the English court, escheated to the crown, and became its property. In the latter years of the same reign, the forfeited estates of Mortimer, and among the rest Cantref Moelynaidd, were restored to the house of Wigmore. From this period, and indeed some years antecedent to it, courts of justice, or rather of injustice, were established in its several castles, investing the Lord Marcher with *jura regalia*, and a power over the life and death of his numerous vassals. At length the male line of the family of Mortimer became extinct, and by the marriage of Anne, the sole heiress of this immense property, with Richard, Duke of York, whose son ascended the throne of England under the title of Edward IV., the paramount lordship of Cantref Moelynaidd once more reverted to the crown, and has ever since, with the short interruption of a year, continued to form a part of its inheritance.

This territory anciently comprised a hundred townships, and extended into Montgomeryshire, including the parish of Cerri, Mochtre, &c. At present it comprehends four hundreds of the county of Radnor, viz., Rhayader, Cefn-y-llys, Knighton, and Radnor; and twelve mesne manors, viz., Presteigne, *alias* Presthend, Knighton, Swydd-wynogion, Swydd-rhiw-ar-allt, Gladestry, *alias* Glandestre, Cnwclâs, Swydd-y-gre, *alias* Ugree, *alias* Treyllan, Uchcoed, Rhustlin, *alias* Rissuli, *alias* Rhosllyn, Cwmdauddwr, Rhayader, Iscoed Sant Harmon, with the comot of Werthrynion. Over these the manor paramount of Cantref Moelynaidd possesses a supremacy to the present day, with, however, the exception only of the borough of New Radnor, the territory of which is comparatively small. The boroughs of Knighton, Cnwclâs, and Rhayader, together with the constablewick of Colfâ and Gladestry, which brings it almost in contact with the town of Kington, are comprehended in its wide extent. The following table contains the names of its manors, townships, and parishes :—

Manors.	Townships and Parishes.
1. Presteigne, *alias* Presthend.	Four distinct wards, viz., Broad Street, High Street, Hereford Street, St. David's Street, Discoed.
2. Knighton.	Cwmgwilla, Farrington, Jenkinhales, Knighton borough.
3. Swydd-wynogion.	Llanbadarn fawr, Cefn-y-llys, (with the exception of the borough, Llan-y-drindod,) Craigin Llandegla, Cefn-pawl, Llanddewi ystrad ennau, Llanbister, part of.
4. Swydd-rhiw-ar-allt.	Whitton, Pilleth, Llangunllo, Llanfihangel rhydieithon, Treyllan in Llandegla, part of.
5. Gladestre, *alias* Glandestre	Gladestry, Colfâ, Wainwen, Hengoed.
6. Cnwclâs.	Cnwclâs borough.
7. Rhosllyn, *alias* Rustlin, *alias* Rissuli.	Gwasteddin, *alias* Gwastadedd, part of, Vaynor, part of.
8. Swydd-y-gre, *alias* Ugree, *alias* Treyllan.	Church, Heyop, Llanbister, Cefn-pawl, Bugaildu, Craigbedda, *alias* Craigbuddwr, Cwmllechwedd, Carreg, Llananno, Llanbadarn fynydd, Pennant, Bugaildn, Madwalled, Golon, Bronllys, Treyllan in Llanddewi.
9. Uwchcoed.	Uwchcoed in Nantmel, Vaynor, Gasteddin fawr, Coedglasson, Tu Sant Harmon.
10. Cwmdauddwr.	Dyffryn Gwy, Dyffryn Elan.
11. Rhayader.	Rhayader borough, Nantmel, Maesgwyn, Gwasteddin fawr, Vaynor, Coedglasson.
12. Iscoed, *alias* Iscoed Sant Harmon.	

It does not appear, from existing documents, that the crown in remote periods invariably observed the custom of appointing deputies, or stewards, for the purpose of collecting and receiving the rents and emoluments of this lordship. These rents, however, were faithfully paid into the royal treasury, and regularly accounted for to the king by his ministers. For though Sir John Doddridge, in his ancient history of the Principality of Wales, asserts that no charter or document can be found, whereby the revenues of the Principality were conferred upon the Lady, afterwards Queen, Elizabeth; yet in her reign, as well as in the reigns of her predecessors, the receivers, or, as they are termed, the ministers of the crown, appear to have accounted for the produce and profits of the different manors within this lordship, or paramount manor. And in the parliamentary survey made in the year 1649, which is deposited amongst the records of the Augmentation Office, they are completely and particularly specified.

In the sixth year of the reign of the unfortunate King Charles I., we find this extensive lordship granted (*inter alia*) to Charles Harbord, William Scriven, and Philip Oden, in fee. This triumvirate, in the following year, transferred, or sold, their interest to Sir William and Sir George Whitmore, who exercised their authority with all the rigour and rapacity of farmers-general. Neither this disgraceful act of venality, nor the consequent abuse of power, incurred the animadversion of the negligent ministers of those days. But so intolerable was the oppression practised upon the inhabitants, that they were induced to resort to a most extraordinary expedient for liberating themselves from lawless extortion and tyranny. Having by voluntary subscriptions among themselves collected a sum of money amounting to £741 12s.—great riches in those days—they made a loyal tender of it to the king, accompanied with a detail of their grievances, and also a humble petition, that the crown would be graciously pleased to re-purchase with this money the said lordship or manor paramount of Moelynaidd, " that they might (to use their own language) become again the tenants of the Kings of England." This singular transaction, proving at once the existing poverty of the royal exchequer, and that the administration of Charles was not that arbitrary thing which some historians represent it to have been, took place in the ninth year of the same reign. The receipt for the said sum is expressed in the following words, viz. :—

" 28th day of August, in the ninth year of the reign of King Charles I., paid by the tenants of Gladestry, Moelynaidd, and others, the sum of £741 12s., who themselves of their own free will have brought and given to the lord the king, with the intention that the same lord the king should re-assume the said lordships, of late alienated, for a royal estate, and that they themselves might continue tenants of the Kings of England, as they formerly had been, by the hands of Charles Price, Gent., collector thereof."

In consequence of the payment of this sum, the king re-purchased the said lordship of those to whom he had lately sold, and a confirmation of their ancient rights and liberties was granted to the inhabitants in return; and this lordship, thus re-purchased, was secured by letters patent issued under the great seal of England, together with his royal assurance that this confirmed grant should never again be revoked, but suffered to descend undiminished to their latest posterity; and this lordship, thus re-purchased, seems to have ever since continued to constitute a part of the crown revenue.

Notwithstanding this transaction, so honourable in all respects, as well to the king as to his tenants the inhabitants of Cantref Moelynaidd, yet we find, in no long time after, the principles of his ministers to have been so depraved as to listen to a petition of Thomas Harley, Esq., for a lease to be granted to him of a considerable part of these premises, and, among other things, of the cottages built thereon, together with the liberty of inclosing, and adding four acres of the wastes to each cottage. The inhabitants, taking alarm at this apparent violation of their late contract with the king, and apprehending that such a lease, if carried into effect, would eventually render void and useless the reinstatement of themselves and their posterity within the pale of the royal tenantry, lost no time in opposing the execution of this design, dispersed copies of the king's confirmation of their rights and liberties, and presented a strong petition to his majesty, reminding him of his sacred promise never again to alienate this his royal patrimony, so recently re-purchased for him with the money of his tenants, representing the great detriment and damage that would result to them from the operation of such a lease, if granted, whilst no additional benefit would be received by himself, and concluding with a humble prayer that no such lease be granted, but that they might be suffered to remain in the unmolested possession and enjoyment of their ancient rights and privileges.

The privy council were staggered at the firmness manifested by the petitioners; and, in order to gain time, proposed that each party should be heard in support of their respective pretensions. On the part of Mr. Harley, it was urged that the royal revenue would be more easily collected, and more punctually received, by the responsibility of one person than of many; that these cottagers, having four acres of land annexed in addition to each cottage, would thereby acquire a stake in the country, and consequently become more peaceable, industrious, and loyal; that the allegations of the petitioners were more specious than solid, and rather the effect of envy at his prosperity than a mark of affection to their sovereign, bringing to his mind the well known fable of the fox and the grapes; that frequent abuses of the royal wastes had been committed, many inclosures made, and houses built, which were afterwards alienated and sold to the great benefit of individuals; and that, finally, it savoured of high presumption in tenants of the crown to dictate to their lord and sovereign the manner how he should dispose of his property.

To these arguments the petitioners replied, that having with a large sum of money liberated themselves from the tyranny of the Whitmores, they little expected to be so soon re-plunged into a similar state of oppression by the Harleys; that the alleged benefit of the cottagers was a mere pretext made for the purpose of disguising the ambitious designs of the aspiring house of Brampton Bryan, which, by the powers delegated by this lease, would convert the said premises into a source of its own private emolument, enlarge them to an indefinite extent, and thereby gain such an ascendancy in the county as would control and domineer over its native inhabitants; that if trespasses had been committed on the royal wastes, they were done without their knowledge or connivance, and that they alone were sufferers by such encroachments; that the abuse of a privilege, enjoyed for centuries, and repeatedly and solemnly confirmed, was no argument for its abolition; that their ancestors, ever since the accession of their noble Lord of Moelynaidd to the regal sceptre of this kingdom, in whose just cause they profusely shed their blood in the field of Mortimer's

Cross, had been admitted to the honour of being the tenants of all its sovereigns, successively, which honour they, their descendents, had by no act of their own forfeited, but which, withdrawn from them in this reign by the pecuniary exigence of their lord for a short space of time, they had re-purchased of the alienators for the use of his majesty, and received a solemn confirmation of the grant, secured by letters patent under his great seal, together with his royal assurance that this grant of their ancient rights and privileges should never again be revoked, but suffered to descend unimpaired to their latest posterity; and that, finally, time, which never fails to develope the hidden motives and principles of human conduct, would demonstrate to the world who of the two contending parties, themselves or their competitors, best deserved the marks of the royal favour and patronage.

The issue of this contest proved the final prevalence and triumph of truth and justice over falsehood and oppression. The ministers of those days, though equally faithless to their king and country, dared not violate a privilege so long enjoyed, so honourably recovered, and so recently and solemnly ratified and confirmed by his majesty. The dispute terminated in favour of the petitioners, whose challenge, in the close of their reply, subsequent events proved to have been dictated by a spirit truly prophetic. For the inhabitants of this county, when the great rebellion broke out, associated in support of the royal cause, presented their liege lord with a sum of money, and even detached a body of infantry to relieve the city of Hereford, when besieged by Sir William Waller; whilst the whole house of Brampton Bryan espoused the side of the Parliament, and strenuously exerted all its power and influence to promote and carry into effect the arbitrary and illegal proceedings of the Commonwealth, by depressing the king's friends, confiscating their estates, and sequestrating their livings.

In the twelfth year of King Charles I., (1637,) the Earl of Pembroke and Montgomery was appointed steward in and over the paramount manor, or lordship, of Cantref

Moelynaidd. In the time of the Commonwealth of England, this situation was conferred upon its strenuous partizan, Robert Harley, Esq., or Sir Robert Harley, Knight, whose conduct in it was marked by many instances of extortion, violence and oppression, exercised upon the royalists. The same gentleman also held the trust at the era of the restoration of the royal family. From this period to the present time, various grants of this appointment appear to have been made in succession, by letters patent under the great seal of the exchequer, to noblemen and gentlemen of rank and influence. The following is a catalogue of the names of the stewards, and of the dates of their appointments:—

Stewards of Cantref Moelynaidd.

Names.	Dates of Appointment.	
	AN. REG.	A. D.
Earl of Pembroke and Montgomery ..	12 Charles I.	1637.
Sir Robert Harley, Knight	11 Charles II. ..	1671.
Sir Henry Osborne, Knight..........	24 Charles II. ..·	December 19, 1673.
Charles Lord Herbert	33 Charles II. ..	October 9, 1681
Marquis of Powis.................	1 James II.	September 1, 1682.
Sir Rowland Gwynne, Knight	4 James II.	April 6, 1688.
Robert Harley, Esq.................	2 William III...	November 26, 1691
Robert Harley, Esq.................	4 William III...	June 19, 1701.
Robert Harley, Esq.................	1 Anne	1702.
Thomas Lord Coningsby	1 George I.	December 7, 1714.
Duke of Chandos..................	6 George I.	February 4, 1721.
Henry Lewis, Esq.	20 George II.....	June 30, 1746.
Henry Lewis, Esq.	1 George III. ..	April 21, 1761.
Edward, Earl of Oxford............	7 George III. ..	February 8, 1768.
Edward, Earl of Oxford, nephew of the preceding	George III. ..	

Among the customs of this paramount manor, or lordship, the steward has power to hold a court baron every three weeks, and pleas to the amount of £1 19s. 11d., the same to be determined by a jury of six men.

The wages, or fee, accompanying the appointment of steward, is £6 13s. 4d., in addition to which the Earl of Oxford received, by a dormant warrant from the treasury, the sum of £100 per annum. The duties required of the several stewards in succession seem not to have been varied. Independent of his wages, or fee, the steward is entitled, under his patent, to all fees arising from and out of the different courts, which are numerous, but which are seldom or ever holden, except for the purpose of electing and swearing in burgesses or voters for the borough, though, for the better preservation of the rights of the crown, as well as of the privileges of the inhabitants, they are required to be holden frequently.

The grant also confers upon the steward " free and several fisheries, as well as the privilege of hawking, hunting," &c., within the different districts of which Cantref Moelynaidd is composed, with full power to depute and to give liberty to others so to do. In the appointment, however, a special reservation seems always to have been made by the crown to itself, " of all the amerciaments, fines, issues, and other profits arising from all courts leet, courts baron, and courts of record, holden within the same." And these the steward is not only expressly directed to account for to the crown, but " from time to time render a good and faithful account thereof, in such manner and form as other stewards, or keepers, of the king's courts of right, and by the laws and statutes of the kingdom, and by the course and custom of the exchequer, ought and are bound to do." . . . .
" And shall make and deliver to the mayors, bailiffs, and other officers of the said manors, true and perfect schedules, or extracts, of all such fines, issues, and amerciaments, and other profits, of the said several courts, respectively, at fit and convenient times in every year, that they may the better collect and answer the same."

He is also directed that he " shall cause to be delivered, yearly, duplicates of the said schedules, or extracts, upon parchment, under his hand, to the auditor of South Wales for the time being, before he holds his audit for the county, so that the said mayors, bailiffs, and other officers, may be charged therewith upon their accounts."

With respect to the grants which have been made of the privileges of these manors, or lordships, in the year 1753, May 30th, the Earl of Oxford obtained a lease from the crown to extend the term of a former one, then in existence, for twenty years from the 6th of April, 1764.

By this lease (*inter alia*) all mines and minerals, of

what kind soever, found, or to be found, dug, acquired, or recovered in any place within the lordship of Cantref Moelynaidd, in the county of Radnor, as well opened as to be opened, or left and not occupied, or at any time heretofore used, were granted to his lordship, with full and free power to open the soil, and carry away any metals or minerals found therein, together with all privileges whatsoever to the said mines belonging, excepting and reserving out of the said grant to the crown all royal mines whatsoever.

The same letters patent also conveyed to him all and all manner of heriots, yearly, from time to time happening or renewing, within the several manors of Glandestre, Presthend, Rhosllyn, Cnwclâs, Cwmdauddwr, Iscoed, Swydd-rhiwarallt, Uwchcoed, Rhayader, Knighton, Swydd-y-Grè, and Swyd-wynogion, or within any of them, with their appurtenances, being parcel of the lordship of Cantref Moelynaidd, in the said county of Radnor; rendering a tenth part of all the clear yearly profits of the said mines and minerals; such profits to be accounted for upon oath, twice in every year, before the auditor of South Wales, and paid into the hands of the receiver-general of the crown. And with respect to the heriots, it was ordained that every seventh year a particular account of the profits should be delivered unto the auditor of South Wales.

In the year 1784 the property reverted to the crown, and was again granted to the brother of the former lessee, the Reverend John Harley, D.D., Dean of Windsor, and afterwards Bishop of Hereford. This lease expired in the year 1815, and was renewed with his widow.

In the reign of George II., (2nd November, 1758,) a lease of a very different and singular description was granted, for thirty-one years, to Richard Austin, Esq., (*inter alia,*) of the soil and ground of all wastes and waste lands, commons and common of pasture, situated, lying and being in, or belonging to, the several manors, parishes, townships and places, being parcels of, or dependent on, the lordship of Cantref Moelynaidd, in the county of Radnor, that is to say, in Llanddew-ystradennau, Llanbister, Bugaildu, Heyop, Llanbadarn-fynydd, and Llananno, within the manor of Y Gre Treyllan; in Llanddewi, Llanfihangel, Rhyd Ieithon, Llangunllo above, Llangunllo below, Whitton, Pilleth, and Treyrllan in Llandegla, within the manor of Rhiwarallt; the township and liberties of the boroughs of Knighton and Rhayader, Glandestre, Gwyddel, Gwainwen, Hencoed, and Colfâ, within the manor of Gladestre and Colfâ; Llanhir, within the manor of Iscoed; Sant-Harmon, within the manor of Uwchcoed; Cwmdauddwr, within the manor of Cwmdauddwr; and in Nantmel, within the manor of Rhosllyn, or Rissuli; together with all cottages, buildings, barns, stables, out-houses and edifices, and all yards, gardens, orchards, fields and inclosures whatsoever, which are or have been encroached, built, taken or inclosed from the said wastes, waste lands and commons aforesaid; and all waifs, estrays, goods and chattels of felons, and fugitive felons of themselves, condemned persons, and persons put in exigent; and all hunting, hawking, fishing, fowling, and all other royalties, privileges, pre-eminences, profits, commodities, advantages, hereditaments belonging thereto; excepting and reserving to the crown all manors, messuages, lands, rents, royalties, courts, courts baron, courts leet, fines, heriots, and all other hereditaments, which had heretofore been granted to any person or persons upon leases, letters patent, grants, term and terms of years, estate and interest therein, and were then subsisting and unexpired; rendering and paying a third part of the yearly profits, to be accounted for on the oath of the lessee, or his steward, before the auditor of South Wales, at the feast of St. Michael the Archangel, or within twenty days afterwards, and paid at, or into the receipt of, the exchequer at Westminster, or into the hands of the bailiff or receiver of the crown, at the same period of the year, or within sixty days then next following.

It might easily have been foreseen by all but venal and corrupt ministers, that the execution of a lease of this arbitrary nature, which tended to reduce the inhabitants to a state of subjection not very different from that which they endured under the dominion of the Lords Marchers, and laid a foundation for numberless impositions and oppressions, would have excited the strenuous opposition of a people tenacious of their rights, and inheriting the spirit of their ancestors. Accordingly, such was the effect it produced. An alarm was immediately spread over the whole county; copies of the grant, confirmed by King Charles I., were circulated; committees formed, and subscriptions collected, for the purpose of supporting a legal and constitutional resistance to a measure fraught with ruin and injustice. The lessee was terrified at the attitude which the county assumed; and having calculated that the trouble and expense of enforcing the concessions of the royal grant would far exceed the profits and emoluments likely to result from its execution, suffered it to lie dormant, and never once dared to act upon it; and the lease having expired in due course of time, has not since been renewed.

To the paramount manor, or lordship, of Cantref Moelynaidd, a peculiar privilege is annexed. It confers on its steward the power of holding those courts, or rather the borough courts within its jurisdiction, for the purpose of nominating burgesses, who thus become qualified to vote for a representative in Parliament for the borough of New Radnor. Nor are these courts ever holden but for this purpose. New Radnor being the shire town, is entitled to return one burgess to Parliament, in conjunction with the contributory boroughs of Knighton, Cnwclâs, Cefn-y-lls, and Rhayader. These four last exist as boroughs by prescription. The boroughs of Pain's Castle and Presteigne form a part of the manor of Cantref Moelynaidd; but the privilege of holding courts within these several places, for qualifying their inhabitants with the right of voting, is not extended to them, and in the year 1690 their claims were disallowed by the House. The manner of nominating burgesses, and qualifying them for voting for a representative in Parliament, is as follows:—

In the borough of New Radnor, which is considered as the parent borough, the burgesses are elected by a majority of the bailiff, aldermen, and twenty-five capital burgesses of the borough; and the number is not otherwise limited than that the persons so elected must be inhabitants within the borough at the time of such election, but their removal afterwards does not deprive them of their elective franchise. In the contributory boroughs of Rhayader, Knighton, and Cnwclâs, which three are within the manor of Cantref Moelynaidd, and of Cefn-y-llys, which is private property, the burgesses, when regularly elected, are chosen in the following manner:—

By prescription, courts leet are occasionally holden by the steward of Cantref Moelynaidd, or by his deputy steward, presiding over these boroughs. At these courts the jury, who have been previously summoned, and who ought to be burgesses of such respective boroughs, are impannelled, and present the names of such persons, whether inhabitants or not, whom they think proper to select as fit and proper persons to be made burgesses. This presentment being accepted by the steward, the persons so presented are generally sworn in immediately, if they be present in court, but if not, at a subsequent court.

In the borough of Knighton there is an established prescription, that any two inhabitants, burgesses, who are present at the holding of the leet, may object to any person so presented. There is also another custom in this borough. The eldest son of a deceased burgess has a right to claim of the steward to be admitted and sworn in a burgess, on the payment of one shilling, which privilege is stated, in the customs of this borough, as delivered to Sir Robert Harley, Knight, steward of Cantref Moelynaidd in the reign of King Charles II. (1662.)

Besides the manor paramount, or lordship of Cantref Moelynaidd, there is included in this county another superior and respectable lordship, called Elfael, which claims to itself the two remaining hundreds, viz., Pain's

Castle and Colwyn. These form a large tract of territory, distinguished to this day by the appellation of Upper and Lower Elfael. Agreeably to the law of gavelkind, this territory was divided and subdivided among the descendents of the *reguli*, or Lords of Fferllys and Moelynaidd, till the era of the Norman conquest, which gave a total alteration to the line of succession, not only of every cantref in Wales, but even of every considerable estate in England. Gilbert de Newmarche, having subdued Brecknockshire, was inflamed with the usual ambition of conquerors. He turned his arms against Cadwgan, the son of Ellistane Glodrydd, and lord of the whole of Radnorshire, wrested from him Cantref Muallt, which his father had taken from Bleddyn ab Meynarch, and extended his usurpations across the river Wye to Elfael, uniting a considerable part of that cantref to his lordship of Brecknock. After his decease, this became the portion of his daughter and only heiress Sybil, who was married to Milo, Earl of Hereford. This nobleman bestowed it on his daughter Bertha, married to Philip de Braos, who, in right of his wife, became Lord of Brecknock, in the reign of Stephen, King of England. One of his descendents, viz., William de Braos, was at the same time possessed of the several lordships of Brecknock, Buallt, Abergavenny, Elfael, Huntington, Radnor, Knighton, &c., whose daughter Maud, married to Roger de Mortimer, carried all the Radnorshire property to the family of the house of Wigmore, in which it remained until it devolved by marriage to the house of York, and afterwards to the crown.

A List of the Names of Manors in the County of Radnor as they at present exist, together with those of their Proprietors.

Manors.	Proprietors.	Manors.	Proprietors.
Radnor Foreign	Bailiff and Burgesses of New Radnor	Golon	J. Chas. Severne, Esq.
Radnor Forest .	T. Frankland Lewis, Esq.	Boughrod	Francis Fowke, Esq.
		Llanstephan ...	Francis Fowke, Esq.
		Clasbury	Colonel Wood
Downton		Cefn-y-llys....	
Newcastle	Crown	Llanwenny	T. Frankland Lewis, Esq.
Bilmore, *alias* Stanner		Ismynydd	
Evanjobb	Earl of Oxford	Trewern	Sir Benj. Walsh, Bart.

HISTORY OF RADNORSHIRE. 101

Barland and Burrfâ		Coed Swydd... Y Gre	The same Crown
Stanage	Charles Rogers, Esq.	Rhiwarallt	Crown
Norton[1]	Earl of Oxford	Rhosllyn	Crown
Badland	Earl of Oxford	Iscoed	Crown
Blaiddfâ	Richard Price, Esq.	Cwmdauddwr	
Kinnarton	Rev. John Rogers, Clerk	Grange[2] Ismynydd	Robert Peele, Esq. Walter Wilkins, Esq.
Gladestry	Crown	Clâs Garmon or	Bishop of St. David's.
Upper Elfael	Trustees of Boughrood Charity	Sant Harmon[3]	Perc. Lewis, Esq., Lessee
Clascwm	Percival Lewis, Esq.	Michaelchurch.	Wm. Trumper, Esq.

Forests, &c.

The county of Radnor contains three forests, viz., the forest of Cnwclâs, the forest of Blaiddfa, and the forest of Radnor. Some add a fourth, viz., Colwyn forest.

By an inquisition of the forest of Radnor taken on the third day of October, 1564, in the sixth year of the reign of Queen Elizabeth, before Robert Davies, James Price, and Edward Price, Esquires, by the corporal oaths of Stephen Howell, Clement Donne, David ab Rhys ab Evan, Arthur James ab Evan, William ab Watkin Dafydd, David ab Howell, Rhys ab Meredith ab Rhys, Meredith ab Owen, Lewis ab Evan, John Evan Rhys, Howel Evan ab Rhys, Howel ab Evan ab Philip, it appears, that it then consisted of 3000 acres, of which 2000 were heath, foggy and moorish grounds, 800 were lanes, roots, and bushes of small orls and thorns, and 200 acres fit for pasturage; that the yearly rent was nineteen pounds; extending in length about three miles, viz., from Maes Moelyn to Sarnau Cerrig, and one mile and a half in breadth, viz., from Quarrel Rhys ab Dafydd to Stalbaig; that the forest of Radnor was granted by King Henry VIII. to William Abbot, Esq., for his natural life, under whom Stephen Vaughan is farmer of the said forest; that the inhabitants of the parishes of New Radnor, Old Radnor, Cascob, Blaiddfa, Llanfihangel Rhydieithon, Llandegla, Llanfihangel Nantmoylen, have right to common of pasture thereon, paying for every beast and cattle, 2d., for every score of sheep, 3d., called chenil, or cwmdogaeth.

[1] The only customary manor in the county.
[2] A crown rent of £6 paid to his majesty's auditor.
[3] A court baron for holding pleas to the amount of £2, but now discontinued.

102   HISTORY OF RADNORSHIRE.

Originally Radnor forest was a boundened forest, that is, if any man or beast entered the said forest without leave, the former was to lose a limb, and the latter to be forfeited, unless a heavy ransom were paid, and other grievous exactions submitted to. These acts of oppression were exercised with unprincipled severity, and instances are recorded of the cattle of the parishioners having been driven within the limits of the forest by the foresters, in order that the said cattle might be forfeited, or a large fine paid for their ransom. A petition complaining of these grievances was presented to Queen Elizabeth, in remedy whereof, a decree of the Court of Exchequer was passed in the fifteenth year of her reign, (1573,) which confirmed the right of the inhabitants of the seven parishes aforenamed, and established a new rate of payment, viz., for every beast or cattle above the age of yearling, 6d.; for yearlings, 2d. each; for every score of sheep, 2d.; for every calf under the age of yearling, and yet grazing, 2d.; for every foal and filly under a year old, and grazing, 4d.; and for every score of lambs grazing 8d.; but for mere sucklings of either, nothing. All strayers to be proclaimed at the parish church, and to be restored to the owners, upon making reasonable satisfaction for their trespass and keep. By this comprehensive and liberal decree, every possible complaint had its appropriate remedy, and every dispute that could have arisen its final adjustment.

A Catalogue or Inventory of Crown Lands, in the County of Radnor, specifying the Premises, Names of Tenants, Gross Annual Rent, number of Years in Arrear, &c.

Tenants' Names.	Names of Premises.	Gross Annual Rent.	Years in Arrear Geo. III. 1784.
		£ s. d.	
James Watt, Esq.	Gladestry Mill[1]	0 18 4	12 yrs.
Evan Stephens, Gent. .	Rhayader Mill	0 17 4	1 ,,
Rev. J. W. Davies	Cnwclâs Mill[2].................	1 2 0	3 ,,
Richard Austin, Esq. .	Clôs Mawr in Gladestry	1 0 0	24 ,,
Mrs. Baskerville	Cefn-y-gaer Mill	0 15 0	13 ,,
Richard Biddle, Gent.	Melyn Hothnant	0 3 4	1 ,,
Walter Wilkins, Esq. .	Mill in Ysmynydd...............	0 3 4	4 ,,

[1] The same rent reserved in the grant made by Charles I. to Eden, Scriven, and others.
[2] Ditto.

HISTORY OF RADNORSHIRE.

		£	s.	d.		
Marma. Gwynne, Esq.	Aberedw Mill	0	13	4	16	,,
J. C. Severn, Esq.	Knill Rectory Stipend	0	3	0	5	,,
Robert Peele, Esq.	Grange Cwmdauddwr	6	0	0	3	,,
	Tenths of the said Grange	0	2	6		
The same	Land, &c., in Llansantfrede	0	6	8		
Dean of Windsor	Messuage and Garden in Llanbir	0	3	4	9	,,
Earl of Oxford	Ackwood and Cwmbergwynne	3	0	0		
The same	Northwood and Harleighwood	8	0	0		
Dukes of Chandois	Agistment of Radnor Park[3]	3	6	8	13	,,
Richard Austin, Esq.	Cow Mead[4]	0	12	0	17	,,
Edward Lewis, Esq., or Duke of Chandois	Lleyfield Land, et alibi[5]	1	11	0	13	,,
Stephen ab Howell	Pluck Park	0	0	6	24	,,
Thomas Lewis, alias Edward Lewis, Esq.	Lady's Field	0	12	0	24	,,
— Lewis, Esq.	Radnor Forest	11	0	0	6	,,
Cymortha	Gladestry Horn-hield	7	15	0½	2	,,
Griffith Jones	Escheat Land in Gladestry	1	0	0	24	,,
Præpositus	Rents of Assize in ditto	2	16	8		
Dean of Windsor	Heriots of Presthend	10	0	0		
Bailiff	Bailiff of the Tolls of ditto	4	1	0	24	,,
Bailiff	Bailiff of Presthend	6	9	0	4	,,
Præpositus	Rhistlin alias Rhosllyn	7	7	11½		
Præpositus	Uwchcoed	7	14	11½	1	,,
Rev. J. W. Parsons	Land about Pen-y-bont[6]	0	7	8		
Præpositus	Bryn-y-bont	7	14	11½		
Dean of Windsor	Land in Rhayader, and Tolls[7]	3	6	8		
Præpositus	Rhayader	4	19	8		
Præpositus	Cwmydauddwr	4	16	8		
Richard Wright, Esq.	Lord's Land in Knighton[8]	0	7	4	2	,,
Bailiff	Cnwclâs	5	6	4½	2	,,
Sir Benj. Walsh, Bart.	40 acres of Land near Swydd-yr-allt[9]	0	15	0	4	,,
Præpositus	Swydd-yr-Allt	11	6	5½	2	,,
Præpositus	Swydd-y-Grê	23	10	2½		
Præpositus	Swydd-Wynogion	10	6	8½		
Bailiff	Knighton Borough	8	4	4		
Earl of Oxford	Tolls of Knighton[1]	3	6	8½		
Robert Davies, et alii	Rents of Assize in Presteigne	0	3	4½	24	,,
Mr. John Cooke	ditto ditto	0	4	1¼	4	,,
Mr. Edward Price	ditto ditto	0	19	10		
Mr. Ezekiel Palfrey	Land, and a Tenement in Llanddewi	0	6	8		
Richard Austin, Esq.	Site of Radnor Castle	0	1	0		
Richard Austin, Esq.	Land in Clascwm named Allivies	0	3	8		
Edward Allen, Esq.	2 Sheds in Knighton Borough	0	0	6		
Edward Burton, Esq.	A Close on Cefn y gaer hill	0	2	6		
Louisa Price	Tenement in Presteigne	0	0	2		
Duke of Chandois	ditto ditto	0	2	0		
Jno. Hancock, et ali.	ditto Ave Mary Lane, Presteigne	0	0	3½		
— Clarke	ditto in Presteigne	0	0	1½		
Evan Meredith, Esq.	ditto ditto					

[3] Granted in fee to Young and Favell; purchased by Pl. Lewis, Esq.
[4] In Austin's lease.
[5] Granted in fee to Young and Favell; purchased by Pl. Lewis, Esq.
[6] Same rest reserved in grant of Charles I. to Eden, &c.
[7] In Dean of Windsor's lease.
[8] Same rent reserved in the grant of Charles I.
[9] Ditto.
[1] In lease granted by James II., 1686, to Francis Haynes of Worcester, the same rent is £13 6s. 8d.

104   HISTORY OF RADNORSHIRE.

Earl of Powis	ditto ditto			
Dean of Windsor	Lead Mines, &c., within Cantref Moelynaidd	0	10	0
The same	Whittersey Land in Cnwclâs Borough	0	6	8
The same	Lord's Mead in Cnwclâs	0	3	4
The same	Weretissa Land	0	0	6
The same	Site of Cnwclâs Castle	0	0	8
The same	4 acres of Land named Bronyrhiwgwydd, and Llwyney Goodin	0	0	6
The same	2 parcels of concealed Land named Wyrgloddgam, and Black Mead	0	3	8
The same	Herbage of Cnwclas Forest	0	13	4
The same	2 parcels of concealed Land in Knighton	0	2	0

The following are the extracts from *Domesday Book* concerning the district of Radnor :—

In Hezetre Hundred.
Rex ten. Radrenore. Herald. Com. ten. Ibi 15 Hidæ. Wastæ sunt 7 fueȓ. Tȓa e. 30 Car. Hugo Lane dicit q^d Wills Com. hanc Tȓam sibi dedit q^{d}o dedit ei Tȓam Turchil antecessoris sui.

The king holds Radnor. Earl Harold did hold it. It contains fifteen hides, which are and were waste grounds. In this land are thirty carucates. Hugh Lasne saith, that Earl William gave this land to him, when he gave him the land of Turchil his predecessor.

In Hezetre Hund.
Osbernus fil. Ricardi ten. 7 tenuit Bradelege de 1 Hida 7 Titlege de 3 Hidis 7 Bruntune de 1 Hida 7 Chenille de 2 Hid. 7 Hercope de Dimid Hida 7 Hertune de 3 Hid 7 Hech de 1 Hida 7 Clutertune de 2 Hid. 7 Querentune de 1 Hida 7 Discote de 3 Hid. 7 Cascope de dimid. Hid. In his 11 ⓄD est Terra 36 Car. sed wasta fuit 7 est Nunq$_b$ geldavit. Jacet in Marcha de Wallis.

Osbern, the son of Richard, holdeth and did hold in Bradley one hide, in Titley three hides, in Brampton one hide, in Knill two hides, in Hercope (or Herrock) half of a hide, in Harton three hides, in Hech one hide, in Discoyd three hides, in Cascob half of a hide, in Clatterbrook two hides, in Querentune (or Kinnerton) one hide. The land of these eleven manors contains 36 carucates. It was and is at present waste. It is situated in the Marches of Wales, and was never assessed.

In Lenteurd Hund. Sciropscire.

Isdem Osbernus ten. Stanege. Ibi 6 Hidæ. Tȓa e. 15 Caruc. Wasta fuit 7 est. Ibi 3 Hidæ.
Isdem Osbern. ten. Cascop 7 tenuit. Ibi dimid. Hid. Tȓa e. 2 Caruc. Wasta fuit 7 est. Ibi

In Lantardine Hundred, Shropshire.
The said Osbern holdeth Stanege, consisting of six hides. The carucates are fifteen. Three hides were and are at present waste grounds.
The said Osbern holdeth Cascop, and did hold it, containing one-

Silva 7 una Hida.

In Hezetre Hund.
Radulphus de Mortemer ten. in Pelelei 2 Hid. In Ortune 2 Hid. In Mildetune 3 Hid. In Westune 2 Hid. In tot. 9 Hidæ sunt wastæ in Marcha de Wales. Tra ē 18 Car. Septë ṁ fuer. 7 qnq̇ tainai tenuerunt.

In Hezetre Hund.
Rad. de Mort. ten. Duntune 7 Oidelard de eo. Ælmar 7 Ulchet tenuer. pr. 2 ṁ 7 poter. ire quo voleb. Ibi 4 Hidæ. Duæ ex his non geldabant. In dnio sunt 2 Car. 7 3 villa. 7 3 bord. cum. dimid Car. Ibi 6 servi 7 piscar. Silva dimid 6 in lg̃ 7 5 q̇ lat. Ibi sunt duæ Haiæ. Vaƚƚ. 30 sol. Hanc tram ded. W. com. Turstino Flandrensi.

half of a hide; two carucates of which were and are at present waste. It contains also a wood, and one hide.

Ralph Mortimer holdeth in Pilleth (or Bilmore) two hides, in Norton two hides, in Milton three hides, in Weston two hides. These nine hides are waste grounds in the Marches of Wales. They contained eighteen carucates of land, and comprised seven manors, or lordships, occupied by five officers, servants, or tenants.

In the Hundred of Hezetre.
Ralph Mortimer holdeth Downton and Oidelard under him. Elmar and Ulchet did hold it by two manors, or lordships, and will be free to go whithersoever they please. It contained four hides. Two of these are exempt from paying taxes. In demesne are two carucates, and three villani, and three bordarii, with half a carucate. There are six servants and fishermen. Half of a wood, extending six miles in length, and five in breadth. There are two parks. The whole is valued at thirty shillings per annum. This property was given by Earl William to Turstin of Flanders.

CHAPTER VI.

PAROCHIAL ANTIQUITIES.

1.—*Hundred of Radnor.—Cascob.*

The usual explanation of this word, viz., Cae-yr-esgob, the Bishop's Meadow, is, in our judgment, inadmissible; because it is neither descriptive of the situation of the place, as all Welsh names of parishes are, excepting those which begin with *Llan*, nor singularly appropriate, since any other lands may have been episcopal, as well as this; and especially, because the contraction of Cae-yr-esgob into Cascob militates against the idiom of the Welsh language. In *Domesday Book* it is called Cascope. Attention to this orthograpy of the word would have led to its true etymology, viz.,—Cas, a fortress, and Cope, an eminence. The justness of this etymology is confirmed by tradition, which reports that a small fortification of earth formerly stood on the summit upon which the church is erected; or, perhaps, the name Cascob might mean the eminence impending over the brook Cas, which runs through the parish, and discharges itself into the river Lug.

This parish is situated partly within the liberties of New Radnor, and partly in the townships of Litton and Cascob, in the hundred of Wigmore, in the county of Hereford, and contains the townships of Cascob, and Litton and Cascob; the former township being in the county of Radnor, and the latter, with the remaining part of the township of Cascob, being an insulated portion of the county of Hereford. At the time of compiling *Domesday*, it was situated, at least a part of it, in the hundred of Hezetree, in the county of Hereford; and the land mentioned consisted of half of a hide, belonging to Osbern, the son of Richard.

The portion comprehended within the liberties of New Radnor is by far the most considerable part of the parish, being five-sixths of the whole, and is called the township of Cascob. The assessment of its poor-rates, and the land-tax, are kept and paid distinct from the portion in the townships of Litton and Cascob, which is denominated Wigmore land, and formerly belonged to Mortimer, Earl of Marche. The money raised by the parish rates for this part in 1803, was £39 18s. 11d., at 3s. 4d. in the pound. In these rates, this last is associated with the remainder of the township, which is comprehended in the parish of Presteigne.

The township of Cascob consists of two manors, viz., Achwood and Cwmgerwyn, formerly a part of the Marches of Wales, but now belonging to the king, being specifically reserved to the crown in the charter granted to the borough of New Radnor. These manors where holden by lease, for many years, by the Earl of Oxford, and his ancestors. An Act of Parliament was passed in the fifty-third year of George III., (A.D. 1813,) for inclosing the common and waste lands in this township.

The portion of the parish in the townships of Litton and Cascob is on the north-east side, and contains by estimation about five hundred acres of land, whereof about two-fifths are inclosed, and the remainder is an open common, called Lanfawr. The whole of this township, consisting of probably twelve hundred acres, is an insulated part of the county of Hereford, being bounded on all sides by the county of Radnor. The money raised by the parish rates for this part, in 1803, was £45 5s. 4d., at 4s. 6d. in the pound. The manor is part of that of Stepleton, and belongs to the Earl of Oxford.

The principal landed proprietors in the parish are John Whitaker, Esq., who served the office of High Sheriff for the county of Radnor in the year 1809; and Hugh Stephens, Esq., who was High Sheriff for the same county in 1818.

According to an inquisition taken 3rd October, in the sixth year of the reign of Queen Elizabeth, (A.D. 1564,) by virtue of the Queen Majesty's commission, addressed to commissioners for the survey of the forest of Radnor, the parish of Cascob, in conjunction with those of New Radnor, Old Radnor, Blaiddfa, Llanfihangel-nant-moylyn,

Llandegla, Llanfihangel-rhydieithon, is entitled to send cattle, &c., to be depastured on the forest of Radnor, on paying to the forester at the the rate of 2d. for every beast or cattle, and 3d. for every score of sheep or goats.

This parish is not distinguished by military positions. Its situation within the protection of the castle and garrison of New Radnor precluded all contention; consequently, no vestiges of ancient fortifications are to be found, nor even a tumulus of any kind, throughout the whole extent of it, except on the highest part, where it meets the boundary of New Radnor, where stands a beacon, or low mound of dark peat earth, called the Black Mixen.

On several parts of the open commons are vestiges of corn ridges, which indicate that anciently the land had been ploughed, and kept in a state of tillage; and on several parts likewise, when turned up by the plough, are discovered the remains of charcoal heaps, proving that a considerable portion of the land had been originally covered with wood, which the inhabitants had converted into charcoal.

The population of the whole parish, including the remainder of the township of Litton and Cascob, was 197, according to the return in 1801. In the year 1811, the return was as follows:—Township of Cascob, 19 houses, 39 males, and 49 females; Cascob, in the township of Litton and Cascob, 7 houses, 25 males, and 22 females;— in all, 26 houses, and 135 persons. The return at that time for Cascob, and the whole of Litton and Cascob, was 35 houses, and 183 inhabitants.

The names of the farms and fields are chiefly Welsh; and, from the circumstance of a Welsh Church Bible having been found in the parish chest, which had been made use of, there is reason to conclude that the language, if not spoken, was at least understood in the parish in the reign of Queen Elizabeth; though at present it is not to be met with within perhaps fifteen miles of the place.

In the return made in the reign of Charles I. of the several sums of money set upon every parish or township in general within the county of Hereford, for the furnishing of one ship of 350 tons for the safeguard of the seas, and defence of the realm, the township of Litton and Cascob were assessed at £7 14s. 6d. They were likewise in the year 1636 assessed the sum of 7s. weekly, towards the relief of the inhabitants of the parish of Presteigne, then infected with the plague.

Ecclesiastical Account.

The church of Cascob, which is situated in the township of Cascob, and distant five miles W.N.W. from Presteigne, the nearest post-town, consists of a single aisle and low tower. Its internal length is 56 feet, and breadth 19; its external length, including the tower, is 72 feet, and breadth 25. The tower, in its original state, was probably considerably higher than at present. It contains two bells, the larger of which has been broken, and rendered useless. The inscription on the smallest is,—

IH. WR. W. 1633. + JESUS BE OUR SPEED;

on the larger is,—

SA. NOOA ANNA ORA PRO NOBIS.

Of this last, the former part is doubtful, being rather illegible. In the church-yard are tomb-stones, with inscriptions, to the memory of the ancestors of Thomas Smith, Esq., who served the office of Lord Mayor of the city of London in the year 1810; and of Hugh Stephens, Esq., of London who was High Sheriff for the county of Radnor in 1818.

The parish of Cascob is in the diocese of St. David's, and archdeaconry of Brecon. The benefice is a discharged rectory, valued in the King's books at £7 0s. 7½d. The patron is the Bishop of St. David's, and the church is dedicated to St. Michael. The annual wake is holden on the first Sunday after Michaelmas-day. According to the diocesan report in 1809, the yearly value of the benefice, arising from glebe land, composition for tithes, augmentation, and surplice fees, was £143 6s. 8d.

The parish register books commence in 1624, but from

1641 to 1662 the entries are irregularly made; which show that the place was affected by the disorders of the usurpation, which laid this living for several years under sequestration, ejected its lawfully appointed minister, and suspended its accustomed duty.

The rectory house has between thirteen and fourteen acres of glebe land in the township of Litton and Cascob.

The rector whose name first occurs in the register book is the Rev. Charles Lloyd, A.M., and it is met with in the year 1678. Prior however to the commencement of the register, the Rev. Richard Lloyd was rector of this parish, whom the Republicans ejected in the year 1649, and sequestrated the living.

List of Incumbents.

Names	When Collated	Names	When Collated
Rev. Charles Lloyd, A.M.	1678	Rev. Henry Probert Howarth[2]	1746
Rev. John Medley, A.M.[1]	1699	Rev. Richard Lloyd[3]	1775
Rev. Walter Williams	1732	Rev. Geo. Albert Barker, B.A.[4]	1797
Rev. John White	1737	Rev. William Jenkins Rees, A.M.[5]	1813

COLFA.

This name is derived from Cól, a sharp hillock, or peak; and Fa, a place, or Fach, little. If the latter, it signifies a low peak, or eminence. This parish is situated near

---

[1] The rectory house was built by this gentleman in 1711. He was also Rector of Blaiddfa, Archdeacon of St. David's, and last Prebend of Llangammarch, in the county of Brecon; for, being annexed to the treasurership of Christ's College, at Brecon, it was for ever after united to the bishopric, in lieu of mortuaries.

[2] He was also Rector of Gladestry, in this county, and brother of Sir Humphrey Howarth, of Maeslough, who represented the county of Radnor in Parliament from 1722 to 1755. The family of Howarth is ancient and respectable.

[3] This gentleman, though blind, regularly performed his official duties, and instructed youth.

[4] He was master of the College School, in Brecon, and succeeded to the rectory of Cefn-y-llys, in 1805.

[5] The present worthy incumbent, to whose assistance and contributions the author of this work is greatly indebted. In 1815, and subsequent years, very considerable improvements were effected by this gentleman to the rectory house. He was likewise the means of the tenement of Little Tu-iscob, in this parish, being purchased by the Governors of Queen Anne's Bounty, for the augmentation of the benefice, in 1819.

the source of the river Arro, or Arrow, which runs through it, and borders it on the west for almost four miles. It is bounded on the other points, viz., on the north, by the parish of Llanfihangel-nant-moylyn; on the south, by Bryngwin and New Church; and on the west, by the parish of Glascwm; and contains about fifteen hundred acres of inclosed and cultivated land, and about six hundred acres unclosed and uncultivated, being hills. The quality of the soil of those lands which border the river Arrow is good and productive, comprising some valuable meadowing and pasturage; the hilly part is extremely well adapted for the rearing of young cattle, and for the purposes of the dairy. The township of Colfa extends considerably beyond the limits of the parish of Colfa, including a large portion of common and inclosed lands in the parish of Llanfihangel-nant-moylyn, viz., Black-yatt, Bailyonnen, Bailybeddw, Rhiwy, and Tyn-y-rin; part of Llanwennau farm, Blaeneddw Wells house and farm, and part of Caer-myrddu, together with part of Llandegla's Ross, extending to the marshes, or morass, in which the river Eddw has its source.

According to the return in 1801, the population of this parish was 188. In the year 1803 the parochial rates amounted to £137 10s. 10d., at 8d. in the pound.

There are several small charities belonging to the poor in Colfa, viz., £90 charged upon a tenement called *Lower Ffynonau*, in this parish, the property of Mr. James Lovett, the interest of which is distributed annually amongst decayed persons who have never received parochial relief.[6] There is also a portion of land on which were till lately two almshouses, which have imprudently been suffered to dilapidate. The land on which they were erected, together with the gardens, lie contiguous to the green road leading from Lower Ffynonau to Cnwc Bank. The site is now open to a field called *Maes*.

[6] £7 per annum are paid to the poor of this parish (Colfa) not receiving parochial relief, arising from a farm, *Ty-yn-y-wain*, in the parish of Llandegley; the remaining £14 being equally divided amongst the poor of Llanvihangel Nantmelan and Llandegley.

The parish of Colfa exhibits no vestiges of antiquity druidical or military;—no barrows, camps, nor castles. Whatever more relates to it will be included in the description of the parish of Gladestry, to which it was in former times united.

The Ecclesiastical Account

is necessarily limited to a similar brevity. The church of Colfa is a small edifice, consisting of a nave and chancel. The benifice is a chapelry, annexed to the vicarage of Glâscwm, and dedicated to St David. It is not in charge, and is of the certified value of £10 per annum. The Bishop of St. David's is the patron. The annual wake is holden on the first Sunday after the 1st of March. According to the diocesan report in the year 1809, the yearly value of this benefice, arising from composition for tithes, and surplice fees, was £24 19s. One-third part only of the tithes belongs to the incumbent, the remaining two-thirds are annexed to the bishopric of St. David's, and leased to Perceval Lewis, Esq. The church of Colfa is distant seven miles west from Kington.

GLADESTRY, OR GLANDESTRE: Wallice, *Llanfair Llethonow*.

The Welsh name of this parish, viz., Llethonow, seems to be derived from the root *lledanu*, to expand; the village being situated in an open recess of the surrounding hills. This interpretation answers to the English name glade, or glen; or, perhaps, it may come from *llethineb*, which signifies humidity, the hills attracting the clouds, and producing a damp and moist atmosphere. Yet the climate of Gladestry is by no means damper than that of similar situations.

This parish is bounded on the north and north-east by that of Old Radnor; by Michael-church and Huntington on the south; on the west by Colfa and Llanfihangel-nantmoylyn; and by the parish of Kington on the east. It consists of four townships, viz., Gladestry, Wainwen, Hencoed, and Gwithel, and contains about four thousand acres, partly inclosed. In the year 1810 an Act of Parliament was obtained for inclosing a common, in conjunction with the parish of Colfa, which has an interest in the same. The united parishes of Gladestry and Colfa constituted in former times a bailiwick, subject or belonging to the paramount manor or lordship of Cantref Moelynaidd; and till very lately a court leet was holden annually at Gladestry, and also a court baron monthly, for the recovery of small debts contracted within the bailiwick. The right of the estrays belongs, by prescription, to the freeholders, and a freeholder in one of the said townships was alternately and annually returned at the court leet to take the estrays, as also to serve the office of chief constable; the same person generally holding both offices.

The old mansion called the court of Gladestry was a spacious edifice, bearing marks of antiquity, and adapted for British hospitality. It belonged to Sir Gale or Gylla Meyric, who in the reign of Queen Elizabeth was attainted of high treason, condemned, and executed; when this estate, and also a piece of land in the same parish, called *Clôs mawr*, became escheated to the crown. This ancient mansion was originally fortified, like many other manorial habitations of our ancestors; and, from the house to the turnpike-road leading from the village of Gladestry to the town of New Radnor, there lately extended a spacious avenue, having a row of majestic oaks planted on each side. These have been eradicated, and the approach to the mansion, which is now converted into a farm-house, altered. This estate was given by the crown to Sir Robert Harley, Bart., and lately sold by the present Earl of Oxford. It is now the property of James Crummer, Esq., of Howey Hall, in this county. Clôs mawr was leased by the crown at £1 per annum, to Griffith Jones, Esq., of Trewern, in the adjoining parish of Llanvihangel Nantmelan, who was Sheriff for this county in 1553, an ancestor of the present Sir Harford Jones, of Boultibrook, near Presteigne. It is now lost to the crown, through neglect of claiming the rent in due time. It is situated on a part of a farm called Hanton, or Hendton, which lies contiguous to the turnpike road leading from the village of

Gladestry to the town of New Radnor, and now divided into small parcels or crofts.

This parish, like Colfa, exhibits no vestiges of druidical relics; and originally commanded, as well as protected, by various camps in the neighbourhood, and subsequently by the strong castles of Radnor and Huntington, it contains few or no sites of military positions. Contiguous to the manorial house, or court, of Gladestry, are the remains of a camp, surrounded by a strong rampart, or breast-work, but now garden ground.

The townships of Gladestry, Wainwen, Hencoed and Colfa united, constitute the manor of Gladestry.

Gladestry Mill is the inheritance of the crown of England, and is at present leased to James Watt, Esq., at the gross annual rent of 18s. 4d. The same rent was reserved in the grant made by Charles I. to Eden, Scriven, and others. In the year 1784, twelve years of arrears were due. Gladestry Hornhield, an inheritance of the crown, was leased to Griffith Jones, Esq., at the yearly rent of £7 15s. 0½. In 1784, two years of arrears were due.

Ecclesiastical Account.

The church of Gladestry is dedicated to St Mary, and consists of a nave and chancel, with a north aisle, and a tower containing five bells. The chancel is lighted by five windows,—one on the east, and two on the north and south sides each. A window on the north side contains a few fragments of painted glass. The lavacrum is in the south wall of the chancel. To the east wall of the church is affixed a monument to the memory of the Rev. Francis Wadeley, rector of this parish, with the family crest, over a shield quartered two lions rampant, and two bends. The inscription is as follows:—

"Within the rail, on the north side of the communion table, lies interred the body of the Rev. Francis Wadeley, Rector of this parish, and Prebendary of the Collegiate Church of Brecon, who died in 1748, *ætat* 70."

Charitable Donations.

A lady, of the name and family of Hartstongue, left

an estate at Weyddel, in the parish and township of
Gladestry, to establish and support a free school for the
benefit and education of the children of this township,
and also of the lower part of the parish of Llanfihangel-
nant-moylyn.

[Mr. Gaitskell, of the Council Office, Downing Street, has kindly
furnished the following information in reference to the Lord-Lieutenants
of Radnorshire:—" 1700.—I find that Thomas, Earl of Pembroke,
was Lord-Lieutenant of South Wales on the 30th of October, 1702,
including the counties of Brecon, Caermarthen, Cardigan, Glamorgan,
Pembroke and Radnor, but I cannot find when he was actually appointed,—I presume it must have been between the years 1692 and
1694. Edward, Earl of Oxford and Mortimer, appointed Lord-Lieutenant of the county of Radnor, 16th July, 1766. The Right Hon.
Thomas Harley, appointed 15th April, 1791. Lord Rodney, appointed
21st March, 1805. Sir John Benn Walsh, Bart., appointed 11th
August, 1842."]

DISCOED.

THIS name is written in *Domesday Book* Discote. The
right orthography of it is Iscoed, which signifies, " beneath
the wood." The land is described in *Domesday* as a
manor, or lordship, situated in the hundred of Hezetree,
in the county of Hereford, and containing three hides.
It then belonged to Osbern, the son of Richard, who
came with the Norman conqueror into England, or rather
preceded him, being the son of Richard Fitz-Scroope,
governor of the Norman garrison of Hereford in the reign
of Edward the Confessor. The lordship of Discoed was
afterwards annexed to the monastery of Wormesley, in
Herefordshire.

The parish of Discoed is situated near the river Lug,
and bounded by the parish of Presteigne on the south,
and by Whitton on the north.

LLANFIHANGEL-NANT-MELIN, OR NANT-MOYLYN.

This parish is bounded on the east by New Radnor, on
the west by Llandegla, Glascwm, and Colva, on the south
by Gladestry, and on the north by Llandegley. It con-

sists of three townships, viz., Trewern, Gwiller, and Llanfihangel. The farms called Baily onnau, and Baily beddw, belonging to Black-gate farm, together with Rhiwy, and Tyn-y-rhin, being part of Llewenny, or Llanwen-nnau farm, and also Blaen-eddw farm, house, and well, with part of Caer-myrddu, are included in the township or parish of Colfâ.

Trewern was the seat of a family of the name of Hartstongue. The old house was a spacious mansion, and built in the style of architecture that prevailed about three centuries since, when lords of manors lived among their tenants, and exercised hospitality. The modern dwelling is a brick-house, and erected about a century ago. It is now converted into a farm-house. To this estate a lordship, or manor, called Busmore, is annexed, of which the family of Hartstongue were the proprietors. About fifty years since it was sold by Sir Henry Hartstongue, Bart., who at that time resided in Ireland, and in whom it became vested to Benjamin Walsh, Esq., whose son, Sir Benjamin Walsh, is the present owner. Previous to the sale of it, a court leet was accustomed to be held at Trewern and Noyadd. A court leet is now held at Trewern annually, Mr. D. James of Presteigne being the steward.

The Rhiwy estate formerly belonged to the late Lord Coningsby, of Hampton Court, near Leominster, Herefordshire. In this neighbourhood his lordship was used to spend three or four months every summer, during several years, and his residence was Rhiwy House. This estate was sold by his descendant, Lord Malden, now Earl of Essex, a few years ago, to Thomas Frankland Lewis, Esq., of Harpton Court, in this county. To this estate is annexed a manor, or lordship, as also was in former times to the Rhiwy property; so that this small parish of Llanfihangel-nant-moylyn contains, if not more, certainly as many lordships as any in the county.

Nor is it less distinguished by the remains of antiquity. In a direct line to the north-east of the church, on a farm belonging to John Whittaker, Esq., of Newcastle Court, stands a large tumulus, or barrow, situated on an eminence, and surrounded with a deep moat or ditch, and high agger. This fortification seems to have been originally formed for the purpose of repelling an enemy advancing from New Radnor. At a short distance from the church westward is a circular or elliptical camp, thrown up to defend and protect the village from an attack on that side; and upon a considerable eminence impending over Blaenedw Wells, on the left of the turnpike-road leading from New Radnor through this village to Pen-y-bont and Rhayader, is a large tumulus, or barrow, environed by a deep trench and elevated agger, and commanding extensive prospects, particularly to the west and south-west. These fortifications seem admirably adapted to having been outposts to the castle of New Radnor, to the defending of the narrow pass Llanfihangel-nant-moylyn, and to the keeping of an enemy in check, who attempted to advance through that defile towards the castle. An intelligent friend, to whom the author is greatly indebted for much valuable information relating to this and some neighbouring parishes, conceives that these fortified points served as outworks to the castle of Colwyn; but the distance between these two fortresses is such as precludes the adoption of this conjecture, in the object of their primary formation: secondarily, indeed, they might have served to that purpose, and have been the link in the chain which connected the castles of New Radnor and Colwyn, when they both belonged to the same powerful chieftain, viz., to William de Braos, Lord of Brecknock and Buallt. After all, the author cannot hesitate to declare his opinion, that these ancient fortifications were long anterior to the era in which it is known castles began to be erected in this district, and that they were originally formed by the Silures, and used by that brave people as a means of obstructing the progress of the Roman invaders, and of defending their country from hostile incursion.

The parish of Llanfihangel-nant-moylyn contains about 5,000 acres of land, partly inclosed.

This parish, in conjunction with those of Llanfihangel Rhydieithon, Llandegla, Blaiddfa, Cascob, Old Radnor, and New Radnor, in all seven parishes, is entitled to send cattle, &c., to be depastured on the forest of Radnor, on paying to the forester at the rate of 2d. for every beast or cattle, and 3d. for every score of sheep or goats. This right, or privilege, derived from remote antiquity, was confirmed by an inquisition taken in the sixth year of the reign of Queen Elizabeth (A.D. 1564) by virtue of the Queen's Majesty's commission, addressed to commissioners for the survey of the forest of Radnor.

According to the return made in the year 1801, the resident population of this parish was 314. The money raised by the parish rates of the three townships conjointly, in the year 1803, was £190 4s., at 5s. 9d. in the pound.

Charitable Donations.

The children of the lower division of this parish have a right to be educated in a free school, established by a lady of the name and family of Hartstongue, and supported by the rent of an estate at Wyddel, in the parish of Old Radnor, and township of Gladestry.

At the foot of Radnor forest, and at the eastern extremity of Llandegla's Ross, is a farm-house, called Gwaen-yr-arglwydd, that is, the lord's meadow, and supposed to have once belonged to an ancient regulus of the district, but whose name tradition has not preserved.

The principal landed proprietors in this parish are T. Frankland Lewis, Esq., who resides at Harpton Court, in the parish of Old Radnor, John Whittaker, Esq., and Sir J. B. Walsh, Bart.

Ecclesiastical Account.

The church of Llanfihangel-nant-moylyn is a very low and mean edifice, constructed with the perishable stone of the country, and externally white-washed. Its internal part contains nothing worthy of notice. It is situated on the bank of a small stream, which runs in this dingle

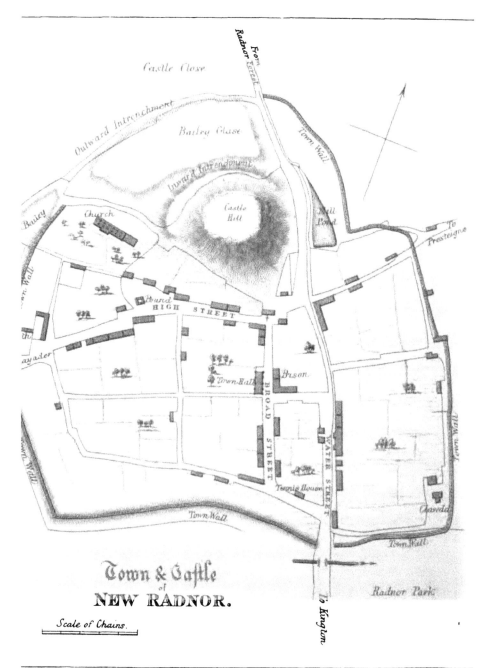

between the hills, and empties itself considerably below the village into the river Somergill.

The benefice of Llanfihangel-nant-moylyn is a discharged vicarage, valued in the king's books at £4 13s. 4d. The king is the patron, which his majesty inherits from Edward IV., Lord of Moelynaidd. The church is dedicated to St. Michael. The annual wake is held on the first Sunday after Old Michaelmas Day.

This parish anciently belonged to William de Braos, Lord of Brecknock and Buallt. His ancestor conferred the tithes of it upon the knights of St. John of Jerusalem. In the reign of Henry VIII. these alien donations were abolished, and the tithes of this parish received a partial distribution, one-third of the great tithe and all the small being assigned to the vicar's share, and the remaining two-thirds to impropriators. According to the diocesan report issued in the year 1809, the yearly value of this benefice, arising from augmentation, tithes, glebes, and surplice fees, was £112 13s. 6d. The yearly tenths are 9s. 4d.

NEW RADNOR.

No historical mention is made of this place prior to the reign of Edward the Confessor, when Earl Harold, afterwards king, transferred the ruins of Old Radnor to the site where New Radnor now stands, called it Radrenove, formed the town, and erected the castle. The description recorded in *Domesday Book* is as follows:— " Rex tenet Radrenove. Comes Haroldus tenuit. Ibi sunt 15 Hidæ Wasta fuit & est." From this it appears that New Radnor constituted a part of the royal demesne of the Norman sovereigns of England.

Its area was an oblong square, containing within its walls an extent of about 26 acres of ground. The regular disposition of the streets, as they were at first formed, may be traced in some measure by the appearance which they at present exhibit. There are three longitudinal streets, distinguished by the modern names of High Street, Broad Street, and Water Street, which were intersected by five transverse ones. The castle was erected above the town, which it perfectly commanded, as well as the entrance of the defile which leads into it, between two hills, from the west. It was a square structure, flanked at the four angles with circular towers, and inclosing a strong keep. Some remains are still existing. The intrenchments are nearly entire; the outer ward, called Bailiglâs, or the green court-yard, is still distinct from the inner one, or keep, and in its original form; the walls of the town had four gates, obtending the four cardinal points of the compass. Their site, together with the moat, is very visible, particularly on the west and south sides. There is also to be seen beyond the western extremity of the parish, and about a mile's distance from the town, an intrenched dyke, which was continued from one extremity of the narrow vale to the other, and evidently thrown up to serve as an outwork to the castle, and for the purpose of guarding the defile. In the year 1773, on digging on the site of the castle, six or seven small Gothic arches, of excellent masonry, were discovered; and, in the year 1818, many more of a similar construction, together with several military weapons, such as halberts, spears, swords, battle-axes, &c.

The history of this town and castle is briefly this. Founded by Earl Harold, after his successful irruption into Wales, and received into his own immediate possession, or courteously presented by him to his master and king, Edward the Confessor, they became, after his death, and at the Norman conquest, a portion of the royal demesne of William I. How long they continued in the tenure of the Norman sovereigns of England is a matter of uncertainty. A soldier of fortune, who accompanied the conqueror on his expedition into England, asserted his claim to the possession of New Radnor on a promise made to him by William Fitz-Osborn, the first Norman Earl of Hereford, as well as the greatest favourite of that monarch in the kingdom. Whether William I. thought proper to ratify the alleged gift of his kinsman, and suffered the pretensions of his follower to prevail over his own, there is no existing document that ascertains the fact. The determined character of this monarch, and the general analogy of his other proceedings, render the negative the more probable, and seem to justify the inference, that the town and castle of New Radnor, together with its annexed territory, thus considered of great importance in its earliest state, remained the royal demesne of the succeeding sovereigns of England.

The political and military importance of the town and castle of Radnor was acknowledged and felt during a long series of years, because the possession of them was made an object of constant solicitude and contest. In all the wars carried on betwixt the two contending nations, the English and the Welsh, in the civil broils of the latter, and in the baronial contentions of the former, as well as under the tyrannical despotism of the Lords Marchers, this town and castle participated with various vicissitudes. In the year 1091 the fortifications were repaired and garrisoned by Reginald, or Ralph, de Mortemer. In 1102 Walter, Bishop of Hereford, was deputed hither upon an important mission, and received within its walls. In 1188 the town of Radnor was the first place in all Wales where the crusade expedition was preached by Baldwin, Archbishop of Canterbury, accompanied by Glanville, Chief Justiciary of England, Giraldus Cambrensis, &c., where they were met by Prince Rhys, and other natives of Wales, of the first rank and distinction. Among those who here took the cross were a son of Cadwallon, Lord of Moelynaidd, and a man of singular strength and courage, named Hector. In the year 1195 Prince Rhys, in revenging the oppressions committed by the Lords Marchers, took the town and castle of Radnor, and defeated Mortemer and De-Saye, with immense slaughter, in a neighbouring field, now denominated War-close. His continuance in this place militating against the further prosecution of his plans, he left it; and, in the following year, the town and castle were fortified and garrisoned by Richard, Duke of Cornwall, afterwards Richard I., King of England. Thus far they remained the property of the English crown; but they were afterwards mortgaged by King John to that opulent and powerful baron, William de Braos, Lord of Brecknock and Buallt, whose daughter Maud, united in marriage with Roger de Mortemer, brought these possessions into the house of Wigmore. In the year 1230 they were taken from the family of Mortemer by Llewelyn ab Jorwerth, Prince of North Wales, but afterwards given in dowry to Ralph, or Reginald, Mortemer, who had married Gwladus-ddu, the only surviving child and heiress of that prince. In the year 1265 Llewelyn ab Gruffudd, siding with the barons, defeated Sir Roger Mortimer, Lord of Wigmore, and by right of inheritance proceeding from his mother, Prince of Wales, took and destroyed the town and castle of Radnor. The possession, however, of both, after the death of Llewelyn, and the final conquest of his principality by Edward I., was restored and confirmed to the family of Wigmore and Marche. For, in the year 1360, the attainder against that family having been repealed, Roger Mortemer, who was restored to the earldom of Marche, and to all his grandfather's inheritances and honours, died possessed of Radnor, the castle, and territory thereto belonging. After the accession of the Earl of Marche, and Lord of Moelynaidd, to the throne of England, who was crowned king by the title of Edward IV., this property was conveyed by marriage of the widow of Sir Edmund Mortemer to the house of Northampton, and subsequently, by means of a similar union, to the house of Buckingham. By the attainder of the duke of the last-mentioned family they reverted a third time to the reigning sovereign of England in the person of Henry VIII. A century prior to this reversion they had sustained, from the impetuous assault of the fierce Glyndwrdwy, a catastrophe more ruinous than any that preceded it, from the direful effects of which they have never since been able to recover. For its houses and buildings were levelled to the ground, and the lands on which they were erected lay for a long time entirely unoccupied; its fortress and its walls were

SEAL FOUND AT RADNOR.

demolished; and its inhabitants either slaughtered, or compelled to abandon their property; whilst the most valuable manuscripts, the charter and records of its privileges, liberties, and franchises, conferred by the Lords of Moelynaidd, the Kings of England, and the Lords Marchers, who were also Lords of Radnor, perished in the flames. The severe edicts enacted by Henry IV. against the inhabitants of the districts, who rather favoured than obstructed the enterprize of their countryman, and who excited the hatred of this jealous monarch by being intimately connected with his imprisoned rival, the rightful heir to the throne, which he had violently usurped, finished the work of desolation.

The political consequence, therefore, which Radnor once possessed, gradually diminished, in the same ratio in which the trade and prosperity of the towns of Presteigne and Kington increased. Hence, about a century ago, the weekly markets of the former were discontinued, because the neighbouring farmers found a greater demand, and consequently a higher price, for their produce, in the towns of Kington and Presteigne, than in it. About the year 1778, attempts were made by a few patriotic gentlemen to revive the markets at Radnor, which were supported for four or five years with considerable zeal and success; but either through the want of proper accommodations in the town, or the badness of the roads, or the paucity of customers, or through the combined operation of all these causes together, they were again dropped, and the thriving town of Kington seized, and retains, the mercatorial monopoly.

The town of Radnor has four fairs in the year. The first is held on the first Tuesday after Trinity Sunday, the second on the 14th day of August, and the third and fourth on the 28th and 29th days of October.

Borough and Liberties.

New Radnor is a very ancient borough by prescription. Its first charter of incorporation now in existence was granted by Queen Elizabeth, in the fourth year of her

R

reign, A.D. 1562, at the request of Thomas Hobby, Esq. This charter conferred privileges of great value, a manor, and liberties extending into twelve townships; being bounded on the north by a part of the parish of Cascob, on the east by the parish of Presteigne and township of Hereton, on the south by the parishes of Gladestry and Colfâ, and on the west-south-west and north-west, by the parishes of Clâscwm, Llandegla, and Llanfihangel Rhydieithon; and computed to embrace in length from east to west about eleven miles, and in breadth from north to north-west about nine miles. This extent of territory is called the manor of New Radnor, and the manor and lordship of Radnor Foreign. The bailiff of New Radnor for the time is the lord of the manor of New Radnor, and T. F. Lewis, Esq., of Harpton court, is lord of the manor of Radnor Foreign.

In the fourth year of the reign of George II., (A.D. 1731,) the capital burgesses of the borough of New Radnor were by death, and through neglect of filling up the vacancies, reduced to the small number of seven only, so that the business of the borough was entirely suspended. A new charter was therefore sought, and granted, confirming, explaining and enlarging the powers and prerogatives of that of Elizabeth. This charter ordained, that the town of New Radnor, and manor of Radnor Foreign, being part of the lordship of Radnor, and Radnor's land, and parcel of the possessions of the late Earl of the Marches, and lying in and near the said borough and town, should be a borough incorporate for ever, by the name of the bailiff, aldermen, and burgesses of the borough of New Radnor; that they should be qualified to acquire lands, &c., to grant and demise lands and goods, to sue and be sued, and to have a common seal. It was further ordained, that there should be one bailiff, two aldermen, and twenty-five capital burgesses, whereof the bailiff and aldermen for the time are three; to whom and their successors were granted the town and suburbs, and all former liberties, &c., at the rent of £37 8s. 1¾d., to be yearly paid at the exchequer, at the feast of St. Michael, into the hands of the receiver-general.

It was further ordained, that they should have a council-house within the borough and town aforesaid, called the Guild-Hall, and in the same should consult, and decree laws, statutes, ordinances, &c., concerning the government of the borough, town and manor, and concerning themselves, their professions, officers, artificers, lands, tenements, hereditaments, and all the other inhabitants, and that they should inflict on offenders such punishments as were not repugnant or contrary to the laws of the realm.

It was also ordained, that the said capital burgesses shall have power to nominate and elect in the month of September yearly, on Monday next after the exaltation of the Holy Cross, one of themselves to be bailiff for the year ensuing; which person so elected shall be sworn faithfully to perform that office, on Monday after the feast of St. Michael; and that on the same day, viz., on Monday next after the exaltation of the Cross, the said capital burgesses shall elect yearly two others of themselves to be aldermen, which two persons shall be sworn anually on Monday next after the feast of St. Michael, faithfully to perform that office, in the presence of six capital burgesses; and that, when any person holding the office of bailiff or alderman dies, or is removed from either of the said offices, the said capital burgesses shall proceed to a new election, and that the bailiff or one of the aldermen shall preside at all elections.

It was further ordained, that the bailiff, aldermen and burgesses shall have power to elect one honest and discreet man, learned in the laws, to be the recorder of the borough; and also, that they shall elect a town clerk or prothonotary, who may appoint a deputy; and also, that they shall yearly, on the said Monday next after the exaltation of the Holy Cross, elect two chamberlains, who, with all other inferior officers, may be sworn before the bailiff and six capital burgesses on Monday next after the feast of St. Michael.

It was also ordained, that there shall be two serjeants-at-mace, to carry the maces and to execute all processes; that the borough and jurisdiction shall extend to the ancient limits; that there shall be a coroner to return all inquests at the next great sessions; that one of the said burgesses shall be elected and sent to parliament; that the bailiff, aldermen, capital burgesses, common council, and all other inferior officers, must abide, reside, and inhabit within the borough aforesaid, the liberties, and precincts thereof; that there shall be holden on every Monday a court of record, for all manner of actions, the damage whereon exceeds not the sum of 40s.; that the bailiff shall take recognizances, and the town clerk shall be king's clerk, to receive, &c., the said recognizances, and that the bailiff, aldermen and capital burgesses (or common council) shall make cognizance of all pleas, &c.

It was further ordained, that there shall be a court-leet and view of frankpledge, and return of all writs; that there shall be a jail; that the bailiff shall be a justice of the peace during his bailiwick, and one year after; and also, that the two aldermen shall be justices during their continuance in office; that there shall be a jail delivery; that the bailiff shall be clerk of the market, and receive all fines, waifs, deodands and felons' goods, heriots, &c.; and that there shall be an assize of bread; and that the authority of the county magistrates shall be superseded in the borough and manor, liberties and precincts of the same, unless in default of the said bailiff, aldermen, &c.

It was also ordained that there shall be a market on every Tuesday; and five fairs, viz., on Tuesday after the feast of the Holy Trinity; on the 3rd day of August; on the feast of St. Luke the Evangelist; on the 29th of April, and on the 1st of October, in every year; during which fairs a court of pie-poudre was to be held, with all free customs to such court belonging; that the bailiff and aldermen shall have a mercatorial guild, together with all customs to such guild belonging; that they shall have power to assess and levy tallage; that the bailiff, aldermen and burgesses shall be free from all toll, lastage, passage, portage, stallage, and other exactions throughout the king's dominions; that they shall not be compelled to appear before any justice of the peace, &c., save before the chief justice of the county; that they shall have power to admit inhabitants to be burgesses; that no burgess shall be sued out of the liberty on any pleas, &c., being done within the borough; that they shall have power to purchase lands under certain restrictions, notwithstanding the statute of mortmain.

It was also ordained, that the bailiff, aldermen and burgesses shall not proceed to the determination of any treason, murder or felony, or any other matter touching the loss of life; that they and their successors shall have all the soils, commons and waste grounds in the borough and manor aforesaid; that they shall enjoy all former grants made to them; that such grants, privileges, &c., are hereby confirmed, renewed and restored; that no sheriff or other officer shall enter the liberties of the said borough, to execute anything pertaining to his office; that no person that is not free of the guild shall trade in the borough and manor aforesaid, unless in the time of markets and fairs; that all residents whatever shall be at scot and lot with the burgesses, and subject to the same contributions; that no *quo warranto* writ shall be issued; and lastly, that this grant or letters patent shall be made and sealed, without fine or fee, in the hanaper, or elsewhere; although the true yearly value of the premises, or any part of them, be not particularly specified or mentioned.

Exceptions.—" Excepted and reserved to us, our heirs and successors, our castle of Radnor, and the advowson of all churches being within the borough town and manor aforesaid: and excepted all those woods called Achwood, Cwmberwyn and Northwood, being of the yearly rent of 37s. 6d.; and also the park called Radnor Park, and demesne land of the castle, being of the yearly rent of 11s. 8d.; and also excepted the lordship and manor of Newcastle, and the rents and services of the tenants of the lordship of Newcastle, together with the mill called Holbatch Mill, being of the yearly rent of £3 14s. 8d., and likewise the forest of Radnor, being of the yearly rent of £16 or £19."

Such is the renewed charter of the borough of New Radnor and manor of Radnor Foreign; which, it must be acknowledged, contains very liberal grants and privileges, and all that deservedly; for the procuring of this new charter cost the exchequer a no less sum than £1284.

Under this new charter of George II. the first bailiff was Stephen Harris, Esq.; the first recorder Thomas Lewis, Esq., of Harpton; the first capital burgesses were Samuel Vaughan, Edward Burton, John Whitmore, James Lewis, John James, Charles Evans, Thomas Stephens, of Kinnerton, Herbert Lewis, Esq., of Harpton, Hugh Stephens, of Cascob, Christopher Lewis, William Lewis, of Pantives, John Griffith, Samuel Vaughan, Thomas Prothero, Henry Morgan, of the Stones, Thomas Jones, of the Rhiw, Edward Phillips, Solomon Vaughan, John Griffiths, of Llanfihangel, Richard White, James Gould, Richard Gould, and John Lewis, of Forsidat.

The first bailiff under Queen Elizabeth's charter was Thomas Mar. Powell ab Stephen; the two first aldermen were Phillip Bunsey, and Rees Lewis; the burgesses, Phillip Luntly, Thomas Lewis, Griffin Jones, John Madox, John Lewis, Walter Vaughan, of Harpton, Steph. Powell, Morgan Price, John Price de Kinnerton, Clement Downe, John Havard, John Watkins de Lywennau, Edw. Howell, John ab Price, Wm. Greene, Roger Powell, John Price ab John, Hugh Davies, John Powell, David Donne, Rees Harris, Phillip Powell, and Stephen ab Stephen Madox.

By the provisions established under these two charters, the borough and manor foreign of Radnor still continue to be governed. The following are the names of the bailiffs, recorders and town clerks of the borough of New Radnor, from the year 1686 to the present time:—

1686. Walter Cuthbert,	*Bailiff*	1695. David Powell,	*Bailiff*
1687. Richard Stones,	,,	1696. Ditto,	,,
1688. John Stephens,	,,	1697. Ditto,	,,
1689. John Davies,	,,	1698. Ditto,	,,
1690. Ditto,	,,	1699. Hugh Lewis,	,,
Charles Cuthbert,	*Town Clerk*	1700. Ditto,	,,
1691. John Davies,	*Bailiff*	1701. Ditto,	,,
1692. David Powell,	,,	1702. Ditto,	,,
1693. Ditto,	,,	1703. Ditto,	,,
1694. Ditto,	,,	1704. Ditto,	,,

1705. James Duppa, *Bailiff*
1706. William James, „
Robert Price, *Recorder*
1707. David Powell, *Bailiff*
1708. Griffith Payne, „
1709. Roger Tonman, „
1710. Thomas Lewis, „
1711. Henry Bull, „
1712. David Powell, „
1713. John Miles, „
1714. Samuel Burton, „
1715. Wm. Chamberlayne, „
1716. James Duppa „
1717. Thomas Lewis, „
1718. Henry Bull, „
1719. John Miles, „
1720. Herbert Lewis, „
1721. James Bull, „
1722. Peter Rickards, „
1723. John Boulter, „
1724. David Williams, „
Rev. David Williams „
1725. James Duppa, „
1726. Herbert Lewis, „
1727. John Stephens, „
1728. John Whitmore, „
1729. Herbert Lewis, „
1730. Roger Stephens, „
John Stephens, „
Howel Lewis, *Town Clerk*
1731. John James, *Bailiff*
1732. Samuel Vaughan, „
Thomas Lewis *Recorder*
1733. Herbert Lewis, *Bailiff*
1734. Samuel Vaughan, „
1735. Herbert Lewis, „
1736. John James, „
1737. Ditto, „
1738. Ditto, „
1739. Stephen Harris, „
Evan Meredith, *Town Clerk*
1740. Thomas Lewis, *Bailiff*
1741. Herbert Lewis, „
1742. John James, „
William Price, *Town Clerk*
1743. John James, *Bailiff*
1744. Ditto, „
1745. Ditto, „
1746. Rev. Mr. Lewis, „
1747. Herbert Lewis, Junr., „
John James, *Town Clerk*
1748. Herbert Lewis, Junr., *Bailiff*
1749. Ditto, „
1750. Thomas Lewis, „
1751. Rev. Tho. Lewis, „
1752. Thomas Lewis, „
1753. John James, „
Thomas Williams, *Town Clerk*
1754. William Lewis, *Bailiff*
1755. Solomon Vaughan, „

1756. John Vaughan, *Bailiff*
1757. John Stephens, „
Henry Lewis, *Recorder*
1758. Thomas Davies, *Bailiff*
1759. John Stephens, „
1760. Thomas Davies, „
1761. Benjamin Allford, „
1762. William Jones, „
1763. Edward Hunt, „
1764. John Gittoes, „
John Lewis, *Recorder*
1765. Benjamin Evans, *Bailiff*
John James, *Town Clerk*
1766. John Lewis, *Bailiff*
Thomas Lewis, *Recorder*
1767. Benjamin Allford, *Bailiff*
1768. John Muscott, „
John Lewis, *Recorder*
1769. James Watkins, *Bailiff*
1770. William Evans, „
1771. Edward Philipps, „
1772. Charles Miles, „
1773. Clement Payne, „
1774. Edward Hunt, „
1775. Charles Miles, *Bailiff*
1776. John James, „
1777. David Williams, „
1778. John Stephens, „
1779. Thomas Lewis, „
1780. Benjamin Evans, „
James Baskerville, *Town Clerk*
1781. Thomas Lewis, *Bailiff*
1782. James Baskerville, „
John Meredith, *Town Clerk*
1783. William Evans, *Bailiff*
1784. Edward Hunt, „
James Baskerville, *Town Clerk*
1785. Edward Cooper, *Bailiff*
James Lewis, *Town Clerk*
1786. John Lewis, *Bailiff*
Rich. Urrich, *Deputy Recorder*
1787. John Gittoes, *Bailiff*
John Lewis, *Recorder*
1788. James Lewis, *Bailiff*
T. W. Lewis, *Dep. Town Clerk*
1789. Thomas Williams, *Bailiff*
James Lewis, *Town Clerk*
1790. Hugh Jones, Clk., *Bailiff*
James Price, *Town Clerk*
1791. John Lewis, *Bailiff*
Hugh Jones, Clk., *Dep. Recorder*
1792. David Williams, *Bailiff*
John Lewis, *Recorder*
1793. James Price, *Bailiff*
T. W. Lewis, *Town Clerk*
1794. Richard Watkins, *Bailiff*
James Price, *Town Clerk* to 1819
1795. John Taylor, *Bailiff*
1796. Richard Williams „
1797. John Hunt, „

1797. William Frankland, *Recorder*
1798. John Stephens, *Bailiff*
1799. Ditto, ,,
1800. David Williams, ,,
1801. Richard Williams, ,,
T. F. Lewis, *Recorder* to 1819

1802. William Jones, *Bailiff*
1803. David Williams, ,,
1804. Thomas Bright, ,,
1805. Richard Williams, ,,
1806. Jeremiah Griffiths, ,, to 1819

Members of Parliament.

Radnor is considered as the mother borough, and being the shire town is entitled, in conjunction with the contributory boroughs of Knighton, Rhayader, Cnwclas, and Cefn-y-llys, which exist as boroughs by prescription, to return one burgess to Parliament. The manner of nominating burgesses, and qualifying them for voting for a representative in Parliament is as follows:—

In the borough of Radnor, the burgesses are elected by a majority of the bailiff, aldermen, and twenty-five capital burgesses of the borough; and the number is no otherwise limited than that the persons so elected must be inhabitants within the borough at the time of such election; but their removal afterwards does not deprive them of their elective franchise. Nothing but the circumstance of receiving parochial relief disqualifies from being made a burgess any inhabitant who is regularly proposed, and goes through the requisite forms. On that account their number is very considerable; those of New Radnor alone at present exceed 200.

In the borough of Rhayader, the ancient rights and customs of which were ascertained by order of the commons of England in the year of 1649, and in those of Knighton and Cnwclas, all of which are within the manor of Cantref Moelynaidd, and also of Cefn-y-llys, which is now private property, the burgesses are, when regularly elected, chosen in the following manner:—By prescription courts-leet are occasionally holden by the steward, or deputy steward, presiding over these boroughs. At these courts the jury, who have been previously summoned, and who ought to be burgesses of such respective boroughs, are impannelled, and present the names of such persons, whether inhabitants or not, whom they think proper to select as fit and proper persons to be made burgesses. This presentment being accepted by the steward, the persons so presented are generally sworn in immediately, if they be present in court, but if not, at a subsequent court.

In the borough of Knighton there is an established prescription, that any two inhabitants, burgesses, who are present at the holding of the leet, may object to any person proposed or presented to be made a burgess. There is also another custom in the said borough; the eldest son of a deceased burgess has a right to claim of the steward to be admitted and sworn in a burgess, on the payment of one shilling; which privilege is stated in the customs of this borough, as delivered to Thomas Harley, Esq., steward of the same, in the second year of the reign of Charles II., A.D. 1662.

In all these contributory boroughs, it is at the time of holding their respective courts that the nomination of new burgesses to be elected is to be made. The number of burgesses belonging to the four contributory boroughs is estimated at 1000, the total is about 1200.

The privilege of returning one burgess for the borough of Radnor, in conjunction with its four contributory boroughs, viz., Knighton, Rhayader, Cnwclâs, and Cefny-llys, is founded on the statute of the 27th and 35th of Henry VIII. This privilege, however, was not immediately exercised and enjoyed, either from the novelty of the institution, or from the predilection of the inhabitants for their accustomed form of government; or, if exercised and enjoyed, no historical account of such elections has been preserved and transmitted to posterity. The first election, of which notice has been handed down to us, took place at the Restoration.

We have just stated that the first recorded election of members of parliament for the borough of New Radnor occurred at the period of the Restoration; the parishioners, however, assert, upon the strength of an authenticated tradition, that Sir Philip Warwick, the faithful friend and loyal attendant of King Charles I. in all his

s

troubles, represented the borough of New Radnor in parliament for several sessions.

List of Members of Parliament for the Borough.

A.D. CHARLES II.
1660. Sir Edward Harley, Bart.
1661. Sir Edward Harley, Bart.
1678. Sir Edward Harley, Bart.
1681. Thomas Harley, Esq.

JAMES II.
1685. John Wynne, Esq.
1688. Richard Williams, Esq.

WILLIAM AND MARY.
1690. Robert Harley, Esq.
1695. Robert Harley, Esq.

WILLIAM III.
1698. Robert Harley, Esq.
1701. Robert Harley, Esq.
1702. Robert Harley, Esq.
1705. Robert Harley, Esq.
1708. Robert Harley, Esq.
1710. Edward Harley, Esq.
1713. Edward Harley, Esq.

A.D. GEORGE I.
1714. Thomas Lewis, Esq.
1722. Thomas Lewis, Esq.

GEORGE II.
1727. Thomas Lewis, Esq.
1734. Thomas Lewis, Esq.
1741. Thomas Lewis, Esq.
1747. Thomas Lewis, Esq.
1754. Thomas Lewis, Esq.

GEORGE III.
1761. Thomas Lewis, Esq.
1768. Edward Lewis, Esq.
1774. Edward Lewis, Esq.
1780. Edward Lewis, Esq.
1784. Edward Lewis, Esq.
1790. David Murray, Esq.
1796. Lord Malden
1799. Richard Price, Esq.
1802. Richard Price, Esq.
1807. Richard Price, Esq.
1812. Richard Price, Esq.
1818. Richard Price, Esq.

A contest for the borough of Radnor was carried on in the year 1678, between Richard Deerham, Esq., and Sir Edward Harley, Bart., a petition presented to the House, and referred to the Committee of Privileges.

A contest for the borough was carried on in the year 1688, between William Probert and Richard Williams, Esqrs., a petition presented to the House, alleging this singular complaint, that the bailiff rejected the votes of the out-resident burgesses, saying that they had no right to vote when any of the twenty-five capital burgesses of Radnor were candidates, and referred to a committee. No determination was passed upon that point.

A contest for the borough was carried on in the year 1690, between Robert Harley, Esq., and Sir Rowland Gwynne, Bart., and a petition was presented to the House, signed by the burgesses of the boroughs of Presteigne and Pain's Castle, who, being inhabitants of a part of the paramount manor of Cantref Moelynaidd, as well as the inhabitants of the boroughs of Knighton, Rhayader,

Cnwclâs, and Cefn-y-llys, claimed an equal right of voting at the election of a member for the borough of Radnor. Their claim was disallowed by the House, and the right of election was then determined to be in the burgesses of Radnor, Knighton, Rhayader, Cnwclâs, and Cefn-y-llys only. This resolution was entered upon the journals of the House, and has ever since been deemed law.

The bailiff of the borough of New Radnor is the returning officer at the election of its representative.

The sheriff's county courts, for the recovery of small debts under 40s., are holden in the town and borough of New Radnor in alternate months with Presteigne: formerly with Rhayader; but the court, for a certain misdemeanour, was removed thence to the town of Presteigne, by the statute of the 34th and 35th of the reign of Henry VIII. The quarter sessions for the borough of Radnor are holden on the Monday in the second week after the Epiphany, on Low Easter Monday, first Monday after the Feast of Thomas a' Becket, and the first Monday after Michaelmas Day.

Parish.

The parish of New Radnor is bounded on the west by the parish Llanfihangel-nant-Moylyn, on the north by the parishes of Llanfihangel Rhydieithon, and a part of Cascob, and on the east and south by the parish of Old Radnor. Its average length is three miles, and its breadth the same. It is divided into four parts, whereof the town and township of New Radnor are the principal; the other parts are included in the townships of Harpton, Badland, and Walton, the remainder of which are situated in the parish of Old Radnor. It is situated in the borough of New Radnor, and in the manor and lordship of Radnor Foreign. The bailiff of New Radnor for the time being is the lord of the manor. This privilege was granted by charter in the fourth year of the reign of Queen Elizabeth. It contains by estimation about 2,600 acres of old inclosed land, and about one-half of the same quantity of waste lands, and new allotments, partly inclosed. An Act of

Parliament for inclosing the commons and waste lands was obtained in the year 1811, and the award thereon was completed three years afterwards. Tradition still preserves the remembrance of a battle having been fought in War-clos, a field at a short distance eastward from the town, on an estate belonging to Percival Lewis, Esq., of Downton, which is supposed, on very probable grounds, to have been the scene of the action between Rhys ab Gruffudd, Prince of South Wales, and Roger Mortimer, Earl of Wigmore, and Hugh de Saye, Chief Justiciary, in the plain below the town, in the year 1195, when the two latter were totally defeated.[7]

In the year 1734 the number of inhabitants was 416. The last return, in the year 1811, was 380.[8]

Each township is assessed separately to the king's taxes. The money raised by the parish rates, in the year 1803, was £209 2s. 3d., at 3s. 7d. in the pound.

Downton, situated on the left hand of the turnpike road leading to Kington, about half a mile from the town of Radnor, is a place of great antiquity, which *Domesday Book* describes in the following manner:—

" In Hezetre Hundred, Com. Hereford. Rad. de Mort. ten. Duntune. 7 Oidelard de eo. Ælmar 7 Ulchet tenuer. per 2 ⅏ 7 poter. ire quo voleb. Ibi 4 Hidæ. Duæ ex his non geldabant. In dnio sunt 2 Car. 7 v 7 3 bord. cum dimid. Car. Ibi 6 servi 7 piscar. Silva dimid. 6 mlg̃ 7 5 q̧ lat. Ibi sunt duæ Haiæ. Val͠b 30 Sol. in tanto. Hanc tr͞a ded. W. com. Turstino flandrensi."

In Hezetre Hundred, & county of Hereford. Ralph Mortimer holds Downton, and Oidelard of him. Ælmar and Ulchet did hold it, being 2 manors: And they are free to go whithersoever they please. It consists of 4 Hides, two of which are not assessed. In demesne are two Carucates and five villains and 3 borderers, with half of a Carucate. There are 6 servants and

---

[7] Two tumuli, apparently sepulchral, are to be seen on the flat land near Harpton Court.

[8] The following returns complete the account of the population down to the present time:—A.D. 1801—329; 1811—380; 1821—426; 1831—472; 1841—478; 1851—481. This statement, however, includes part of the township of Upper Harpton, comprising three houses and nineteen persons.—W. J. W.

Chancel Screen, Old Radnor.

fishers. A moiety of a wood 6 miles long and 5 broad. There are two parks, or inclosures. It was valued in the whole at 30s. This land Earl William gave to Turstin, a Fleming.

Ecclesiastical Account.

The church of New Radnor is situated upon an eminence above the town, and distant two miles and a half south-west from Llanfihangel-nant-Moylyn, two miles and a half south-east from Old Radnor, and the same distance north-east from Kinnerton Chapel. It consists of a nave and aisle on the south side, separated from the nave by five octagonal pillars supporting six pointed arches, and a chancel. The partition that divides the nave and chancel is a low timber frame under a pointed arch. On the south side of the nave are three windows, containing each three lights, divided by stone mullions under trefoil arches. A similar window is on the north side, the arch of which consists of three quatrefoil lights. The chancel contains three windows of ordinary construction. It also has a tower flanked by low buttresses, and at present covered with a tiled roof, but was originally higher, and, as appears by Speed's sketch of it taken in the year 1610, embattled. The tower contains four larger bells, and one smaller, with a clock. Its south side has three ranges of lights. The lavacrum is on the south side of the lateral aisles, which on the east appears to have formerly contained a small chapel, entered by two doors. The internal length of the church is 24 yards; its breadth, 11. Its length externally is 25½ yards; breadth, 13. The porch is of timber, but the entrance into the church is under a pointed arch of stone; and opposite to the entrance door is a large hewn stone font. The internal length of the chancel is 11½ yards; breadth nearly 6 yards.

Upon the whole, this church, which, as Leland says, was erected by William Bachefield and Flory his wife, bears many marks of antiquity, and appears to have been constructed on a foundation coeval with the castle. The style of its windows corresponds with the order of architecture introduced in the reign of Edward III.

The register commences in the year 1643, from which period to the year 1681 the entries are written in Latin. The most curious of the entries are the following:—

"Since the re-establishment of the church of God in truth & peace by the blessed return of the dread sovereign Lord Charles II., by the grace of God, King of England, Scotland, & Ireland, & France, defender of the faith, &c. By whose especial grace and favour Robert Bidewell Clk was constituted and confirmed rector of this parish of New Radnor, in the twelfth year of his Majesty's reign: A.D. 1660."

"A.D. 1676. His Grace, the Archbishop of Canterbury sent in the year above-written a letter of Inquiry to all the Clergy, what number of persons there were in the several parishes, how many recusants, how many sectaries. There were then in all, small and great, in this parish of New Radnor, four hundred and five persons, of which forty nine were sectaries, recusants none. Simon Jones, Rector."

"A.D. 1734. There were four hundred and sixteen persons in the parish of New Radnor. Walter Williams, C. W."

"1754. Novr. 2. Bap. John Llewelyn, Son of Corporal John Wood of Sir Robt. Rich's Dragoons by Elizabeth his wife. All the soldiers of the Corps being in Novr. 20, then on a detachment and quartrd in this place at the request of Thos. Lewis Esqr. of Harpton to oppress the inhabitants: a thing never before know in the memory of man, and for which he has incurred the great displeasure of the country: Thos. Lewis, Rector."

There are no religious dissenters in this parish.[9]

On the south side of the church, partly covered with earth, were found two images, cut in stone; the one resembling a warrior, clad in armour, holding a long spear in his right hand, and a shield in his left; the other a female. There is no inscription upon either. The figures are two yards in length each. About seventy years ago they lay flat upon the ground. It is probable that they formed the ornamental sculpture of some tombstones which have been demolished.

Charitable Donations.

A.D. 1668. Thomas Ecclestone by will gave £5 to the poor, which is lost.

[9] A chapel, belonging to the Calvinistic Methodists, has recently (1833) been erected in this town.

Coffin-Lids, New Radnor Church.

John Bedward, in 1688, by will gave £40 to the poor, which is also lost. This is called the *Vron* charity, being settled on an estate called the *Vron*. Thomas Lewis, Esq., late of Harpton Court, deceased, by will has directed this charity to be paid whenever the parish can prove its claim.

Henry Smith, of the city of London, Esq., by indenture dated the 24th day of April, 1627, duly enrolled in the High Court of Chancery, settled and directed the payment of from four to five pounds a-year, the sum not being fixed owing to repairs, &c., to be distributed amongst the most indigent housekeepers and other industrious poor in the parish of New Radnor, payable out of an estate and lands called Longney Farm, near Gloucester, as a perpetual charity.

John Green, of the city of Hereford, Gent., by will dated the 10th day of December, 1788, in the Prerogative Court of Canterbury, settled and directed the payment of £300, the interest of which to be distributed as follows:—" £10 a-year for ever to a charity school in the parish of New Radnor, (viz., for fifteen boys from New Radnor, and five boys from Glascwm,) and £3 a-year for ever to be given in bread, monthly, amongst the most indigent housekeepers and other industrious poor in the said parish; and the remainder to purchase pulpit, desk, and altar cloths; and also a hearse and a pall for the parish of New Radnor."

The two last donations are recorded on a benefaction table suspended on the south side of the church, in the front aisle, and they are duly administered.

John Hugh, time and manner unknown, left £50 to the poor, the interest of which was for many years regularly paid by Jeremiah Griffiths, of Downton; but a dispute arising between him and the parishioners, he deposited £50 in the exchequer, till the parish could purchase land with it, where it has remained for more than thirty-seven years.

Richard Price, Esq., of Knighton, the representative of this borough in parliament, gives £5 annually towards the instruction of poor children. He also causes the sum of £40 to be annually distributed among the poor of this parish.

List of Incumbents.

	A.D.		A.D.
Rev. Thomas Lake[1]	1649	Rev. John Jenkins	1708
Rev. Hugh Watkins	1654	Rev. John Pugh	1714
Rev. Robert Bidewell	1660	Rev. David Williams	1715
Rev. Simon Jones	1675	Rev. Chamberlayne Davies	1741
Rev. John Hergest	1683	Rev. Thomas Lewis	1745
Rev. John Howells	1685	Rev. — Woodhouse	1796
Rev. James Gwynne	1692	Rev. Thomas Hodges	1800
Rev. Roger Griffith	1706	Rev. J. Merewether, D.D., Dean of Hereford	1828

OLD RADNOR.

This parish is denominated, in Welsh, sometimes Maesyfed hên, and sometimes Pen-y-craig. The former name has been already interpreted. The latter is descriptive of the situation of its church and palace, for it anciently had a palace, viz., on the summit of a high rock. It is bounded on the north by New Radnor, on the east by the parish of Kington, on the south by Gladestry, and on the west by Llanfihangel-nant-Moylyn. It is a very extensive parish, consisting of the several townships of Bareland and Burfâ, Ednol, Evenjobb and Newcastle, Harpton and Woolpits, Lower Harpton, in the county of Hereford, Kinnerton and Salford, Old Radnor and Burlingjobb, Walton and Wymaston. It contains seven manors, viz.—1. Radnor Forest, of which T. F. Lewis, Esq., of Harpton Court is the lord; 2. Newcastle, which belongs to the crown; 3. Bilmore, *als.* Stannier, Jno. Morris, Esq.; 4. Evenjobb, and Burlingjobb, of which the Earl of Oxford is the lord; 5. Bareland and Burfâ; 6. Badland, belonging to the Earl of Oxford; 7. Kinnerton, of which the Rev. John Rogers, rector of Stowe, in the county of Salop, is the proprietor.

The antiquities still existing in this parish, though in a mutilated form, are extremely interesting, and may be referred to the druidical and Silurian ages. The four upright stones at Hindwell deserve a priority of notice.

---

[1] Ejected by the republican sequestrators. The other dates refer to the time of collation, respectively.

Besides this relic of antiquity, there are three or four others, which, though of a different construction and use, may be referred, if not to the druidical institution, yet to the Silurian age, and indicate the military tactics and civil jurisprudence of that people. On the road leading from New Radnor to Walton are three tumuli, tommenau, or barrows, placed triangularly; one of them is* of a considerable magnitude. These were for defence, and, perhaps, for the sepulture of the hero who fell in battle contiguously to the spot. To Old Radnor, tradition, in some degree confirmed by history, assigns a castle, or palace, the remains of which still exist, but in a very mutilated condition. These consist of a circular piece of ground, situated in a field on the south side of the churchyard, from which it is separated by the road, and surrounded by a deep fosse, or moat. This round area was the base of a large barrow, or tumulus, which served as the keep of the castle, or palace, that formed the superstructure. This conjecture is warranted by the circumstance of foundations of buildings having been frequently dug up in this place, as well as on the adjoining grounds, which latter circumstance seems to verify the tradition, that there once existed at Old Radnor a populous and considerable town. The name also, viz., court-yard, in the Welsh language, *llys*, corroborates the tradition of the existence of a castle, or palace, in which the ancient reguli of this district resided, the outward apartment of which was circular, and constituted the audience-hall, and the court of judicature; from this there extended, towards the east, an oblong range of building, which was the chief's own retirement; and around this principal building were others of various forms and dimensions, occupied by his vassals and tenants.

These buildings of every kind and denomination fell the victim of civil dissensions, and were destroyed in the year 990, when the first historical mention is made of Maesyfed, or Radnor, or Pen-y-craig, by the chroniclers of Wales. At that time, they and the adjacent lands belonged to Edwin, the son of Eineon, the son of Owen,

T

the son of Howell Dha. Edwin was also rightful heir to the Principality of South Wales, the throne of which had been violently seized by his usurping uncle Meredith, the younger brother of his father Eineon, who perished immaturely in the field. Edwin endeavoured to recover his right by hiring, as was customary in those times, an army of Saxons and Danes, with the assistance of whom he ravaged Meredith's territories in South Wales. To retaliate these outrages upon Edwin, Meredith destroyed with fire the buildings at Radnor, and ravaged in a cruel manner the adjacent lands. Whether Maesyfed, or Radnor, formed a part of the possessions of Elystan Glodrydd, Lord of Fferllys and Moelynaidd, no documents appear to ascertain; it certainly lay within the limits ascribed to that chieftain, who undoubtedly left to his son Cadwgan the whole of what is now comprehended under the name of Radnorshire. The Mercians, or Saxons, had made no permanent settlement in this or in any other part of the district, till after the second and successful expedition of Earl Harold into Wales, when he took possession of what is now called Old Radnor, and transferred the seat of his government to a place more commodious in situation, which he named Radrenove, or New Radnor, expelling from the adjacent lands the ancient occupiers, and substituting in their room his followers and adherents, who immediately imposed upon the different townships of this parish new names, all of which, Burfâ alone excepted, which remained a British post for some time after, are derived from Saxon origin. And this is the era in which Radnor first began to be distinguished by the epithets Old and New.

Camden entertained the opinion that Maesyfed hên, or Old Radnor, was anciently a place of very considerable note, and that on its site stood the Roman city Magos, where the commander of the Pacensian regiment, or cohort, lay in garrison, under the Lieutenant of Britain, in the reign of the Emperor Theodosius the Younger; and that from this circumstance the inhabitants of this part of the district acquired the name of Magasetæ, and

Magasetenses. That Old Radnor has been a place of some celebrity the preceding paragraphs evince; but every circumstance attached to it serves to show the absurdity of supposing that a Roman garrison was ever placed there. The fixing of Magos at Radnor is an idle fiction supported by no argument whatever. Horsley says that no Roman road led to or from Old Radnor;— granted. But there certainly was a military road of the Silures which connected Radnor with their camps of Burfâ, Cwm, and Newcastle. In *Domesday Book*, Radnor is described by the general term *Wasta*, by which is meant, not land unappropriated, but land uninclosed, as the greatest part of Wales at that time was. For ninety-six years prior to the compilation of *Domesday Book*, the lands of Radnor were the property of the great-grandson of Howell Dha, King of all Wales.

It is not to be concealed that there exists a current tradition, that the town and castle of Old Radnor were demolished by Rhys ab Gruffudd, Prince of South Wales, in the reign of King John; and that with these ruins were erected the town and castle of New Radnor. But this supposition is rejected by all historians, who concur in asserting that New Radnor was first formed by Earl Harold in 1064.

The other remains of antiquity by which this parish is distinguished consist of military positions, or camps. The principal of these are two, viz., Burfâ and New-castle. The former is situated on the river Hindwell, and distant about a mile east from the church of Old Radnor. The latter on the road from Presteigne to New Radnor, contiguous to a place called Beggar's Bush.

The principal landed proprietors of this parish are T. Frankland Lewis, Esq., member of parliament for Beaumaris. His seat is at Harpton Court, situated on the western side of the turnpike road leading from New Radnor to Walton, or Well-town. Hampton, in ancient times, belonged to a family of the name of Vaughan, descended from Eineon Clyd, Lord of Elfael, who was the son of Madoc, the son of Idnerth, the son of Cadwgan, the son of Elystan Glodrydd.

The manor or reputed manor of Bilmore, otherwise Stanner, purchased by Mr. Morris of Mr. James Poole in 1789, who purchased it of Mr. Harford Jones in 1781, who purchased of Jno. Watkins, and Mary Ann Addison Smith, London; some lands detached belonged to Stephen Comyn. Harford Jones married Elizabeth Brydges, daughter of Elizabeth Bridges, of Colwall, and John, &c., of London, 1760, two Harfords before the present one; 1713, Colonel James Jones; Brydges, 1729; Harford Jones married Elizabeth Brydges in 1730.

Lords of the Manor of Bilmore.

A.D.
1713. Colonel James Jones
1729. —— Brydges
1730. Harford Jones, by marriage

A.D.
1760. Harford Jones
1781. James Poole, by purchase
1789. John Morris, by purchase

Some detached lands were purchased by Harford Jones of Jno. Watkins and Mary Anne Addison Smith, which belonged to Stephen Comyn.

Ecclesiastical Account.

The church of Old Radnor is erected upon a rock. Hence its name in the British or Silurian language, viz., Pen-y-craig, is significantly expressive of its situation, on the northern side of a lofty eminence. It is a venerable edifice, consisting of a chancel, in which have been chantries, a nave, and two aisles, an embattled tower, with three ranges of lights on each side, one in each range, containing six bells, and a staircase turret on the north-west side. The roof is ceiled with oak, on which are carved the armorial bearings of the ancient Lords of Radnor. The beautiful screen extends entirely across the nave and aisles.

The area of the nave and aisles is paved with tiles of an hexagonal figure, and decorated with the figures of birds, the representation of crests and arms, and other fanciful devices. These are to be met with in some dwelling-houses in the town of Presteigne, and especially in the habitations usually reserved for the use and accommodation of the judges of assize.

There also stands on the north side of the chancel a richly carved old case of an organ, despoiled of its pipes. The old bellows lies in the chantry behind. At the east end of the south aisle are several monuments dedicated to the memory of the family of Lewis of Harpton Court, in this parish; more particularly that of the late Thomas Lewis, Esq., commonly known by the name of the Old Burgess Lewis, because he not only lived to a great age, viz., eighty-three years, but also because he represented this borough in parliament eight successive parliaments, from the year 1714 to the year 1768.

No document or memorial exists which might ascertain the precise era in which this church was erected.

The benefice of Old Radnor is a rectory and vicarage, with the chapels of Kennarton and Ednol annexed. Kennarton is the Querentune mentioned in *Domesday Book*, as belonging to Osbern, the son of Richard. The Dean and Chapter of Worcester, in whom are vested the whole of the tithes, are the patrons. For in the reign of Henry VIII., both the patronage of the church, and the tithes of the parish of Old Radnor, which came to the crown by the accession of the Lord of Moelynaidd to the throne of England in the person of Edward IV., were granted by the foreign sovereign to the reverend the Dean and Chapter of Worcester, for the purpose of augmenting their income. Ever since that time, the whole of the tithes have been let by lease, renewable every seventh year, to a lay gentleman resident in the neighbourhood. The present lessee is T. Frankland Lewis, Esq., of Harpton Court, at a low rent, out of which is paid the salary of the vicar.

List of Incumbents.

	A.D.		A.D.
Thomas Powell	1809	H. F. Mogridge, M.A.	1834

Population.

A.D. 1801—1243; 1811—1220; 1821—1331; 1831

—1526; 1841—1503; 1851—1263. Part of the township of Upper Harpton, containing twenty-four houses and 124 persons, is in the parish of Llanfihangel-nant-Moylyn, in this sub-district, but is here returned as in 1841.[2]

PRESTEIGNE, *Wallice*, LLANANDRAS.

The etymology of this name has given rise to a variety of conjectures, as widely differing from each other as they seem to do from the truth. Some contend that it is of Saxon origin, and ought to be written Preston, signifying priest town. But what was there in any age of a singularly sacerdotal or monastic character about the place? Besides, Presteigne had no existence during the Saxon Heptarchy. It was not then in being.

Others deduce the name from the Welsh language, viz., Prysg-duon, the translation of which is black copses. The objections to this etymology are, *first*, the ungrammatical connection of the compound Prysg-duon, violating an essential rule of syntax; *secondly*, its unappropriate designation; and, *lastly*, because the place already has a Welsh name, viz., Llanandras, in constant use, and there appears no reason for multiplying its appellations, which would lead to confusion.

The truth is, Presteigne was not in existence, nor known to the Welsh and Saxons, anterior to the Norman invasion, for no mention of it occurs in *Domesday Book*. In that national record notice is taken of every place by which it is surrounded, together with the names of the proprietors, and the extent of the property.

" In Hezetre Hundred, Osbern, son of Richard, holds and did hold Bradelege (Bradnor, containing 1 hide); Titlege (Titley, 3 hides); Bruntune (Brampton, 1 hide); Chenille (Knill, 2 hides); Hercope (Hyop, half of a hide); Hertune (Hereton, 3 hides); Hech (Heath, 1 hide); Clatertune (Clatterbrook, 2 hides); Querentune (Kinnerton, 1 hide); Discote (Discoed, 3 hides); Cascope (Cascob, half of a hide)."

[2] The returns for this parish, and the insertion of other corrections, are due to the kindness of the Rev. Walter Jones Williams, M.A.

Mention is also made of Pilleth, Norton, Weston, &c.; whilst Presteigne itself is passed by unrecorded and unnoticed. And the reason of this can be no other than because, prior to the time in which *Domesday Book* was published, Presteigne had no distinct and separate name of its own, but was included in, and formed a part of, the several hamlets here specified. At the time of the publication of *Domesday Book*, Presteigne had not an existence—it was not in being; and Clatterbrook, Discoed, Heath, and Hereton, possessed the pre-eminence. At present these have fallen from their original superiority, holden in a comparatively inferior estimation, and absorbed in the name Presteigne; whilst the latter has not only emerged from its original obscurity, and sprung from its state of non-existence, but also lifted up its head far above them all, and become the metropolis of the county of Radnor.

From the preceding statement, it is evident that, for the derivation of the name Presteigne, we must not look to the Saxons. To what people then is this name to be ascribed? Most assuredly to the Norman usurpers, from whose practices and institutions the name Presteigne springs. Whatever lands these Norman hunters chose to denominate wastes, they declared should be forests. There are in the county three of their forests, viz., Radnor, Blaiddfâ, and Cefn-y-llys, which formerly were more extensive than at present. On these forests their tenants and vassals had the liberty to depasture their cattle, on paying a certain rate for the privilege, which rate, *mutatis mutandis*, exists to this day. To collect and receive this rate particular officers must have been appointed, who would naturally fix their abode in places contiguous to these forests. The situation of the town of Presteigne, built at the foot of the royal forest of Radnor, and in the vicinity of the forest of Blaiddfâ, was an advantage not easily to be overlooked or neglected. Nor is its name less applicable to this purpose. It is a compound word, of Norman Latin, and is derived from " Presa," the fee for depasturing cattle on the royal wastes, and "Teigni," officers. So that the first colonizers and inhabitants of Presteigne were foresters, officers appointed to collect and receive the royal revenue arising from the herbage of the forests.

The parish of Presteigne is very extensive, containing not fewer than six large townships, viz., Presteigne, in the county of Radnor, and Stapleton, Willey, Brampton, Rodd, and Nash, and Combe, in the county of Hereford. Its situation in respect of the adjoining parishes is nearly as follows:—On the east and south-east sides are Lingen, Kinsam, and Byton; on the south and south-west are Stanton, Titley and Knill; on the west and north-west, Old Radnor, Cascob and Whitton; on the north and north-east, Norton and Brampton-Brian. It extends eight miles in length, and seven miles in breadth. The quantity of acres it contains cannot be exactly known, as the form of the parish in many places is much indented and irregular. Two-thirds of the common lands remain still uninclosed, and no certain measure of them is known.

Near the town of Presteigne, on the south-east quarter, is Clatterbrook, named in *Domesday* Clattertune, where formerly stood a town in a situation seemingly preferable to Presteigne, for it is sheltered from all obnoxious winds. This is supposed to be the Clatterbrigg, or Claftsbrigg, where Gruffudd, the victorious Prince of Wales, put to death the prisoners he took in the sacking of Hereford, viz., the bishop, sheriffs and other persons of distinction.

On one of the adjacent eminences, called Wardon, situated on the north-west side of the town, it is reported a castle anciently stood, of which no remains are at present visible. Stapleton Castle was the residence of Elias Walwyn, the associate of Sir Edmund Mortimer, of Wigmore. He was extremely active and instrumental in betraying and slaying the unfortunate Llewelyn ab Gruffudd, the last Prince of Wales, in the neighbourhood of Buallt, in Brecknockshire, in the year 1282.

Another spot in this valley, entitled to historical notice, is at a little distance from the town of Presteigne, on the

HISTORY OF RADNORSHIRE.

The Butter-House, Knighton.

road leading to Leominster, and to this day denominated Market Lane, Broken Cross, Chicken Lane, &c. The reason of these several denominations is this: in the years 1610, 1636 and 1637, the inhabitants of this parish and town were victims of a disease at once loathsome and destructive. A great and alarming mortality ensued. So excessive was the horror conceived of this disease, and such the precaution used to guard against its contagion, that nobody cared to approach near to the scene of infection. The business and intercourse of the town and parish were suspended. The market was removed from the town to the place before described; thither the country people brought necessaries, such as prepared provisions, medicines, changes of linen, &c., left them, and departed. As soon as they were gone, the infected came, and distributed the articles thus brought for them. This dreadful situation at length excited the commiseration of gentlemen of rank and power; and Sir Robert Harley, and John Vaughan, Esq., magistrates of the county of Hereford, issued the following precept and warrant, directed to the chief constables of the hundred of Wigmore, and to either of them:—

"Forasmuch as the Lord hath visited the neighbourhood of the Town of Presteigne, within the county of Radnor, with that grievous infection of the Plague: And now being certified from two of the Justices of the Peace of the same county, of the poverty of the inhabitants thereof, &c. These are therefore, by virtue of an act of Parliament made in the first year of the reign of King James, of famous memory, for the charitable relief and the ordering of persons infected with the plague, to will and require you to collect and gather weekly within the feudal rights and townships underwritten, within your hundred, the sums on them assessed; and the same to pay to John Price of Combe, Gent., at his dwelling house there, every Friday weekly, and to begin the payment thereof upon Friday next ensuing the date hereof. And if any person or persons do refuse to pay such sum or sums of money, as shall on them be assessed, that then you certify to us, or some of our fellow Justices of the peace of this county, that further order may be taken therein, either for distress for the same, or for the imprisonment of the bodies of the parties refusing according to the tenour of the said Act.

Thereof fail you not the due performance, as you will answer the contrary at your perils. Dated at Pembridge, under our hands and seals, the Twentieth of September 1636.

Ro. HARLEY (L. S.)
JOHN VAUGHAN (L. S.)

	s.	d.		s.	d.
Stapleton	2	6	Titley parish	5	0
Willey	2	0	Mouldley Waples Stanton	5	0
Upper Kinsum	2	0	Leintwardine parish	5	0
Rod, Nash and Brampton	10	0	Brampton parish	2	7
Combe and Byton	9	0	Wigmore parish	2	7
Lower Kinsum	2	0	Leinthall parish	2	7
Knill and Barton	4	0	Aymstry parish	5	0
Litton and Cascob	8	0	Lingen parish	2	0

There is also a third place in this valley, surpassing all the rest in singularity of occurrence, and not less deserving of historical perpetuity. This is called the "King's Turning," by which is meant the turning out, or departing, from the straight road by King Charles I. In the time of the great rebellion, after the fatal loss of the battle of Naseby, in the year 1645, the royal cause declined rapidly. The king had come into the Marches of Wales for the purpose of recruiting his army among the loyal inhabitants; he was closely pursued by his enemies, yet safely conducted by Sir David Williams, of Gwernyfed, to Radnor, where he slept one night. The following morning he marched to Hereford; and on the succeeding day came from thence through Leominster and Weobley, to the neighbourhood of Presteigne, and slept two successive nights at the Lower Heath, in this parish, in a house belonging to Nicholas Taylor, Esq. Having by this halt sufficiently eluded his pursuers, he resumed his march, but "turned" or changed the line of his route, by riding from hence over the hills to Norton, Knighton, Newtown, Chirk Castle, and so on to Chester.

On this occasion is reported a traditionary tale in this parish, which, as it is an additional confirmation of the courage and loyalty which the inhabitants of this county universally evinced during the time of the great rebellion, deserves to be recorded for the example and benefit of succeeding ages. Numerous were the obstructions with which they impeded the progress of the king's pursuers; and among other devices, the deception of false intelligence was practised. Determined to punish this malignancy, the republican soldiers had recourse to plunder and oppression. On a certain day, whilst Mr. Legge, of Willey Court, and all his male domestics, were occupied in the hay-field, these reforming marauders took the opportunity of pillaging his house, and brutally treating the females that were preparing dinner for the labourers. Mr. Legge, wondering that the dinner was so long protracted beyond the usual hour, returned to his house to know the cause, and found it completely plundered, and his domestics bitterly lamenting the base usage they had received. His indignation stimulated him to immediate revenge. He assembled his workmen, who armed themselves with pitch-forks, and, commencing at their head a pursuit, he overtook the villains, attacked them without hesitation, killed one on the spot, and wounded and dispersed the rest. The pitch-fork with which the soldier was run through the body, and nailed to the ground, remained for many years with the family a favourite relic, and was as singular in its formation as in the use to which it was then applied, for the tine was fastened to the steel by a screw. The instrument has been seen by many aged persons now living, who relate the story, or the achievement.

The manor of Presteigne was anciently holden of the priory of Limbrook. At the dissolution it was seized by King Henry VIII., and annexed to the crown, or to the eldest sons of the Kings of England. In the year 1649 a survey was made of the manor of Presteigne, with the rights, members and appurtenances thereof, late parcel of the possessions of King Charles I., by virtue of a commission granted upon an act of the Commons of England assembled in parliament, for sale of honours, manors and lands belonging heretofore to the late king, queen and prince, under the hands and seals of five or more of the trustees in the said act nominated and appointed. The following is the inventory then published:—

150 HISTORY OF RADNORSHIRE.

	£	s.	d.
The quit rents due to the aforesaid manor in free soccage tenure are Court barons and court leets, fines and amerciaments, upon alienation, &c.	7 4	2 10	11 0
Heriots due communibus annis	4	0	0
Tolls belonging to market and fair day are comm. ann.	12	10	0
Of which tolls a part is granted to Sir Edmund Sawyer, Knight...	2	0	0
The other part on market days said to be granted to the Bailiff...	10	0	0
Hartley Wood, containing by estimation 40 acres, bounded west-by-north by Mer; north by Elias Taylor; North Wood, west by mountains; north by R. and N. Mer; 240 acres; value of both per acre, 3s.; improvement of both above the rent reserved per annum, is	38	0	0
The last mentioned premises were leased to Sir Thomas Trevor for 99 years, for the use of the then Prince of Wales, 14 Jac. 10th January. The mountainous land between the highway to Discoed, and Ruddock's land, from the lands of Walter Gorney to those of Evan Vaughan, containing about 60 acres, was conveyed to Mrs. Taylor, valued per acre, 3s.			
So the value above the reserved rent is	8	18	10
The advowson to the parsonage is in the lord of the manor, worth £200 per annum; present incumbent, John Skull, aged 70. Edward Price, of Knighton, leased the Great Close at Gorney, lying between the highway to Discoed and Ruddock's land, late parcel of the Earl of Marche's lands, to Edward Gorney from 25th March, 1584, for 20 years, at the rent of 18d. per annum; expired in 1604. Thomas Price, Ar., leased the said lands to Hugh Lewis, Ar., from 1604 for 21 years, at 18d. per annum; expired 1625. And from that time, Meredith Morgan, Ar., leased the same to Sir Edmund Sawyer, Knight, for 40 years, which expired 1665. Meredith Morgan passed his time to Nicholas Taylor, Ar., at the said yearly rent, fifteen years of which are yet to come. Then follows a list of the common freeholders, chiefly owners of premises in the town of Presteigne, total of which is	7	2	2

An abstract of the present rents, future improvements, and all other profits of the said manor of Presteigne:—

	£	s.	d.
The quit rents and royalties..	11	12	11
The rents upon the several leases holden			
Total amount of the present profits per annum	19	14	1
The yearly value of the heriots is	4	0	0
Herriots in Presteigne due to the representatives of the Dean of Windsor...	10	0	0
Tolls of the markets and fairs to the Bailiff			
Rents of assize leased to Robert Davies, et alii........................	0	3	4½
Do. do. John Cooke.....................................	0	4	1½
Crown lands, Edward Price, tenant...	0	19	10
Tenement in Presteigne, Louisa Price, tenant	0	0	2
Do. in Ave Mary Lane, Presteigne, Jno. Hancocke, et alii, tenants	0	0	3½
Tenement in Presteigne, — Clarke, tenant			
Do. do. Earl of Powis, tenant........................	0	0	1½
Do. do. Evan Meredith, Esq., tenant...............	0	0	1½
Do. do. Duke of Chandos, tenant	0	2	0

	£	s.	D.
Concealed land in Presteigne, called Frieth, Dean of Windsor, tenant	0	1	2
The yearly value of tolls of markets and fairs	12	10	0
The improvement of the several leases is	42	18	10
Total amount of the future improvements per annum is	79	2	11

Ex. per Will. Webb,
Supr. Genl.
1649.

HEN. MAKEPEACE,
JOHN MARRYOTT,
PETER PRICE,
Jo. LLOYD.

The present lord of the manor of Presteigne is the Earl of Oxford. This parish exhibits no traces of ancient military positions—a proof of its more recent occupation and culture; but is surrounded on all sides by camps of importance and magnitude, viz., Newcastle, Burfâ, Wapley, &c.

In the reign of Queen Elizabeth, a considerable manufactory of woollen cloth, which afforded employment to a numerous poor, was established and conducted with great success by John Beddowes, Esq., a gentleman as eminent for his charity as for his industry. From this period the town of Presteigne rapidly increased in the number of its inhabitants and of its houses. For carrying on this business several ranges of back buildings were erected in Harper's Street, on the right side of the Broad Street, and on the left of the High Street, and vestiges of several fullers' mills still remain in the vicinity of the place. It appears also from the register, that 250 years ago the population of the town exceeded the present by one five in twenty. Notwithstanding this apparent prosperity, when the sickness of 1636 invaded Presteigne, the inhabitants were unable to support themselves, and they became objects of the commiseration and charity of the surrounding townships.

Presteigne is a borough by prescription, and was formerly, it is said, one of the contributory boroughs of New Radnor. How it came to lose its elective franchise, whether by petition on the score of inability to contribute to the salary of its representative, or by forfeiture, or whether it ever enjoyed this privilege, are matters of equal uncertainty. In the year 1690, the burgesses of

Presteigne claimed a right of voting at the election of a member to serve in parliament for the borough of New Radnor, when Sir Robert Harley and Sir Rowland Gwynne were candidates; and, on being rejected by the returning officer, they presented a petition to the House of Commons. In the same year the house determined that the right of election for the borough of New Radnor was in the burgesses of Radnor, Rhayader, Cnwclâs, Knighton, and Cefn-y-llys only, and consequently their claim was disallowed. This resolution has ever since been considered as law. It is governed by a bailiff, who is not elected by the inhabitants, but nominated and imposed upon them by the steward of Cantref Moelynaidd. So that the good people of this town may still boast, as their ancestors did formerly, of being governed by the King of England, who nominates the steward of Cantref Moelynaidd, and the latter nominates the bailiff who governs the town of Presteigne. The Great and Quarter Sessions are holden here, as also the County Courts (instead of Rhayader, which forfeited them), alternately with New Radnor.

Cock-fighting was formerly a favourite and popular diversion, pursued by gentlemen of figure and respectability. About the middle of the last century, a main of cocks was fought at the *Oak Inn*, in Broad Street, in this town, for a considerable wager, by . . . . Esq., of Boultibrook, in this parish, and . . . . . Baskerville, Esq., of Aberedw Court, in the parish of Aberedw, in this county, and added one to the many fatal instances of ungoverned passion which the partaking of this brutal and barbarous diversion never fails to kindle and inflame. High words arose betwixt the two contending parties; they withdrew into the yard of the inn to settle their dispute: swords were drawn, and the former gentleman was run through the body, and died on the spot. The bringing of weapons so dangerous to such a place can only be accounted for on the score that a personal combat had been previously concerted by the parties. The Baskervilles were desperate fellows at pinking their opponents. Sir Ralph Baskerville, of Aberedw Court, and Lord Clifford, of Clifford Castle, near the town of Hay, quarrelled about the limits of their respective estates, and fought (1270) on the Radnorshire bank of the Wye, when the latter was slain. It is supposed by several that the huge sculptured stone in the church-yard of Llowes was erected in commemoration of this battle. Sir Ralph obtained a pardon from the Pope, not for killing his man in a fair duel, but for fighting in the church-yard—an act of the most enormous profanation.

Ecclesiastical Account.

The church of Presteigne consists of a nave, two aisles, a chancel, a tower, and a vestry. The aisle on the south side is separated from the nave by eight octagonal pillars, sustaining seven pointed arches; the aisle on the north side by six octagonal pillars and two circular columns. The entrance from the nave into the chancel is under a high pointed arch, which is not exactly in the centre of the present church. The aisle of the chancel is divided from it by three octagonal pillars supporting two pointed arches. On the capitals of the different pillars are suspended the crests of Owen, Bradshaw, Cornewall, and Taylor, heretofore the most respectable and opulent inhabitants of this parish. The families of the former, and also of Price, are commemorated on marble monuments fixed to the east wall of the greater chancèl, between which, and over the communion-table, is placed an altar-piece of curiously wrought tapestry, representing the entrance of Christ into Jerusalem. The arch between the church and chancel is decorated with the figures of Moses and Aaron; and on the opposite end are delineated Time and Death, the tyrants of the whole human race. On each side of the altar-piece is a very elegant oak pillar of the Corinthian order, and on a monument fixed against the north wall of the chancel is the following remarkable inscription:—

"Here lieth the body of Francis Owen, of Brampton, in this parish, Gent. He died March 12th, 1686, aged 80, who had the happiness not only to see, but to cohabit with, his father, grandfather, and great-grandfather, from whence he was lineally descended; and as many generations issuing from his loins, in a lineal descent downwards, viz., his son, grandson, and great-grandson: he himself making the seventh generation of his family in his own memory and house of Brampton."

Walter Devereux, Earl of Ferrars, was Chief Justice of South Wales in the reign of Henry VIII. He was possessed of several estates in the county of Radnor, and among others Pipton, in the parish of Gladestry, and the rectory of Presteigne, and the great tithes of Norton, an adjoining parish. Being also lord of Tamworth, he is supposed to be the person at whose expense the south side of Presteigne Church was erected. His arms were —*Argent*, on a chevron engrailed *azure*, two griffins combatant of the first, collared *gules*, hoofed and langued *gules*, on a chief of the second three mullets pierced *or*. He was executed in the year 1554, in the reign of Queen Mary, for the ostensible crime of high treason, but really on account of the favour he showed to the Protestant religion.

The tower is square, flanked at the angles with shelving buttresses, embattled at top, with pinnacles at the four corners, and a cupola supporting a weather-cock. It has three ranges of windows, with two lights in each, and contains a clock, chimes, and six musical bells, on which are the following inscriptions:—

" I.—A.D. 1717. Prosperity to the Church of England.
" II.—Abraham Rudhall, of Gloucester, cast us all.
" III.—Peace and good neighbourhood.
" IV.—Samuel Sandford, Rector, A.D. 1717.
" V.—A.D. 1717. William Jones, Richard Pugh, Timothy Haswell, James Ashley, churchwardens.
" VI.—Me resonare jubet pietas, mors, atque voluptas."

It has also two sun dials, and is about 60 feet high. The tower originally stood in a separate situation from the old church, as evidently appears from the particular mode of its construction, and, from the different style of its architecture, seems to have been built at different times. The old church ascended in height only to the first story.

The chancel was built against the upright walls of the former fabric by Mortimer, lord of Wigmore, in the reign of Edward I., soon after the royal grant of Moelynaidd and Elfael received confirmation, who by this act of munificence endeavoured to conciliate the affections of his new vassals.

There remains no existing record to authenticate the assertion that this south aisle was built by Lord Tamworth; but it is founded on the mere tradition of the inhabitants. The lordship of Tamworth Castle is a title almost coeval with the conquest, and was conferred on Robert de Marmion, Lord of Fontney, in Normandy, who came into England with the Conqueror. The castle of Tamworth, and the territory adjacent, had been the royal demesnes of the Saxon kings. This title, passing through the families of De Marmion, De Freville, De Ferrars, and of Northampton, successively, was conveyed by the marriage of Lady Charlotte Compton, the only surviving issue of James, fifth Earl of Northampton, in the year 1751, to the Hon. George Townshend, eldest son and heir to Charles, third Viscount Townshend, of Raynham, in the county of Norfolk. The noble family of De Ferrars having intermarried with the powerful families of De Braos, Lord of Brecknock and Buallt, and of Mortimer, Earl of Marche and Wigmore, respectively, became possessed of considerable estates and several castles in the county of Hereford, and on the borders of Radnorshire. A part of this property, consisting of tithes leased to Richard Price, Esq., representative in parliament for the borough of Radnor, at present belongs to Townshend, Lord de Ferrars, the heir of that house. His arms are quarterly of six,—1. *Azure*, a chevron *ermine*, between three escallop shells *argent* (Townshend). 2. France and England, quarterly, within a border *argent* (Plantagenet of Woodstock, Duke of Gloucester). 3. *Sable*, a lion of England, between three helmets, proper, garnished *or* (Compton). 4. Paly of six, *or* and *azure*, a canton *ermine* (Shirley). 5. Quarterly, 1 and 4 *argent*, a fess *gules*, three torteaux in chief (Devereux); 2 and 3, Varre *or* and *gules* (Ferrars of Chartley). 6. *Gules*, seven mascles conjoined, 3, 3, and 1 (Ferrars of Groby and Tamworth.) The arms of Townshend, Ferrars of Chartley, and Ferrars of Groby and Tamworth, are sculptured on the three buttresses which flank the south front of the church. Two of them are defaced by the injuries of time and weather, the middle only remains visible, which is that of Townshend. The crest of Ferrars of Tamworth was,—on a wreath an unicorn passant *ermine*, armed, hoofed, maned and tufted *or*.

In the year 1604, in the reign of James I., Sir Robert Harley, the only surviving son of Thomas Harley, Esq., was made forester of Bringewood Forest, with a salary of £6 2s. 8d. per annum, with the pokership, £1 10s. 5d. per annum, and also forester of Prestwood, 18s. per annum. *Query*, if Prestwood be the same with Presteigne.

The church-yard is a spacious and extensive area, containing about half of an acre of land, and accommodated with gravel walks, planted on each side with trees. The walk on the north side of the church is 120 yards long, and eight broad, where lately flourished a grand avenue of fine sycamore trees, which were felled and sold by an avaricious rector of this church. On the right hand of the walk that leads to the grand entrance into the church, which is an arched porch sustaining the tower, stands a mutilated stone cross.

This is, perhaps, the most valuable benefice in all South Wales, being worth, at a moderate calculation, £1000 per annum. The late rector, the Rev. John Harley, advanced its income to £1500 per annum. It consists of a vicarage and rectory united, with the chapelry of Discoed annexed. The rector enjoys all the tithes of every denomination of this well cultivated and extensive parish. Formerly the vicarial and rectorial tithes were disunited, and possessed by different persons. For in the eighth year of the reign of King Charles I., the Rev. John Scull was presented to the vicarage only; but in the fifteenth year of the reign of King Charles I., the impropriate tithes of this parish, being forfeited to the crown by the feoffees of St. Antholine's, London, who purchased impropriations to maintain and establish factious and seditious lectures, were by royal letters patent given to the said Rev. John Scull, D.B., the first clerical rector of this church, and to his successors for ever, in *puram eleemosynam*, for the good of the souls of the parishioners of the said parish. This royal grant was procured by Mr. Scull at a considerable expense, aided by the friendly advice and interest of Lord Willoughby, so that he became the greatest benefactor to this church since its foundation. But in the despotic administration of the Rump Parliament, he was deprived of all the emoluments of his living, and died in extreme poverty in the year 1652. The income of this rectory was, by a set of hypocritical parliamentary rascals, under the influence of Oliver Cromwell, given to one Knowles, an Anabaptist, and Lucas, a London tailor, and enjoyed by them till the day when Oliver's carcase was exhibited at Tyburn. In the first year of the restoration of King Charles II. the said rectory was again bestowed upon the church, to which in the same year was presented the Rev. Philip Lewis, A.M., the second clerical rector of this benefice. This account is extracted from the register book of the parish.

"Ego Phil. Lewis, Rect. Presteigne, hæc apposui in successorum gratiam X Cal. Junii, vid. 23° die Maii 1670.

"Joannes Scull, Baccal. in Sacr. Theolog. impensis ter centum librarum et ope domini et comitis de Willoughby, (cui erat a sacris) obtinuit ab optimo, et in ecclesiam munificentissimo, rege Carolo primo, rectoriam impropriatam ecclesiæ de Presteigne in puram elemosynam; hoc est, effecit ut piissimus rex per literas patentes constituerit ex rectoria impropriata et vicaria prius existente, (cujus vicarius erat dictus Joannes Scull) unam individuatam et consolidatam rectoriam præsentativam, &c. ut ex literis patentibus constat. Quas literas patentes videat licet, cujus intersit. (In the third part of the originals of the fifteenth year of King Charles I., transcribed out of the High Court of Chancery, and remaining in the custody of the Treasurer's Remembrancer in the Exchequer, c. vii. Roll.) Joannes dictus denominatus erat in istis literis rector ecclesiæ dictæ, et imperturbatus ita remansit, donec (usque) in Carolo primo cecidit ecclesia Anglicana, in eaque rectoria de Presteigne: nam atrum et sacrilegum nomine Parliamentum, sed re conventio diabolica, concessit rectoriæ de Presteigne reversionem, vel reventus, parochianis de St. Anthling factiosissimis Londini. Sic exutus est rectoria rector meritissimus do'ius Scull, et fit Presteigne rectoria præda sacrilegis de St. Anthling, (   ) James de Trippleton, aliisque: Interim moritur ex mærore

158 HISTORY OF RADNORSHIRE.

prædecessor meus do'ius Scull, destitutus, devestitus, et denudatus omnibus suis et beneficiis, et officiis. Sit sibi pax. Optime meruit de hac ecclesia, et de omnibus qui ei successerint: In memoriamque ejus hæc apposui gratus successor.

"Huic divino et reverend, viro surrogarunt perduelliones sacrilegi Knowles, nescio quem anabaptistam, et Lucas, sartorem Londinensem, quorum nomina fœtent.

"Tandem ecclesiæ Anglicanæ conculcatæ, et exulantis regis, et direptæ plebis, et eversarum legum misertus Optimus Maximus restituit et throno et nobis Carolum secundum 29° Maii annoque Dei 1660.

"Eoque anno benevolentia erga me moti primi Parochiani de Presteigne, imprimis Thomas Ecclestone me monuere, imo adegerunt, ut me Regis serenissimi pedibus supplicem offerrem, et eorum nomine (nam etiam supplices eo literas composuerat amicus meus Franciscus Richards, quibus omnes alii subscripserant parochiani) peterem ad rectoriam de Presteigne nunc vacantem Præsentationem.

"Excitatus ergo eorum votis adii Aulam, supplices libellos ope viri (mihi usque colendi, cui, quicquid sum debeo,) Reverendissimi Doctoris Georgii Morley, nunc Episcopi Wintoniensis, (cui etiam sum Capellanus,) obtuli Regi, qui gratiose mihi rectoriam dictam concessit, ad eamque me præsentavit: Multum quidem negotii mihi fecere Edw. Harley, Britton, aliique competitores, sed illis non obstantibus 6ᵗᵒ die Mensis Augusti anno 1660 admissus sum ad vicariam de Presteigne cum impropriatis eidem annexatis dotibus per Doctorem Chaworte Vicarium Generalem. Cum Jurisperiti me monuissent Præsentationem ad rectoriam nomine præsentationis renovare, id quoque obtinui et perfeci et tandem 24ᵗᵒ die Octobris anno 1664 inductus sum ad rectoriam ecclesiæ parochialis de Presteigne per Rever. in Christo Patrem Herb. Hereford, sit laus Deo. Georg. Winton. Gilbert Londin. Johan. Sarisb. Docto. Gibbs, Johan. Richards. Nichol. Taylor. Evan. Davies, Thom. Owen, aliosque. Et denuo aliquid dandum est et ingenio et non numerandis expensis meis.

"Hæc apposui in gratiam successorum ut noscant scopulos quibus ipse allisus sum, et petant non ut ipse male consulens, Vicariam sed Rectoriam, et ut inspiciant literas dictas irrotulatas ut supra.

"Natus modicis sed honestis parentibus Rich. et Anna Lewis paroch. de Llandrindod (individuæ Trinit. sacræ) in viculo de Brin heire de Mellenith; educatus scholæ de Presteigne; Oxoniæ ab Doc'io optimo Roberto Waring alitus in Æde Christi, Magistri artium dignitate cohonestatus in Aula Sanctæ Mariæ. Jam denuo rector de Presteigne hæc scripsi anno ætatis meæ XLiii, anno rectoriæ meæ 9ⁿᵒ., anno Do'i 1670.

"PHILIP LEWIS."

This rich benefice is valued in the king's books as low as £20. The patronage of it is vested in the Earl of Oxford. The church is dedicated to St. Andrew, and situated on the right bank of the river Lug, celebrated for its fine trout and grayling fishing. It is distant 150 miles west-north-west from London.

The charitable donations and benefactions left to this parish are very liberal, as will appear from the following list:—

John Beddowes, Esq., in the year 1568, gave certain

lands and tenements to the value of £30 per annum, for the maintenance of a free grammar school, for the education of children born in this town and parish.

Ellen Harris, widow, of London, by her last will in the year 1630, gave the sum of £4 to be distributed yearly, viz., 4 marks for 4 quarter sermons, and 13s. 4d. to be distributed among the poor of the parish on the four sermon days, and the other 13s. 4d. to the churchwardens of the said parish for ever.

John Matthews, of Clerkenwell, London, gave £50 to be lent to five or six poor tradesmen of this parish for two years to each tradesman, use free. He gave £52 to be distributed in 12d. loaves to twelve old people of the parish, every Sunday for ever. He gave six coats to six poor children every year. He gave six bibles to six poor children every year for ever.

Nicholas Taylor, Esq., of this parish, gave the interest and use of £30 for placing one poor boy or girl of this parish an apprentice for ever.

Margaret Price, widow, late of Pilleth, gave the interest of £50 for ever, for the placing of one poor boy an apprentice every year. She gave the interest of £10 for the clothing of two poor people yearly.

Richard Rodd, Esq., of the Rodd, in the county of Hereford, gave £5 to the poor of Presteigne.

Jane Bull gave 12s. per annum, to be distributed in bread to twelve poor people upon Candlemas-day.

Thomas Ecclestone, of Presteigne, Esq., gave to the poor of Presteigne £50 as a fund towards the building of a small house for their accommodation for ever. He likewise gave £5 to purchase some ornament for the church.

Nicholas Taylor, Junr., Esq., of this parish, by will, dated December 2, 1672, gave £20 to be added to the £30 given by his father for binding apprentices. He also gave £30 to buy cloth for the poor at Christmas, in all £80.

Ambrose Meredith, of Stapleton, gave one-half of the annual rent of two parcels of lands, and one cottage with a garden, lying and being at the Slough, to be distributed by the minister and churchwardens among the most needy and poor of the parish, on the feast of St. John the Baptist, St. Michael, Circumcision, and Annunciation. The other moiety he gave to bind an apprentice.

Thomas Cornewall, Esq., baron of Burford, lord of Stapleton and Lougharness, gave to the poor of this parish several sums of money and goods forfeited to the said lord of the manor by felonies, murders, and other crimes, viz., by a felony committed at Cascob, £2 12s.; by a murder committed at Combe, £6. By another forfeiture of blood, applied to the benefit of the school, and the purchasing of leathern buckets for the engines, and to other charitable purposes.

Sir Thomas Street, of the county of Worcester, one of the judges of assize on this circuit, gave £20 to bind seven apprentices, which sum was forfeited by William Whitcombe, Esq., of London, high sheriff of this county, for non-attendance at the great sessions.

Littleton Powell, Esq., of Stanage, one of the six clerks of Chancery, gave a large, noble, silver flagon, weighing 74 ounces and 3 drams, valued at £25, to be used in the administration of the holy sacrament of our Lord's Supper.

Thomas Owen, Esq., of Brampton Parva, gave the altar-piece in the great chancel, and two silver salvers, gilt, to contain the bread at the holy communion.

One large, handsome silver chalice—donor unknown.

Nicholas Scarlet, of Presteigne, gave 40s. per annum, to be distributed among the poor of this parish.

Giles Whitehall, Esq., of the Moor, in the year 1734, gave to the township of Presteigne a fire-engine, and 12 leathern buckets.

Edward Price, Esq., of Aylesbury, in the county of Bucks, in the year 1774, gave a handsome chandelier to the church; also, he gave the interest of £50 to be distributed in bread to the poor of the parish on Christmas-day and Easter-day, for ever, by the minister and church-wardens thereof. The said Edward Price was buried in the great chancel.

Arms on Brass in Presteigne Church.

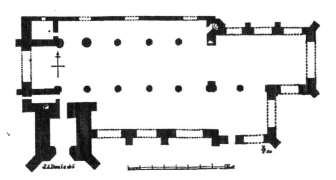

Plan of Presteigne Church.

List of Incumbents.

Rev. Roger Bradshaw, Vicar 1600	Rev. Timothy Thomas, D.D. 1727
Rev. John Scull, D.B., Vicar 1611	Rev. Joseph Guest 1751
Rector 1640	Rev. Archdeacon Harley..........1770
Rev. Philip Lewis, A.M., Rector ..1653	Rev. William Whalley............1789
Rev. William Morgan 1702	Rev. James Bull.................1799
Rev. Samuel Sandford............1717	Rev. John Harley 1812
Rev. Archdeacon Comyn..........1721	Rev. James Beebee...............181

The original appointment and names of the first trustees of the free school, founded by John Beddowes, Esq., in the reign of Queen Elizabeth, A.D. 1568.

Trustees' Names.

Thomas Wigmore, Esq.   Nicholas Meredith.   Philip Gough, Junr.
Peter Lloyd, Esq.   Rev. Roger Bradshaw. John Jennings.
John Weaver, Esq.   John-ab-Owen.   John Jenkins.
John Blayney, Junr.   Roger Vicares.

List of Schoolmasters.

Rev. Miles Hawkins 1595	Rev. Eusebius Beeston 1700
Rev. John Gomey 1658	Rev. Humphrey Griffiths 1779
Rev. Robert Treyloe 1663	Rev. John Grubb...............
Rev. James Bailey 1682	

HUNDRED OF KNIGHTON.

THE territory now denominated the hundred of Knighton was in ancient times included in those portions of Cantref Moelynaidd, and Cantref-y-clawdd, which embraced the two mesne manors of Knighton, and Swydd-y-wgre, and a small portion of that of Swydd-wynogion, and contained the three cwmwds of Dyffryn Tafediad; Is-mynydd and Uwch-mynydd; and Swydd-wynogion. It is situated on the north-eastern extremity of this county, and is bounded on the east by the river Tame and Shropshire, on the west by the hundred of Rhayader, on the south by the hundreds of Cefn-y-llys and Radnor, and on the north by the line that separates the two counties of Radnor and Montgomery. It contains seven parishes, including one market-town, two contributary boroughs, and one independent lordship, viz., Bugaildu, Cnwclâs, Heyope, Knighton, Llanano, Llanbadarn-fynydd, Llanbister, Llanddewi-ystrad-ennau, and Stanage. Heyope, Knighton, and Stanage, are Saxon names, the rest Welsh. The reason why this hundred was denominated Knighton is obvious, because the important borough and market-town of Knighton are situated within it.

BUGAILDU.

This name signifies "The Shepherd's House," and alludes to the occupation of the inhabitants in ancient times, who, in common with the rest of their countrymen, chiefly led a pastoral life. This parish remains to this day distinguished by its healthy and extensive sheep-walks, and for its superior breed of that most useful and profitable animal. It is situated near the source of the river Tame, and is bounded on the north and east by that river, on the south-east by the parishes of Knighton and Heyope, on the south by Llangunllo, on the south-west by Llanbister, and on the west by Llanbadarn-fynydd, and on the north-west by the parish of Cerri, in the county of Montgomery. It contains four townships, viz., Bugaildu, Pennant, Crug-bydder, and Madwalled, or Buddwalledd, and extends in length fourteen miles, and two miles in breadth, including an area of about 18,000 acres of which one third remains uninclosed and common,—thus constituting the largest parish in this county. In assessing and collecting the parochial rates it is divided into two divisions, viz., the upper and the lower; but each division pays its own taxes separately. Situated in the crown lordship of Cantref Moelynaidd, and in the cwmwd of Uwch-mynydd, the manorial rights of this parish are vested in the Earl of Oxford, the lessee, and part of the borough of Cnwclâs is comprehended within its limits.

The use of the Welsh language in this parish has been totally superseded by the universal adoption of the English tongue. The names of hills, fields, and houses still remain evidences of the original speech of the country. As recently as the year 1730, the service of the church was performed in the Welsh language monthly, since which time it has invariably been done in English. An increased intercourse with England, a more general interchange of the commodities and produce of these two countries respectively, and, above all, the introduction of that jurisprudence with which the inhabitants of Wales found it necessary to be familiarized, as well as the diction in which all legal pleadings, deeds, conveyances, processes, &c., are executed, soon undermined that predilection for their mother tongue which was before their distinguishing character, and rendered the study and acquisition of the English language necessary, not only as an accomplishment, but also as a matter of indispensable interest.

With respect to the population of this parish, very little difference can be perceived within the last century. The number of persons baptized and buried at the two periods is nearly equal.

Ecclesiastical Account.

The church of Bugaildu is situated in the deanery of Moelynaidd, archdeaconry of Brecon, and diocese of St. David's, on a gentle eminence contiguous to the river Tame, and distant from Knighton eight miles north-west, from the church of Heyope five miles north-west, from Llangunllo seven miles north, from Llanbister seven miles north-east, and from Llanbadarn-fynydd six miles east. It is a small structure, consisting of one aisle, and a tower, the roof of which terminates in a point. The interior is decent, and becoming a place of worship. At the west end thereof a handsome and commodious gallery has recently been erected. It contains no sepulchral monuments, and but one, yet pious, inscription, "Remember the Poor." It is dedicated to St. Michael. Its external length is thirty-seven yards. The tower contains three bells, on which are the following inscriptions:—

I.—" Edward ab Evan, Edward Whettall. 1664."—Diameter at the mouth, 2ft. 8in.

II.—" All praise and glory be to God for ever. 1664."—Diameter, 2ft. 5in.

III.—" God save the King. Vive ut post vivas. 1661."—Diameter, 2ft. 2in.

No inscription on the chalice, which is silver. On the flagon is the following, —" Long live the Prince and Princess of Orange."

This benefice is a vicarage, estimated in *Liber Regis* at the clear yearly value of £7 15s. 7½d. Improved value, £35 per annum. The total emoluments at present amount to the annual sum of £143 9s. 6d. The yearly tenths are 15s. 6¾d. The patron is the Bishop of St. David's. All the tithes of the township of Bugaildu, that of Hay excepted, are the property of the vicar. In lieu of the tithe of Hay a penny modus is paid. The tithes of the other three townships belong to the Dean and Chapter of St. David's, and Penry Powell, Esq., holds them, by virtue of a lease renewable every seven years.

The feast is holden on the first Sunday after St. Michael's-day, O.S., and observed with the customary festivities, sometimes perverted to purposes of intemperance and excess.

The vicarage house is an old and inconvenient habitation, to which are attached a barn, stable, and beast-house; likewise about twelve acres of glebeland, situated between the village and the river Tame, and contiguous to the house.

List of Incumbents.

A.D.		A.D.
Elias Owens 1665	Richard Beeston 1740
—— Watkins 1700	John Prichard, Junr. 1765
John Prichard, Senr. 1738	Samuel Newland Evans 1776

Charitable Donations.

In the year 1741, the Rev. John Davies, D.D., devised by will the principal sum of £100, vested in the vicar and churchwardens, and now secured on an estate called the Graig, in this parish, the interest whereof is duly distributed among poor householders not receiving parochial relief, on St. Thomas'-day, annually.

In the year 1741, Vavasor Griffiths, Esq., left by will the sum of £20, vested in the minister and churchwardens, and now secured on the above-mentioned estate, the interest whereof is duly distributed among poor householders not chargeable to the parish, on St. Thomas'-day, yearly.

In a year unknown, and whether by will or deed also unknown, Philip, or Robert, Lord Wharton, left the annual sum of £10, or, as tradition says, £20, secured on an estate called Maesgwin, in this parish, for the purpose of teaching the poor children of this parish, and also of the parishes of Llanbister and Llanbadarn-fynydd, now vested in the Earl of Oxford. The number of scholars on the foundation is unlimited, yet they never exceed ten.

In this parish was born the learned Joan Du, *Anglice* Black Jack, who for his surprising attainments in astronomy and mathematical science, far surpassing the expectations of the age in which he lived, was deemed by the common people a conjurer. He was the counterpart of the celebrated Roger Bacon. Isaac Casaubon, prebendary of Canterbury, satirized John Du in a doggerel poem, entitled "A Dialogue between John Du and the Devil," which Du answered, and completely silenced his opponent. He lived highly respected in the court of Queen Elizabeth, of whom he was the mathematical instructor.

CNWCLAS CASTLE AND BOROUGH.

This place is invariably denominated by the common people "the Cnwclâs," as if by way of eminence; being at present a contributory borough, and having been in ancient times a formidable castle. Its name signifies "the green hillock," an interpretation truly descriptive of the feature of the situation. Our account of it will be divided into two parts: first, the castle; second, the borough.

Of this hillock, so formed by nature, and placed in so

commanding a situation, that little doubt can be entertained of its having attracted the notice of the Silurian commanders, no recorded account exists prior to the era of the Norman conquest. But though the precise date of its original appropriation to military purposes it is impossible at this remote period, through want of documents, to ascertain, yet it does not seem improbable, from the circumstance of its vicinity to Caer Caradoc, its impregnable nature, and its situation on the bank of the river Tame, that its use, as an important fortification, was coeval with that last scene of the patriotic struggle of the brave Caractacus; that in subsequent times it protected the vale of the Tame from the hostile incursions of the Saxons and Normans, advancing from Cheshire and Salop; and that the possession of so important a post was an object of frequent contention. After signal success, obtained chiefly through the fatal dissensions which reigned among the native *reguli*, this hillock was seized upon, and fortified with a castle, by Roger Mortimer, Earl of Wigmore and Marche, and the Norman Lord of Moelynaidd and Elfael. Few or no remains of this formidable fortress have survived the combined ravages and spoliations of war and time. The site, and some low foundations of walls only, are at present discernible. The hillock rises by a steep ascent from the bank of the river Tame, on which it is situated, to the height of one hundred yards. Its summit, which is distant about three hundred yards from the bed of that river, is of an oval or elliptical form, and of considerable extent, and is encompassed by a double intrenchment; commanding a view of the river, the vale through which it flows, and the opposite hills of Shropshire, at the distance of about a mile. At the foot of this castle hill is a piece of pasture land, which, from time immemorial, has sustained the denomination of "the bloody field," or "meadow." Hence it is conjectured that, on this piece of land, a severe battle had once been fought, but whether prior or posterior to the erection of the castle cannot be ascertained. In confirmation of this traditional report, it has been urged that, on the opposite side of the river, on a farm called Monachtu, was discovered a small tumulus, which, on its being opened some years ago, presented to view a stone of astonishing dimensions, weighing several tons, and of a quality very different from the stones of this country, and covering an entrance into a vault, which was divided into five compartments. In each of these recesses were deposited human skeletons, arranged side by side in complete regularity, and having teeth as white as ivory, and containing bones of a large size. It is conjectured that these skeletons composed the remains of those warriors who fell in the battle of "the bloody field" above mentioned. The discovery of this sepulchral repository furnishes a clue to ascertain the country of the interred, and the date of the interment. The interred were natives of Wales, the whiteness of whose teeth is remarked by every historian. The interment, viz., in a tumulus, or barrow, was prior to the introduction and establishment of Christianity in this part of the kingdom, for by that happy event the ancient manner of burial was superseded. Hence may be inferred, that the slaughter committed in "the bloody field," supposing these bones to have belonged to the slain in that action, preceded, in point of time, many centuries, the construction of the castle of Cnwclâs. To what era, therefore, can it be so justly assigned as to that which has been signalized by the long and vigorous resistance maintained by the brave Silures to the all-conquering Romans? A traditionary remembrance of several other battles fought in this vicinity, at different times, is still preserved by the inhabitants.

It has already been observed that this important post, the castle of Cnwclâs, was an object of frequent contest. Its possession was also secured by much art and ingenuity; for water, for the use and comfort of the garrison, was conducted into it by means of leaden pipes from a well or spring upon an opposite eminence, toward the west, called Gifron. It must be confessed that the ingenuity of this contrivance bespeaks a more modern and refined era than that which distinguished the ancient Britons, and must in justice be referred to the times of the Mortimers, Lords of Moelynaidd, in whose possession it remained, with little interruption, till it finally merged in the crown, by the accession of the Duke of York—who, by his maternal line, was descended from that powerful house—to the throne of England, under the title of King Edward IV., when the restoration of internal peace to the distracted kingdom superseded the use of its military designation, and its walls, no longer wanted to repel the assailing foe, supplied materials for constructing the more tranquil and friendly habitations of social man. In the reign of Richard III., Philip ab Howel was Lord of Cnwclâs, and assisted Henry, Earl of Richmond, in defeating the tyrant and usurper in the battle of Bosworth field, and in obtaining the English crown.

The town, or rather village, of Cnwclâs consists of a few scattered houses, situated at the foot of the hillock on the bank of the River Tame, mean and inconsiderable in appearance, having a small garden, and perhaps a meadow, attached to each. At the public house, in this village, was born a man who made a considerable figure in his time; for he was a radical reformer. This person was the noted Valvasor Powel, a sturdy republican, and a violent impugner of the doctrine and discipline of the Established Church, to whom was committed, during the anarchy of the Long Parliament, and the usurpation of Oliver Cromwell, the whole of the ecclesiastical government of this and some of the adjoining counties. Armed with the authority of Parliament, and assisted by Sir Robert Harley, President of the Radnorshire Committee, this associate and coadjutor of the famous Hugh Peters, chaplain to the Protector, succeeded in sequestrating the tithes in every parish in this county, stripping the churches of their ornaments, and ejecting the regularly ordained ministers.

The original establishment of English boroughs, howsoever distinguished, by prescription, or by charter, was a political favour conferred either in return for obligations already received from the inhabitants, or as a means of securing future ones. The proximity of the borough of Cnwclâs to that of Knighton, being distant only two miles and a half west-by-south, seems to evince a strong desire in the Norman impropriators of procuring and meriting the good will and affections of the ancient inhabitants of this part of the county of Radnor, by investing them with privileges and civil distinctions, which, however intensely coveted, and highly appreciated in the present times, were, in the infancy of the British constitution, deemed as generally a burden as an honour, if we may reason from the numerous and voluntary petitions for being exonerated; whilst the continuance of Cnwclâs as a contributory borough, from its first institution to the present era, not only contradicts the insignificance which the first view of this village presents, but also bespeaks an absence of those causes which have operated to the disfranchisements of similar establishments, both in England and Wales.

Cnwclâs having been a baronial and royal castle, and the seat of baronial judicature, was deemed competent, in the reign of King Henry VIII., to be made one of the contributory boroughs of New Radnor; and all such persons as are duly elected burgesses at its several courts holden for that purpose, possess the right of parliamentary suffrage. The manner of conferring this privilege is as follows:—By prescription, court-leets are occasionally holden by the steward, or deputy-steward, presiding over this and the other contributory boroughs. At these courts the jury, who have been previously summoned, and who ought to be burgesses of this particular borough, are impannelled, and present the name of such persons, whether inhabitants or not, whom they think proper to select as fit and proper persons to be made burgesses. This presentment being accepted by the steward, the persons so presented are elected burgesses, and generally sworn in immediately, if they be present in court, but if not, at a subsequent court.

The borough of Cnwclâs is extensive: it reaches into

the two parishes of Bugaildu and Heyope. The courthouse, in which the burgesses are elected, is situated in that of the former. Its boundaries were ascertained on the 2nd day of November, 1787, by the oldest inhabitants then living, viz., William Matthews, Richard Matthews, John Morris, William Jones, William Jones, Junr., Thomas Griffiths, Richard Davies, and many others, who signed the following descripton thereof, viz.:—" From the bridge near the Pound follow the course of the brook upwards to a piece of land belonging to Lower-hall Farm called the White-leasow, about one acre of the east side of which is within the borough; follow the hedge on the north side of White-leasow, to a piece of land lately inclosed to Lower-hall Farm, about two acres of which are within the borough; proceed up to the east hedge about twenty-two yards above the corner of the Upper Bwlch, belonging to Lower-hall Farm, and cross that field straight to an old ditch on the Gifron Hill, south of the Gifron Well, leaving about four acres of the Upper Bwlch within the borough; follow that old ditch, which appears to have been thrown up as a landmark, through the middle of the Goitrey Birches to the lower hedge, about three acres of which are within the borough; follow the said hedge to the bottom of the piece below Goitrey House, then cross to an oak tree in the lane hedge, following the lane hedge to the bottom of the Goitrey Farm, about four acres; then over the edge of the rock to John Wood's tenement, turning down between the house and the garden to the water that comes from the mill, following that to the river Tame, below the Llwyneu; cross the river into the Graig cow pasture, and follow it on the north side to a meadow belonging to the Graig Farm, called the Dôl, about two acres of which are within the borough, as also another piece of excellent pasture about five acres adjoining to the river Tame, belonging also to the Graig; follow an old bed of the river across the Graig lands to the wear in Dôl-fawr belonging to Monachtu Farm; thence follow the water-course through the fold at Monachtu, cross the corners of two meadows, including about one acre and a half to the north side of the Charity land, and down the Long-leasow to an old bed of the river, following that to the bottom of Monachtu Farm, leaving about twelve acres below the house within the borough; thence down to an old bed of the river in Skyborreu Farm, leaving about two acres on the north side of the river within the borough; then cross the river to the hedge on the sluice leasow, down that straight hedge almost to a corner on the north side of the Barn Meadow, and thence across to the lane hedge, which follow to Graig-y-swydd, or Swydd."

A considerable portion of this hamlet remains to this day a part of the royal patrimony of the Kings of England. The site of Cnwclâs Castle, the herbage of Cnwclâs forest, Whittersley land, within the borough of of Cnwclâs, are all three the property of the crown of England, and now leased by the Earl of Oxford, or by the representatives of the Right Rev. Dr. Harley, late Bishop of Hereford; the former at 1s., the second at 13s. 4d., and the latter at 6s. 8d., being the gross annual rent. Whittersley land originally consisted of seventy acres, and was holden by Thomas Price, in the reign of Queen Elizabeth, at the yearly rent of £14, and latterly by Mr. Philip Gouch, Gent.; likewise a piece of land called Lord's Mead, leased by the late Bishop Harley, at 3s. 4d. gross annual rent. Also Cnwclâs mill, leased by the late Rev. J. W. Davies, at the gross annual rent of £1 2s., being in the year 1784 three years in arrears. Likewise Cnwclâs borough, leased by the bailiff thereof, at the gross annual rent of £5 6s. 5½d., being in the year 1784 two years in arrears. Also Gwartuissa land, leased by the late Bishop Harley, at the gross annual amount of 6d. Likewise four acres of land called Brynrhiwgwith, and Llwyneugoden, leased by the late Bishop Harley, at the gross annual rent of 6d. Also two parcels of concealed land, called Wyr-glodd-gam, and Blackmead, leased by the late Bishop Harley, at the gross annual rent of 3s. 8d.

KNIGHTON.

The town of Knighton is beautifully situated at the head of a deep and narrow vale, on the southern bank of the river Tame, urging its winding course under a stone bridge, between high hills and wooded knolls, and leaving on each side a breadth of land rich and fertile. It consists of several streets, some narrow, but all upon a descent, and therefore clean, and unobstructed with that filth which is generally suffered to accumulate in small country towns. They are also all paved, and contain several good houses, which, viewed at a distance, as towering one above another, and contrasted with the romantic scenery of the vale, present to the traveller many picturesque objects. It is a place of trade and business, and of considerable resort. Its shops furnish the town and neighbourhood with every article of general use and consumption. Its market is on Thursday, and was, before the pursuit of agriculture became so general as at present, wont to supply many of the inhabitants of Cantref Moelynaidd with grain; and its fairs, which are on Saturday before the second Sunday in March, 17th May, 2nd of October, and 9th of November, are well served with cattle, sheep, horses, pigs, corn, iron-ware, hops, salt, linen and woollen cloth, and various other commodities. It is governed by a bailiff, the manner of whose election and appointment shall be described hereafter, and is distant from the town of New Radnor ten miles north-east, and from London one hundred and fifty-five miles north-west. In short, Knighton ranks among those neat, clean, lively and well-supplied little towns, for which the Principality of Wales is distinguished.

Nearly in the centre of the town still remains an old mansion, once occupied by a branch of the Chandos family, of the name of Brydges. To this habitation was attached, in former times, on the side next to the street, an open terrace walk, which was entered from the second story. To this balcony the family often resorted for the purpose of inhaling the refreshing breeze, enjoying the distant prospect, and contemplating the busy and careworn faces of those who resorted to the fairs and markets, without incurring the risk of compromising their personal dignity by a nearer and more familiar association.

At the east end of the town stands the mansion formerly inhabited by the Crowther family, who once possessed considerable property in this parish, and in the neighbourhood. It has usually been denominated the "Great House." It appears to have been originally built in the form of the letter H, and in the construction of its roof, and of its chimneys, bears a strong resemblance to the style of architecture which prevailed in the reign of James I. The grand entrance was at the east end, guarded by a very large door, and a porch; this end, which composed at least one half of the mansion, has been taken down; and the present entrance placed on the north side, next to the public road. Adjoining to this house stood the barn, in which the republican marauders received from the hands of Mr. Legge, of Willey, and his servants, the death which their villainous and outrageous excesses deserved.

Farrington, the old stone mansion of an ancient family of the name of Cutler, stands upon an eminence on the south-east side of the town of Knighton, and at the distance of a mile from it. The initial letters, R. C., and the figures 1666, mark the era of the building, and testify the name of its original proprietor, viz., Robert Cutler. The south wing is in a dilapidated state, and the remaining part of the house has been converted into the residence of a farmer.

It was no uncommon thing, two centuries ago, for gentlemen of large fortunes to occupy mansion-houses situated either in the centre, or at one end, of small towns, in which beauty of situation, or fine views, were circumstances little attended to. The probable inducement to a custom so different from that which prevails at present, seems to have been suggested by that assurance of protection and security holden out by an obliged and devoted population in times when sudden commotion and lawless outrage were frequent, which a solitary and insulated residence could not satisfactorily promise. The tranquil and respectful obedience that is now paid to the laws, and the perfect security in which every subject enjoys his own property, render the contiguity of a numerous population no longer necessary to the safety of a rich individual; yet the good old custom of a landed proprietor expending his income in the midst of his tenants still distinguishes the town of Knighton, the inhabitants of which derive many and great advantages from the constant residence of the worthy representative of the borough of New Radnor, during the time he is relieved from his parliamentary duties. This gentleman's house is situated opposite the Town-Hall, commands a full view of the principal street and adjacent country, and possesses every suitable accommodation.

The foundation of the wealth and influence which the two families of Cutler and Crowther acquired in this part of the county of Radnor was wisely laid in the profession of the law, which leads its votaries more directly than any other profession to the temple of affluence, dignity, and fame. Robert Cutler, Esq., served the office of high sheriff for this county in the year 1694. He afterwards removed his residence to Street Court, in the parish of Yerdisland, and county of Hereford, having succeeded to the possession of that mansion, estate, and manor. The office of high sheriff for this county was filled by Brian Crowther, Esq., in the years 1639 and 1645. He was a gentleman of unblemished respectability and honour: many arbitration cases were referred to his decision, and, particularly, a tedious and prolonged litigation between Smallman and John Crowther, his relative, at the instance of the Archbishop of Canterbury. He strenuously supported the royal cause, and consequently was fined by the rebellious parliament for his delinquency.

The castle was situated at the upper end of the town, near where the Butter Cross at present stands—a situation overlooking and commanding the whole place. The mount, now called the "Castle Mount," was the keep or citadel; and this, with the area inclosed by the ditch, occupies the space of an acre and a quarter of land. It was well adapted to purposes of defence before the invention of artillery, and guarded from surprize by the grounds rapidly falling on each side, excepting on the north and north-west, on which points it was strongly fortified by a wide and deep trench. That on the north side has been filled up in the course of time; but that towards the west may still be traced. A strong wall appears to have stood on the inside of the trench, and there were probably, within this wall, some low structures formed for the accommodation of the troops of the garrison. From what can at present be collected of the ancient state of this castle, it seems that it can only be ranked among the inferior fortresses in this part of the kingdom. But as persons of some distinction, in the Saxon and Norman times, resided in castles of little note, so it is probable that some petty lord or chieftain held this fortress as a fief under the Mortimers, and subject to their control in the wars and factions of those ages. Each baron of the realm, as Roger Mortimer, on receiving the royal summons, was obliged to bring into the field a certain number of *milites*, or knights, who held lands, &c., under him, on the favourite tenure of knight-service. To one of these knights did Roger Mortimer, to whom the King of England had granted the lordships of Moelynaidd and Elfael to be holden *in capite*, commit the custody of this castle, and the government of this town, which from this circumstance derives its present name, " Knighton," or the town of the knight.

The justness of this derivation is doubted by some, who allege in opposition to it that Knighton was an inhabited place, not only prior to the era of the invasion of this district by Roger Mortimer, and recognized as such by Roderic Mawr about the year 840, and by that prince denominated Tref-y-Clawdd, or the town on the dyke; but that even this appellation was a modern one, suggested by the recent formation of the dyke, and that it succeeded its pristine denomination, which was Cnuch-din. All that ridge of mountains extending from the parish of Llangunllo to and above the town of Knighton was formerly designated by the general term *Cnuch:* now the word *Cnuch* signifies a joint or copula that connects,—a term apparently descriptive of the site of this town, which joins together or connects two opposite hills, on its south and south-east quarter; and *din* means a fortification: so that *Cnuch-din,* now converted to Knighton, signifies a fortified juncture.

The reader is to bear in remembrance that the word is not to be met with in *Domesday Book,* where it certainly would have been inserted, had it been of Saxon or Norman origin. On this silence of the authoritative register of England is grounded the probable inference that the name Knighton is of Welsh extraction.

The last Lord of Cantref Moelynaidd, which included the town and castle of Knighton, and considerable tracts of land in this parish, was Edmund, the last Earl of Marche and Wigmore. By his death, which happened in the beginning of the reign of Henry VI., the male line became extinct, and all his possessions devolved to Richard, Earl of Cambridge, who had married his sister Anne. Upon the attainder of this last mentioned nobleman, for being implicated in Jack Cade's conspiracy, Cantref Moelynaidd, and all the castles and lands annexed to it, merged in the crown; and, by the accession of the Duke of York to the throne, by the title of Edward IV., they have ever since formed a part of the royal patrimony of the Kings of England. For some years past they have been leased out by the crown to the Earl of Oxford.

The town of Knighton was endowed, like the other towns appendant to the castles of Norman barons, with the privilege of being corporate, and of exercising a peculiar civil jurisdiction within itself. This approached, as nearly as possible, to the forms of English jurisprudence. It was not, however, till the reign of Henry VIII. made one of the five contributary boroughs, which conjointly return one member to the British Parliament. The constitution of this borough in the article of creating burgesses differs in some particulars from that of the other boroughs; for, if any of the burgesses living within the said borough die, his eldest son is of course and by custom to be admitted and sworn burgess in the said borough at any court-baron he shall require the same, paying a penny to the crier for the same. And the burgesses have the power to nominate and elect any person to be a free burgess, whether freeholder, tenant, foreigner, or otherwise, the same being approved with general consent. But if two of the said burgesses then present in court do oppose any person to be a burgess, then the same person is not to be admitted or sworn a burgess of the said borough. The other customs are,—

I.—The borough to have a bailiff and burgesses. A court-baron to be holden in the Town-Hall upon a Friday once in every three weeks, and upon a Wednesday once in every three weeks, and likewise two leets to be holden, the one a month after Michaelmas, the other a month after Easter, in the Town-Hall aforesaid, where the bailiff and burgesses do their suit and services; and that one shilling is paid yearly to His Majesty, the lord of the borough, for the ground whereon the said Town-Hall was built.

II.—The bailiff and burgesses have the benefit of the butchers' and other standings belonging to the said hall, and all the tolls of corn and grain exposed there for sale upon fairs and market days, and to let or lease the said standings for a term of years.

III.—The bailiff, upon every Lord's-day next before Michaelmas yearly, between the hours of eleven and twelve o'clock in the morning, is to return and put in writing three names of the burgesses then inhabiting in the said town or borough, at the usual and accustomed place, to be approved by the burgesses then present; but, if disliked, then some of the burgesses then present inhabiting within the said borough are immediately to nominate and return three other burgesses inhabiting within the said borough; which said several returns are to be presented at the next court-leet after Michaelmas yearly, after the calling of any action to the steward, who is to order a trial by poll of the two returns, and out of that return which has the majority of voices, to swear one of the three bailiff for the year ensuing, wherein no foreign burgess is to have any voice. But if no dislike against the bailiff's return be expressed, then his nomination to stand good, and one of the three burgesses so presented to be sworn bailiff, and no other. A foreign candidate for the bailiwick must be resident within the borough at least a month before the election day. The steward to be sworn a burgess thereof. Burgesses are exempted from toll.

IV.—The bailiff to return all jurors to be impannelled at every court, who must be burgesses, and to choose a serjeant for delivering summonses; but he must in his person summon burgesses; and he, or his deputy, to execute distringases, warrants, precepts, issuing forth of the said court; and to collect and receive the lord's chief rents, and perquisites of the said courts; all waifs, estrays; and at Michaelmas yearly account for the same.

V.—The bailiff to have the profit accruing from the wool weights in the Town-Hall upon fairs and market days; and also one half of the pitching due at fairs and markets; and all profits for sealing of leather with the town seal.

VI.—Four constables out of the company of burgesses to be sworn; two of whom to be appointed by the bailiff, and two by the steward.

VII.—The bailiff and burgesses stand seized of one parcel of wood ground, called Garth Wood, lying within the said borough, and have right to cut and dispose of it to their own use and uses, and none else.

VIII.—The burgesses and tenants have a right to license any poor, old, or decayed person to build cottages for habitation upon any part of the waste land or commons belonging to the borough; which commons are purtenances to the several messuages or tenements of the burgesses and freeholders.

IX.—The chief rents due from the burgesses and tenants to His Majesty, who is lord and owner of the borough, amount to the sum of £8 4s. 4½d., and the

2 A

herriot upon the decease of any tenant of the said borough is 2s. 6d. No herriot due from a tenement not being a messuage place.

X.—The extent of the said borough is from an elder tree or bush growing on the back side of Francis Mason's house, who is now deceased; thence to an ash, late of one Meredith Edwards, barber, deceased; and thence to the further side of the Black Meadow, beyond the river Tame, and so over Tame to Cappero Meadow, late in the possession of Jeremiah Bayliss; thence to a stone bridge in the highway leading from the town of Knighton to Presteigne; thence to an oak in a parcel of land of Mr. Barbley; thence to the top of the Frieth Wood; thence to a crab tree near St. Edward's Well; so over a common, called the Garth, unto a gutter near Whitterley, with the compass of the Lord's Meadow, late in the possession of Richard Evans, deceased; and so to the farther side of a meadow called Clâsby; thence over the river Tame; and so to a house wherein Thomas Hodges now deceased, formerly dwelled; and so to the elder bush aforesaid.

The author of this work has been informed, that the borough lands above detailed have long since become private property, excepting the part which belongs to the crown; and that the courts formerly holden by the bailiffs and burgesses, for the recovery of small debts, are now discontinued.

Some of the inhabitants of this borough had once a license to coin halfpence. There is one of them still to be seen, with this inscription,—front side, " James Mason, of Knighton, his halfpenny" in the border; in the centre is a " Maiden's head " within a shield, being the arms of the Mercers' Company; reverse, 1668.

The parish, which includes the townships of the borough, and Cwmgelau, together with the lordship of Farrington, is small, not exceeding two miles in extent. It is supposed that two-thirds of it, and more, are in a state of cultivation, the remainder being woods and hills. The parochial assessments amounted to £377 9s. 9d., at 2s. 3d. in the pound on the rack rental, in 1803.

The lordship of Farrington, within this parish, is a mesne manor, within Cantref Moelynaidd. The King of England is lord of it, and the Earl of Oxford under him, as steward of Cantref Moelynaidd. The rest of the parish, as a manor, is part of the great lordship of Moelynaidd.

There is in this parish, in a field a little below the town, a mount called Bryn-y-castell. It is a very large tumulus, of an oblong square form, fortified on the east, south, and west sides with a very deep fosse and rampart, and on the north by an abrupt precipice, which terminates below, near the river Tame. The summit of the tumulus is somewhat excavated, and it has much the appearance of having once contained some temporary structure. It does not appear to have been the keep of a castle, or at all appendant to a fortification of larger extent, as no traces of any such are to be found near it.

The country around Knighton abounds in military vestiges of past times. Studded with British and Roman camps, and containing fragmented pieces of ancient weapons, both defensive and offensive, together with human bones frequently turned up by the spade and by the plough, it indicates a scene marked by bloody hostility, and which bears honourable testimony to the bravery of the inhabitants, and to their obstinate resistance to the yoke of their invaders. Whether the Romans penetrated so far into this district, or whether the line of the Tame was the boundary of their conquests on its north-east quarter, as the line of the Ieithon was on its south-west, are questions at present indeterminable; but there is presumptive proof, which cannot be controverted, that Caractacus, if he did not make the vale of the Tame the scene of one of his campaigns, certainly drew much of his resources from its vicinity; and, as Knighton is of very short distance from Caer Caradoc, it would seem almost unpardonable to omit the mention of so celebrated a position of that great general,—not for the purpose of swelling this work with a detailed description of a place not included within the limits of its subject, but of submitting to the consideration of the candid reader what appears, to the mind of the author, an additional argument, which corroborates the general conjecture that, on this very spot, terminated the high spirited, long continued, and well supported struggle which the intrepid Caractacus, and his brave Silurians, maintained for the space of nine successive years, for the preservation of the independence of their country against the conquerors of the world. No traveller, who shall have arrived in Knighton, can possibly refrain from extending his visits to a camp which he will find to have been fortified as well by art as by nature, and which incontestibly demonstrates the discrimination and judgment of its constructors. It is surrounded by a triple belt of ramparts, accommodated with a well of fresh water in the centre, approached by two entrances, east and west, and occupies an almost inaccessible eminence, containing twelve acres of land. Lastly, it constituted the third angle, Coxwall Knoll and Stretton being the first and second, of the last series of triangular positions which this great commander had formed for the defence of his country. When to these circumstances we add its appropriate name, Caer Caradoc, can we entertain a doubt of the superior claims which this celebrated position has to the honour of having been the site of the last conflict of Caractacus? Vain and fruitless is the opposition urged by Coxwall Knoll, which has so many military positions of the same commander considerably in the rear of its line. The stone of large rotundity which was lately found within it, and supposed to have been flung thither by a Roman balista from the opposite camp at Brandon, affords no argument in favour of its pretensions. Stones were often the only instruments of offence which the ill-equipped Silurians possessed; and the rotundity of their figure was an artificial effect, not for the purpose of adapting such missiles to the strings of a balista, which would have been worse than useless labour, but for capacitating them for rolling down the precipice with accumulated force against the Roman cohorts. This stone, then, appears to be rather of British than of Roman application; and, consequently, the argument founded upon it falls to the ground. Nor is the alleged claim of Rhyd Esgyn, in the parish of Guilsfield, in the county of Montgomery, recommended to our acceptance by stronger pretensions. A thousand other similar situations are equally entitled to prefer the same claim, some of which possess features more commensurate to the description given by the Roman historian, Tacitus, than the Montgomeryshire encampment; whilst the appropriate and significative appellation, Caer Caradoc, implying at once a fortification, a battle, and the hero's name, together with its local situation, and other accompaniments, cannot fail of striking conviction into the mind of every impartial investigator, that this, and no other, was the identical spot on which the brave defender of Siluria received his final overthrow. It is no invalidation of this inference to urge that two other intrenchments bear the same appellation; for only one of them has any plea to stand in competition; and that one, viz., at Church Stretton, has already been attributed to Caractacus, and included in his plan of the campaign within the territory of the Ordovices; whilst the other, in the parish of Sellack, in the county of Hereford, is excluded from all pretensions of being considered as a camp of the Silurian commander; having been constructed eleven centuries posterior to his era, by Caradoc, a prince of South Wales, in the reign of William the Conqueror. The preference here given to Caer Caradoc being the site of this last conflict, rather than the encampment of the same name at Church Stretton, is grounded on this circumstance, little attended to by historians: The Silurian general was disappointed in his expectations of the effectual succours stipulated to be supplied by the Ordovices, and found himself under the necessity of retreating. The execution of the new plan which he in consequence adopted, of carrying on the future operations of the war through the mountains of Radnorshire and Brecknockshire into Monmouthshire, where was the capital and the principal seat of the Silurian government, was prevented only by being forced by the enemy to a battle at Caer Caradoc, and there totally defeated.

The last piece of curious antiquity that remains to be noticed, is the remarkable dyke, constructed in the reign of Offa, the eleventh King of Mercia, by the united labours of Saxons and Welsh, and destined to perpetuate the discriminating boundary between their respective countries. It enters this parish from the hundred of Clun, in the county of Salop, and, skirting the west side of this town by a garden wall belonging to Richard Price, Esq., M.P., it passes along the ridge of Friedd Hill, leaving Jenkin Allis to the east; thence proceeds along Reeves' Hill in a straight line from north to south, into the parish of Norton. Many outrages, bloody frays, and cruel violences, were committed on each side of this boundary line by the two contending nations.

It would be improper to conclude this article with omitting to notice a place in this parish, once venerated by antiquity, and continued till lately to be honoured and respected by the youth of the town of Knighton, of both sexes, but which modern refinement has doomed to neglect and oblivion. This place is called Craig Donna, situated about a mile from the town, in a wooded declivity, on the left side of the road leading to the borough of Cnwclâs. It consists of a huge, stupendous rock, containing a very capacious chasm, and watered by a limpid and murmuring stream. Hither the young people of Knighton were wont, till of late years, to resort on Sunday evenings, to drink the water of this pellucid spring, sweetened with sugar, and to hold social and friendly converse with one another. This custom undoubtedly originated in the veneration which was anciently paid to the occupier of this rock, whose name was *Donna*, a sainted recluse. He lived in the seventh century; the chasm in the rock was his bed; the spring supplied his beverage; and the roots that grew nigh and spontaneously were his food.

In the third year of King James II., on the 13th day of January, 1688, Francis Haynes, of the city of Worcester, obtained a crown lease of lands, tolls, herriots, and other premises in this borough and parish to a considerable amount, viz :—

Tolls of Knighton of the yearly value of	£13	6	8
6 acres Stubble Close, called Skill Garth	2	10	0
Jenkin Hales, 26 acres	1	10	0
Friedd, being woodlands, 70 acres	10	10	0
Cwmbigel, 18 acres waste land	4	10	0

by letters patent for the term of thirty-one years; likewise all herriots, and also two small closes of concealed land, of the yearly value of 2s. Two other small closes of concealed land, of the yearly value of 1s. 2d. He was to have all arrears due. There is also in Cefnferfin a parcel of concealed land, of the yearly value of 2s., and also concealed land called Tir Gwillim, of the yearly value of 1s. 5d. All these lands are now leased to the representatives of the late Bishop Harley.

The following is a list or catalogue of the crown property within the town, borough, and parish of Knighton, as it stands at present, viz :—

Knighton borough, £8 4s. 4½d., in arrears, in 1784, one year. This is leased by the bailiff.

Tolls of Knighton, £3 6s. 8d., leased by the Earl of Oxford.

Lord's Mead in ditto, 7s. 4d., leased by R. Wright, Esq. In arrears two years in 1784.

Two parcels of concealed land in Knighton, 2s.

Two small closes in ditto, 1s. 2d. A parcel of concealed land in Cefnferfin, 2s.

Concealed land called Tir Gwillim, 1s. 5d. All leased to the representatives of the late Bishop Harley.

Two sheds, in Knighton borough, 6d., leased to Edward Allen, Esq.

The crown rents of Haynes' lease, were for the tolls, £3 6s. 8d.; for the lands, £2 4s. 8d.; for the woods, &c., rented at £10 10s., a crown rent of 3s. 1d.

Ecclesiastical Account.

The church of Knighton is a plain, modern structure, erected in 1752, and uniformly pewed. The tower, which is square and ancient, had originally a roof of lead, but now slated. It contains six bells. The church is dedicated to St. Michael, and an ancient festival in commemoration of its consecration was annually observed on the 1st of October, which of late years has grown into disuse.

This benefice is a perpetual curacy, not in charge, stated in *Liber Regis* to be of the certified value of £10 per annum. It is situated in the deanery of Clun and Wenlock, in the archdeaconry of Salop, and in the diocese of Hereford. The warden of Clun Hospital is the patron. It has been twice augmented by Queen Anne's bounty, and there is a glebe annexed to it. A handsome parsonage house was lately built near the church, on a very picturesque and well chosen spot. The great tithes of this parish, which, prior to the dissolution of religious houses in the reign of Henry VIII., belonged to the monastery of Malvern, in the county of Worcester, were purchased in the reign of James I. from Sir Francis Maurice, Knight, and Francis Philips, Esq., by Henry Howard, Earl of Northampton, for the endowment of his hospital at Clun. Out of the annual rent of these tithes a certain proportion is reserved and allotted for the service of the church. The occupier of the tithes was the late Thomas Johnes, Esq., Cwmgwillau, leased to Mr. J. Brown. In the church-yard is a plain tomb,

In
Memory of MARY, Wife of
HENRY BARNSLEY, Gent.,
ob. the 12th day of Feb. 1774.
Aged 80.

The Barnsleys of Knighton were a younger branch of the Barnsleys of Yerdisley Castle, in the county of Hereford. They possessed a considerable property in and near this town, the greater part of which passed into the family of Price, by the marriage of John Price, Esq., with the daughter and heiress of Henry Barnsley, Esq., the last gentleman of the family of that name that resided in this neighbourhood.

On the outside of the church, adjoining the chancel, is the cemetery belonging to the respectable family of Price.

Charitable Donations.

Mr. Thomas Meyrick left by will, date unknown, a rent-charge on land, now vested in Job Strangward, of £2, for teaching poor children.

In the year 1769, Lieutenant-Colonel Winwood bequeathed a free gift in land, of the yearly value of £2, now vested in Job Strangward, for teaching poor children.

In the year 1774, Mrs. Mary Barnsley bequeathed, by will, the sum of £50, the annual interest of which to be expended in teaching poor children. This money is now vested in Henry Price, Esq.

In the year 1774, Judith Price, and John Price, gave a rent-charge of £4 5s., secured by deed upon land, now vested in Richard Price, Esq., to be laid out in purchasing bread for the poor.

In the year 1752, Andrew Clarke left, by will, the yearly sum of £2 10s., secured upon land, and now vested in John Lewis, for the benefit of the poor.

List of Incumbents.

Roger Powell	1600	Edward Davies	1731
Robert Milward	1603	Robert Davies	1761
William Sneade	1717	Robert Morris	1813
Vaughan Davies	1719		

The most remarkable article inserted in the parish register is the following list of persons who did penance, and were excommunicated :—

"*Excommunicated.*
Barnaby Lloyd did penance. Elizabeth Felton did penance.
Richard Young did penance. Dorothy Penson did penance."
Catherine Hodges did penance. No dates to the preceding.
"1763.
Obadiah Dower did penance, and was excommunicated.
1778.
Excommunicated, James Cartwright and Robert Lewis."

LLANBADARN FYNYDD.

It is bounded on the south by the parish of Llanbister, on the south-west by Llanano, on the east by Llanfihangel-Bugaildu, and on the north by the brook Nantu, and the line that divides the two counties of Radnor and Montgomery. It consists of one township only, but contains two divisions, viz., the lordship of Ywgre, and the lordship of Golon. The part belonging to the latter lordship includes two-thirds of the whole parish, and contains double the number of inhabitants; yet it serves the overseership of the poor but alternately with the part included in the lordship of Ywgre. The present lords of the mesne manor of Golon are C. Severn, Esq., of Penybont, who married the heiress of the late John Price, Esq., banker, of that place, and D. Fields, Esq., of Cae-bach. In former times this manor and lordship were vested in the ancient family of the Fowlers, of Abbey Cwmhir, in this county, and were alienated forty years ago. The manor of Ywgre, as part of the paramount manor of Cantref Moelynaidd, belongs to the King of Great Britain, and is very extensive, including several parishes and townships. Some years ago, a litigation happened between the freeholders and the cottagers resident in this manor, respecting the right of common. The former felt themselves aggrieved by the encroachments made on their sheep-walks by the latter, and, taking the law into their own hands, levelled their inclosures, and pulled down their cottages. The latter, presuming upon the illegality, or at least the informality, of these proceedings, not having

2 B

been authorized by an order issued from a court-leet, as that form it seems was requisite, brought an action against the trespassers, and obtained a verdict. The freeholders have never been able to set aside this decision, no court-leet, of which the Earl of Oxford is the steward, having ever since been holden. This policy of countenancing and sanctioning private inclosures has invariably been pursued by the Oxford family, ever since its first appointment to the stewardship of Cantref Moelynaidd. In the reign of Charles I. the scheme was defeated by the spirited resistance of the freeholders; but the renewal of it in the the reign of George III. seemed to have been attended with that success which the chicanery of law, and the withholding of the legal means of redress, usually afford; or at least, through want of courage on the part of the plaintiffs to lay the grievance before His Majesty in council, as their ancestors had done.

The principal landed proprietors are Sir David Dundas, Knight, William Fields, Evan Stephens, Davies, and Cheese, and Arthur Hague, Esqrs.; Mr. Richard Griffiths, of Gwainlâs, and Mr. George Oliver, of Dôl. Only the two last mentioned gentlemen reside in the parish.

This mountainous region, forming a chain of natural fortifications, superseded the necessity of constructing for its defence artificial mounds, or tumuli. There is, however, one large tumulus, bearing at present the denomination of Castell-y-Blaidd, *i. e.*, the castle of Blaidd, the original proprietor, who was the *regulus* of this district, subject to his superior lord or prince, the *regulus* of Moelynaidd and Fferllys. It is situated on the left-hand side of the road leading from Llanbadarn-fynydd to Llanfihangel-Bugaildu, and is nearly equidistant from each. This Blaidd was contemporary with Brochwell Ys-Gythrog, Lord of Pengwern, or Shrewsbury, and shared with him and others in the honour of inflicting ample and merited vengeance upon the traitorous and murderous Saxons, for their wanton destruction of the venerable monastery of Bangor, and their bloody mass-acre of its innocent monks. (A.D. 617.) He was also great-great-grandfather to Meyric, who, in conjunction with Meredudd, the great-great-grandson of Cadwgan, eldest son of Ellistan Glodrudd, Lord of Moelynaidd and Cerri, fell in the great battle of Buddywgrè, fought with Roger de Mortimer, which terminated in the loss of the territory, or manor, anciently denominated Swydd-y-wgre. (A.D. 1144.) No druidical circles have been met with, nor any relics of antiquity discovered.

About a century ago the Welsh language was generally spoken in this parish, and even used in the Divine Service of the Church; and though many old people still continue to speak, and more to understand, the tongue of their forefathers, yet, to the present race of young people in general, it is become unintelligible and obsolete.

The many void houses which are seen scattered plentifully over this parish, together with their dilapidated remains, must appear on first view to the spectator a melancholy object, and suggest the conviction that the number of its inhabitants must have alarmingly decreased within the last century. But this appearance is owing to the too prevalent practice of uniting many small farms into one, and suffering the buildings to fall into decay and ruin. But to infer from this circumstance that the population must thereby have diminished is to draw a premature conclusion; because the cottages erected on the wastes and commons exceed the number of dilapidated dwellings on the cultivated lands. The race of little farmers, who in former times supported themselves and families with credit, has here, as in all other parishes in the kingdom, become extinct, whilst the rapid and overwhelming spread of pauperism excites universal alarm. The last return of population consisted of 226 males, and 234 females. The parochial assessments made in the year 1803 amounted to the sum of £277 13s. 5d., at 5s. 3d. on the rack rental. There is, in this parish, a mineral spring, called Ffynon-Dafydd-y-gôf, *i. e.*, the well of David the Smith, who was the discoverer. This water is strongly impregnated with sulphur, and has proved exceedingly efficacious in all cutaneous and scorbutic affections.

Ecclesiastical Account.

The church of Llanbadarn-fynydd is dedicated to St. Padarn, or Paternus, who flourished in the sixth century, and was one of the most indefatigable propagators of Christianity in Wales. It is rude and mean in its form and construction, and contains simply one aisle, and one little bell, which is suspended in a box of wood at the west end of the edifice. Altogether, it bears a stronger resemblance to an antique barn than to a temple destined to the public worship of God. Its external length is 65½ feet, and its breadth, 25 feet. It contains nothing worthy of notice, unless it be an old Gothic window at the east end, and has neither monuments nor inscriptions.

This benefice, of which the Chancellor of Brecknock is the patron, is a perpetual curacy, not in charge, annexed to the vicarage of Llanbister. The incumbent derives from the tithes of the parish the sum of £10 per annum only, which he receives from Colonel Brookes, of Noyadd, in the county of Cardigan, to whom the remainder belongs. The whole tithes, it is said, were anciently the property of the prebend of the prebendary of Llanbister, in the Collegiate Church of Brecknock, during his continuance in the said prebend, of whom one of the ancestors of Colonel Brookes leased them, with the right of having the lease renewed by paying a certain stipulated fine.

The benefices of Llanbadarn-fynydd and Llanano being consolidated, whatever lot of Queen Anne's bounty is granted to the one is equally applicable to the augmentation of the other. Six augmentations have been granted, and the money of four of them has been laid in the purchase of land; viz., of Cerrig-croes, in the parish of Lanhir; of Maeshordu, in the parish of Llanbister; of Pant-glâs, in the parish of Llanbister; and of Bedw, in the parish of Llanfihangel-Bugaildu. The two first of these grants consisted of £400 each, and the two last of £200 each. The remaining two are deposited in the three per cent. consols. The total emolument of this benefice amounts at present to the annual sum of £50 3s.

The oldest parish register is dated 1724, and contains no article meriting transcription, unless it be the burial of Edward Preece, aged 105 years, in 1736. The salubrity of the air in this parish is favourable to the longevity of its inhabitants, among whom the age of 100 years and upwards is a common occurrence.

This parish has no vicarage house, nor any dissenting place of worship. There are, however, in it six dissenters, viz., four Anabaptists, and two Wesleyan Methodists.

List of Incumbents.

—— Morgan...................   Jacob Wood 1740

Charitable Donations.

In the eighth year of the reign of King James I. the Rev. Robert Barlowe left a legacy of £10, in money, the legal interest of which is distributed yearly by Mr. John Smith, in whom the principal is vested, among the poor inhabitants not chargeable to this parish.

Another legacy of £10, in money, was bequeathed by Mrs. Margaret Lloyd, the legal interest of which sum is distributed yearly by Mr. Lloyd Jones, in whom the principal is vested, among the poor of this parish not receiving parochial relief.

The parish of Llanbadarn-fynydd is situated in the cwmwd of Uwch-mynydd, cantref of Elfael, now called the hundred of Knighton, and contains somewhat more than six thousand acres of inclosed and cultivated land, and two thousand acres that are uninclosed, and uncultivated.

The lineal descendents of Blaidd, the constructor of Castell-y-Blaidd, in this parish, are as follow, viz.,— Riryd, who begat Madawc, who begat Meyric, who was slain in battle by Roger Mortimer. His grandfather, Riryd, was first cousin and general to Madoc ab Meredudd, Prince of Powis.

LLANANO.

The tutelary saint of this parish and church is Ano, who lived about the end of the seventh century.

Benjamin Thomas, Esq., M.D., of Kington, in Herefordshire, Evan Stephens, Esq., solicitor, in Newton, Montgomeryshire, whose paternal seat is Crughallt, in this parish, recently rendered conspicuous by a fine grove of timber, and Evan Stephens, Esq., land-surveyor, in the town of Presteigne, Radnorshire, are the chief proprietors. The latter gentleman is owner of the site of Castle Dynbod.

This strong and once impregnable fortress stood on the summit, and at the northern extremity, of a high hill called Crugyn, having a steep and inaccessible precipice towards the river Ieithon. It occupied an area of 180 feet in circumference, but what the superstructure was originally, it is now impossible to ascertain, as the foundation of exterior walls is scarcely discernible, yet appearances indicate a quadrangular base, with massy towers on the angles. On the eastern side is still standing a solitary fragment of the outer wall, eighteen feet in height and twelve feet thick, projecting considerably over its base, and rendered by its elevated situation an interesting object to the spectator placed at a great distance. Other fragments, weighing several tons, formerly undermined, now lie prostrate in the moat beneath, bidding defiance to the spoilation of man, and to the destructive operation of time. Around the castle, but diverging to the south, is a deep foss of considerable breadth, inclosing a circular plat or yard of 210 paces, formerly strengthened by a stone wall, having apparently towers at intervals for observation as well as defence. Here probably stood the keep. Along the declivity eastward are three parallel intrenchments cut deep in the rock, and at a few paces further south-east are three more intrenchments, designed undoubtedly to guard the more accessible approach. In front of the fortification are several tumuli, hillocks, and inequalities of ground, resembling ancient places of interment after some sanguinary contest. Whether these sepulchral memorials contain the bones of the slain in the siege of this fortress, in the year 1640, when it was taken and demolished by Llewelyn ab Gruffudd, Prince of Wales, in the course of his expedition into this country against Roger Mortimer, Earl of Marche, and Lord of Moelynaidd and Elfael, or in any preceding attack—for it does not appear that it ever was subsequently rebuilt—is one of those uncertainties in which the history of this district is in general enveloped. For no memorial whatever exists, excepting that which records this catastrophe, furnishing any information respecting its origin, its transactions, or its destiny. Some light, perhaps, might be collected from the etymology of the name, if its orthography were reduced to a certainty; but as this is not the case, and as the pronounciation is various, the name being written Dynbod, Dinboeth, and Daybod, each mode bearing a different signification—the first meaning a fortified mansion, the second an inflamed fortress, in allusion to the probable manner of its destruction, the third perhaps a corruption of Talebote, the name of a soldier of fortune who accompanied William the Conqueror in his enterprize against England—the difficulty of tracing its history seems insurmountable. This difficulty is increased by the complete substitution of the use of the English language instead of the Welsh, which has taken place in this parish, in the course of the two last centuries, whereby all traditionary knowledge respecting its antiquities is irrecoverably lost.

At the foot of a hill named the Rallt is a spring of mineral water called Ffynnon Newydd, or New Well, which has often proved efficacious in scorbutic and scrofulous complaints.

Besides Castell Dynbod, this parish contains also the the remains of an ancient fortress, called Ty-yn-y-bwlch, *i. e.*, the house in the narrow pass or defile, situated on an almost inaccessible rock in a narrow defile, and overhanging the river Ieithon. Tradition ascribes this to have been one of the residences of the descendants of Ellistan Glodrudd, the *reguli* of Moelynaidd, Cerri, and Elfael.

About one mile north-west from Crychallt, the family seat of Evan Stephens, Esq., stands a conventicle belonging to the religious denomination of Baptists, called the New Chapel, erected in the year 1805, on the spot where formerly the Society of Friends, or Quakers, had a meeting-house, and burial-ground attached. On the decline of the latter society, and the remaining members of which having abandoned the place, the former took possession of the ground, and founded thereon a neat chapel, which, in the year 1814, was endowed by Mr. Williams, of Maes-yn-helem, in this parish, with several acres of excellent meadow land on the bank of the river Ieithon.

Ecclesiastical Account.

The church of Llanano is a small antique structure, consisting of a nave, chancel, porch, and low tower. The nave is separated from the chancel by an old and curious screen, resting on corresponding pillars of wood, neatly wrought or carved, having niches for images, which, perhaps, were demolished at the Reformation.

This benefice is a perpetual curacy, not in charge, annexed to the vicarage of Llanbister, and estimated in *Liber Regis* to be of the certified value of £10 per annum. The Chancellor of the Collegiate Church of Brecknock is the patron. The tithes of this parish are holden by the lay impropriator of Llanbister, who pays the curate of Llanano the above sum of £10 per annum for performing the duty of the church, which salary has been augmented by two lots of Queen Anne's bounty, viz., one of £200 in the year 1749, and another of the same amount in 1781; so that the aggregate amount of the curate's emoluments exceeds the annual sum of £40.

Charitable Donation.

In the eighth year of James I. the Rev. Robert Barlowe left a rent-charge upon land, amounting to the yearly sum of 6s. 8d., now vested in Mr. John Smith, for the benefit of the poor inhabitants of this parish not receiving parochial relief.

List of Incumbents.

Jacob Wood 1759
Morgan Jones 1789
John Thomas ....
John Foley ....
John Rees Lewis ....

The resident population of this parish, as it appears from the return made in the year 1801, consisted of 208 individuals. The money raised by the parish rates, in the year 1803, amounted to the sum of £99 3s. 8d., assessed at 3s. in the pound on the rack rental.

LLANBISTER.

This parish is very extensive, in length exceeding twelve miles, and of a very irregular breadth, averaging from three to five miles; and contains about 16,000 acres of inclosed land, and nearly the same uninclosed and hilly. It is divided into two portions, viz., the upper and the lower division. The upper division consists of two townships, viz., Golon and Cefn-y-pawl, both attached to the chapel of Abbey Cwmhir. The lower division consists of the townships of Bronllys, Carogau, Cwm-llechwedd, and Llanbister, with the hamlet of Cwm-y-gâst, which is attached to the parish of Llangunllo. It is bounded on the north by the parish of Llanbadarn-fynydd, on the west by Llanano and Golon, by the parish of Bugaildu on the east, and by Llanddewi-ystrad-Ennau on the south. Its resident population, according to the return made in the year 1801, consisted of 940 individuals. The money raised by the parish rates for the service of the year 1803 amounted in the lower division to the sum of £475 15s. 10½d., and was assessed at 3s. 6d. in the pound on the rack rental.

In this parish, particularly in the reputed lordship of Golon, which is included in the ancient mesne-manor of Swydd-y-wgre, a singular custom prevails, viz., the payment of a certain tax or tribute, called Clwt-y-Cyllell, or knife money, which is imposed on a certain corner of a field on some estates, consisting of a certain number of groats, amounting from 4d. to 13s. 4d. There is a payment likewise of chief rent, for grass and water. These two payments amount to the annual sum of £22 18s. 2½d.

Of antiquities this parish has no great cause for boasting. No vestiges of ancient fortification could be discovered, nor any druidical remains were visible. In the year 1805, at a place named Cyfaelog, near to the village of Llanbister, was dug up a great quantity of freestone out of some ruins; particularly a curious old baptismal font; whence it is conjectured that a religious edifice once stood here, which, perhaps, was dedicated to St. Cyfeilioc.

Two family mansions seem to merit notice; more particularly a venerable mansion called Llynwent, which, though a very considerable portion of it was taken down in the year 1782, still contains many parts that bespeak a high antiquity, and considerable importance. It exhibits at this day door-cases and windows arched with freestone, sculptured with rosettes, and various figures. The timber frames also are curiously wrought and fluted. This house seems to have been erected in the reign of Queen Elizabeth, if not at an earlier period; for, in the year 1563, Morgan Meredith, Esq., of Llynwent, served the office of high sheriff for the county of Radnor, and again in the year 1585, or his son.

Long prior to this era, and in an age when family feuds produced the most direful disasters among relatives, an act of the most atrocious nature was committed at Llynwent. During the unguarded moments of a festive carousal, two cousins-german, namely, John Hir, or John the Tall, son of Philip Fychan, and David Fychan, quarrelled about the extent of their patrimonial inheritance, as parcelled out by the law of gavelkind, and fought with swords, in which combat, the latter was run through the body, and died on the spot. His death, however, did not pass unrevenged; for the sister of the slain, named Ellen Cethin, who resided at Hergest Court, in the county of Hereford, a woman of masculine strength, and intrepid spirit, hearing of the disastrous issue of this family dissension, and of the murder of her brother, repaired to the adjoining parish of Llanddewi on the day in which it had been previously fixed to hold a trial of archery. Disguising herself in men's clothes, she challenged the best archer in the field. This challenge was no sooner known than accepted by John Hir, who, entitled to the first shot, fixed his arrow in the centre of the target. Exulting at his success, and confident of the victory, he was followed by Ellen Cethin, who, instead of pointing the head of her arrow in a line with the target, directed its flight against the body of her cousin-german, John Hir, which it pierced, and went through his heart.

Two miles north-east of the village of Llanbister is an antique family mansion, called Croes-Cynon. This name frequently occurs in places not at present distinguished by stone crosses. Cynon, or Cynan, was a Welsh saint, who flourished in the sixth century. His cross, or oratory, was erected at Croes-Cynon, his hermitage scooped in the rock named Craig-Cynon, and his beverage was composed of the water of Nant-Cynon; all these three are in this parish, and commemorate, if not the personal residence of this saint, at least the profound esteem in which he was holden by its ancient inhabitants.

Ecclesiastical Account.

The position of the church of Llanbister suggests another probable derivation of its name. Erected upon an acclivity of dimensions so small as to render it necessary to place the quadrangular steeple on its eastern side, why may not the church be indebted for its name to this circumstance? for Llan-bas-tir signifies a church built on shallow ground. In Mr. Carlile's *Topographical Dictionary of Wales*, the church of Llanbister is erroneously described to be situated on the bank of the river Tame, from which it is distant at least twelve miles north-west. This is, undoubtedly, a typographical error, which has substituted the river Tame instead of the river Ieithon. In the year 1701 this church was repaired, and reduced to its present height. It consists of a nave, chancel, and a low tower containing three bells, two of which are very ancient. Near it is a piece of land on which it was originally intended to have erected the church, but tradition reports that the accomplishment of this design was prevented by the intervention of supernatural agency. The tradition that a supernatural being carried away in the night whatever was built of the church during the day is still kept alive, because the warden claims an annual rent of 2s. 6d. for the vacant and unconsecrated site of the originally intended church.

This benefice is a discharged vicarage, estimated in *Liber Regis* at £6 11s. 5¼d., but certified to be of the clear yearly value of £38. The yearly tenths are 13s. 1½d. The Bishop of St. David's is the patron. The tithes are impropriate, and belong to the prebend of the prebendary of Llanbister, and are leased to Colonel or Mrs. Brookes, and estimated in *Liber Regis* to be £34. The vicar's portion is one fourth of the whole. His present emoluments are supposed to amount to the sum of £120 per annum. The church of Llanbister seems to be not only the most ancient, but also a mother-church; for the churches of Llanbadarn-fynydd, Llanano, Llanddewi, and Llanfihangel, are all governed by the terrier of Llanbister. The parish register commenced in the year 1681.

Charitable Donations.

In the eighth year of James I. the Rev. Robert Barlowe gave the sum of £1, now vested in Mr. John Smith, to be yearly distributed in bread to the poor inhabitants of this parish.

In the reign of Queen Elizabeth a certain prebend of this church gave the sum of £1, to be annually distributed among the poor inhabitants of this parish.

In 1734 Mr. Silvanus Williams bequeathed the sum of £2 10s., being the annual interest arising from the principal, £50, for the purpose of teaching poor children to read the Bible, and clothing them; this charity is now vested in Mr. Evan Williams.

List of Incumbents.

A.D. 1649.—This living was sequestered by the republican commissioners.

Philip Lewis	166	Charles Morgan	1750
Walter Vaughan	1738	Jacob Wood	1756
Joshua Thomas	1746	David Lloyd	1789

LLANDDEWI-YSTRAD-ENNAU.

This parish is divided into two townships, viz., the church, or Llanddewi-ystrad-Ennau, and Maes-tre-rhôs-Llowddi. The money raised by the parish rates for the service of the year 1801 was, for the township of the church, £146 5s. 4d., and assessed at 2s. 4½d. in the pound; for the township of Maes-tre-rhôs-Llowddy, £103 11s. 4d., and assessed at 4s. 9d. in the pound. The vale of Llanddewi is narrow, but singularly beautiful and fertile. No part of the county surpasses it in abundance and variety of produce. Llanddewi Hall and estate formerly belonged to the ancient family of Hanmer, and about the year 1726 passed over by purchase to Edward Burton, Esq., of Fron-lâs, in the parish of Llandegel, who devised the property to a gentleman of Shrewsbury who bore the same name, but was in no way related.

We proceed now to describe the existing remains of the antiquities that are so numerous in this parish, and take our first stand on the extensive common of Moelynaidd, which gave its name to a territory consisting of one hundred townships, and extending from the river Wye to the Severn. That name lives now only in this common, on which formerly resided the fifth royal tribe of Wales, and which has been the scene of most sanguinary and decisive contests. This fact is rendered indisputably evident by the line of intrenchments still visible, and which commences a quarter of a mile north-west from the river, Cwmaron, or Cwmarafon, presenting a camp of an oval or elliptical form, extending in circumference about 4104 yards, and being 76 yards in length, and 54 in breadth, situated on an open plain, with an avenue to the west, and having the principal entrance defended by a double ditch and rampart on the east. Proceeding in the same line one mile westward, Cwm-Cefn-y-Gaer, another more extensive encampment, presents itself, of a circular form, occupying the summit of an elevated hill, and containing an area of at least twelve acres of land; its south side is obtended by an extensive valley, and a champaign country lies opposite, with the Gaer Pool contiguous. Advancing along the summit of the hill, opposite to Llanddewi, and impending over the river Ieithon, we discern another stupendous camp, exceeding the latter in dimensions, called the Gaer, a parallelogram, with the angles rounded, and evidently of Roman origin by its construction, being in the vicinity of a Roman ystrad and station. It occupies the brow above the village of Llanddewi, which in that direction, with Coed Lladron on the west, seems impervious to the military and destructive machinations of man.

The author still persists in thinking that these works were originally constructed by the Silures, whose bravery and determined spirit their number and contiguity sufficiently demonstrate; and that the third here mentioned, and designated Gaer, was, after the expulsion of the Silures, occupied by the Romans, and used by them, either as an exploratory camp, to which purpose its elevated situation, commanding extensive prospects, is admirably adapted, or by its impregnable formation by nature, especially on its western side, confronting the country of the assailants, as an instrument to secure and extend their conquests. In a period many centuries subsequent to this transaction, and on a similar calamity, when the Normans and Saxons under the conduct of Hugh Lupus, Earl of Chester, in the year 1141, and of Hugh Mortimer, Lord of Wigmore, in the year 1144, invaded the lordships of Cantref Moelynaidd and Elfael respectively, the inhabitants, commanded by the descendants of Ellistan Glodrudd, the British *regulus* of Fferllys, Moelynaidd, and Cerri, viz., Idnerth, Madoc, and Cadwallon, successively, flocked to these camps, and defended their country, till the demon of discord infected the minds of their natural guardians, and paralyzed their efforts. Howel and Cadwgan, the two brave sons of Madoc, quarrelled, fought, and perished by each other's sword. Eineon Clydd, Lord of Elfael, seized upon the person of his elder brother and superior lord, Cadwallon, and sent him a prisoner to Henry II., King of England, with whom the Princes of Powis, the constitutional defenders of this district, had formed a traitorous alliance. The country, thus left defenceless and destitute of succour, fell a victim to the rapacity of Hugh Lupus (1142); and though afterwards recovered, it was again invaded by Hugh Mortimer, who took Rhys ab Howel (1144) and many others prisoners, and slew in battle Meyric ab Madawc ab Riryd ab Blaidd, together with Meredith ab Madoc ab Idnerth (1145). After a long series of reverses, victory and success once more smiled on this country, whose lord, Cadwallon, now escaped from prison, and reconciled to his brother Eineon Clydd, formed a coalition with his valiant relative Rhys, Prince of South Wales. Their combined exertions frustrated the ambitious schemes of Henry II., King of England, defeated the Anglo-Normans in several encounters, (A.D. 1165,) regained the possession of all Moelynaidd and Elfael, and assisted their countrymen in distant parts to emancipate themselves from the yoke of Norman oppression. About ten years after this event, (A.D. 1175,) Prince Rhys, reflecting on the debilitated state of Wales, and the disunion of its princes, persuaded his two nephews, or cousins-german, Cadwallon and Eineon, to follow his example, and submit to do homage to the King of England. This submission, however, was unable to restrain the rapacity of the Normans; and Moelynaidd continued to be for many years an object of hostility and contest. At length Roger Mortimer, son of Hugh, and Earl of Marche, having raised a numerous force of veteran troops, invaded this cantref, or territory, and after several battles of various success, (A.D. 1194,) overpowered the two sons of Cadwallon, seized their estates, and fortified and garrisoned the castle of Cwmarafon, erected some years before, and in which he is said to have resided, and kept his baronial court in great state and splendour.

The castle of Cwmaron is situated on a small elevation, about two miles hence, bordering on the river of the same name. The site presents a square grass plat of ground, each side containing forty-four yards, and remarkably green, indicative of human occupation, and having a farm-house of that name on the eastern angle. It is surrounded with a foss of great depth, and a high rampart. Adjoining, on the south side, stands a large tumulus, the circular base of which is surrounded by a deep excavation, cut in a schistous rock. No part of the superstructure of the castle at present remains, so that it is impossible to ascertain the form, or materials, of its construction. On the south-east is a deep romantic glen, through the centre of which runs the river Cwmaron along a fertile bottom, whose opposite sides, broken by rugged precipices, bear a striking contrast to the barren common of Moelynaidd adjoining. In the farm-house on the spot is preserved a cannon ball, weighing nine pounds, found a few years since on the premises. It is conjectured that with this ball the republicans, in the time of the usurpation, battered and demolished the walls of this fortress.

There were also found two earthen pipes, sixteen inches long, supposed to have been used for the purpose of conveying water into some part of the castle. The retention to this day of its Welsh appellation gives an air of probability to the traditional conjecture, that this was a military post of defence used by the Silurian inhabitants. The advantages of the situation attracted the notice of the Norman invaders in the eleventh century, who erected a kind of fortress on the spot, which was soon after indignantly destroyed by the Welsh; re-edified by Hugh Lupus, in a second invasion of this district, made in the year 1143; devolved by marriage on Hugh Mortimer, in 1145; dispossessed by Cadwallon ab Madoc, in 1175, but retaken by Roger Mortimer, in the year 1194. Llewelyn ab Gruffudd, Prince of Wales, in the year 1260, dispossessed the Mortimers of the whole of Cantref Moelynaidd and Elfael, and consequently of this castle; but after his death, in 1282, this territory and castle were conferred by Edward I. on Roger Mortimer, Earl of Marche and Wigmore, on whose attainder for high treason, in the reign of Edward III., this castle and lordship escheated to the crown of England. The royal pardon having soon after restored this powerful family to their honours, privileges, and estates, this property remained in the possession of the Mortimers till the accession of the Duke of York to the throne, under the title of Edward IV., when it became the patrimonial inheritance of the Kings of England.

On the summit of an eminence a little west of the village of Llanddewi, and in a line opposite to the Gaer encampment, is a remarkably large tumulus, or barrow, composed entirely of earth, and surrounded by a deep foss and high rampart of the same. It forms a very conspicuous object at a considerable distance, and is named by the common people Bedd-y-Grè, *i. e.*, the grave of the Grè. It is situated in a cwmwd which still retains the name of Swydd-y-Grè, *i. e.*, the office or jurisdiction of the Grè. No rational or satisfactory account has yet been given, or perhaps can be given, at this remote period, devoid of all memorials relating to the subject, of the origin, use, and destination of this stupendous tumulus. Tradition reports it to be the sepulchre of a chieftain of this name, who, if we may argue from the uncommon magnitude and solitary aspect of this barrow, must have been a person of the most illustrious, if not royal, rank and distinction. It is a pity, therefore, tradition did not also add some particulars respecting the character and services of a hero of whom history is totally silent. This objection militates so strongly against the admission of this hypothesis, as to induce several inquirers to contend that the word *Bedd* ought to be written Budd, and that Budd-y-Gré was originally a military station, as the appendage of a surrounding moat evinces, and being opposed to the fortification on the right bank of the Ieithon, denominated Gaer, and signifying in the English language, according to the *Cambrian Register*, the race of victory, was the scene of a victorious combat. This opinion derives considerable weight from comparing these two fortifications upon the Ieithon with two exactly similar ones on the right and left banks of the river Usk, above the town of Brecknock, one of which is also designated Gaer; and both the one and the other being originally works of the Romans, as the name testifies, point out the different and opposite lines of attack in which that people invaded the kingdom of Siluria, planting with one detachment the Roman eagle on the western bank of the Usk, whilst with the other they took a position on the eastern side of the Ieithon. It appears, therefore, that Budd-y-Gré was attacked by the Gaer, and, on that occasion, either obtained a decisive victory, or sustained a complete defeat; demonstrating, whatever the event may have been, the vigorous and spirited resistance of the inhabitants.

About three miles south-west, on a hill named Camlo, is a huge carn, which was opened a few years since for the purpose of investigating its contents. It consisted of thirty or forty cart-loads of unhewn stone. Its circumference was composed of a circular range of coarse stones rising gradually to the centre, which is always most protuberant, and approaching in configuration to a cone. On this being cleared, a rude chest or coffer of stone, of an oblong figure, presented itself, about four feet long and two feet wide, placed in the direction of north and south, and covered with two large flat stones. On these being removed, a vacant space of nearly the depth of one foot appeared. This having been perforated, a stratum of ashes of a reddish colour, and beneath it another stratum of a blue colour, were exhibited. To the latter succeeded the native soil. The chest displayed a rude construction of two large stones on the sides, and one at each end, the angles being strengthened and supported by others of a large dimension. To examine the whole more minutely, it became necessary to remove the earth from the external sides of the chest to its base, or foundation; which being done, a deposit of burnt bones, carefully concealed in an arched concavity made in the earth, was discovered; and the stones with which this deposit was surrounded bore evident marks of ignition, and that so intense, that the whole appeared remarkably red, and of a brittle quality, and were in a great degree vitrified.

This hill possesses two other carns, which are of considerably inferior magnitude to the one now described.

Ecclesiastical Account.

The church of Llanddewi-ystrad-Ennau is situated in a pleasant bottom, almost encircled by hills, and in the centre of the village, consisting of a few houses, one of which is Llanddewi Hall, the seat of the Hanmers and Burtons. It is a neat modernized edifice, and consists of a nave and chancel, containing two small tablets erected in commemoration of Phillips and Burton. It is dedicated to St. David.

This benefice is a perpetual curacy, not in charge, annexed to the vicarage of Llanbister, stated in *Liber Regis* to be of the certified value of £14 per annum. The prebendary of Llanbister is the patron. According to the diocesan report published in the year 1809, the total emoluments of this benefice, arising from augmentation, fixed stipend, and surplice-fees, amounted to the yearly sum of £35 15s.

Charitable Donations.

In the eighth year of the reign of King James I. the Rev. Robert Barlowe bequeathed by will, to the use and benefit of the poor of this parish, a rent-charge upon land of 10s. per annum, now vested in John Smith.

Likewise the sums of £1, and of 10s., were bequeathed to the use and benefit of the poor of this parish, and are now vested, the former in Edward Griffiths, the latter in James Moore, by two persons whose names are unknown, in the year unknown, and whether by will or deed, also unknown.

Crown Rents.

Land and a tenement in this parish, of the gross annual rent of 6s. 8d., in the occupation of Mr. Ezekiel Palfrey.

A close on Cefn-y-gaer Hill, of the gross annual rent of 2s. 6d., in the holding of Edward Burton, Esq.

STANAGE.

This name is a Saxon compound, derived from *stan*, stony, and *hoge*, a hill. It is synonymous with the Latin appellation *mons lapidosus*, and with the British Pencerrig, and signifies a "stony summit."

Stanage is a distinct and independent lordship, situated on the point of junction between the three counties of Radnor, Hereford, and Salop, and is included in the former. It constitutes a part, however, of the parish of Brampton-Brian, in Herefordshire; but appoints its own overseer, and maintains its own poor; and is only considered with the parish of Brampton-Brian, as to the payment of church-rates, and the ballot for the militia, the quota of it serving with that of the rest of the parish for the county of Hereford. Its average length is about three miles, width about two. The number of inhabitants is probably less than it was a century ago, as many cottages have been pulled down. The poor-rates seldom exceed the sum of £180 per annum. The tithes of Stanage are appropriated to the Hospital of Clun, in the county of Salop, founded by Henry Howard, Earl of Northampton, in the reign of James I., King of England. There is at present no charity school established at Stanage. The inhabitants have a right to send their children to a school at Brampton-Brian, founded in the year 1720, and endowed by Edward Harley, Esq., auditor of Her Majesty's Exchequer, and brother of Robert Harley, Esq., the great statesman in the reign of Queen Anne.

Stanage, though compelled by the fate of war to receive for a long series of years an appellation taken from the

Saxon language only, is supposed on probable grounds to be a lordship of much higher antiquity than the era of the Saxon invasion, occupied and inhabited by some of the British *reguli* of this district, the site of whose habitation still remains entire and unmutilated at Lower Stanage. It is placed in the hollow of the valley, and upon the brink of the river Tame, where they enjoyed at once conveniency of water, and security from winds. It consists of a large tumulus surrounded with a trench, and of an oblong area of ground, likewise encircled and fortified with a trench.

The circular tumulus was the court of judicature; and it also served occasionally as the audience hall of the chieftain, whose more appropriate and retired apartments for himself and family were erected upon the oblong area. Here stood the principal building; and around this were several others of various forms and dimensions, for the accommodation of his followers, who lived immediately about the person of their chief, or in little bodies along the windings of the valley, that they might be within reach of the usual signal of the lord, which was the striking of the shield, or the blowing of the horn. There is also, on the adjoining hill, called Reeves' Hill, an intrenchment, or camp, of nearly a square form, of which a sketch is given. It is now planted with trees. This fortification served either as a place of retreat to the chief when forced by the enemy from his habitation below, or as an exploratory camp, to which latter purpose it seems well calculated, for it commands a most extensive prospect, comprehending the Wrekin Hill, near the town of Wellington, in Shropshire, the Stretton Hills, the Brown Clee, the Titterstone, and the Stopperstone, together with Walcot Park, near the town of Bishop's Castle, to the north-west.

It is a circumstance much to be regretted, that no authenticated list of the British Lords of Stanage, or explanation of the origin of the numerous military vestiges, of remote antiquity, in which this neighbourhood abounds, has been transmitted to posterity. No document exists to guide and animate the researches of the antiquary, who is left to the operation of probable deduction alone. As the site of the last conflict of the renowned Caractacus with the Roman invaders of his country, namely, Caer Caradoc, lies at a short distance, and as the line of the river Tame must have formed a part of his nine campaigns, or of the campaigns of his brave successors, who revenged his captivity, and long resisted the Roman yoke, the supposition that the contemporary *regulus* of Stanage, whose name is unrecorded by fame, served in one of those campaigns, and that the camp on Reeves' Hill served as a point of retreat to his troops discomfitted in the attack made by the enemy on Coxall Knoll—both of these intrenchments lying within sight of, and at a short distance from, each other—carries with it no inconsiderable degree of probability.

The first printed authority which mentions Stanage is *Domesday Book*, in which it is thus described:—

" Osbornus fil. Ric. tenet Stanage. Ibi 6 Hidæ. Tr̃a e. 2 Car. Wasta fuit 7 est. Ibi 3 Hidæ."

Thus rendered into English,—

" Osbern, the son of Richard, holds Stanage. There are six hides. The land consists of two carucates. It hath been, and still remains, waste. There are three hides."

The six hides, and the three hides, above mentioned, comprehend both the Upper and Lower Stanage. Osbern was a Norman officer of fortune, who accompanied William the Conqueror into England, and was a favourite of that monarch, who gave him Stanage as a reward for his services. How long this lordship remained in the possession of his descendants is unknown. In the thirty-ninth year of Henry III. it belonged to Sir Brian de Brampton, of Brampton-Brian Castle. After his decease it devolved to his only son and heir, Sir Walter de Brampton, from whom it descended to his only son and heir, Sir Brian de Brampton. This gentleman had two daughters, viz., Margaret, the eldest, who was married to Robert Harley, and conveyed the Brampton-Brian estate to that family. The second daughter was named

Elizabeth, and received the hand of Sir Edmund de Cornewall, grandson of Richard, Earl of Cornewall, King of the Romans, brother to Henry III., King of England, and Lord of Radnor. To this gentleman were allotted, by virtue of his marriage with this lady, the lordships of Stanage, Stepleton, near the town of Presteigne, and Downton, near the borough of Radnor. Of a descendant of the Cornewalls, who were also Barons of Burford, the lordship of Stanage was purchased by John Powell, Esq., a merchant of London and Hamburgh, who served the office of high sheriff for the county of Radnor in the year 1641. His son, Samuel Powell, Esq., succeeded to this property; he also was high sheriff for this county in the year 1654. The last proprietor of Stanage of this name and family was Folliott Powell, Esq., who served the office of high sheriff for this county in the year 1725. Soon after this gentleman's decease, it was conveyed to the family of Richard Knight, Esq., of Croft Castle, in the county of Hereford; and at the marriage of his daughter and sole heiress with Thomas Johnes, Esq., it passed into the possession of that gentleman. His son, Thomas Johnes, Esq., of Hafod, in Cardiganshire, member of Parliament for the county of Radnor, and subsequently for the county of Cardigan, sold it, in the year 1779, to the present worthy and hospitable proprietor, Charles Rogers, Esq., who, being a younger son of an ancient family, established since the reign of Henry II., King of England, at the *Home*, near the town of Bishop's Castle, in the county of Salop, and having added to his fortune by commercial pursuits in the city of London, has fixed upon Stanage, as a seat of retirement and ease from the bustle of the world, which all wish to enjoy in the decline of life. His constant residence at Stanage is sufficient to entitle him to the denomination of a Radnorian gentleman; but he has other pretensions to this distinction, for he is descended by the maternal side from an ancient and a respectable family of the name of Clarke, once possessing considerable property, and many years residing in the parish of Blaiddfa, in this county.

Two gentlemen of this family were high sheriffs for this county, viz., John Clarke, in the year 1715, and John Clarke, in the year 1738. The present proprietor and Lord of Stanage served the office of high sheriff for this county in the year 1805, and endeavoured at great expense, and with the commendable perseverance of three years successively, to promote the interests of the district, and increase the comforts of the inhabitants, by a generous and patriotic attempt to discover that most useful fossil, coal, in the neighhourhood of Presteigne.

From this brief detail of the descent and transmission of this property, it appears that the lordship of Stanage has, from the earliest times, passed successively through some of the most powerful and opulent families established in this part of the kingdom, and came twice into the possession of commercial gentlemen; thereby evincing the benefits that result from an extended trade to individuals, as well as the nation in general.

Stanage House is situated on the summit of a ridge between two hills, commanding a most delightful and extensive view to the east over the richly cultivated counties of Hereford and Salop, and on the old site, and partly on the foundations of a large mansion, to which the ancient park of Stanage belonged, and of which a small part yet exists.

PAIN'S CASTLE HUNDRED.

The territory, now denominated Radnorshire, lying between Brecknockshire and Montgomeryshire, two districts conquered almost simultaneously by Bernard de Newmarche and Baldwin, was soon after their conquest exposed thereby to the inroads of the enemy. It continued, notwithstanding, to make a vigorous resistance, under the government of its native *reguli*, among whom, the patriotism of Idnerth ab Cadwgan ab Ellistan Glodrudd shone with conspicuous lustre. Assaulted, however, on all sides, and deprived of the succour of South Wales, which now had no head, and receiving no assistance from the Princes of Powis, who had formed an alliance with the king and nobles of England, it was unable, alone and defenceless, to preserve its independence, and to avert any longer its dismemberment. The first act of hostility was directed against Cadwgan, the father of Idnerth, and conducted by Bernard de Newmarche, Lord of Brecknock and Buallt, and by Paganus de Cadurcis, or Payne of Cahours, now Quercy, in the province of Guienne, in the kingdom of France. These two generals, companions in arms, passed over the Wye, and succeeded in possessing themselves of Glasbury and Pain's Castle. This conquest was secured by erecting, in the year 1100, a very strong and formidable fortress, called after the name of its founder, Pain's Castle, which, in a subsequent era, viz., four centuries after its construction, was deemed of such great importance as to merit the singular honour of perpetuating its own appellation by affixing it to the hundred now under consideration. Paganus, or Pain, who, some time after, was killed in a tournament, and whose body was conveyed to Gloucester, and interred in the cathedral church of that city, by the side of his friend and ally, Bernard de Newmarche, where is a stone with this inscription, "Hic jacet Paganus de Cadurcis," *i. e.*, "Here lieth Pain, of Cahours, or Quercy," left this property to his son Thomas. He died without male issue, and his only daughter and heir conveyed it by marriage to the family of De Braos, whose ancestor had married Bertha, grand-daughter of Bernard de Newmarche, and daughter of Milo, Earl of Hereford, and, in virtue of that marriage, was created Lord of Brecknock and Buallt. These possessions, by a similar right of conveyance, subsequently passed to the family of Mortimer.

This transfer of the patrimonial inheritances of the Welsh *reguli* of Elfael and Moelynaidd was facilitated by a series of disastrous events in addition to those already related. The death of the brave Madoc ab Idnerth, who preserved Radnorshire and Cerri entire; the impolitic divisions of this property in conformity to the law of gavelkind; the bloody quarrels among his children in consequence of that distribution; and the base assassination of his younger son, Eineon Clyd, or Eineon Glawd, *i. e.*, Eineon the venerable, or Eineon with the fair countenance, effected by the Flemings and Normans, on the mountains of Cardiganshire, as he was returning from Aberteifi, where he assisted at the celebrated festivities holden in that town by his father-in-law, Prince Rhys; —these were sad reverses, which must have contributed greatly to the success of the rapacious enterprizes of the Normans. Accordingly, we find that Philip de Braos, Lord of Buallt, Robert de Todeni, Lord of Clifford, together with Ralph de Baskerville, Lord of Eardisley, completed the overthrow of Cantref Elfael, and divided among themselves the remaining estates of Eineon Clyd, or Glawd, particularly Clyro, Boughrood, Colwyn and Aberedw. Some time after this seizure, a spark of honour was rekindled in the breasts of the usurpers of his patrimony; for, through the liberality of Walter, Bishop of Hereford, Eineon's eldest son, Walter Fychan, was reinstated nominally in the possession of Cantref Elfael, but substantially only in a certain portion of it; in whose descendants, of the name of Vaughan, this property remained for several generations, and indeed to a very recent period; of whom, was Roger Vaughan, Esq., of Clyro, who served the office of high sheriff for the county of Radnor in the year 1580, and subsequently for that of Hereford. It became then subdivided, partly by marriage, and partly by purchase, among the families of Whitney, Williams, Howarth, &c., and at present rests principally with Walter Wilkins, Esq., of Maeslough, in the parish of Glasbury.

Pain's Castle hundred contains twelve parishes, viz., Bettws Clyro, Boughrood, Bryngwin, Clâsbury, Clyro, Llanbedr, Llanddewi-fach, Llandeilo-graban, Llanstephan, Llowes, Michaelchurch, or Llanfihangel-ar-Arrwy, and Newchurch. All these were anciently comprized within those divisions called Cantref-y-Clawdd, and Cwmwd Penwyllt, and are at present situated within the Cantref Elfael.

BETTWS CLYRO.

This small parish is included in the parish of Clyro, and chiefly distinguished by having on its north-eastern quarter a Roman road, advancing from Gaer, a Roman camp in the parish of Llanfihangel-ar-Arrwy, or Michaelchurch, upon the Arrow, to a place named Pen-yr-heol, in this parish, and thence diverging towards a farm-house called Tu-yn-yr-heol, in a southern direction, towards the river Wye, which it crossed near to the bridge of the town of Hay.

Bettws Clyro maintains its own poor, and collects its parochial assessments separately and distinctly, which, for the service of the year 1803, amounted to £197 4s. 0½d., raised at 1s. in the pound. Its population consisted in the year 1801 of 164 individuals.

The benefice of Bettws Clyro is a chapelry, not in charge, annexed to the vicarage of Clyro, of no certified value, and consolidated with the benefice of Clyro, under the same institution and induction.

BOUGHROOD.

It contains on an average about 1000 acres of inclosed and cultivated land, and nearly 500 acres uninclosed and uncultivated.

This parish has passed through the hands of divers proprietors. In the year 1140, it was the property of Eineon Clyd, the younger brother of Cadwallon, Lord of Moelynaidd, who was murdered on his return from Cardiganshire, as before related. The possession of it was then seized by the Norman usurpers; and, pursuant to a new division of the spoils, it devolved upon the Bishop of Hereford, who had the generosity to restore it to the rightful heir, Walter Fychan, son of Eineon. A part of the wall of the old castle of Boughrood, in which Eineon and his descendants for several generations resided, was standing a short time since, and the moat with which it was surrounded remains to this day. This castle, together with the lordship of Trewern Boughrood, constituted a part of the property of Sir Richard Chace, whose only daughter and heir was the third wife of John Price, Esq., of Knighton, in this county, the grandfather of Richard Price, Esq., the present representative of the borough of Radnor in Parliament. Their issue was two sons, viz., Chace Price, Esq., member of Parliament, first, for the borough of Leominster, in the county of Hereford, and afterwards for the county of Radnor; and Richard Price, Esq., late of the borough of Knighton. The former gentleman, being a *bon-vivant*, died in embarassed circumstances, and had contracted a large debt to government. An extent was issued for the recovery of this debt, and the Boughrood estate was sold to discharge it.

An estate called the Noyadd, in this parish, remained for centuries in the possession of the Whitney family, obtained originally by the marriage of Hugh Whitney, Esq., of Whitney Court, in the county of Hereford, with Catherine, daughter of William Vaughan, Esq., of Maeslough, in the parish of Clâsbury.

According to the return made in the year 1801, the resident population of this parish consisted of 285 individuals. The parochial assessments for the service of the year 1803 amounted to the sum of £226 14s. 6d., assessed at 1s. 6d. in the pound.

Ecclesiastical Account.

The church of Boughrood consists of a nave and chancel, divided by a timber partition, a tower containing three bells, a porch having a lavacrum on the right of the entrance. The interior is dark, irregularly pewed, and contains nothing remarkable. It is dedicated to St. Cynog.

The benefice of Boughrood is a discharged vicarage, estimated in *Liber Regis* at £12 6s. 8d.

The prebend of Boughrood, in the Collegiate Church of Brecknock, to which is annexed the perpetual curacy of Llanbedr, Pain's Castle, is estimated in *Liber Regis* to be worth annually 13s. 4d.

List of Incumbents.

John Williams, A.M. 1739   Benjamin Howell............. 1778
Thomas Owen 1750   Benjamin Howell, recollated 1778

Charitable Donations.

In the year 1686 the Rev. Mr. Powell bequeathed by deed the annual sum of £5, charged upon certain lands, and vested in trustees, viz., Sir Edward Williams, Bart., Hon. and Rev. John Harley, D.D., John Morgan, Esq., Walter Wilkins, Esq., M.P., Charles Powell, Philip Williams, Walter Jefferys,

Samuel Hughes, John Bullock Lloyd, Esqrs., Rev. John Williams, clerk, for binding out poor children of this parish apprentices.

William John bequeathed by will, and vested in the parishioners, a rent-charge of £1 4s., secured upon land, to be distributed yearly among twelve poor parishioners of this parish.

CLASBURY.

Although the river Wye is in general the separating boundary of the two counties of Radnor and Brecknock, yet this parish violates this arrangement, and stretches itself on both sides of that line, having its parochial church on the Brecknockshire, and a considerable part of its territory, viz., the township or portion of Pipton, on the Radnorshire quarter. Thus, the Radnorshire portion of Clâsbury, which lies on the right bank of the Wye, being a part of the conquered territory which Bernard de Newmarche, the Norman Lord of Brecknock and Buallt obtained of Cadwgan, the Welsh Lord of Elfael, Moelynaidd, and Cerri, was annexed to his larger property that was situated on the left bank of that river; and, on the formation of the four new counties of South Wales, in the reign of Henry VIII., King of England, this baronial arrangement was adhered to, and the Radnorshire and Brecknockshire Clâsbury were made to constitute one parish, each, however, maintaining their own poor, raising their own quota of militia, and assessing their own rates, severally, distinctly, and separately, and the inhabitants of both having an equal right to the use and service of the church, which is situated on the Brecknockshire side of the Wye; the boundaries between the two counties in this parish being Ffordd-fawr and Llwyneubach, one half of a mile from the river, southwardly; then turn east and west; then turn angularly south-west, by Clâsbury Church, to the left; cross the turnpike road, and return through the Sconces into Wye.

Few vestiges of antiquity are discoverable in this parish. There are, in certain situations, small encampments, and barrows of Welsh construction, of which tradition is totally silent. Nor is it supposed that any castle was ever erected here. The proximity of those two formidable fortresses, Colwyn and Pain's Castle, afforded sufficient security. The conquest of this parish by Bernard de Newmarche, obtained over Cadwgan ab Ellistan Glodrudd, broke a link of that chain which for centuries connected the Severn and the Wye together, and which conferred the appellation of Fferllys on the interjacent country. Having passed through the family of De Braos, by means of a matrimonial union with the grand-daughter of the first Norman Lord of Brecknock and Buallt, it reverted, through the liberality and a sense of justice with which a prelate of the see of Hereford was even in those days impressed, to Walter Fychan, son of the original proprietor, Eineon Clyd, and remained in the possession of his descendants till the year 1500, when William Vaughan, Esq., of Maeslough, in this parish, departed this life, leaving behind him two daughters, co-heiresses, viz., Catherine and Sybil, to whom the father had devised eight messuages, eight gardens, or farms, one grist mill, 300 acres of meadow land, 200 acres of pasture, 100 acres of wood, furze, heath, &c., in the several parishes of Clâsbury, Llowes, and Boughrood, in fee. His eldest daughter, viz., Catherine, was married to Hugh Whitney, Esq., of Whitney Court, who, for a certain consideration, alienated his interest in Clâsbury. In the year 1582 died Sybil, the second daughter, and wife of Charles Lloyd, Esq. They left no male issue, but one only daughter, who conveyed by marriage this property to Humphrey Howarth, Esq., of Caebalfa, in the parish of Clyro, but originally of White House, in the parish of Michaelchurch, or of the parish of Clodock, in the county of Brecknock. His son, Sir Humphrey Howarth, Bart., having greatly involved himself in embarassment, by severe contests for the representation of this county in Parliament, and by other expensive pursuits, was under the necessity of mortgaging this extensive property to Walter Wilkins, Esq., member of Parliament for this county, by whom, in due time, the mortgage was foreclosed, and the estate of Maeslough purchased. This gentleman has erected, on or near the site of the old house of the Vaughan family, a large mansion. The parochial assessments collected in the Radnorshire part, for the service of the year 1803, amounted to the sum of £41 11s. 8½d.

Ecclesiastical Account.

The church of Clâsbury consists of a nave, chancel, porch, and a square tower containing six bells. The chancel contains several handsome monuments commemorative of the loyal and respectable family of Williams, of Gwernyfed, and also of Devereux, of Tregoed, with their several escutcheons.

On the north side of the church are four windows, each containing two lights. The east window contains three lights, divided by stone mullions supporting cinquefoil arches. The space above, under the point of the arch, is filled in a similar manner. It is dedicated to St. Peter. The church-yard is very spacious, and, standing on the declivity of an eminence, commands a beautiful and picturesque view of the river, and of the adjoining country.

This benefice is a vicarage, remaining in charge, and estimated in *Liber Regis*, at £10 per annum. The great tithes of this parish were conferred by Bernard de Newmarche, its conqueror, on the monks of Gloucester, as a means of atoning for his military spoliations. These tithes still continue to enrich the clergy of that cathedral church, and the patronage of this benefice is vested in its bishop. Although there are two chapels in the Brecknockshire division of this parish, viz., Felindre and Pipton, they have been suffered to fall into decay and ruin, and the whole duty has been transferred to the church of Clâsbury.

List of Incumbents.

John Williams 1720
John Williams, Junr. 1750
Thomas Owen .... —
Thomas Stock, A.M. 1778
Thomas Stock, reinstated 1787
Charles Boravare Penaly Lowther 1804
Charles Bradley Warry .... 182?

The first vicar of this parish of whom any written account has been transmitted was Alexander Griffith, of the family of that name, resident at the Gaer, in the parish of Llowes, in this hundred. He was educated at Hart Hall, in the University of Oxford, and lived in the troublesome time of the Great Rebellion. On all occasions he manifested himself a strenuous supporter of the royal cause, and a firm adherent to the Church of England. He wrote and published many treatises, as well on subjects of polemical divinity, as on the jarring politics of the day, and was the author of the "Hue and Cry" after Vavasor Powell, the grand apostate and rapacious sequestrator of the benefices of this county, and of Wales. His publications, particularly the latter, alarmed and annoyed the republicans and fanatics of those innovating times, who, in order to silence and ruin him, invented the grossest and most unfounded calumnies, and cited him to appear before their court of unjust inquisition, on a charge of drunkenness and lasciviousness. From such a tribunal, in which the same persons were prosecutors, witnesses, and judges, no innocence ever escaped. He was ejected, and his benefice of Clâsbury sequestrated, in the year 1649.

Charitable Donations.

In the year 1605 Walter Meredith bequeathed by will certain houses, of which the rent-charge is £3 per annum, for the purpose of clothing six old persons of this parish one year, and eight young persons the following year.

Mrs. Seagood devised the sum of £4, being the yearly interest of the sum of £100 in money, vested by will in Lord Viscount Hereford, for the use and benefit of the poor of this parish.

In the year 1612 Sir David Williams, Bart., of Gwernyfed, devised the annual sum of £3 5s. 5d., arising from tithes, partly to purchase bread for the poor, and partly for the preaching of an annual sermon in the church of Clâsbury, vested in the parishioners of Gendwr by will.

CLYRO.

This parish, which, after it had fallen under the power of the Norman Lords of Brecknock and Buallt, reverted at a subsequent period to Walter Fychan, son of Eineon Clyd, Lord of Elfael, the original proprietor, remained several centuries in the possession of his descendants. Roger Vaughan, Esq., of Clyro, who served the office of high sheriff for the county of Radnor in the year 1580, when ship money was exacted by the Parliament, belonged to this family; so likewise did the Vaughans, of Harpton, in the parish of Radnor, and of Bugaildu, in this county, and of Courtfield, in the parish of Goodrich, in the county of Hereford, persons of affluence and respectability. The family seat in this parish, called the Court of Clyro, was anciently a venerable mansion, but is now converted into a farm-house. The ancient embattled gateway and arch which open the approach to the house still remain entire on the north side.

Near to the village of Clyro, partly to the south-east of the church, on a small eminence, containing about two acres of land, are the remains of extensive buildings, which appear to have once covered the whole area, and were encompassed with a deep trench or moat. A subterranean arched passage led from the centre of these ruins towards the river Wye. The summit on which these dilapidated remains of buildings appear, and which commands a most beautiful and enchanting prospect of the river, both towards the east and west, and of the adjoining country, is now called the Castle Bank. It admits of much doubt whether this was the real site of Clyro Castle; the ruins rather favour the supposition of a monastery, or of some religious house; and this conjecture is further corroborated by the vicinity of an extensive and a valuable farm, called "Tir-y-mynach," *i. e.*, Monk-land, which is now let at nearly £600 per annum. Most probably this estate, or farm, constituted Clyro Grange, a part of the property with which the Abbey of of Cwmhir, in this county, was endowed; and these ruins, if not the remains of a castle, formed the occasional residence of the abbot, or cells for the habitation of monks, subject to his visitation.

About a mile to the north-east of the village, and near to a respectable looking old farm-house, erected about three centuries ago, called Court Evan Gwynne, stands a very large tumulus, or barrow, about 40 feet high, and nearly 100 yards in circumference, and is surrounded by a deep moat and high rampart. It originally contained a quantity of building, and the foundations of walls are still visible. To what use this fortification was originally applied, whether for the purpose of repelling the Roman or Norman invaders of this district, or both, is a matter enveloped in obscurity. It overlooks the town and castle of Hay, on the opposite side of the river, and also commands a view of the Gaer encampment, in the parish of Llanfihangel-ar-Arrwy, or Michaelchurch, in this county, and also of the hills around Dorston and Peterchurch, in the county of Hereford.

On the south side of the marsh, called Rhôsgoch, so named from its red appearance, is an extensive farm, called Llys-Ifor, or Ifor's palace. This habitation has been in ancient times encompassed by a deep trench of considerable depth, and by a high rampart, or vallum. The voice of tradition assigns this property to have formerly belonged to an inferior chieftain, or *regulus*, of the name of Ifor. Who could this second ranked prince have been but Ifor, the father of Cynhyllyn, of whom descended Ellistan Glodrudd, *regulus* of Moelynaidd and Fferllys, or perhaps rather Ifor, the son of Idnerth, and younger brother of Madoc, Lord of Moelynaidd and Elfael, who, by virtue of the law of gavelkind, inherited a certain portion of this division of Radnorshire? In a military point of view, the site of this ancient fortification is in no degree imposing, and seems better calculated for the station of an ambush, which might surprize and annoy an enemy occupied in the siege of Pain's Castle, distant about two miles and a half towards the west, than a defensive position to secure the country from incursions. The name only implies that it was the court or palace of Ifor, guarded in front by the marsh before-mentioned.

At Gwern-fythen House, in this parish, lived Sir William Whitney, Bart., who inherited this estate, with many others in the neighbourhood, either by marrying the Welsh heiress, or derived it from his ancestor, Hugh Whitney, Esq., who married Catherine, daughter and heiress of William Fychan, Esq., of Maeslough, as before related. Several gentlemen of this family served the office of high sheriff for the county of Radnor, as Sir Robert Whitney, Bart., in the year 1562; and Sir William Whitney, Bart., in the years 1608 and 1616. The proprietor of Gwernfythen estate had by Anne, his wife, ten sons, all of whom attained the state of manhood, and to each of whom the father left by will respectable freeholds, equally dividing, according to the law of gavelkind, perhaps at the impulse of his wife, from whom in all probability this property descended, all his landed estates among them,—all of which have long since passed into other hands.

A Roman road entering the chapelry of Bettws Clyro, at Pen-yr-heol, intersects this parish, and by Tu-yn-yr-heol, proceeds through it to the river Wye, and the town of Hay.

This parish contains four townships, or hamlets, viz., Clyro, Bettws Clyro, and Bronydd, in which the parochial assessments are paid collectively, and for the service of the year 1803 amounted to the sum of £508 4s. 0½d., raised at 1s. in the pound. According to the return published in the year 1801, the resident population of this parish consisted of 602 individuals.

Ecclesiastical Account.

The church consists of a nave, chancel, tower, and a porch, and is dedicated to St. Michael.

The benefice of Clyro is a discharged vicarage, with the chapel of Bettws annexed. It is estimated in *Liber Regis* at £6 per annum. The tithes are divided between the prebendary of Clyro, who is the impropriator, and the vicar. The clear annual income of the latter, some years since, was £40. The total amount at present exceeds £189 per annum. The yearly tenths are 12s.

The prebend of Clyro, in the Collegiate Church of Brecknock, is valued in *Liber Regis* at £7 6s. 8d. per annum, and is in the patronage of the Bishop of St. David's. No church register existed prior to the year 1700.

List of Incumbents.

William Jones .... 1728 Edward Edwards, A.M. 1764
William Stephens, L.B. .... 1749 Richard Drake Venables, D.D. .. 1800

Charitable Donations.

In the year 1773 Mrs. Gwynne devised by will the sum of £600, and directed it to be laid out in the purchase of land, and vested it in Mr. James Price, her executor, the yearly rent of which to be paid to a schoolmaster, for teaching, clothing, and apprenticing poor children of this parish.

BRYNGWIN.

The cwmwd to which it anciently appertained was denominated Castell-Maen, *i. e.*, Huntington Castle-manor, in the county of Hereford. It contains about 3000 acres of inclosed and cultivated land, and 2000 acres of hills uninclosed and uncultivated. By the return published in the year 1801, the resident population of this parish then consisted of 277 individuals. The parochial assessments for 1803 amounted to the sum of £221 18s. 8d., raised at 8s. 4d. in the pound.

A Mr. Griffith is at this time in actual possession of an estate, and resides in the farm-house, called the *Portway*, which his ancestors have enjoyed, in a direct line, for the last four centuries. This, however, is not the only circumstance which renders this estate an object interesting to the local historian. A superior claim to notice arises from having a Roman road running through it, as its name indicates, and assimilates it to others of a like appellation in many counties of England, particularly Herefordshire. The commencement of this road, in the county of Radnor, may be traced in the vicinity of the Roman camp called *Gaer*, in the parish of Llanfihangel-ar-Arrwy, or Michaelchurch on the Arrow, whence it scuds along the level summit of Brilley mountain, commanding a most extensive and picturesque view of the country on both sides, and also of the course of the Arrow, when at the western extremity of the mountain it descends the brow with a gentle sweep to a place called Bwlch-ar-heol, *i. e.*, "the defile, or pass on the Roman road," where it divides into two branches, the one of which proceeds to the parish of Clascwm-Llansantfraid, and, finally, to the river Ieithon, in the parish of Llanfihangel Helygen; the other advances in a straight line to Pen-yr-heol, and Tu-yn-yr-heol, in the parishes of Bettws Clyro and Clyro, and joins the Roman road leading from the town of Hay.

On the south-eastern side of this parish, in the bottom of a valley, is a large morass, called Rhôs-goch, *i. e.*, "the red morass," extending in length one mile and a quarter, and about half a mile in breadth; producing a most excellent kind of peat, nearly equal in heat and durability to coal, and exceeding it in inflammability.

Ecclesiastical Account.

This church consists of a nave, chancel, a low tower containing two small bells, and a porch. The east window consists of three lights, divided by stone mullions supporting trefoil arches. The space above, under the pointed arch of the window, is filled up in the same manner. In the south-east angle of the exterior wall of the chancel is fixed a long stone, on the east side of which is sculptured a female figure, and on the south side a male, without any inscription. The church is dedicated to St. Michael.

In the church-yard, which commands an extensive prospect, is a stone of considerable length, and about one foot in breadth, different in quality from the stones in this vicinity, originally placed erect, but now by the violence of time and weather inclining much towards the west, on which are sculptured several crosses and figures.

The benefice of Bryngwin is a rectory, estimated in *Liber Regis* at £11 6s. 8d. per annum; but the total emolument of the rector's annual income exceeds at present £200. The yearly tenths are £1 2s. 8d. The parish register commences about the year 1600.

List of Incumbents.

Humphrey Price 1640
James Powell 1668
Onslow Barrett 1796
Rowland Rogers 1749
William Powell 1780
Samuel Powell 1796
Samuel Davies ....

Charitable Donations.

In the year 1706 Richard Jones, Esq., devised by will a rent-charge of

£2 10s. per annum, secured on land, and now vested in Mr. William Gore, for the use of the poor of this parish.

The sum of £2 per annum was also devised by will, bearing no date, by a person unknown, for the benefit of the poor of this parish.

LLANBEDR, PAIN'S CASTLE.

Pain's Castle is a township of itself, and is united in all respects, civil and ecclesiastical, with Llanbedr, thereby forming one parish, and including in one return the number of its population, and the amount of its parochial assessments. According to the return published in the year 1801, the resident population consisted of 78 individuals. The money raised for the service of the year 1803 amounted to the sum of £350 10s. 8d., assessed at 13s. 8d. in the pound. The town consists of four streets, or roads, intersecting each other at right angles, subtending the four cardinal points, and containing several old and respectable farm-houses, viz., the Castle, belonging to Walter Wilkins, Esq., M.P.; the Upper House, the property of J. C. Severn, Esq.; and Pen-y-dre, the residence of Mr. Prosser—which two latter houses are of very antique appearance; and the New House, belonging to the son of the James Williams, Esq., of the town of Hay.

The situation of the castle seems judiciously selected for the purpose of commanding and controlling the vicinity. It was a fortress of considerable strength and importance, having a very lofty keep, or citadel, surrounded by a moat twenty feet deep, and encompassing an area of an acre and a half, intrenched in the same manner, and communicating with the former. It was also secured by an exterior intrenchment of considerable depth and extent, part of which, viz., that towards the east, has been defaced, and is now covered with buildings, inclosing about twelve acres of land. It wanted, however, one appendage of ancient fortification, viz., water, of which there appears at present no source of supply sufficient to fill the trenches.

This formidable fortress was begun by Paganus de Quercis, (A. D. 1130,) who accompanied the Conqueror into England, and completed by his son, Thomas de

Paganus. His daughter and sole heir conveyed it by marriage, together with other immense possessions in the counties of Monmouth and Glamorgan, to William de Braos, Lord of Gower, Brecknock and Buallt, and of Bramber, in the county of Sussex—a baron of great power, wealth, and influence. It was frequently taken and retaken in the Welsh wars, particularly by Prince Rhys; and besieged by Gwenwynyn, Lord of Powis, who sustained a total discomfiture. These repeated attacks, and the subsequent spoliations of the country people, have reduced this once frowning and terrific stronghold to the mean and despicable appearance which it now exhibits; nothing more remaining of it at present than a few loose fragments of its external walls.

The mountain between Pain's Castle and Glâsbury, over which the turnpike road leading from the former to the latter passes, is called the Beacons. It remains uninclosed, and extends about five miles from east to west. It has several points which command extensive views, which might have served as beacons, and used to convey intelligence to the castle, and to other fortresses in the neighbourhood. No sort of intrenchments, however, nor tumuli, or artificial mounds for observation, have been discovered upon it.

Ecclesiastical Account.

The church consists of a nave, chancel, porch, and a low tower containing three bells.

This benefice is a perpetual curacy, not in charge, under the prebend of Boughrood, stated in *Liber Regis* to be of the clear yearly value of £8; but its present emoluments amount to £50.

LLANDDEWI-FACH.

This small parish extends along the banks of the river Bach-Howey. According to the return published in the year 1801, its resident population consisted of 116 individuals. Its parochial assessments collected for the service of the year 1803 amounted to £58 1s. 6½d., raised at 1s. 6d. in the pound. No vestiges of antiquity have been discovered in this parish.

Ecclesiastical Account.

The church consists of a nave only, and has a small turret containing one little bell. This benefice is a chapel only, annexed to the vicarage of Llowes, stated to be of the yearly value of £24.

LLANDEILO GRABAN, *alias* LLANDEILO CRIBIN.

Nearly two miles from Craig-pwll-du, and on the north side of the Bach-Howey, a river which at the place of its disemboguement separates the parishes of Llandeilo Graban and Llan-y-styffan, is a rising and almost circular eminence called Twyn y Garth. Upon the summit of this hill is a small camp, nearly circular, containing only one ditch, but in a high state of preservation. The only entrance is on the east side; and about eighty yards distant from it, only inclining to the north-east, are two carneddau. The ascent to the camp is very steep upon all sides, and three or four thousand men might defend it against an army. On the south side of the camp is a piece of land, nearly square, inclosed by a slight ditch, and seemingly coeval with the intrenchment. One side of it is protected by the rampart of the camp.

On viewing this camp in connection with one of the rocks of Craig-pwll-du, a celebrated cataract on the river Bach-Howey, a variety of interesting reflections is suggested to the mind of the antiquary. It is handed down by tradition, and even gravely asserted by Welsh chroniclers, that the traitor and usurper Gwrtherin Gwrthenau after his deposition retreated into the wilds of Radnorshire, denominated Elfael, and there for some time eluded the vengeance of his countrymen. Now, it may confidently be asked, in what place in Elfael could a more gloomy spot for a castle be selected than Craig-pwll-du, which bears to this day the appellation of *Domini Castra*, or the "Lord's Castle," especially when we recollect that this dingle was at that time with lofty and majestic oaks impervious to the view? Or what camp in all this district is equally calculated to give confidence and security as that above described?

The population of this parish has remained nearly stationary for this century past. According to the return published in the year 1801 the number of its resident inhabitants was 372. The parochial assessments raised for the service of the year 1803 amounted to the sum of £118.

Ecclesiastical Account.

The parish church consists of a nave, a chancel, a square tower of stone containing three bells, and a porch. The nave is separated from the chancel by a timber frame, or screen; the roof is ribbed with oak; the pews have an antique appearance, and want that neatness which is derived from uniformity. This benefice is a perpetual curacy, holden under the prebend in the Collegiate Church of Brecknock. It has been augmented by two lots of Queen Anne's bounty, viz., £200 in the year 1718, and £200 in 1778. This money was laid out in the purchase of land in the year 1785. The total emoluments of this benefice amount at present to the yearly sum of £69.

The prebend of Llandeilo Graban, in the Collegiate Church of Brecknock, was seized in the year 1649 by the parliamentary sequestrators, and perverted from its original destination to their fanatic purposes. It is estimated in *Liber Regis* to be of the clear yearly value of £9 13s. 4d. The yearly tenths are 19s. 4d.

List of Incumbents.

Henry Penry, licensed in 1736... 1717　　Thomas Williams, 14th August... 1802
John Powell 1722

Charitable Donations.

In 1726 Mr. David Beddoes bequeathed by will the principal sum of £100, which has been laid out in the purchase of land, and £5 per annum, and has directed it to be distributed among the poor inhabitants of this parish. No trustees appointed.

In 1686 Thomas George bequeathed by will, for the benefit of the poor of this parish, the sum of £10, secured on land. No trustees appointed. No further information can be given.

In 1686 William George bequeathed by will the sum of £40, the annual interest of which he directed to be distributed among the poor inhabitants of this parish. No trustees. No further information can be given.

An unknown person left, supposed by will, date unknown, a rent-charge upon land of the value of 10s. per annum, and directed to be distributed among the poor inhabitants of this parish.

LLANSTEPHAN.

The author has not succeeded in discovering any vestiges of remote antiquity, either druidical or military. It certainly must have possessed some of the latter description, as there is a respectable farm-house, called Tu-yn-yr-heol, *i. e.*, "the house on the Roman road," which penetrated into this parish from Bettws Clyro. There also stands, upon a lofty eminence of steep ascent, another respectable farm-house, called Ciliau, *i. e.*, "Retreats," or "Recesses," denoting it to have been a scene of military retreat in some distant and unknown age—perhaps at the time when Bernard de Newmarche and his Norman followers crossed the Wye, and attacked this district; or its original name may have been Guiliau, i. e., "Vigilatories," a designation which the site is well calculated to answer, for it commands a prospect as wide and extensive as it is fine and picturesque.

According to the return of the population of this parish in 1801, the number of resident inhabitants was 246. The parochial assessments raised for the service of the year 1803 amounted to the sum of £196 11s. 6d., at 1s. in the pound.

The lord of the manor of Llanstephan is Francis Fowke, Esq., proprietor of Boughrood Castle.

Ecclesiastical Account.

The church consists of a nave, a chancel, a low tower containing four bells, and a porch. The communion table is a stone slab. The chancel, which contains the lavacrum, and sepulchral tablets commemorating a family of the name of James, of Tu-yn-yr-heol, is separated from the nave by a timber frame, under a pointed arch of stone, and a roodloft of fine oak, very elegantly carved, with rosettes and vine leaves intertwined, supported by oak pillars handsomely pilastered.

This benefice is a perpetual curacy, not in charge, estimated in *Liber Regis* at the clear yearly value of £9. The Archdeacon of Brecknock is the patron. All the tithes are alienated from the church, and possessed by lay impropriators. The curacy has been augmented by two lots of Queen Anne's bounty, viz., £200 in August, 1747, and £200 in September, 1754. Its total emoluments amount at present to the annual sum of £80.

List of Incumbents.

Thomas James	1739	John Edwards	1792
Jenkin Jenkins	1749	Thomas Williams	1799

Charitable Donation.

In the year 1681 Mr. Thomas Havard bequeathed the annual interest of the principal sum £60, viz., £3, now vested in the minister and churchwardens, and directed it to be distributed among the poor inhabitants of this parish.

LLOWES.

The parish of Llowes contains some ancient vestiges of the military kind. Besides numerous encampments of the ancient inhabitants of this district, there is a respectable farm-house called "Gaer," erected on the area of a Roman camp of considerable magnitude, and contiguous to the Roman road which proceeds from "Gaer," in the parish of Michaelchurch, and passes by " Pen-yr-heol," and through this parish to Tu-yn-yr-heol, and so on to the Wye. It is said that the Danes entered Herefordshire, and penetrated along the line of the Wye as far as Buallt. It is reasonable to suppose that, in the course of that surprizing march, some of these encampments were occupied by that fierce and warlike people.

According to the return of its resident population, published in the year 1801, the number of its inhabitants was 363. The parochial assessments raised for the service of the year 1803 amounted to the sum of £202 5s. 1½d., at 7s. 6d. in the pound.

The greater part of this parish was once the property of Sir Humphrey Howarth, Bart., who represented this county in Parliament. His ancestor married the daughter and heiress of William Vaughan, Esq., of Maeslough, a descendant of Walter Fychan, son of Eineon Clyd, the ancient *regulus* of Elfael. Sir Humphrey's seat and park were in this parish. The name of Howarth, it is said, was originally Havard. The family resided, according to the report of some, at White House, in the parish of Michaelchurch, in this county, and of others, at Caebalfa. Both these traditions may be true at different periods. Sir Humphrey Howarth, Bart., proprietor of Maeslough, had an only daughter, who was married to the Rev. Mr. Davies. This marriage produced an only son, viz., Manwaring Probert Howarth, who died in the Fleet Prison, leaving a son who is lately arrived from the East Indies. Sir Humphrey had a brother, whose son Henry was rector of Gladestry. He left behind him several children: 1. Henry, the barrister, who was drowned in the river Thames, when his talents were at the point of attaining the height of his profession; 2. Humphrey, late member of Parliament for the borough of Evesham; 3. Edward, now Sir Edward, general of artillery; 4. Mrs. Allen, wife of —— Allen, Esq., of the Lodge, in the county of Brecknock. Henry, rector of Gladestry, in this county, had a brother to whom were born two sons, both of whom were promoted to high rank in their respective professions, one having been a general, and the other an admiral. Both departed this life in the town of Hay, Brecknockshire, about twenty years since. The late Sir Humphrey Howarth, Bart., the last proprietor of Maeslough of the name, married the relict of Sir David Henry Williams, Bart., of Gwernyfed, in the parish of Clâsbury, in the county of Brecknock, and in her right enjoyed for life the estates of Gwernyfed, Lodge, &c.

Ecclesiastical Account.

The church consists of a nave, a chancel, separated from the nave by a timber railing, a low square tower containing two bells, and having three ranges of lights on each side, and crowned with a weather-cock, and a porch. In the chancel, on the south wall, are suspended the armorial bearings of the ancient and respectable house of Howarth. The family vault lies beneath.

A tombstone in this church-yard contains the only Welsh inscription that is recorded in this county, which is as follows:—

"William Bevan, o Fedwllwyd, dan y
garreg sydd yma yn gorphwsfa: Oedran
oedd 84 mlynyddau, ac yma dewis ar
byd hwn yn 17 dydd Ebrill, a blwyddyn
1684. Miserere mei, Deus."

In the church-yard is a singular monument of remote antiquity. This consists of a stone of immense weight and dimension, placed erect, and measuring in height about seven yards from the surface of the ground, and in breadth about two yards, and nearly six feet in thickness, and carved or sculptured into the similitude of a human body. On its breast is delineated a large circle, divided into four semilunar compartments, separated by rich sculpture. In the centre of the circle is a lozenge. The lower part of the body is decorated with lozenges and triangles. Its arms have been broken off by accident, or by violence, or by the corroding hand of time. This amputation affords just matter for regret; as, if these parts had remained unmutilated and entire, they might have given a clue to discover the hidden meaning of this astonishing piece of emblematical sculpture. The consequence of this loss is the indulgence of conjectures. Some, among whom was the late Theophilus Jones, Esq., suppose that this formidable figure represents Malaen, the British Minerva, the goddess of war. A Christian cemetery must be deemed an extraordinary situation for the erection of the image of a pagan deity. The traditional report respecting the origin of this monumental stone is replete with absurdity, extravagance, and ridiculousness, and outrages every degree of probability. For it asserts that a certain female, of gigantic strength, called Moll Walbec, threw this immense stone out of her shoe across the river Wye from Clifford Castle, which she had constructed, distant about three miles. The British and original appellation of Moll Walbec was Malaen-y-Walfa, *i. e.*, "the fury of the inclosure."

This benefice is a discharged vicarage, estimated in *Liber Regis* at the clear yearly value of £28. The yearly tenths are 17s. The Archdeacon of Brecknock is the proprietor of the tithes, and patron of the benefice.

List of Incumbents.

William Stephens, L.B. 1735   John Jones 1764
The total emoluments may amount at present to the annual sum of £70.

Charitable Donation.

In the year 1704, Mrs. Susannah Howarth devised a rent-charge of 10s., now vested in Thomas Griffith, by will, for the purpose of purchasing bread for the poor of this parish.

MICHAELCHURCH.

The Welsh appellation of Michaelchurch is Llanfihangel-ar-Arrwy, that is, the church or parish of St. Michael on the river Arrow, it being situated along the banks of that river. From the return of its resident population, published in the year 1801, it appears that the number of its inhabitants then consisted of 172 individuals. The parochial assessments amounted to £97 17s. 0½d. for the year 1803, at 6s. in the pound.

There are in this parish the vestiges of an ancient encampment of very large extent; the area contains several acres of land. It commences in an arable field, on the right hand of the road leading from Kington to Hay, almost opposite to a farm-house called Postles, and reaches in a northern direction to the river Arrow. Its immediate vicinity abounds in tumuli, or barrows, and in redoubts composed of earth and stones, and commanding the fords and watering-places of that river. It is designated by the military name Gaer, and consists of two divisions, the Upper and Lower Gaer, as they are at present denominated. Its ramparts in several places have been levelled by the plough.

Ecclesiastical Account.

The church is a small chapel, erected on the bank of the river Arrow, and annexed to the vicarage of Kington, in the county of Hereford.

NEWCHURCH.

According to the return of its resident population, published in the year 1801, the number of its inhabitants then consisted of 115 individuals. The parochial assessments for the service of the year 1803, at 7s. in the pound, amounted to the sum of £83 3s.

A branch of the great Roman road connecting the two British divisions of Cymru, viz., Ordovicia and Siluria, commences at Mortimer's Cross, in the county of Hereford, and proceeding through the parish of Lyonshall, to Gaer, in Michaelchurch parish, pursues its course along the summit of Brilley Mountain, aud takes a gentle sweep down its western-side, till it arrives at a place where stands a house called Gwylfa-ar-heol, "the sentinel's station or watch-tower," on the Roman road. This site is most judiciously chosen, and admirably adapted for this purpose. For here three roads meet, viz., that which leads from Gaer above-mentioned; the other diverges towards the parish of Clâscwm, towards the north; and the third advances in a straight line to Pen-yr-heol, in the parish of Bettws Clyro, in a direction towards the west; of all and of every one of which this station at Gwylfa commands a complete and distinct view; so that a body of men advancing in either of these directions must have been immediately discovered.

Contiguous almost to Gwylfa-ar-heol stands a farm-house called at present Redborough. The proximity of a name so completely English to a Welsh name that has existed since the time of the Roman invasion naturally excited some astonishment and doubt. The result of a long attempt to solve this phenomenon amounts to this: Redborough seems to be a corruption of the Welsh word Arhyd-y-bro, *i. e.*, "along the bank of the river," the adjoining lands answering to that description..

The river Arrow in this parish receives an accession of water from a small rivulet that issues from the morass of Rhôsgoch, in the parish of Bryngwin, and runs in a north-easterly direction. The dingle through which it meanders is called Cwm-gwillo. About half a mile from the source of this rivulet is a conspicuous tumulus, or barrow, ascending to the height of thirty feet from the surface of the surrounding ground, and situated on an estate called Tal-beddwyn, or Twlch-beddwyn. It stands on an eminence, and has been encompassed by a deep trench or foss, which is now almost obliterated by the plough. Its summit and sides are planted with firs and other forest trees, which produce an ornamental effect. It is distant from Pain's Castle about three miles, of which it commands a full and distinct view. This tumulus was probably intended to command and secure the vale of Cwm-gwillo, and perhaps to convey intelligence to the garrison of Pain's Castle. The estate on which it stands is the property of the Rev. Samuel Beavan, of Tu-yn-y-cwm, in this parish, but now of the city of Hereford, rector of Newchurch.

On the summit of the Little Mountain, at the eastern extremity of the parish, is an ancient encampment of an oblong form, or rather elliptical figure.

Ecclesiastical Account.

The church consists of a nave, a chancel, separated from the nave by a timber frame, a low tower containing three bells, and a porch. A timber frame terminates the tower.

This benefice is a discharged rectory, estimated in *Liber Regis* at £5 6s. 8d., but the total emoluments of the rector amount at present to the annual sum of £112 8s., including an estate purchased by Queen Anne's bounty, and called Cae-triggin. The church is dedicated to St. Mary.

HUNDRED OF RHAYADER.

This modern division of the county of Radnor takes its name from its principal town, Rhayader, and constitutes the largest and most important portion of that extensive territory which in ancient times was designated by the appellation of Cantref Moelynaidd, once the residence and property of the British *reguli* of this district, afterwards the acquisition and inheritance of the powerful barons of Wigmore and Marche, and lastly the royal patrimony and estate of the Kings of England. It is also the only modern division of the county which has preserved and transmitted the ancient name by which this territory was distinguished; for Rhaiadrgwy hundred is described as being *olim* Cantref Moelynaidd, as if it were more peculiarly included within it. It now forms the greater part of what is at present called the upper division of the county of Radnor, comprehending one borough and market town, one independent lordship, or hamlet, and six parishes, viz., Abbey Cwmhir, Cwmdauddwr, Llanfihangel-fach, or Helygen, Llanhir, Nantmêl, Rhaiadrgwy, and St. Harmon, and is situated within the cwmwd of Glyn Ieithon, and the mesne manor of Rhiw ar Allt. It is separated from the several hundreds of Knighton, Cefn-y-llys, and Colwyn, by the river Ieithon; and on the west it is bounded by the rivers Wye and Elan, which separate it from Brecknockshire; on the north by the parishes of Llangurig and Llanidloes, in the county of Montgomery.

This hundred constituted a portion of that extensive territory which, reaching from the river Wye to the Severn, once belonged to ancient *reguli* of this district, the Lords of Moelynaidd and Fferllys. The most eminent and illustrious of these was Ellistan Glodrudd, who, by virtue of his marriage with the grand-daughter and heiress of Tewdwr Trefor, became Earl of Fferleia, or Hereford, and possessed all the lands lying between the two before-mentioned rivers, and also Upper and Lower Gwent, in Monmouthshire. He was the first of all the native princes that established and confirmed his royal descent and pedigree from the ancient sovereigns of Britain. He was unfortunately slain at Cefn, or Mynydd Du-goll, in the county of Montgomery, where his barrow, or tumulus, remains to this day visible, in attempting to quell an insurrection, which event obviously suggests the following remark, viz., the wonderful coincidence between the death of the last *regulus* of this extensive territory, the greater and more important part of which quickly after fell under the dominion of the Saxons and Normans successively, and that of the last prince who swayed the sceptre of North Wales, immediately succeeded by the total annexation of his country to England; the one losing his life by the rebellion, and the other by the treachery, of their respective subjects. After the death of Ellistan, this hundred descended to his son Cadwgan, and from him to Ifor, Idnerth, Madoc, Cadwallon, the founder of Abbey Cwmhir, Maelgon, &c., successively. From this family it devolved upon the sons of Rhys ab Gruffudd,

Prince of South Wales, who erected the castle of Rhaiadrgwy, and endowed his abbey of Strata Florida with certain parcels of lands situated in the upper part of this hundred, and now denominated the Grainge of Cwmdauddwr. When the Princes of Wales became no longer able to protect their dominions from the never-ceasing encroachments of the rapacious Normans, and when the fate of war, and the direful effects of intestine broils, had extinguished the family of the *reguli* of this district, this hundred, together with the great and paramount lordship in which it is included, and whose name it still retains, became subject to the Earls of Marche and Wigmore, and at the accession of the heir and representative of that warlike and powerful house to the throne of England it merged in the crown, the King of Great Britain being the lord of the manor of Moelynaidd; so that this county, from the remotest era to the present period, has always remained a royal patrimony, and the tenure of its manor is the most honourable, being free soccage.

MONACHLOG, OR ABBEY CWMHIR.

This name signifies "the abbey situated in the long dingle." It is itself a hamlet included in the parish of Llanbister, and comprises two of the four townships of that parish, viz., Golon and Cefn-pawl, yet is totally independent of that parish, both in its civil and ecclesiastical jurisdiction, assessing its own rates, supporting its own poor, and maintaining its own minister. It appears therefore in all respects entitled to be considered as an independent and a distinct parish. The money raised by the parochial rates in the year 1803, in these two townships, was £185 18s. 6d., at 2s. 6d. in the pound on the rack rental; the resident population of them, according to the return made in the year 1801, was 400. They contain about 2500 acres, one half of which is under cultivation; and unite on the north-east with the parish of St. Harmon; with Llanano on the north; with Nantmêl on the south; and with Llanddewi-ystrad-Ennau on the south-east. These townships are diversified with hills and valleys, and abound in woods and fertile inclosures in a more copious proportion than most of the adjoining districts; thus clearly evincing the superior industry and improving culture of the monks, whose numerous groves of majestic oaks formed the grand and beautiful characteristic of their domains, while the gloomy recesses of a winding and watered valley inspired devotion. The dingle or vale of Cwmhir exactly corresponds with this description; for it is a delightful and fertile bottom, watered by the river Clywedoc, and is environed by an amphitheatre of hills of stupendous grandeur, clothed with wood.

South-west of the river Clywedoc stood the mill of the monastery; and contiguous to this appear the ruins of ancient dwellings. On the banks of the river are also vestiges of walls in several parts, together with a barrow, or tumulus, in the environs. The whole monastic establishment has evidently been defended by a strong mound, or intrenchment, crossing the valley abruptly at equal distances above and below, extending through the village, and inclosing a space of about ten acres, which perhaps comprized the ancient and usual privilege of sanctuary. On the summit of a stupendous hill on the north-east side of the abbey is a large excavation, out of which has been extracted the stone used in the construction of the old monastery. This has been called Fowler's Cave, and anciently formed a part of an extensive park, which tradition reports to have been seven miles in circumference, and stocked with upwards of 200 deer. One of the old gates and fragments of pales, together with the site of two deer-houses, remain still visible.

The authenticated history of this district may be traced to so early a period as the reign of Henry II., King of England, and his contemporary, Rhys, Prince of South Wales, and cousin-german of Cadwallon, the founder of Abbey Cwmhir. Hence it may justly be inferred that the lordship of Golon, with the dependent manors of Cwmhir and Dolelfeu, were the most extensive manorial properties in the county of Radnor, including in its wide circuit the township of Cefn-pawl, part of the parishes of Llanbadarn-fynydd, Llanbister, Llanddewi-ystrad-Ennau, Llanano, Nantmêl, and St. Harmon. In a certain part within this territory was contained the ancient manor of Gwrthrynion, whither the base Vortigern is supposed to have retired; and the whole of it once formed the property of the monks of Abbey Cwmhir. At the dissolution of the abbey, in 1546, these domains were conferred by King Henry VIII. on Walter Henley, Esq., in the county of Monmouth, and John Williams, *alias* Lord Cromwell, of Thame, in Oxfordshire, one of the Lords President of the Court of the Marches. Before the conclusion of the sixteenth century they came, either by marriage or by purchase, into the possession of an ancient and a respectable family of the name of Fowler, in the county of Stafford. Members of this family have served the office of high sheriff for the county several times, and represented it in Parliament many sessions. In the year 1600 Sir Richard Fowler, Bart., of Abbey Cwmhir was high sheriff. The same gentlemen was appointed to the same office in the year 1615. His son, Sir Richard Fowler, Bart., of Impton, in 1626. The same gentleman, of Abbey Cwmhir, was appointed to the same office in the year 1655. John Fowler, Esq., of Bronydre, in 1690. Sir Hans Fowler, Bart., of Abbey Cwmhir, served in the year 1765 the office of high sheriff for this county. In the year 1714 the representation of this county in Parliament was severely contested by Sir Richard Fowler, Bart., and Thomas Harley, Esq. Notwithstanding the latter gentleman had represented the county ever since the year 1698, and was backed by court interest, and had presented to the house a petition against the return, yet Sir Richard Fowler obtained a large majority of voices, and continued the sitting member. In the year 1722 a severe contest for the honour of representing this county was carried on between Sir Richard Fowler, Bart., and Sir Humphrey Howarth, Knt. A petition was presented to the house, and the latter gentleman declared duly elected. About the year 1760 one moiety of this great estate, including the manor of Golon, was alienated from the family of Fowler, and sold to Charles Gore, Esq., and afterwards purchased by the late John Price, Esq., banker, of Penybont, in this county. This gentleman had an only daughter and heiress, who by marriage conveyed this property to John Cheesement Severn, Esq. On the death of Sir Hans Fowler, Bart., who departed this life March 1st, 1771, leaving no male issue, the other moiety of this estate devolved on Thomas Hodges Fowler, Esq., descended from the female line. This gentleman also died without issue. This estate, therefore, by virtue of intermarriages, has recently become the property of the present Lord Hastings, Earl of Huntington.

One mile from the abbey stands Tu-faenor, or Manor House, a venerable mansion of the lordship, and where the court-leets are holden. This house is supposed to have been erected in the reign of James I., but recently repaired and modernized by J. C. Severn, Esq.

In the township of Cefn-pawl was a remarkably large fish-pond, which supplied the monks of Abbey Cwmhir with fish; it is now in a ruinous condition; and not far distant is a Roman causeway in a narrow defile, called Bwlch-y-sarnau. This causeway is part of the Roman road leading from Caer-fagu, a Roman station in the parish of Llanfihangel Helygen, Radnor, to Caersws, in the parish of Llandinam, Montgomery; thus opening a communication between the Silures and the Ordovices. Near it is a hill named Garn, the summit of which is crowned with a British carn.

Ecclesiastical Account.

The chapel of Abbey Cwmhir is situated on a bank of the river Clywedoc, about 140 paces to the north from the site where the venerable old monastery of Cwmhir once stood. It was erected in the year 1680, or, as some say, in the third year of the reign of Queen Anne, at the expense of Sir William Fowler, Bart., on a picturesque spot, where tradition reports the monks had a fish-pond, and endowed by that gentleman with a small charge imposed on each of his tenants within the two townships before-mentioned. It is dedicated, as the monastery was, to St. Mary, and consists of one aisle.

This benefice is a perpetual curacy, or chapelry, estimated in *Liber Regis* to be of the certified value of £4 10s. per annum, being the aggregate amount of the rate assessed upon the tenants. Having been augmented by several lots of Queen Anne's bounty, its total emoluments exceed at present the yearly sum of £50. Neither the incumbent of the chapel, nor even the vicar of Llanbister, are entitled to any portion of the tithes of this hamlet, all of which, having been originally annexed to the monastery, are now impropriate, and belong to the proprietor of Abbey Cwmhir, who is also patron of the chapel.

List of Incumbents.

Joshua Thomas............... 1736
Llewelyn Davis............... 1750
John Davis 1775

CWMDAUDDWR (LLANSANTFRAID).

This is the most western parish, not only in the hundred of Rhayader, but also in the county of Radnor, and derives its name from being situated between the two rivers Wye and Elan. It is bounded on the north by the parish of Llangurig and the county of Montgomery; on the east by the river Wye; on the south by the river Elan; and on the west by that river and the brook Clarwen. It consists of two townships, viz., the Grainge and the Parish. It is also designated by two other divisions, viz., Dyffryn-Wy and Dyffryn-Elan; that is, the vale of the Wye, and the vale of the Elan. The Grainge includes that portion of the parish with which Rhys, Prince of South Wales, endowed his newly founded Abbey of Strata Florida, in the county of Cardigan, and constitutes a royal manor, holden of the crown of England by Robert Peele, Esq., of Cwmelan, in this parish, at the gross rent of £6.

The principal landed proprietors of this parish are Robert Peele, Esq., of Cwmelan, Thomas Lewis Lloyd, Esq., of Nant-gwyllt, Hugh Powel Evans, Esq., of Noyadd, Thomas Prickard, Esq., of Dderw, David Oliver, Esq., of Rydoldog, —— Davis, Esq., of Gwardolau, &c. The Cwmelan estates were purchased of the late Thomas Johnes, Esq., some years ago, by Thomas Grove, Esq., a gentleman of the county of Somerset, amounting to 10,000 acres of land, called the Grainge of Cwmdauddwr.

Nant-gwyllt House was added to by the late Thomas Lewis Lloyd, Esq. It is a strong, commodious mansion of stone.

Noyadd, which signifies Hall, or Court, is situated in a delightful valley on the left bank of the Elan, and resembles in its construction the letter H.

Rhydoldog House was erected by the late Jeremiah Oliver, Esq., of the city of London.

In former times, as well as at present, this parish was distinguished by containing mines and minerals. At a place on the hills, about three miles west from the town of Rhayader, near the line of the old road that led to Aberystwyth, named Gwaith-y-mwynau, *i. e.*, the miners' works, great quantities of lead ore, impregnated with silver, were found in the reign of Charles I., which were melted and coined for the pay of the royal army; and recently a lead mine was worked at Cwmelan, by the late Thomas Grove, Esq., its proprietor.

The antiquities also of this parish are interesting; and the first that deserves our attention, as it was undoubtedly the first in construction, is the tommen or tumulus which at present is designated by the appellation of Tommen Llansantfraid, though not so originally; for there is ground for believing that its existence was prior to the age in which that saint lived, and that its primitive construction was druidical. Contiguous to it, and only divided by the road leading towards Noyadd, is a place named Bryn, with accumulations of earth adjoining. The word is often applied to signify a druidical court of judicature. The addition, however, to the Tommen, of a deep foss and a high rampart, made in a subsequent age, gives it the character of a military position, destined to defend and protect the adjoining cell of Dominicans, or Blackfriars, placed at the western foot of Rhayader bridge, as well as afterwards the church of St. Fraid, situated in front of it, and also the castle of Rhayader, to which it served as an outpost. The cell of the Dominicans, here mentioned, was suppressed in the thirty-first year of the reign of Henry VIII. Its temporal endowments are unknown. Contiguous to this cell, and on the right hand of the road leading to Aberystwyth, is another tumulus, or barrow, the summit of which is excavated.

On the top of the hill, not far distant from the turbary, is a huge stone, set erect in the ground, and having upon it the figure of a cross. It is supposed to be commemorative of the base assassination committed by the Flemings and Normans on Eineon Clyd, *regulus* of Elfael, brother of Cadwallon, *regulus* of Moelynaidd, on his return from Cardigan, where he had assisted in the celebration of the festivities and tournaments instituted by his father-in-law, Rhys, Prince of South Wales.

Near to Gwaith-y-mwynau there is a considerable tumulus, or barrow. The use and designation of this work may be collected from its local situation; for from thence may distinctly be seen the castle of Rhayader, to which fortress, therefore, it must have served as an outpost to give intelligence to the garrison of the approach of an enemy in a quarter from which most danger was to be apprehended, namely, from the Flemings and Normans, who had at that time over-run and possessed Cardiganshire.

Proceeding onwards from Abercython in a straight line parallel to the course of the Elan, and through a valley richly cultivated and picturesque, about three miles in a westerly direction, we arrive at Nant Madoc, where the ruins of Capel Madoc are at this day distinctly to be seen, near to which in ancient times a monastery stood. Among other temporalities, of which its endowment consisted, was an adjoining estate named Coed-y-mynach, or Monks' Wood, which supplied its inmates with fuel for culinary and other purposes. Frequent visits subsisted between them and the neighbouring monks, either for the purpose of their mutual peace and edification, or for consulting together on their temporal interests; and it is recorded that the inhabitants of this religious establishment were accustomed, on certain periodical seasons, to visit their brethren in the abbey of Strata Florida, in the county of Cardigan, marching over the hills in procession, and making the rocks re-echo their loud and chaunted hymns. Their road over the mountains may at this day be traced.

The next piece of antiquity that occurs in point of time is situated on the confines of this parish, where it comes in contact with Cardiganshire, at a place named Abernant-y-beddau. It consists of a huge stone set erect in the ground, and bearing upon it this inscription:—

"Mae tribedd tribedog
Ar Lannerch dirion feillionog,
Lle claddwyd y tri Chawr mawr
O Sir Frecheiniog
Owen, Milfyd, a Madog."

There are crown lands in this parish, holden by the prepositor, the gross annual rent of which is £4 16s. 8d. The tenths of the Grainge in this parish, belonging to the crown, are holden by Mrs. Margaret Lewis Lloyd, of Nant-gwyllt, at the gross annual rent of 2s. 6d.

Ecclesiastical Account.

The old church of this parish was built in the form of a barn—low, long, and dark. Its roof was covered with shingles. The present church, a neat and handsome structure, was erected in the year 1778.

This benefice is a discharged vicarage, estimated in *Liber Regis* to be of the clear yearly value of £25. The aggregate emoluments of the vicarage, arising from augmentation, composition for tithes, and surplice fees, amount at present to nearly £100 per annum. The tithes are divided between the prebendary and the vicar; but in the township of the Grainge the vicar enjoys only the third part. The parish register commences in the year 1678, and contains several articles written in Latin.

List of Incumbents.

Howel Price	1660	Hugh Edwards	1741
John Davies	1683	Thomas Edwards	1783
David Lewis	1724	—— Evans	
Morgan Richards	1741		

Charitable Donations.

In a year unknown, and whether by will or deed unknown, a rent-charge of £2 12s. per annum upon land, now vested in Mr. Evan Thomas, was bequeathed by John Davies, supposed to be the vicar collated in 1683, for the benefit of poor inhabitants of this parish who have attained the age of 50 years, and of such as are blind, dumb, and maimed.

In a year unknown, and whether by will or deed unknown, a rent-charge of £2 per annum upon land, now vested in Mr. Thomas Lewis, was bequeathed by Jeremiah Powell, for the benefit of the poor inhabitants of this parish.

About the year 1719, whether by will or deed unknown, a certain messuage called Llawryllan, and lands annexed, were given and devised by the Rev. Charles Price, vicar of Llanarth, in the county of Cardigan, in trust, to his heir-at-law, and to the vicars of Cwmdauddwr and Nantmêl for the time being, for the purpose of providing education for poor children of this parish, and for the preaching of five divinity sermons in the church of Cwmdauddwr on the first Sunday in May, and on the first Sunday of the four succeeding months, yearly. The school is kept in the town of Rhayader, by the sub-curate thereof, who is also master of the free school of Rhayader, and likewise vicar of this parish.

ST. HARMON.

The common appellation of this parish is St. Harmon, but the proper name is St. Garmon, the initial letter G being softened into H. The money raised for the service of the year 1803 amounted to the aggregate sum of £216, at 8s. 3d. in the pound. In each township the king's taxes are collected separately.

It contains three manors or lordships: viz., Clâs, which belongs to Perceval Lewis, Esq., of Downton; Rhiworiad, the hereditary right of the Prince of Wales, or of the crown of Great Britain, now leased by the Earl of Oxford; a small portion included in this belongs at present to J. C. Severn, Esq., of Penybont, but was formerly a part of the demesne of the ancient family of Fowler, of Abbey Cwmhir.

This parish contains numerous druidical relics, rude fortifications, and sepulchral memorials, such as distinguished the ancient inhabitants of Siluria. On the extreme point of an elevated hill, named the Garn, is a most perfect carn, accompanied with a stone chest, human bones, black earth, and other corresponding appendages. On Foel Howell is an ancient tumulus, the remains of the castle or sepulchre of Hywell ab Madoc, *regulus* of Moelynaidd. Moel Bryn contains three mounds, or barrows, probably seats of judicature in ancient times. Contiguous to Nant-y-Saeson is a single stone of huge dimensions, placed erect in the earth, and also two large and two small stones arranged quadrangularly, named " Dau fraich, a dau law," that is, the two arms and the two hands, near to a place called Hendrew. On the verge of the common named "Waun Marteg," and near to the river of that name, are three tumuli, placed in a triangular position. On the Cnuch estate is a tumulus called Crygin; and near to a farm-house named Pen-y-pistill is another, of much larger dimensions, named Cae Crygin; and near to a farm-house called Nantserth-ucha, that is, the upper steep brook, is a third tumulus, named Crygin Sero. Many of these barrows are placed in so direct a line of position as to be visible from each other, and therefore in ancient times they may have been rendered subservient to vigilatory purposes, and for spreading intelligence through the country, and not used as sepulchral memorials of the illustrious dead, as is generally supposed by the commonalty of these parts. The greater part of them appear to have been military, and constructed for the defence of the country.

On the moor which divides the parishes of St. Harmon and Llangurig, or that separates the county of Radnor from that of Montgomery, was slain, in one of those violent and bloody commotions which too often agitated the ancient inhabitants of Wales, and contributed to ruin the country and destroy its independence, Gwynne, the brave son of Llewelyn ab Iorwerth, Prince of North Wales.

There is also, on the bank of the river Marteg, at the eastern extremity of the parish, near to the confines of the parish of Llanbister, a remarkable and conspicuous tumulus named Bedd Garmon, *i. e.*, the grave of Garmon, where perhaps the tutelary saint of this parish, or of some person of that name of distinguished note, lies interred. Probability favours the former supposition, as tradition has transmitted an account that St. Garmon had an hermitage adjoining to the church-yard of this parish.

About 150 years ago, so universal was the use of the Welsh language in the county of Radnor, and so superior its purity in so recent a period as the life-time of the late Lewis Morris, Esq.—a most competent judge—that is, in the year 1747, that in all its churches Divine Service was performed in that tongue alone. So great a revolution has since taken place, that the church of St. Harmon, situated in a remote and sequestered corner of the county, the inhabitants of which have little or no direct intercourse with England, remains in the present day the only one in which Christian worship is celebrated, and religious instruction dispensed, in the aboriginal language of Britain. But even here it is in a rapidly declining state; and the English tongue, now almost become the prevailing medium of oral and epistolary communication, threatens its radical abolition.

The numerous cottages which of late years have been

erected on the wastes indicate an increase of population in this parish. According to the return published in the year 1801, it consisted of 661 individuals.

Ecclesiastical Account.

The church of St. Harmon is situated on the right bank of the river Marteg, nearly in the centre of the parish. It consists of a nave, chancel, porch, and a low turret containing one small bell. The whole edifice is in a very dilapidated state. The old church, like all other old churches in Wales, was built in a barn-like fashion—low, long, and dark. Its antique appearance gave some colour to the tradition that it was coeval with the saint to which it was dedicated. Some years ago, when Chase Price, Esq., was candidate for the representation of this county in Parliament, its ruinous condition rendered its reduction in size necessary. But the temporary relief which this measure gave has ceased, and the whole fabric requires to be taken down and rebuilt from the foundation.

The ancient inhabitants of this parish were distinguished, among other qualities, by a grateful remembrance of their sanctified benefactors. For, besides their care in perpetuating the name of their patron saint by making it the appellation of their parish, they preserved in their church, with holy reverence, the pastoral staff, or crook, of St. Gurig, which, in those days of simplicity and superstition, possessed the much prized virtue of curing most of the diseases incident to the human constitution. This venerated relic was committed to the devouring flames at the time when the heretical reformation of the errors and corruptions of Popery took place in this kingdom.

This benefice is a discharged vicarage, estimated in *Liber Regis* to be of the clear yearly value of £5 15s. 2½d.

The prebendary of St. Harmon, in the Collegiate Church of Brecknock, is stated in *Liber Regis* to be of the yearly value of £3 17s. 3½d. The yearly tenths are 7s. 8½d. This prebendary, or sinecure, was sequestrated or abolished by the republican fanatics in the year 1649.

A few years ago was established a Methodistical conventicle; also, a chapel of the Baptist persuasion was erected at a place named Nant-gwin. These dissenters from the Established Church are not supposed to be on the increase.

List of Incumbents.

William Jones, ejected by the parliamentary commissioners, and the benefice sequestrated, 1649

Robert Lewis 1739   John Dyer, A.M............... 1785
Llewelyn Davis................ 1745   Timothy Davies 1786
John Lewis 1774   Evan Powell 1793

Charitable Donations.

James Edward Morris bequeathed at a time unknown, and whether by will or deed unknown, a sum of money, the gross amount of which is £10, for the relief of decayed labourers not chargeable to the parish.

Another account says that the yearly interest of £10, left by James ab Edward, supposed to be the same with James Edward Morris, is yearly distributed by Evan Edwards and the churchwardens.

In the year 1781 Mr. Evan Davies, of Sychnant, in this parish, bequeathed by will a legacy of the gross amount of £20, for the benefit of poor and

HISTORY OF RADNORSHIRE. 241

decayed labourers not chargeable to the parish. Both these pecuniary bequests are at present vested in Mr. David Davies.

A small estate in this parish, named Penbedw, was bequeathed by Lady Hartstronge, relict of Sir Standish Hartstronge, Bart., about the year 1702, for the purpose of endowing a free school in the parish of Llanelweth, in this county.

LLANFIHANGEL-FACH, OR HELYGEN.

This name signifies the parish of St. Michael the Less, or the parish of St Michael abounding in willows. One of the most interesting vestiges of antiquity by which this county is distinguished occupies a situation in this parish. A Roman station, containing a Roman cohort of soldiers, commanded by a prefect, established and fortified on the left bank of the river Ieithon, in this parish, and not in the adjoining parish of Llanhir, as some have erroneously supposed, became in process of time a large and populous place, surrounded to a considerable extent with buildings erected by the natives, who had intermixed with the new colony, and assimilated their manners to those of their conquerors. This celebrated station, which by the Romans was named Magos, but Caerfagu by the Silures, Camden, through error of judgment, fixed at Old Radnor, and other antiquaries, with as little foundation for their conjectures, at other places. But if coincidence of distances, identity of name, and many other concurring circumstances, have any weight in determining questions of this kind, this fortified mansion, commanding the line of the Ieithon and the adjoining country, must appear to the mind of every impartial investigator as having juster claims and stronger pretensions to be considered the very spot on which the Roman governors of Britain constructed the Silurian Magos, and facilitated its communication with their other numerous stations in Britannia Secunda by the formation of roads. Two of these immediately communicated with the river Wye, one at Llechrhyd, in the parish of Llanhir, in this county, and the other at a place in the parish of Clyro, opposite to the town of Hay. Another road passed by the church of Llanbadarn-fawr, leaving the village of Penybont on the right, and, intersecting the country in

2 I

a line parallel with the river Clywedoc, proceeded by Bwlch-cefn-din, near to a farm-house called Cwmtelmau, where it communicated with Gaer, in Llanddewi parish, by Abbey Cwmhir, through Bwlch-y-sarnau, that is, the defile or pass in the Roman road, and so on in a straight line to the river Severn, opposite Caersws, in the county of Montgomery.

According to the return made of its resident population in the year 1801 the number of its inhabitants was 102. The money raised by the several parochial assessments for the service of the year 1803 amounted to the sum of £24 0s. 2d., at 2s. 6d. in the pound.

Ecclesiastical Account.

The church is dedicated to St. Michael, whose memory is little honoured in the meanness of its structure, and in its total want of those appendages of accommodation generally found in places set apart for religious worship. For this has no baptismal font, nor pulpit, nor ground dedicated to funeral rites. The children born in the parish are obliged to be conveyed to the churches of Nantmêl and Llanhir, at a considerable distance, to receive the sacrament of baptism, whither the dead are also transported for Christian burial. With respect to the other sacrament of our holy religion, the total neglect of its administration is connived at here, because there is no communion-table. And yet the non-payment of tithes is not connived at, but rigidly enforced. This benefice is a perpetual curacy, annexed to the vicarage of Nantmêl.

List of Incumbents.

Evan Lewis	1702	Hugh Price	1762
Thomas Jones	1758	Daniel Williams	1805

LLANHIR.

The signification of this name, written as above, is the Long Church, or Parish. This parish contains two townships, viz., Cil Ci, that is, the Retreat of the Dog; and Traws Coed, that is, Across the Wood.

The inhabitants possess a right of depasturing their cattle, sheep, &c., on the common of Llandrindod; and they have hitherto resisted every application for joining in a petition to Parliament for leave to inclose their commons and waste lands.

The parochial assessments raised in the two townships of this parish are collected separately and distinctly, and the aggregate amount of them for 1803 was £200 17s. 8d., at 8s. in the pound. According to the return made of its resident population in the year 1801 the number of its inhabitants consisted of 519 individuals. Since this period its population seems to be on the increase.

The property in this parish which Howel ab Cadwallon granted to the monks of Abbey Cwmhir, in this county, for the purpose of endowing a chantry, and for the providing of lights, consisted of four acres of land, and was called Ryllerhôs, or Kyllerrhôs.

There is also in this property, belonging to the crown, a messuage and garden, leased by the late Hon. and Rev. Dr. Harley, Bishop of Hereford, and now by his representative, at the gross annual rent of 3s. 4d. In the year 1784, this rent was nine years in arrears.

Ecclesiastical Account.

The church is a humble structure, consisting of a nave, chancel, and low tower, and is dedicated to All Saints.

This benefice is a perpetual curacy, not in charge, annexed to the vicarage of Nantmêl, estimated in *Liber Regis* to be of the certified yearly value of £22. The tithes are equally divided between the Chapter and Chanter of St. David's, and the vicar of Nantmêl. The total emoluments of this curacy amount at present to the annual sum of £71.

List of Incumbents.

Evan Lewis 1702
Hugh Price.................... 1755
H. P., recollated.............. 1762
William Williams 1782
John Williams 1804

Charitable Donations.

In 1718 Mr. John Davis left a rent-charge of £2 upon certain lands, sometime vested in the late Rev. Thomas Jones, to be distributed among the poor inhabitants of this parish.

In a year unknown Messrs. Morris Owen, and Rees Price, left by will a rent-charge of £2 10s. upon certain lands called Garreg, now vested in Richard Price, for the benefit of the poor inhabitants of this parish. This money was regularly distributed till a few years ago. John Price, in whom it was then vested, retarded the payment of the same, and it has been detained ever since.

NANTMEL.

This parish is bounded on the north by the parish of St. Harmon and hamlet of Abbey Cwmhir; by the parishes of Llanfihangel Helygon and Llanhir on the south; by the river Wye and the borough of Rhayader on the west; and by the parishes of Llanbadarn-fawr and Llanddewi-ystrad-Ennau on the east. It is a large parish, extending in length eight miles, and five in breadth, and contains four townships, viz., Coed-glasson, or the green groves; Faenor, or the summit; Maesgwyn, or the white field; and Cwys-tudin, or the furrow of Tudwen. Each of these collect their assessed taxes separately and distinctly, the aggregate amount of which, for the service of the year 1803, was £469. 14s. 5½d., at 6s. 8d. in the pound. It is calculated that about two-thirds are inclosed and cultivated.

The chief mansion-house is Llanbarried.

The vestiges of antiquity that still exist in this parish are numerous and interesting. And as the hill of Cwystudin contains more relics of this description than any other spot of equal dimensions within the parish, it is just that the signification of its name be first settled and defined, before its ancient vestiges be described. This appears the more necessary from the erroneous explanation assigned to it in a work of great popularity, viz., Mr. Carlile's *Topographical Dictionary of Wales*, article, " Nantmêl," where it is printed " Gwastadedd." Now this word signifies a plain; whereas the thing itself is a hill, surpassed, indeed, in height and dimensions by many hills in Wales, but on each side sufficiently precipitous to distinguish it from a plain, or level territory. Besides, to interpret the name of this hill by Gwastadedd violates analogy; for the configuration of the hill resembles an immense furrow turned up by the plough. The current name in the neighbourhood is not Gwastadedd, but Cwystudin; and it is evident that its etymology consists of Cwys, a furrow, and Tudwen, the saint of that name. On the summit and on the sides of the hill are to be seen to this day vestiges of furrows; and there is on this hill, a little to the west of a farm-house named Skyrrhiw, a particular place, now known by the appellation Cwystudwen, having traces of several furrows, and of some buildings, where it is probable this agricultural saint had his dwelling and residence, and which gave name to the hill. Whence it may justly be concluded that Cwystudwen is the real name of the hill, and that its true signification is the furrow of Tudwen.

Near to the above-mentioned place, Cwystudwen, are two remarkable carns, named Carnwen, and Carnfach, that is, the white and the little carn, each being of an elliptical form, and having in the centre an erect stone of superior magnitude. These relics have been much disfigured and altered from their original formation by the spoliations of lazy and avaricious farmers, who have removed many of the stones of which they were composed for the purposes of building, and of road repairing, &c.

On the eastern extremity of this hill, and on a farm named Gifron, is a place which the common people distinguish by the appellation Gwar-y-beddau, that is, the ridge of graves; it consists of three mounds, or elevations, in which tradition reports three brothers, who, returning from the wars, quarrelled, fought, and fell by each others' swords, were interred. It is impossible at this remote period to ascertain the names or the rank of these near relatives; but it is evident from these sepulchral memorials, and other circumstances, that they were of considerable note and distinction. In the adjoining turbary there was found, some years ago, a human skull, having its full complement of hair; probably the preservation of the hair was owing to the astringency of the peat water.

But it is on the central summit of this hill that the most remarkable and interesting vestige of antiquity is placed, and which hitherto has escaped the notice of all preceding antiquaries. On the south side stands a farm-house, at present of mean appearance, but which was of considerable note in former times, as its name, Bwlch-y-llys, or the defile leading to the palace or court, implies; and tradition reports it to have been the residence of the *regulus* of this district, and also to have been occasionally occupied by some of the Princes of Wales. No vestige, however, of its ancient grandeur now remains. The whole of its magnificence is confined to the north side, where, in a direct line from the defile, is to be seen the site of the royal palace, or court of judicature. These ruins consist of seven or more large heaps of quarried stones, arranged east and west, and placed in positions opposite to each other. There can be little doubt of this place having once been a court of judicature, instituted probably as early as the druidical times.

Along one side of the lake Llyngwin there is an elevation of ground resembling an embankment, of a semicircular form. For what purpose this was done cannot now be ascertained. Tradition says that in former times there stood a town in this place.

A little to the east of the mansion of Llanbarried is a farm-house named Gwylfa, being a vigilatory appendage to the Roman camp upon the Ieithon, in the parish of Llanfihangel Helygen, and commanding a distinct and extensive view of the adjoining country. And on the left hand of the turnpike-road leading from the town of Rhayader to Nantmêl Church, between Hendre and Dolau, there is a farm-house named Tafarn-eithin. This is supposed to have been the Taberna of the Roman garrison of the camp above-mentioned, and the work around Llyngwin to have constituted their baths.

On the bank of the rivulet Rhydtîr, at a small distance east from the town of Rhayader, whither it is supposed the town formerly extended, and where a church, as tradition reports, once stood upon an adjoining piece of ground named Clytiau, or Pant-yr-Eglwys, that is, the church-yard, is a solitary tumulus, or barrow, destitute of a moat or vallum, and consequently sepulchral. It is named Cefn-Ceidio, which signifies the ridge of Ceidio, who was a Welsh saint that lived about the middle of the fifth century.

Many of the hills in this parish are crowned with British encampments. Many old houses also still retain the appellation of " castles," as Castell-mawr, Castell-newydd, &c., having each in their vicinity a tommen, or tumulus, moated round, or intrenched, and therefore military ; from which circumstance is derived their title to the denomination of " Castell."

The inhabitants of this parish speak the two living languages of this island, though the use of the aboriginal tongue is rapidly declining, Divine Service in the church being performed entirely in English.

Ecclesiastical Account.

The church of Nantmêl is situated nearly in the centre of the parish. This benefice is a vicarage, remaining in charge, and having annexed to it the chapel of Llanhir. It is estimated in *Liber Regis* at £11 17s. 6d. per annum The yearly tenths are £1 3s. 9d. The Bishop of St. David's is the patron. The tithes are equally divided between the Chapter and Chanter of St. David's and the vicar. The present lessee is Hans Busk, Esq.; they are worth £400 per annum. This benefice was sequestrated by the parliamentary commissioners in the year 1649.

List of Incumbents.

Evan Lewis was instituted by Gul. Clement, Surrog. Archiep. Cant., 1702.
Hugh Price, recollated 1762 1755
William Williams 1782
John Williams 1804
William Henson 1818
J. B. Byers ....
Richard Venables...............

Charitable Donations.

In the year 1718 Mr. John Davies devised by will the annual sum of £2, secured upon land, and now vested in Mr. John Griffiths, for the benefit of the poor of this parish.

In the year 1718 Mr. Hugh Phillips, of Pen-y-ffynnon, devised by will the sum of £5 per annum, secured upon land, and vested in the late David Stephens, Esq., and now in his representatives, for the poor of this parish. We are informed that the will specifies that this sum left to the poor of this parish from Pen-y-ffynnon estate should be distributed at the discretion of the minister and churchwardens; but the person in whom it is now vested evades that part of the will, and takes upon himself, or at least pretends to, the distribution of the same.

RHAYADER, OR RHAIADRGWY.

The town of Rhayader contains four streets, intersecting each other at right angles, and pointing nearly to the four cardinal points. Though in this respect the form of this town bears some resemblance to a Roman camp, and though much fortification, exclusive of the castle and its appendages, surrounds the place, yet there are no grounds for believing that it was ever possessed by the Romans, the river Ieithon being the boundary of their progress in this district.

This town is a distinct and independent parish of itself, exempt from *county rates*, maintaining its own poor, and having a resident population of nearly 400 persons. The money assessed and raised by the parish rates amounts upon an average to £160 per annum. It contains a grammar school, and an endowment of about £12 per annum for the education of a limited number of poor children. The school-house, which stands on the confines of the church-yard towards the east, was erected by subscription in the year 1793. The Rev. Mr. Evans, sub-curate of Rhayader, is the present master.

The Town-hall, which is a handsome, modern, square building, strengthened at both ends, east and west, by a strong work of stone masonry, and having two commodious rooms above, supported by arches resting on massy oak pillars, is situated in the centre of the town, and was erected in the year 1762, by subscription. The east and west ends have each a circular arch of stone work, and over the former is affixed a sun-dial, made by that celebrated arithmetician, the Rev. Llewelyn Davies, vicar of St. Harmon. The bridge over the Wye was erected in the year 1780.

It is impossible now to ascertain the era in which Rhayader began to be a distinct town. It probably existed as such long prior to the Norman conquest. The vestiges of antiquity, in which its vicinity abounds, refer the population of the district in which it is included to a much earlier age, even to the druidical times. Tradition reports that the ancient town far exceeded the present one in magnitude, and that its precincts extended to Cefn-ceidio on the east, to Felin-drê on the south, and in the same proportion on the two remaining points; and that the avenues, now denominated lanes, were once inhabited streets. However this may be, it is certain, that the place was ever considered by the Princes of Wales, and by their enemies, as of great importance, the object of frequent contests, and made the victim both of intestine and of foreign hostilities. Rhys, Prince of South Wales, with his civil and military officers, and his army, consisting of at least between five and six thousand men, encamped here for several days; whilst the Prince, in the most solemn manner, in the church of Rhayader, in the presence of a numerous assemblage of spectators, among whom were the chieftains of the district, confirmed the several grants with which he had endowed his newly-founded abbey of Strata Florida, in Cardiganshire. This fact renders the circumstance probable that the adjoining country, in order to be capable of furnishing subsistence to so great a multitude of people, was far better cultivated, and more fertile, than it is at present; and also, that the houses of the town were more numerous and more respectable, to be able to provide suitable accommodation for visitors of the first distinction.

In the year 1340 this town was the property of Roger Mortimer, Earl of Wigmore and Marche, and remained, with little interruption, in the possession of that family, until the accession of Edward, Duke of York, to the throne of England, when it became, together with the rest of Cantref Moelynaidd, a part of the patrimonial inheritance of the crown of these realms.

From the desolating effects of the hostile irruption made by Owen Glyndwrdwy into this district, this town suffered severely, as well as by the oppressive and barbarous edicts issued by Henry IV., consequent upon that irruption. These violent and impolitic measures retained it long under the pressure of poverty, mitigated by the sunshine of royal favour in the reign of the first English monarch of the race of Tudor, and entirely dissipated under the auspices of his son and successor. For here both the county court and the court of great sessions were holden. The hall, or court of judicature, was situated at Pen-y-porth, on the bank which overlooks the bridge over the Wye, and the structure on the opposite side of the street, now the Presbyterian meeting-house, was the gaol or prison. The iron rings and chains which bound the prisoners, and iron bars which secured the windows, remain to this day. The place for the execution of convicts was on the north end of the town, near a house known by the name Pen-y-maes.

This gleam of sunshine was of short duration. A disastrous event happened which deprived the town of Rhayader for ever of this distinguished privilege. A

2 K

Cardiganshire banditti, composed of disbanded soldiers, had long concealed themselves in an inaccessible cavern near where the Devil's Bridge now stands. From hence they sallied out, imposed contributions on the adjoining country, and to their depredations sometimes joined the occasional effusion of human blood. They were distinguished by the name of Plant Mat, or the children of Mat. Leaving their lurking-place in the obscurity of the night, and having arrived on the right bank of the Wye, they waited their opportunity, safely concealed in a thick grove of oaks which grew on an estate named Dderw, in the parish of Cwmdauddwr Llansantfraid; where, being informed by their spy that the judge would repair at a certain hour on the ensuing morning to the church of Rhayader, previous to his entering on the business of the sessions, they sallied forth, crossed the river at Waun-y-capel, met him on Maes-bach, fired their pieces, and shot the venerable man through the heart. During the moments of amazement, with which the suddenness of this transaction overwhelmed the attendants, the villains were able to effect their escape, and returned over the hills to the cavern. The whole country soon rose against them; the murderers were besieged in their rocky den, and, after a desperate resistance, taken, and executed. After this it was ordered by Parliament that the court of great sessions should be removed to Presteigne, where the county court was also henceforward to be holden, alternately with New Radnor.

Rhayader, having contributed both men and money to the support of the royal cause of Charles I., was denounced by the parliamentarians as malignant, and they ordered a court of inquisition to be holden here by commission, for investigating and confiscating the patrimonial inheritance of Charles Stuart, &c. The meadow lands named Gwirglodd, adjoining this town, and situated within the precincts of the borough, together with the town mill, had been previously alienated by James I., who had given or sold this property to —— Lloyd, Esq., of Dôl-goch, in the parish of Cwmdauddwr. At present,

HISTORY OF RADNORSHIRE. 251

Rhayader is a considerable market-town and place of trade, and in it a woollen manufactory has for some years been established.

Rhayader Castle.

This fortress, which in ancient times conferred on the town of Rhayader no inconsiderable degree of importance, and was an object of much contention, advantageously stood on a nook of the river Wye, a very little above the place where the present stone bridge is erected, at the extremity of Maes-bach, or the little common. Of the superstructure no vestige at present remains. Many large stones, the foundations of its walls, the author of this work remembers to have seen on the spot. The rest had been conveyed thence, time immemorial, for purposes now unknown. But the original foundation of the castle may still be traced. The only entrance at present, which preserves a communication with it, is a narrow space on the north-east, between two deep trenches cut out of an exceedingly solid schistous rock; the one trench leads to the river towards the north, the other is more inclined to the east. Along the south foundation runs a foss, about 16 feet deep and 12 feet wide, until it communicates with a steep precipice, whence issues a spring that formerly supplied the garrison, and now the inhabitants of the town, with most excellent water. The bottom of the precipice runs parallel with the bed of the river. These three trenches form three sides of a hexagon, the very figure in which this fortress was constructed. The several tumuli, or barrows, situated in the vicinity of the castle, at irregular distances, have been already enumerated; excepting perhaps one which stands on the brow of the hill to the west, which overlooks the town, and which served as a vigilatory post to communicate to the garrison intelligence of the approach of an enemy. The particular situation of this outwork, and indeed of the fortifications of the town, which extended from the northern bank of the river Wye to its southern, having the castle and the other tumuli in the centre of the line westward, and leaving its eastern side totally unguarded, sufficently explains the reasons which demanded their construction, and clearly indicates the enemy against whom they were intended to guard. The depredations and cruelties committed by the Normans and Flemings who had settled themselves on the sea-coasts of the counties of Pembroke and Cardigan, and the horrid murder which they perpetrated on Eineon Clyd and Morgan ab Meredudd on the hills of Cwmdauddwr, as these *reguli* were peaceably and unsuspiciously returning from Aberteifi, rendered a precaution of this kind absolutely necessary. Influenced by these considerations, Rhys, Prince of South Wales, constructed this castle, for repelling such sanguinary incursions. Eventually, the fortress stood him in a double stead; the fidelity of its garrison, and the strength of its works, serving to counteract the machinations of his personal enemies and competitors. For it was no sooner completed than the sons of Conan, who himself was the illegitimate offspring of Owen Gwynedd, Prince of North Wales, envying the glory and prosperity of Rhys, marched with united forces, and attacked this his favourite castle; but after having lain before it a considerable length of time, they raised the siege, (A.D. 1178,) and returned into their own country, stung with disappointment.

Giraldus Cambrensis relates, in his *Itinerary of Wales*, an extraordinary occurrence to have happened in the castle of Rhayader. (A.D. 1188.) A certain delinquent was imprisoned in this fortress. His wife, anxious for his liberation, found means secretly to convey to him a portable bell, which, as the avaricious and imposing monks informed her, possessed the wonderful efficacy of liberating prisoners from confinement. The governor of the castle, true to his trust, and in equal defiance of monkish indignation and of this alleged virtue, refused to liberate his prisoner, or even to restore the magical bell; upon which, as this historical divine gravely adds, both the town and the castle of Rhayader, excepting only the fortunate wall on which the bell had been suspended, was by divine vengeance in one night consumed by lightning.

We hear no more of the castle of Rhayader for the space of nearly seven years, when the fury of civil war instigated unparalleled enormities, and a most unnatural conspiracy broke out amongst the sons of Prince Rhys, who imprisoned their aged father, and took and burned to the ground this his favourite fortress. Recovering his liberty, and knowing the importance of having a fortified station in this place, which in a manner commanded the communication between North and South Wales, the prince ordered it to be reconstructed and regarrisoned. (A.D. 1194.) It was afterwards consigned to the care of Cadwallon ab Madoc, *regulus* of Moelynaidd and Cerri, who zealously supported his country's cause, and manfully opposed the encroachments of the ambitious house of Mortimer. He fought several severe battles, and was at length defeated and imprisoned through the treachery of his brothers, whom the English had seduced to favour their interests. Having recovered his liberty and his property, chiefly by the mediation of Prince Rhys, he soon died, (A.D. 1230,) and his possessions in Moelynaidd and Cerri were distributed, conformably to the laws of gavelkind, among his children, whom, disunited among themselves, and abandoned by the Princes of Wales, Roger Mortimer, Earl of Wigmore, dispossessed of all their estates in this county. From this period the castle and town of Rhayadergwy became the property of the family of Mortimer. Soon after this event, Llewelyn ab Iorwerth, Prince of North Wales, having defeated Hubert de Burgh, the general of Henry III., and compelled him to retire from Wales, destroyed most of the Norman castles constructed in the Marches, and leading his victorious army to this district, he laid siege to the castle of Rhayader, which he took by assault and burned to the ground, and put the whole garrison of Mortimer to the sword.

Historians are silent whether this castle recovered itself from the effects of this complete catastrophe. This silence militates against the supposition of its restoration to its former splendour and importance. For had it existed during the hostile and furious incursion which Owen

Glyndwrdwy made into this district, then in subjection to the family of Mortimer, some notice would have been taken of it; nor would that bold chieftain, when he marched hence to the gates of Worcester, have left a place of this consequence in his rear, and in the hands of his enemy.

The site on which the old castle stood merged to the crown at the accession of Edward IV. to the throne of England, and is, or ought to be, vested in the Earl of Oxford.

Borough.

Rhayadergwy is an ancient borough by prescription, governed by a bailiff, who is annually elected. Here are holden a court-leet, and a court-baron, at the former of which the burgesses are elected by the town jury. The rights, privileges, customs, boundaries, and extents of this borough, it is thought best to express in the words of the several presentments of these two courts, copies of which are as follow :—

A Court-Leet was holden in the Borough of Rhayader, on the second day of May, in the twelfth year of Charles I., (A.D. 1637,) before Charles Price, Esq., the Deputy Steward of Philip, Earl of Pembroke and Montgomery, the jurors whereof presented and declared,—

I.—That a herriot of two shillings is due to the King's Majesty upon the decease of every tenant dying seized of any messuage, tenement, or lands within the said borough or liberties thereof; and that the like sum of two shillings is due upon alienation of any messuages, tenements, or lands, upon any person or persons within the said borough or liberties thereof, and no more.

II.—That the bailiff of the said borough was accustomed to be elected at His Majesty's leet holden for the said borough after Michaelmas yearly, either out of the residing or foreign burgesses, provided that if a foreign burgess be to be elected, then it is requisite and agreeable to the custom there used that he be residing within the said borough upon the Michaelmas-night next before the said leet, together with his wife, and necessary household stuff, as pot, pan, cat and dog, else not to be admitted to the office.

III.—That the bailiff for the time being, at the leet aforesaid, is to present to the stewards of the same sitting in court, the names of two such of the burgesses as are in election besides himself, with the names of such other of the burgesses as approve the same, out of which choice the said stewards in court are to make election of any one of them to be bailiff, if there be no cross return put in by other of the burgesses for the election of another; and if there be, then the bailiff is to be elected by the major voice of the burgesses, wherein no foreign burgesses have a voice, except they be then resident.

IV.—That the office of bailiff doth partly consist in gathering and accounting for His Majesty's use all such rents, fines, and amerciaments of courts-leet and courts-baron, waifs, estrays, and other forfeitures happening and falling due, and to be found within the said borough and liberties thereof; and to answer and pay the same at His Majesty's receipt, when as he shall be required; in respect whereof the said bailiff is entitled to a fee called merements.
V.—That burgesses be elected when occasion shall require with the steward's approbation by the homage of the residing burgesses at the court-leet, wherein no foreign burgess hath voice to elect or oppose, unless he be residing in town at Michaelmas-night. And in case another burgess doth oppose, then it is requisite by the said custom, that such oppositioner be then in person present, seconded with two such other voices more to oppose the same, or in default thereof, he is himself to produce two more to be present at the next court-baron there to be holden, to oppose the same; else the first election to stand, and the persons elected to be admitted and sworn.

Jurors.

Ludovice Evans, Gent.
Ricdus David Lloyd, Gent.
Evan Joseph.
David ab Evan ab Howell.
Evan ab Hugh.
Johes. Evans.

David ab Evan Mill$^{r.}$
Ludovice ab Howell.
Rice David Faber.
Rice Da^d ab Richard, Junr.
Johannes Thomas.
Edmund ab Hugh.

Johnes Jenkins, Constable.

At a Court of Jury holden for the Manor and Borough of Rhayader, the following presentments declarative of its rights and ancient customs, and in answer to several articles demanded by the States and Commons of England, in relation to the right and property due to the late King and his progenitors of and from the said Manor and Borough, holden the twenty-ninth of November, 1649, before Henry Makepence, John Marriott, Peter Price, and John Lloyd, Esquires,—

I.—The said manor and borough in length, and breadth, and compass, extends from a place called Llidiard-fawr northward to a gate called Llidiard Cae James; thence to a brook called Caeminod eastward; thence along that river called Wye to a place called Llidiard-yr-hendrè westward; and so along that gate to the said Llidiard-fawr northward; and that the late king and his progenitors were lords thereof.

II.—That the freeholders and their tenants hold their services by holding of suit to the court-leet and court-baron, and paying of herriot, together with one hundred shillings chief rent, and that is to be paid by the bailiff for the time being at the audit or receipt next after Michaelmas, and that yearly, to the use of the late king, and now consequently to the states and commons of England.

III.—That the freeholders and their tenants by their rents and services are so entitled in the commons called Maes-y-drè, and Maes-bach, as purtenances to their freeholds, so that they have had, and still have, power to give leave to poor people that want habitation to build upon the same, and to inclose any part of the said commons at their pleasure.

IV.—That John Lloyd, of Dôl, Gent., deceased, did purchase in fee-farm his heirs and assigns for ever, one mill and meadow, Gwirglodd-fawr, and certain other lands within this manor or borough, of King James I., about the first year of his reign, reserving yearly rent to the crown, and that the same is in possession of Eleanor Lloyd, his widow, and her tenants.

V.—This confirms the herriots due upon decease and alienation, and declares the toll of the market to belong to Sir Edmund Sawyer, and that Howell Jones, Esq., is his agent and his under-farmer, to gather the same.
VI.—No copyholders within this manor or borough.
VII.—Courts-leet holden twice a year, viz., within a month of Easter, and within a month of Michaelmas. The court-baron every three weeks. The court-leet to be holden by steward and bailiff, and any thirteen men or more of the freeholders, tenants, and burgesses, to inquire and present their ancient customs within this manor or borough in behalf of the lord and themselves. And the court-baron is to be holden by bailiff and steward, and served by the burgesses, freeholders, and tenants, to serve as jurors betwixt party and party, and that to the number of six men being then sworn. And that the freehold lands are holden in fee-soccage-tenure under the last king, being lord of the said manor and borough, as under his manor of Greenwich. And that the bailiff's fee is called merements, a farthing for pitching every market-day, and a penny every fair-day for pitching; and that there are two markets every week, viz., every Wednesday and Saturday; and one fair on the twenty-third of November; and three days of meeting, or fair-days, on the twenty-sixth of July, fifteenth of August, and sixteenth of September, yearly.
VIII.—That Lewis ab Hugh alienated one messuage, one close and garden, with a little house and piece of ground thereunto, belonging to Hugh Powell, Gent., for which a herriot of two shillings is due.
IX.—That the late king granted to the freeholders and tenants within the same manor or borough, belonging to the lordship of Moelynaidd and Gwerthrynion, of which this manor is a member, a charter under the great seal of England. The records and customs of the court-leet and court-baron are kept by James Price, Esq., of Pilleth.
X.—No works due on the freeholders and tenants within the said manor or borough, but touching the rents and services before-mentioned.
XI.—That there is a church within this manor or borough, which is a chapel belonging to Nantmêl; that the parson's part is sequestrated by the committee of sequestrations; that Robert Powell, an orthodox divine, the present incumbent, doth hold the same by the approbation of the Assembly of Divines, and the Great Seal of England; that the tenth of all the town hay is paid, lambs, wool, and cheese to the said parson or vicar, the same to be equally divided between them, and the same tithe is set out yearly for fifty shillings.

Jurors.

Evan David, Gent.
Morgan Lewis, Gent.
David Jn°. Pyrce, Gent.
Owen Vaughan, Gent.
Lewis ab Hugh, Gent.
James, Lloyd, Gent.
John Evans, Gent.
Edward Lloyd, Gent.
Rees David Richard, Gent.
Evan ab Rees ab Evan Gough, Gent.
Stephen Jones, Gent.
Evan Pugh, Gent.
Dávid ab Evan Pyrce, Gent.

The inhabitants are accommodated with a supply of fresh water, both in the heat of summer and the frosts of winter, conveyed through the middle of the town from a spring at the extremity of Maes-y-dref, by means of an artificial channel, close to their doors. This stream is now named Bwgey, or Bwch-gwy. The comeliness and beauty

of the children of this town have been the subject of observation to every traveller, and is recorded in the following short but ancient adage,—
"Adarn Bwgey, Glanha ynghymry,"
that is,—
"The fairest children Wales can have,
Are those that drink bright Bwgey's wave."

Rhayadergwy having been, from time immemorial, a manor belonging to the Princes of Wales, and under them to the royal tribe of Ellistan Glodrudd, Lords of Moelynaidd, Fferllys, and Cerri, enjoyed privileges, honours, and immunities, in which property of inferior description was not allowed to participate. These marks of favour were continued whilst it remained subject to the Earls of Marche and Wigmore; and when a descendant of that powerful family ascended the throne of England, it became a part of the royal patrimony of the sovereigns of that country, each of whom it has the honour to regard as its lord. But it was reserved for the reign of Henry VIII., who, sprung from Welsh ancestors, patronized the inhabitants of the Principality, and endowed them with the same rights and privileges as his English subjects possessed, to rescue this royal lordship from obscurity, and invest it with a right in common with the other contributory boroughs to vote for the election of a representative in Parliament for Radnor. This privilege was conferred by statute enacted in the twenty-seventh year of his reign. (A.D. 1536.) The manner of electing its burgesses, who are entitled to vote at elections, is as follows : At a court-leet the jury, being impanelled, present to the steward, or deputy-steward, the names of such persons, whether inhabitants or not, whom they think proper to select as fit and proper persons to be made burgesses. This presentment being accepted by the steward, the persons so presented are generally sworn in immediately, if they be present in court, but if not present, at a subsequent court.

Though the rent of land within the limits of this

borough is as high as £5 per acre per annum, yet the number of acres uninclosed and uncultivated exceeds that of those which are inclosed and cultivated; the former amounting to 90 acres, and the latter to 87, as it appears by a survey made in the year 1787. The uninclosed and uncultivated land comprizes Maes-y-dref, Maes-bach, and Waun-y-capel. Part of Maes-y-dref has at times been inclosed, and converted to tillage; in which case it was apportioned among the householders, paying scot, and liable to lot, by a pound rate. The last inclosure took place in the year 1775, not without some grumbling and opposition set up by a few of the neighbouring farmers, who, though neither residents or occupants within the borough, nor consequently liable to pay suit or service thereto, have exercised a custom which, through long connivance, is usurped as a right, of depasturing their cattle and sheep upon these commons, whilst the inhabitants of the borough, in whom the sole right is vested, are terrified from the attempt of establishing and confirming their exclusive claim by the enormous expense to be incurred by an application to Parliament for an inclosure act.

On the western extremity of the common called Maes-y-dref is a most excellent spring of pure and limpid water, named St. Mary's Well. It was heretofore a custom for the young people of Rhayader, of both sexes, to resort hither on Sunday evenings, during the spring and summer seasons, to drink this salutary beverage sweetened with sugar. Adjoining to this fountain there stood formerly, previous to their mutilation, vestiges of druidical construction, such as a cromlech, and an elliptical basin chiselled out of the solid rock, and corresponding with the description given by Borlase in his *History of Cornwall*.

On the south-eastern side of Maes-bach is a small collection of houses named "Pentrè-boeth," that is, the hot suburb or village. The cause of the addition of this epithet has given rise to various conjectures.

Ecclesiastical Account.

The church of Rhayadergwy stands on the north-west side of the town. Rhys ab Gruffudd, Prince of South Wales, escorted by an army amounting at least to between five and six thousand men, arrived in the town of Rhayader, and made a magnificent procession to the church, where, in the presence of an innumerable concourse of people, he ratified and confirmed, in the most solemn manner, the immunities, liberties, and donations with which he had endowed his newly-erected abbey of Strata Florida, in the county of Cardigan. The perpetual property of that territory, now denominated the Grange of Cwmdauddwr, was at this time conferred on the monks of that monastery. The idea of so great a multitude of persons, some of whom were of the highest rank and distinction, assembling in the town of Rhayader, and abiding there some days, at least suggests the opinion that the place at that period must have been much larger in extent, and the country around better cultivated and more fertile, in order to be capable of furnishing the necessary provisions and accommodations which this numerous and diversified assemblage required. This historical fact is alone sufficient to prove the importance and respectability in which this division of the county of Radnor was anciently holden.

A custom prevailed to a recent period for Divine Service to be performed in the church of Rhayader on Christmas-day yearly, at six o'clock in the morning, on which occasion the church was completely illuminated. The abuse of this pious custom, called in the Welsh language " Plygain," caused its abolition.

Another ancient practice, derived probably from the druidical institution, was observed in this town till of late years with rigid tenacity. The attendants on every funeral procession were wont to carry a small stone or pebble in their hand, which, on the arrival of the bier at the turn of the road leading to the church, they threw to a large heap of stones that had accumulated there by similar means, saying, " carn ar dy ben," that is, a stone on thy head. This relic, savouring of superstition, though harmless in itself, was deemed unfit to be continued under the light of Christianity. The act, however, of recording the practice of our ancestors, as it may lead to the knowledge of their principles, will, it is hoped, escape censure.

The church or chapel of Rhayadergwy is dedicated to St. Clement, the contemporary of St. Paul. The benefice is a perpetual curacy, in the diocese of St. David's, not in charge, annexed to the vicarage of Nantmêl, and estimated in *Liber Regis* at the yearly value of £1 15s. The vicar of Nantmêl is the patron. It has been augmented by Queen Anne's bounty.

On digging the foundation of the new tower of the church of Rhayadergwy, erected in the year 1783, a great number of skeletons were discovered about a foot below the surface of the ground, arranged side by side, in a most regular and orderly manner, with their respective heads placed in the same direction; one skeleton only excepted, which was of an immense size, the thigh-bone measuring more than one yard in length. This skeleton was placed in a direction contrary to all the rest. All the teeth in the skulls were sound and whole, and rivalling ivory in whiteness. This discovery gave rise to much discussion. After many conjectures as to the time and occasion of this interment, it was at last unanimously agreed upon that these skeleton bones were the remains of the garrison soldiers of the castle of Rhayadergwy, whom Llewelyn ab Iorwerth, Prince of North Wales, had put to the sword, and the inhabitants of the town buried in this methodical manner under the old belfry of the ancient church. That individual skeleton, which was of gigantic magnitude, and placed in a direction contrary to all the others, was supposed to have been that of the commander of the castle. All these bones were carefully collected, and deposited in one large grave opened in the church-yard, by order of the father of the compiler of this history.

Rhayader mill is crown property, now holden by Evan Stephans, Esq., of Cruchell, in this county. The gross annual rent is 17s. 4d. In 1784 one year was in arrear. The same rent was reserved in the grant made by Charles I. to Eden, Scriven, and others.

In the Dean of Windsor's lease a mention occurs of crown land in Rhayader, supposed to be Gwirglodd-fawr, the gross annual rent of which, together with the tolls, amount to £3 6s. 8d.; and also of the borough of Rhayader, the gross annual rent of which is £4 19s. 8d., due from the prepositor.

The Presbyterians and Calvinistic Methodists have each a conventicle here. The former was the old gaol, near the Tower Hill; the other is in the same street. A meeting-house for the Wesleyan Methodists was erected in East Street; but, for want of support, has now totally declined.

Charitable Donations.

In a year unknown Mr. John Davis left a rent-charge of £2 15s. upon land, now vested in Thomas Price and John Davies by will, for the purpose of teaching poor children.

About the year 1720 David Morgan, Esq., of Bettws Diserth, devised by will a rent-charge of £3 upon land, vested in the late John Davies, for the purpose of teaching poor children.

About the year 1719 the Rev. Charles Price bequeathed by will the annual sum of £11 12s., secured upon land, and now vested in the Rev. ―― Evans, for the maintenance of a schoolmaster in or near Cwmdauddwr Church, distant from Rhayader about a furlong, for teaching a certain number of poor children. This school is now kept in Rhayader.

In the year 1813 the Rev. Henry Williams, A.M., bequeathed by will to the use of the Vice-Chancellor and Heads of Houses in the University of Oxford a sum in the three per cent. consols, reduced by the legacy duty to the sum of £59 8s., for the purpose of establishing a lectureship in the church of Rhayadergwy, and of increasing the salary of the parish clerk, as a compensation for his attendance when the duty is performed.

CEFN-Y-LLYS HUNDRED.

This modern division of the county of Radnor received its name from the celebrated castle so called; and the castle from the palace, or court of judicature, erected and established on an elevated spot impending over the river Ieithon by the ancient Silurian *reguli*. This hundred embraces the central division of the county, having the hundred of Knighton on the north side of it, that of Radnor on the east, Pain's Castle and Colwyn on the south, and that of Rhayader on the west; and comprehends partly the ancient cwmwd of Swydd-wynogion, and partly Swydd-yr-allt, in 'the Cantref of Elfael. It contains nine parishes, viz., Blaiddfâ, Cefn-y-llys, Llan-

HISTORY OF RADNORSHIRE. 261

badarn-fawr, Llandegla, Llan-y-drindod, Llanfihangel-rhyd-Eithon, Llangunllo, Pilleth, Whitton. The parishes of Cefn-y-llys, Llandrindod, Craig township in Llandegla, and Cefn-y-pawl township in Llanbister, are situated in the cwmwd of Swydd-wynogion; whilst Llandegla, Llangunllo, Llanfihangel-rhyd-Eithon, Llanbadarn-fawr, Pilleth, and Whitton, are in the cwmwd of Swydd-yr-allt.

BLAIDDFA.

The parish of Blaiddfâ contains upwards of 4000 acres of land, of which about 1200 are hills, 400 wood, and the remainder inclosed and cultivated. It also contains one forest, which, being in ancient times exposed to the cruel incursions of wolves, has, in consequence of the wise policy of destroying those ravenous animals, become a secure, excellent, and lucrative sheep-walk. This forest is an appendage of the crown, and leased by Richard Price, Esq., the present representative of the borough of Radnor; the under tenants paying a fixed rate, similar to that of Radnor forest, for the privilege of depasturing their cattle, sheep, &c., thereon. The same gentleman holds the lordship or manor of Blaiddfâ.

In this parish, within a few yards of the turn which the turnpike-road leading from Presteigne to Knighton takes in the direction towards Penybont, stands a manorial house of venerable antiquity, commonly named Monach-ty. This name implies a monastery; and the tradition of the neighbourhood seems to sanction this designation. But this is one of those vulgar reports which have no foundation in fact. There is no other proof of the existence of a monastic establishment in this place, than because a part of the estate still retains the British appellation Clôg, which signifies a grange; it being one of the endowments with which Roger Mortimer, Earl of Marche and Wigmore augmented the temporalities of Abbey Cwmhir, and because, in all probability, King Henry VIII., out of his great favour and grace to the Welsh, had permitted the last abbot of Cwmhir to retire to this sequestered spot, and here end his days in solitude and peace. Or perhaps historians may have confounded this place with its neighbouring Monach-ty, situated near Knighton, on the left bank of the river Tame, which undoubtedly was a monastic cell, and to which, as tradition reports, the monks of Abbey Cwmhir, after the dissolution of their society, retired. To which may be added the following solution of this historical difficulty: The error of supposing this house to have been a monastery is to be ascribed to the corrupt appellation by which it has been designated for several years past. The original name was not Monach-ty, that is, an habitation of monks, but Monad-ty, that is, a house in an isolated situation; which signification exactly corresponds with the situation of the place; for it is embosomed in an amphitheatre of hills and woods, and does not visibly appear to the traveller till he suddenly and unexpectedly falls upon it.

The house of Monach-ty bears all the appearance of having been a very respectable manorial mansion. It is built of stone, and flanked with two wings. The interior contains many very lofty, grand, and spacious apartments, especially the great hall, which present an idea of the splendour and magnificence of ancient times. It contains also a dungeon, or a condemned hole for convicts, and consequently a court of judicature, in which offences against the rights, &c., of the manor, and the property of the tenants, were tried and condemned. On the southeast wall of the house, the following coats of arms are sculptured in relievo :—1. A chevron between three lions rampant, and three spear heads, with trefoils. 2. A chevron between three spear heads, and also these two initial letters, J. P., and date, 1638.

The first proprietor of this house and estate of whom any authentic account has been transmitted was James Price, Esq., who served the office of high sheriff for the county of Radnor in the year 1552, being the sixth of Edward VI. The same gentleman was sheriff in the year 1574, being the seventeenth year of Queen Elizabeth's reign. The next proprietor was John Price, Esq., probably the son of the preceding. He served the office of high

Mynachty House.

Pilleth House.

sheriff for this county in the year of our Lord, 1576, and was succeeded in this property by his son, James Price, Esq., who was high sheriff for this county in the year 1599, being the forty-first of Queen Elizabeth. The two initials above plainly bear allusion to this gentleman, whose reparation of, or addition to, the house is thus commemorated. After this period there follows a confused detail of the descent of the estate, owing to the anarchical transactions attendant on the great rebellion in the reign of Charles I. The following copy of an original document issued by one of the generals of that monarch, then acting in this district, and preserved by the Crowther family of Knighton, may perhaps throw some light on this subject:—

"Whereas there hath been an order formerly from his Highness Prince Rupert, directed to Brian Crowther, Esq., high sheriff of the county of Radnor, for putting Charles Prise, Esq., into possession of an estate called Monaughty, till further orders from the King's Majesty, or his Highness, in recompense of £1000 lent upon a statute against Sir Robert Harley, now in actual rebellion: And whereas Mrs. Vaughan, widow, and Mrs. Powell, her sister, have forcibly entered into possession of the said estate, without order: I do require the aforesaid high sheriff to put Mrs. Vaughan and Mrs. Powell out of possession, and to give the possession to the Widow Prise, of Pilleth, administratrix to Charles Prise deceased, till further orders."

The new order of things established by the Commonwealth of England altered the subsequent transmission of this property by alienating it from the family of Price, of Pilleth, probably on account of their loyal attachment and pecuniary assistance afforded to the king, as above related, and transferred to a line of a republican character; for John Davies, Esq., who served the office of high sheriff of this county in the year 1656, being the fourth year of the protectorate of Oliver Cromwell, was then in possession of the house and estate of Monad-ty. At the restoration the property reverted to the family of Price, of Pilleth, and belongs at this time to Richard Price, Esq., of Knighton, representative in Parliament of the borough of Radnor. In this house are to be seen, in excellent preservation, very curious pieces of ancient armour; particularly an helmet and breast-plate of iron; and halberds, originally twelve in number, nine feet in length, the iron heads of which are formed to resemble those of a battle-axe, and adapted for cutting as well as thrusting. The general opinion, however, is, that they were never used as instruments of war, but as preservatives of peace, being carried by the sheriff's men in procession before the two justices of assize for the county when on the circuit.

Blaiddfâ Hall was the seat and property of a respectable family of the name of Clarke. Two gentlemen of this family served the office of high sheriff of this county, viz., John Clarke, Esq., in 1716, and John Clarke, Esq., in 1735. The late Charles Rogers, Esq., of Stanage, was related to this family by the maternal side.

The number of paupers in this parish is small, and the parochial assessments are moderate. The low sum of £38 13s. 7d., assessed at 1s. 4d. in the pound, sufficed for all the demands of the year 1803.

Ecclesiastical Account.

The church of Blaiddfâ is a rude edifice, consisting of a nave, chancel, low tower, and porch. The tower contains one bell. It is dedicated to St. Mary. The benefice is a rectory, estimated in *Liber Regis* at £12 10s. 1d. per annum; but as all the tithes of the parish are annexed to the rectory, the annual emoluments of the rector must be considerable. The yearly tenths are £1 1s. 2½d. The Bishop of St. David's is the patron.

Charitable Donation.

Above a century ago a person named —— Wilkes bequeathed by will a rent-charge of the clear annual income of 1s. upon land, now vested in David Jenkins, for the benefit of the poor of this parish.

List of Incumbents.

——, Brown was rector of this parish, and ejected by the parliamentary sequestrators; the tithes were confiscated and appropriated to the use of the government, 1649.
Henry Meredith, A.M.......... 1732   William Baker 1793
Thomas Bowen................ 1765   Ditto, recollated............. 1796
William Crawford, A.M........ 1769

CEFN-Y-LLYS.

In describing this portion of the hundred, we shall consider it under these three general heads, viz., the castle, the borough, and the parish.

This castle, indeed, has sometimes been denominated

Castell-Glyn-Ieithon, because its situation is upon a bank or ridge that overlooks the vale of the river Ieithon. Its original construction was so admirably adapted for defence as to be almost impregnable against the modes of attack practised in those days, when the use of gunpowder and artillery was unknown. However, in 1262, it was taken by surprize by a detachment of troops sent thither by the order of Llewelyn ab Gruffudd, Prince of North Wales, who had defeated Roger Mortimer in the field, and was laying waste his Radnorshire and Herefordshire estates with fire and sword. The governor of the castle was made a prisoner, and the greater part of the garrison, who were Herefordshire men, were put to the sword. After this capture the right policy which this detachment should have pursued was to have razed the walls of the castle, and levelled them with the ground, and then to have retired into their own country; instead of which they made it their residence, in a country every part of which was possessed by their enemies, who soon besieged them, cut off their supplies, and compelled them by starvation to an unconditional surrender. It remained ever after in the possession of the Norman Lords of Moelynaidd, who established in it that tremendous court of justice, or rather injustice, called the Lords Marchers' Court, which gave them an uncontrolled authority over all the inhabitants, and over the whole property of the country. It became the resort of traitors and unprincipled banditti, who were prepared to swear anything, and against any person, to gratify the will and avarice of their employer. By these nefarious means many an innocent inhabitant of the country has been deprived at once both of his estate and of his life. In the reign of Henry VI. died Edmund, the last Earl of Marche and Wigmore of the name of Mortimer, leaving no issue. This castle then devolved to Richard, Duke of York, and Earl of Cambridge, in right of his wife Anne, the only surviving sister and heir of the aforesaid Edmund; and upon the accession of his son to the throne of England, by the name of King Edward IV., it finally was annexed to the crown of Great Britain.

2 M

Camden, the antiquary, relates that, in his time, viz., about the year 1558, it lay in ruins, and that the site on which it stood then belonged to the Duke of York. Several years ago a silver thumb-ring was dug up in a place called the Castle Garden, and is now in possession of a lady named Mrs. Edwards, of Greenfields. Many persons ascribe it to remote antiquity, and suppose it to have been the signet-ring of one of the Princes of South Wales, probably Rhys, who occasionally resided in the castle of Cefn-y-llys.

Cefn-y-llys is a borough by prescription, and by the 37th of Henry VIII. was annexed as one of the four contributory boroughs which enjoy the right to nominate and qualify burgesses for voting for a representative in Parliament for the borough of New Radnor. Its burgesses when duly elected, are chosen in the following manner :— At a court-leet holden by the steward, or deputy-steward, presiding over this borough, the jury, who have been previously summoned, and who ought to be burgesses of the same, are impanelled, and present the names of such persons, whether inhabitants of the borough or not, whom they think proper to select as fit and proper persons to be made burgesses. This presentment being accepted by the steward, the persons so presented are generally sworn in immediately, if they be present in court, but if not, at a subsequent court. After this, their names are enrolled in the courts above. The borough of Cefn-y-llys is a lordship, or manor, inherited by the crown, but alienated some centuries ago to the ancestors of Sir Standish Hartstronge, Bart., who died in the year of our Lord 1701, and was buried in the Cathedral Church of Hereford. This lordship and borough, together with the lordship of Trewern, which comprises the township of the parish of Llanfihangel-nant-Moylin, and several other considerable estates in this county, were sold about sixty years ago by Sir Henry Hartstronge, Bart., an Irish gentleman, to Benjamin Walsh, Esq., whose son, or rather nephew, Sir John Walsh, is the present proprietor. Previous to the time of this purchase, court-leets were holden at Noyadd,

Cefn-y-llys, and at Trewern; of which courts the late Rev. James Jones, father of the Rev. Benjamin Jones, perpetual curate of Buallt, was steward. A court-leet is still holden in the village of Cefn-y-llys, at a farm-house called Noyadd.

The aggregate amount of the parochial rates in both places was, for the service of the year 1803, £93 13s. 9d., at 3s. 3d. in the pound.

It is doubtful whether the number of inhabitants is now upon the increase; the reverse is most probable, on account of the obnoxious practice of consolidating farms. The resident population, containing the borough and the out-parish, or the upper and lower division, consisted in the year 1811 of 320 individuals.

In this parish, near to the site of the old castle, is a stone bridge over the Ieithon, which connects a communication with several high roads leading to and from the towns of Radnor, Kington, Knighton, Buallt, Rhayader, and the hamlet of Penybont.

Sir B. Walsh, Bart., is the lord of the manor of Cefn-y-llys, and proprietor of the borough.

Charitable Donations.

Mr. Thomas Palmer bequeathed by will, in the year 1712, a clear annual rent-charge of £3 5s. upon land, now vested in the minister and church-wardens of this parish, for the relief of poor housekeepers not receiving parochial assistance.

In the year 1713 the Rev. Hugh Powell bequeathed by will a clear annual rent-charge of £2 15s., now vested in the minister and churchwardens of this parish, for the relief of poor housekeepers not receiving parochial assistance.

Ecclesiastical Account.

The church consists of a porch, nave, chancel, and a low tower. It is dedicated to St. Michael. The benefice is a rectory, estimated in *Liber Regis* at £8 19s. 4½d. per annum. The whole tithes of the parish are annexed to the rectory, which renders it a valuable living. The Bishop of St. David's is the patron.

List of Incumbents.

Matthew Herbert was ejected by the parliamentary sequestrators, and the tithes were confiscated, 1649.
David Lloyd 1717   Daniel Jones, A.B. 1768
Herbert Bradford, A.B. 1747   Thomas Jones 1784

LLANBADARN-FAWR.

Following the sinuosities of the beautiful and meandering river Ieithon, we enter upon the parish of Llanbadarn-fawr, so named to distinguish it from the parish of Llanbadarn-fynydd, in the same county.

Ascending still higher up the Ieithon, along a circuit of considerable compass, we arrive at the hamlet or village of Penybont, a name synonymous to the French *tete du pont*, both signifying the head of the bridge. In former times it bore a different name, and was called Pont-rhyd-y-cleifon, that is, the bridge on the ford of the wounded, implying that a battle was fought in its neighbourhood. In its present state it can boast only of a few houses, and those scattered. Three new ones have a few years ago been added: that which the late John Price, Esq., inhabited, where he acquired by trade an immense fortune, which qualified him to become one of the firmest and most respectable country bankers in the Principality of Wales. This house has lately been enlarged and beautified in a very splendid manner by J. C. Severn, Esq., who married the only daughter and heir of the said Mr. Price, and served the office of high sheriff for this county. The other house is inhabited by Middleton Jones, Esq.

Few are the vestiges of antiquity contained in this parish. On the right hand of the road leading from Penybont to Rhayader, at a short distance from the former place, is a druidical carn. A Roman road from the Roman station Magos, or Caerfagu, upon the Ieithon, in the parish of Llanfihangel Helygen, communicating with the stations in North Wales, passes through this parish, and crosses, first, the Ieithon at or near the bridge of Llanbadarn-fawr, then the turnpike-road leading to Penybont, within half a mile of that village; and, ascending up the country in a line parallel to the river Clywedoc, proceeds to Bwlch-cefn-din, near to Cwmtelmau, and thence near to Abbey Cwmhir; it then continues its course through Bwlch-y-sarnau, that is, the pass or defile of the road, and thence in a straight line to the river Severn, at a place

Opposite to Caersws, in the parish of Llandinam, and county of Montgomery.

There is, near the village of Penybont, a piece of crown land, leased to the Rev. J. Parsons at the gross annual rent of 7s. 8d.

Ecclesiastical Account.

The church of Llanbadarn-fawr, dedicated to Padarn, or St. Paternus, is a small edifice, consisting of only a single nave, or aisle, and contains two sepulchral memorials of marble; the one commemorating the interment of the late John Price, Esq., of Penybont, and the other —— Davies, Esq., of Brincnwelàs.

This benefice is a discharged rectory, estimated in *Liber Regis* to be worth £7 12s. 6d. per annum. The total annual emoluments amount at present to £100. The Bishop of St. David's is the patron. In the year 1651 it was sequestrated by the parliamentary commissioners.

Charitable Donations.

In the year 1813 George Moore, Esq., devised by will a rent-charge on land, now vested in Mr. James Moore, of the sum of 10s., to be distributed among poor housekeepers of this parish who receive no parochial relief.

In the same year Mrs. Bridget Clarke bequeathed by will the yearly interest of £10, now vested in Mr. Evan Powell, to be distributed among poor housekeepers of this parish who receive no parochial assistance.

List of Incumbents.

Thomas Davies	1738	David Griffith	1804
Hugh Price, A.B.	1762	Charles Griffith	1805
William Amos, A.M.	1782	Lewis Price Jones	1823
John Dyer	1785		

LLANDEGLA.

This parish derives its appellation from the name of the patron and female saint Tecla.

As this parish borders upon the forest of Radnor, it possesses a right of commonage on those healthy and extensive sheep-walks. For, according to an inquisition taken in the sixth year of the reign of Queen Elizabeth, (A.D. 1564,) by virtue of the Queen Majesty's commission addressed to commissioners for the survey of the forest of Radnor, the parish of Llandegla, in conjunction with those of Llanfihangel-nant-Moylin, Llanfihangel-rhyd-Ieithon, Blaiddfà, Cascob, Radnor, Old and New, is entitled to send cattle, &c., to be depastured on the forest of Radnor, on paying to the forester at the rate of 2d. for every beast or cattle, and 3d. for every score of sheep or goats.

The parochial rates, which are assessed and collected in the three townships separately and distinctly, amounted to the sum of £166 1s. 9d., at 7s. in the pound, for the service of the year 1803.

There do not appear at this time any vestiges of antiquity, or traces of ancient fortification, or tumuli, in this parish; although in all the neighbouring parishes such vestiges are clearly discernible. It is probable that this parish participated in the fate of the parish of Llanfihangel-nant-Moylin, which fell under the arms of William de Braos, Lord of Brecknock and Buallt, in the eleventh century.

Castell Cwmaron, that is, the castle in the dingle of the river so called, is in this parish, and about two miles distant from the village. It was erected by Roger Mortimer and he is said to have occasionally resided in it. There are grounds for believing this fortress to have been of an earlier date, and to have originally belonged to the *reguli* of Cantref Moelynaidd. No relic of it remains at present; the site only is to be discerned.

There is also in this parish an estate named Swydd, the tenure of which was in ancient times official; that is, this property was granted by one of the *reguli* of the district, and holden by the proprietor, on the condition of performing certain services or duties, and of executing a delegated authority.

Ecclesiastical Account.

The antique appearance of the church of Llandegla renders the supposition probable that some parts of its structure are composed of the fragments of some despoliated monastery, perhaps of Abbey Cwmhir, and removed hither at a time immemorial.

The church-yard is spacious, and contains many memorials of the dead. The following inscription is on a tombstone that commemorates the sepulture of Evan and Alice Williams:—

"They were so univocal, that none could say,
Which did rule, and which did obey,
He ruled, because she would comply: and she,
By so complying, ruled as well as he.
Now they sleep in hopes through Christ again to be
Mutually united to their souls eternally."

HISTORY OF RADNORSHIRE. 271

The prebend of the church of Llandegla, in the Collegiate Church of Brecknock, is stated in *Liber Regis* to be worth £5 per annum. The yearly tenths are 10s. The Bishop of St. David's is the patron.

The benefice of the church of Llandegla is a discharged vicarage, estimated in *Liber Regis* at £35 3s. The clear yearly value of this benefice, arising from augmentation, tithes, glebe, and surplice fees, is about £80.

Charitable Donations.

In the year 1637 the clear annual sum of £4 was devised by Evan ab John Morris, by deed, charged upon land, and vested in Thomas Jones, John Meredith, and Evan Phillips, for the benefit of decayed inhabitants of this parish not receiving parochial relief.

In the year 1721 Samuel Williams devised by will a rent-charge of £3 upon land, vested in the minister and churchwardens, for teaching and instructing the poor children of this parish to read.

In the year 1721 Mrs. Anne Griffiths bequeathed by will the sum of £120, which produces an annual interest of £9, and is now vested in John Griffiths, James Phillips, Thomas Williams, Thomas Jones, Howel Evans, and Richard Williams, to be distributed among the decayed housekeepers and poor of the parishes of Llandegla, Llanfihangel-nant-Moylin, and Colfa. This bequest has been laid out in the purchase of land.

In the same year Mr. Evan Griffiths bequeathed by deed the annual interest of the principal sum of £40, to be distributed in the same manner as the preceding.

In the same year Mrs. Bridget Clarke left by will a rent-charge of 1s. per week, secured upon land left by John Meredith, called the Wern, in this parish, and vested in Thomas Beversley. The same was given for a short time, but afterwards refused on account of its not having been given in the testatrix's life-time, and never received since the year 1733. It has been paid for some Sundays; but the person to whom the estate was left refused payment; upon which an opinion was taken and given against the parish.

List of Incumbents.

Robert Bicknell, ejected by the parliamentary commissioners, 1649
Richard Prothero 1700
Herbert Probert Howarth 1740
James Phillips 1748

LLAN-Y-DRINDOD.

This parish, which bears the name of the Holy Trinity, is bounded on the west by the river Ieithon; on the east by the parish of Llanbadarn-fawr; on the south by Cefn-y-llys; and on the north by Diserth and Bettws Diserth. It contains by estimation nearly 3000 statute acres of land, of which about 2000 are inclosed and cultivated, and the remaining acres, being hilly and common, are uninclosed. It consists of two divisions, viz., the upper and the lower, each of which collects and pays the land-tax and the assessed taxes separately and distinctly.

This parish may with justice boast of the superior

salubrity of its air and climature. It is the Montpelier of Radnorshire, preserving the health of its inhabitants to a great age, and speedily restoring invalids who resort hither for the benefit of the waters to a gladsome state of convalescence. Though, as might be expected in a hilly country, the showers of rain are frequent, and sometimes heavy, yet a moist foggy atmosphere is seldom seen. There are also many pleasant rides about Llandrindod, and some scenes in the neighbourhood by no means destitute of beauty and sublimity. These circumstances, with exercise, contribute, no doubt, to the preservation and restoration of health; and the claim of Llandrindod is substantiated by facts. Of thirteen successive years, two passed without a single funeral; and during the whole of that period, the average number of annual instances of mortality did not amount to three, out of a resident population which, according to the return made in the year 1801, consisted of 192 individuals. In the year 1817, the number of inhabitants was estimated at 180 persons, of whom 87 were males, and 93 females. From the commencement of the year 1800 to the close of 1816 there had been 66 children baptized, viz., 37 males and 29 females; and during the same term of years, some of which were remarkable for dearness and scarcity of provisions, were buried 46 persons, viz., 26 males, and 20 females. The parochial assessments collected and received from the two divisions of this parish, for the service of the year 1803, amounted to the sum of £157 5s. 1d., at 2s. 6d. in the pound.

To the antiquary this parish is a most interesting spot, and affords many a delicious treat. There is on the western extremity of the common of Llandrindod, almost contiguous to the village of Howey, an ancient encampment of an elliptical form, named Caer-du; besides many others interspersed, and enumerated elsewhere. A Roman road which entered this county on the banks of the river Wye, at Newbridge, intersects this parish. The formation seems to have been vigorously opposed by the Silurian inhabitants, who manfully disputed every inch of ground with their invaders, and compelled them to alter the line of its direction in some places. Their combined attacks issued simultaneously from certain and distinct points, viz., Caerneddau, Cefn-y-gaer, and Addfa —all parallel to the road, and commanding a full view of it—and harassed in no inconsiderable degree the Roman caravans which conveyed the ore from the lead mine in this parish, that had been worked, not only from remote antiquity, but also by that people, though at various times discontinued. At length, the Romans succeeded in establishing a fortified camp and station on the right bank of the Ieithon, in the parish of Llanfihangel Helygen, which effectually served to overawe the country, and suppress the desultory and irregular hostilities of its natives. This station is to the present day denominated Caer-fagu, and has the justest pretensions to be the site of the Roman Magos. The Saxons were never able to penetrate into this district. It was, however, reduced by the Norman conquerors of England, and retained in subjection by the family of the Earls of Marche and Wigmore, who, after the total extinction of the native *reguli*, not only seized upon their patrimony, but also assumed their honours and title, viz., Lords of Moelynaidd and Elfael.

In this parish are situated those medicinal springs of long-continued and approved celebrity, called Llan-y-drindod Wells. The principal of these are three, viz., the rock or chalybeate water, the saline pump-water, and the sulphur water.

Walter Wilkins, Esq., of Maeslough, the representative of this county in Parliament, is lord of the crown manor of Is-mynydd, including the parish of Llan-y-drindod.

It is conjectured, on probable grounds, that the number of inhabitants of this parish must formerly have exceeded the present amount, or themselves more religiously disposed; for one church was found inadequate to the expression of their pious feelings and inclinations. The foundations and walls of a very ancient chapel, named Llanfaelog, that is, the church of St. Maelog, who lived in Wales about the middle of the sixth century, were a short time ago dug up in the centre of a corn-field in this parish; but no authentic or even traditionary information could be obtained respecting it. This alleged degeneracy from the piety of their ancestors is not supported by fact; for, as a substitute of the dilapidated chapel, a Presbyterian meeting-house has started up, built by an ancestor of the late Thomas Jones, Esq., of Pencerrig, the grandfather of the present Mrs. Thomas, who, together with his family, constantly repaired thither every Sunday morning for public worship, and it was endowed by his surviving widow.

Ecclesiastical Account.

The church of Llan-y-drindod consists of a single nave, and is dedicated to the Holy Trinity. This benefice is a curacy, not in charge, under the prebend thereof, and estimated in *Liber Regis* at £6 per annum. It has been augmented with two lots of Queen Anne's bounty, of £200 each, and its total emoluments amount at present to £40 per annum.

The prebend of Llan-y-drindod, in the Collegiate Church of Brecknock, is stated in *Liber Regis* to be worth £30 per annum. It was sequestrated by Parliament in the year 1649. The yearly tenths were 10s. 10½d. per annum, but are now discharged. The Bishop of St. David's is the patron.

List of Incumbents.

Jeremiah Griffiths, A.B. 1734   Philip Davies 1768
David Jones, A.B. 1776   John Davies ....

Charitable Donations.

In the year 1684 Mr. Philip Lewis devised by will a rent-charge of 10s. secured on land, and vested in the churchwardens, to be distributed among the poor inhabitants of this parish not receiving parochial relief.

John Bevan Meredith, date unknown, and uncertain whether by will or deed, bequeathed a rent-charge of 10s. secured on land, and vested in the churchwardens, for the benefit of the poor of this parish not receiving parochial relief.

Evan Jones, date unknown, and uncertain whether by will or deed, devised a rent-charge of 8s. secured on land, and vested in the churchwardens, to be annually distributed among poor persons of this parish not receiving parochial relief.

John Jones, date unknown, and uncertain whether by will or deed, bequeathed the annual interest of £10, vested in the churchwardens, for the use and benefit of the poor inhabitants of this parish not receiving parochial relief.

LLANGUNLLO.

This parish derives its name from the saint to whom its church is dedicated. It contains about 6000 acres of land, 1000 of which may be said to be uninclosed and waste; and consists of two divisions, the upper and the lower, bounded by the two rivulets that discharge themselves into the river Lug, near the church. It extends about five miles in length and four in breadth.

There is a peculiarity observed in this parish in the mode of paying its land-tax and county rates. One third part of the upper division pays these assessments to the collectors of the parish of Heyope, which is not included in the same hundred as Llangunllo; and another third part of the same division pays the same taxes to the collectors of the parish of Llanbister, which is comprehended in the hundred of Knighton. This singularity can only be accounted for on the supposition that these parcels of the parish of Llangunllo belonged formerly to persons of power and influence in the several parishes of Llanbister and Heyope, who annexed these payments to the places of their principal and respective residences.

The vale of the Lug does not seem to have been so firmly and obstinately contested as the vale of the Tame; there remain therefore fewer vestiges of antiquity, and traces of fortification. Several circular tumuli of considerable magnitude, containing about an acre of land each, are, however, to be discerned, as in several different places, so especially on the hill between the Bailey House and the Great Gate, and one distinguished by the name of Camp. In what era this camp was first formed no documents specify. As this part of Radnorshire was greatly infested by the Norman adventurers of Salop and Cheshire, it may have been made use of for the purpose of defending the country from their predatory incursions. There is also a remarkable ridge of earth artificially thrown up, named the Short Ditch, being a straight line extending between 200 or 300 yards in length from north to south on the Beacon Hill, partly in this parish, and partly in that of Bugaildu. The manifest designation of this fortified redoubt was to obstruct the march of the enemy invading this district from the north, and its formation effected by Sir Edward Mortimer's men, in the year

1402, for the purpose of opposing the progress of Owen Glyndwrdwy before the battle of Pilleth, if not supposed prior to that event. Another corroborative proof of the existence of a fortified camp, or castle, upon the Bailey Hill, is furnished by the name by which that eminence is designated.

In the year 1804 a considerable quantity of gold coins was found by Mr. West, in the farm-fold of Noyadd-fach, in this parish, covered lightly by the earth. These coins were of the reign of Edward III., and struck in commemoration of a naval victory obtained over the French fleet, denoted by the figure of a man standing in a ship impressed on the reverse of the coin. A few of them were of the reign of Henry IV. There can be little doubt that these coins were secreted in consequence of the great alarm occasioned by the impetuous and desolating incursion made by Owen Glyndwrdwy in the year 1402. The concealment of the coins was done in a hurry, as appears from the circumstance of their being slightly covered over with earth; and was never disclosed, because probably the owners met their deaths, either in the skirmishes that preceded the great battle of Pilleth, or in the field of battle itself. However, the discovery serves to confirm the reality of Owen's successful invasion.

Many silver coins also of the reigns of Elizabeth, James I., and Charles I., were discovered in a piece of ground belonging to a farm called Malagoed, near Creignant, in the year 1814. This field is denominated the Camp.

This parish has long been entirely Anglicised. The language universally spoken here is English. The oldest inhabitant has no recollection of the time when the Welsh language was in use; and yet the farm-houses, and the estates, are all distinguished by Welsh names.

There seems something peculiar in the elocutionary organs of the inhabitants of this parish. Though completely Anglicised, yet they are able to pronounce Welsh guttrals, not knowing them to be Welsh, with facility and distinctness; whilst, on the other hand, their enunciation of English words partakes of the Welsh peculiarity combined with English vulgarity. For instance the word *upper* is pronounced *uvvr*; *fodder, fother*; *little* sounds like *leedle*; and *good* as *coot*. Again, some words are pronounced in such a manner as renders it difficult to distinguish whether they be of Welsh or English extraction, as *Cribyn Llhwyde* they call *Griffin Flyde*.

Some years ago the parish of Llangunllo was noted as well for the number as for the respectability of its landed proprietors, who resided on their respective freeholds, and exercised the duties of hospitality. The pressure of excesssive taxation occasioned by the American and French revolutions has destroyed this link of the social chain, and swept away from this parish this once respectable and useful order of people. Their dwelling-houses, also, which were always open to the stranger and the poor, are fallen into a dilapidated state, and scarcely competent to shelter the depressed tenant from the inclemency of the weather. Even Weston Hall, which was once the residence of a Welsh chieftain, from whom was descended Sir William Meredith, a patriotic and an eloquent member of the House of Commons, is now reduced into so ruinated a condition as to be fit only for the occupation of a pauper, though it has become the joint property of Richard Price, Esq., of Knighton, M.P., and of Mrs. Pritchard, widow, of Dol-y-felin. The site of this mansion still retains some vestiges of its ancient grandeur, and presents many traits of delightful scenery. Of late years, however, some of these habitations have undergone a tenantable repair, or rebuilt upon an inferior scale. Bailey House, indeed, emulates the characteristic feature of better times; situated on the brow of a hill, and surrounded with numerous and fine plantations of trees, this mansion commands a most beautiful and extensive prospect of the vale of the Lug, and presents to the eye of the traveller, wearied with the melancholy view of desolated dwellings, an object singularly refreshing and animating.

In this parish is an antique farm-house, called Mynach Ty, or Monk-house. This was certainly an habitation of that description. Several years ago some stone coffins were dug up in the ground adjoining. The present structure is chiefly composed of timber and lath, the interstices filled up with mortar, and therefore not of so remote a date as monastic edifices in general. Thither at the dissolution, in the time of Henry VIII., the ejected monks of Abbey Cwmhir transferred their establishment, and in this seat of seclusion from the world maintained privately their former religion and habits, in opposition to the recent innovations of Cranmer, &c.

Ecclesiastical Account.

The church of Llangunllo consists of a nave, a chancel, a cross aisle or transept, a tower containing three large bells together with a smaller one, and a porch. It is dedicated to Cynllo, a Welsh saint who lived in the fifth century.

This benefice is a discharged vicarage, estimated in *Liber Regis* at the annual sum of £5 0s. 0½d., and stated in the margin of the said book to be worth the clear yearly sum of £28. An allotment of £200 has been given by the governors of Queen Anne's bounty.

The prebend of Llangunllo, in the Collegiate Church of Brecknock, is stated in *Liber Regis* to be worth the annual sum of £13. Three-fourths of all the tithes of this parish are annexed to the prebend, and leased to Richard Price, Esq., M.P., of Knighton.

In ancient records Llangunllo is designated thus, " Llangunllo cum capellis suis," that is, Llangunllo together with its chapels. In corroboration of this statement the parish church of Pilleth St. Mary is understood by the inhabitants of the former place to have been a chapel under Langunllo, as three-fourths of the tithes of Pilleth, in like manner as a similar portion of the tithes of Llangunllo, belong to the prebend thereof. Llanbister also is conjectured by some to have been another of these chapels, a supposition founded only on the circumstance of a water-spout denominated Pistyll Cynllo, that is, the waterspout of Cynllo, the saint to whom this church is dedicated, being in a situation contiguous to the church of Llanbister. Others entertain the wild opinion that by "the chapels of Llangunllo" are designated some of the perpetual curacies situated on the banks of the river Ieithon, and comprehended within the deanery of Moelynaidd. These unfounded conjectures are further contradicted by the circumstance that no portion whatever of the tithes of these parishes is annexed to the prebendary of Llangunllo.

Charitable Donations.

In the year 1752 Andrew Clarke, Esq., bequeathed a rent-charge of £2, secured on land, and now vested in Mr. John Lewis, to be distributed among the poor of this parish not receiving parochial relief.

In the year 1764 Thomas Meyrick, Esq., bequeathed a rent-charge of £1 1s., secured on land, and vested in Mrs. Anne Meyrick, for the use and benefit of the poor of this parish not receiving parochial relief.

In the year 1769 Thomas Holland, Esq., bequeathed, for the purpose of teaching six poor children of this parish, the annual sum of £2 5s., secured upon land, and vested in the vicar and churchwardens of this parish.

In the year 1763 Mrs. Anne Chamberlayne, wife of Mr. William Chamberlayne, Gent., of Cefn-suram, and daughter of the Rev. James Footman, who was vicar of this parish fifty-one years, gave to the use of the communion a silver salver, bearing an inscription which records the gift and the name of the donor.

The late Mrs. Blashfield, of Treburfâ, in this parish, whose tomb-stone is at the east end of the chancel in the church-yard, with a coat of arms inserted in the gable end of the wall, and inscribed with these words, "In Deo omnes confidemus," let us all trust in God, has bequeathed the sum of £30, of which the annual interest is to be distributed by the vicar and churchwardens to such poor as are not become pensioners on the parish.

The several estates of Pen-y-clawdd, now the property of J. C. Severn, Esq., of Penybont Hall, and of Llehall, of which the owner is David Griffiths, Esq., of the town of Ludlow, are respectively charged with small bequests to the poor of this parish; these are payable annually, but not regularly paid, except on the ground of a free gift. The proprietor of Llehall causes to be distributed annually at Christmas, among the poor of this parish, the sum of £2, which is given under the denomination of a free gift.

A parochial lending library has been established in this parish by the associates of the late Dr. Bray, in the year 1811, of which the vicar is the librarian, and the rector of Cascob, the vicar of Cerri, and the rector of Llanbister are trustees. The books are in number 1807, besides two or three sent from Caermarthen. Copies also of the annual sermons preached at Caermarthen before the Society for Promoting Christian Union in the diocese of St. David's are usually deposited here.

In the year 1811 the vicarage-house of this parish was rebuilt by the vicar at his own expense.

List of Incumbents.

James Footman	1666	Evan Evans	1782
Griffith Orleton	1717	Henry Bevan	1784
Robert Lewis	1739	Morgan Evans	1807
John Meredith	1779		

LLANFIHANGEL-RHYD-IEITHON.

This parish contains about 5000 acres of land, of which nearly 3000 are inclosed and cultivated; the remainder, being part of the forest of Radnor, is uninclosed and uncultivated.

According to an inquisition taken October 3rd, in the sixth year of the reign of Queen Elizabeth, (A.D. 1564,) by virtue of Her Majesty's commission addressed to commissioners for the survey of the forest of Radnor, the parish of Llanfihangel-rhyd-Ieithon, in conjunction with those of Llandegla, Llanfihangel-nant-Moylin, Blaiddfâ, Old Radnor, New Radnor, and Cascob, is entitled to send cattle, &c., to be depastured on the forest of Radnor, on paying to the forester at the rate of 2d. for every beast or cattle, and 3d. for every score of sheep or goats.

There exist at present few or no monuments of antiquity, such as barrows, carns, or cromlechs; nor are there to be seen any vestiges of ancient fortifications or castles. There is, however, in this parish a certain eminence which deserves to be recorded, on account of its designation in ancient times. It is corruptly named Llys-sin; the true orthography is Llys-ty, or Llys-din. No existing record makes mention of it; and therefore the only means left of investigating its original use and designation are to be derived from etymology. Now, the word Llys, in the Welsh language, signifies a palace, or court of judicature; and Ty, or Din, means a house, or place of abode. The name Llys-ty, or Llys-din, signifies the house, or fortified place, where the court of judicature, or palace, for these two were constantly identified, was wont to be holden. Llys-din is exactly synonymous with the Saxon appellation Luston. Now, the name Luston among the Saxons signified the very designation here ascribed to Llys-din, viz., the palace of the lord of the manor, or his court of judicature, which was always holden in the open air.

The Welsh are described by tourists as paying respectful homage to springs and fountains, every one of which is elevated to distinguished notoriety by being dedicated to some favourite saint. This characteristic feature of the natives of Wales is preserved in this parish with considerable zeal. At a certain season of the year, which is here called the Wake, young people of both sexes meet at these wells, quaff the limpid water sweetened with sugar, and conclude the day with the dance, and other innocent amusements.

Ecclesiastical Account.

This church, or rather chapel, is dedicated, as the name imports, to St. Michael; and the additional appendage serves to distinguish it from the other churches or chapels in this county that are dedicated to the same saint. It consists of a nave, chancel, and porch.

This benefice is a perpetual curacy, not in charge, annexed to the vicarage of Llanbister, and stated in *Liber Regis* to be of the certified value of £14 per annum. But at present the total emoluments arising from augmentation, fixed stipend, and surplice fees, exceed the annual sum of £36. The prebendary of Llanbister is the patron.

Charitable Donations.

In the year 1660 Dr. Berglios left by deed a benefaction of 10s., now vested in the minister and Mr. John Moore, to be distributed annually among the poor of this parish not chargeable to it.

In the year 1660 John ab Edward bequeathed by will a benefaction of 10s., now vested in some person unknown, to be distributed annually among the poor of this parish not receiving parochial relief. No further information can be given.

The annual sum of 10s. was left, as it is supposed, by Robert Davies, date unknown, by deed, now vested in John ——, to be distributed among the poor of this parish not chargeable to it.

About fifty or sixty years ago Mrs. Bridget Clarke gave by will a benefaction of 10s., now vested in the minister and churchwardens, and four of the principal inhabitants, to be distributed annually among poor persons of this parish not receiving parochial relief.

List of Incumbents.

Lewis Price	1727	Richard Williams	1762
James Meredith	1749	James Jones	1775
David Jones	1758	Morgan Price	1802

PILLETH.

The first printed authority now extant that mentions Pilleth is *Domesday Book*. It is there spelled Pelelai, and described as situated in the hundred of Hezetre, Herefordshire, and as belonging to Ralph de Mortimer. It then consisted of two hides of land. The article runs thus:—

" In Hezetre hundred.
Rad. de Mortemer ten. in Pelelei 2 Hid."

That is,—

Ralph Mortemer holds in Pilleth 2 hides.

It was here that a battle was fought between the Welsh patriots, under Owen Glyndwrdwy, and the English troops, commanded by Sir Edward Mortimer, and on the field of action are to be seen two straight lined parapets of earth, thrown up to the height of above five or six feet, facing each other, and at a distance of 300 or 400 yards from one another. These two lines of breastwork, or redoubts, were occupied, it is supposed, by the two hostile armies, and that the battle was fought on the level ground that lies between these breastworks,—man to man,—by main strength, and not by manœuvring. It is not ascertained whether on this occasion either party had brought into the field artillery, the use of which in deciding the fate of armies had been known and experi-

2 o

enced in the preceding century, although a cannon ball was found at no great distance from the scene of action. Batteries of artillery might have been advantageously erected on the respective wings of these breastworks, to prevent the line being turned. That Owen was not furnished with these implements of destruction his sudden raising of the siege of Montgomery Castle, and leaving an armed force in his rear, is a convincing proof. The event of the conflict remained not long doubtful; the attack made by the Welsh was furious and irresistible; each Merionethshire arrow told, and the close combat that ensued rendered the heavy bills of Herefordshire in a great measure unwieldy and useless. There fell on the side of the English upwards of 1100 men slain, besides a number of prisoners, among whom was the commander-in-chief, Sir Edward Mortimer. This decisive victory, now distinguished by the name of the victory of Pilleth, opened to Glyndwrdwy a ready access into the heart of the counties of Hereford and Worcester.

On the northern border of this parish, on the bank of the river Lug, are to be seen two tumuli, now overspread with trees. They are situated on an elevated common, not immediately in this parish, but on its borders, in the parish of Blaiddfâ, corruptly named, as before observed, Hendre-garreg. On this place are several detached tenements; and an erroneous tradition prevails that there once existed here a town, which rests on no better foundation than that the inhabitants, perhaps on account of their poverty, enjoy a partial exemption from the payment of chief rent.

Contiguous to the river Lug there also is the site of an ancient castle, surrounded by a rampart and foss, named Castell Ffaled. It is conjectured that Castell Ffaled is erroneously written, and that its true orthography is Castell Cynffaled, that is, the castellated mansion of Cynffaled, a Welsh saint. The castle is an intrenched tumulus situated in a small wood near the side of the road leading from Monadtu Blaiddfâ to Pilleth. It seems to have originally consisted of a timber structure erected upon the summit of the tumulus, which is large, and surrounded by a double vallum. As there is a small brook running through the valley near the wood, water may probably have been conducted into the trenches, which must have added to the strength of the fortress, and embarrassed the progress of the assailants.

The inhabitants of this parish retain in their recollection an event which evinces that a general dissatisfaction prevailed among the people of this kingdom, even in the glorious reign of Queen Anne, similar to that which is too much the character and temper of the present times. A numerous colony of Radnorshire Nonconformists migrated to Pennsylvania, in North America. To their labours are owing the printing and the publishing of the first Concordance that ever appeared in the Welsh language. It was the product of the Philadelphia press. Now, at the expiration of one century, the living language of the inhabitants of this parish is entirely English. The names of houses and lands still retain their Welsh appellations; and, as is the case in many parishes in this county, utensils, and sundry other articles, are distinguished by Welsh names, which the inhabitants in general consider to be English. For instance, they call a mattock, *caib*; an earthen pot, or jar, *steene*; a furrow, *rhigol*; wretched, *truan*; importunate, *taer*; with many more.

This parish contains at present about 2000 acres of land, inclusive of a common, which was inclosed and divided in 1812.

Pilleth Hall, or House, formerly the residence of the respectable family of Price, of this parish, is now the property of T. F. Lewis, Esq., M.P., of Harpton Court, near Radnor. The south wing was taken down some years ago; it is probable that this wing corresponded with that on the north side, and if so, it was originally a complete H house.

Ecclesiastical Account.

The church of Pilleth is dedicated to St. Mary, and consists of a porch, nave, chancel, and tower containing one bell. In the inside of the altar are fixed sepulchral memorials of the ancient and respectable family of Price, of this parish; one of which commemorates the death of Jane Esther Morgan, daughter of James Price, Esq., of Pilleth, and wife of the Right Worshipful Sir John Morgan, Bart., of Kinnersley, Herefordshire. The other is a stone monument, sculptured with two elegant human figures, containing the following inscription:—" To the pious memory of John Pryse, Esqr. of Pilleth, & of Catherine his wife, daughter of Roger Vaughan, Esqr. of Clitherow, in the county of Radnor. *He* died in 1597, & *she* in 1589." A sword and a pair of spurs are suspended on this monument, which are said to have belonged to the said John Price, Esq., who served as a gallant officer in the wars of Queen Elizabeth. Fame, which propagates falsehoods as well as truths, reports that the original spurs, which were of gold, one day disappeared, and a pair composed of a baser metal was substituted in their stead. In the church-yard, on the north side of the church, is a steened and arched well, the water of which was formerly considered beneficial in ophthalmia, and other diseases of the eyes.

Three-fourths of the tithes of this parish are annexed to the prebend of Llangunllo, in the Collegiate Church of Brecknock; and the other fourth part belongs to Richard Price, Esq., of Knighton, M.P., the other impropriator.

This benefice is a perpetual curacy, not in charge, annexed to the vicarage of Llangunllo, and stated in *Liber Regis* to be of the certified yearly value of £4 12s. 6d.

Charitable Donation.

In the year 1703 Lady Anne Child by will left certain parcels of land, of which the clear annual value is reported to be £52 10s., but supposed to be much higher, vested in the Bishop of St. David's, Chanter of St. David's, vicar or curate of Pilleth, and rector of Whitton, for the purpose of teaching the children of the several parishes of Pilleth and Whitton to read and to write, and to place out one child apprentice yearly from each parish. This school, of which the Rev. G. A. Barker, rector of Whitton, is master, is holden at Whitton, the adjoining parish, and is united with the free school thereof.

List of Incumbents.

Robert Lewis 1744   Henry Bevan 1788
James Meredith 1764   Morgan Evans 1807

WHITTON.

This name seems to be altogether Saxon, and to signify the white town, or township. It contains by estimation 1200 acres of inclosed land. Its resident population, according to the return made in the year 1801, consisted of 109 individuals.

HUNDRED OF COLWYN.

About the same time that Paganus de Cadurcis, or Payne of Cahours, that is, in the reign of William Rufus, wrested the hundred of Pain's Castle from the native inhabitants, Ralph de Todeni, who bore the standard of the conqueror of England in the decisive battle of Hastings, and who was governor of Clifford Castle, and Radulphus de Baskerville, governor of Eardisley Castle, invaded the territory now comprehended by the hundred of Colwyn, and secured their acquisitions by bridling the country with the castles and garrisons of Colwyn and Aberedw. These acquisitions were facilitated by the unhappy circumstances in which the Principality of South Wales happened at that time to be involved; for after the death of its prince, Rhys ab Tewdwr, who was slain in battle by Robert de Fitzhamon, the whole country, destitute of a legitimate ruler and confidential defender, fell a prey to intestine commotions on the one hand, and to hostile invasions on the other. After the lapse of some centuries, this territory passed from the family of De Todeni to that of De Braos, Lords of Brecknock and Buallt, and was granted by Edward I. to Roger Mortimer, Earl of Marche and Wigmore, who thereby united the two ancient lordships of Moelynaidd and Elfael. The last surviving heiress of the family of Baskerville, of Aberedw Court, conveyed that estate by marriage to the Rev. John Powell, late of Clyro Court.

The hundred of Colwyn contains ten parishes, viz., Aberedw, Bettws Diserth, Clâscwm, Cregrina, Diserth, Llanbadarn-y-garreg, Llanelwedd, Llanfaredd, Llansantfraid, and Rhiwlen, which shall be described in the order in which they are here enumerated; and also four lordships, viz., Upper Elfael, Graig, Aberedw, and Porth-Cadwgan.

ABEREDW.

This parish presents to the antiquary many interesting vestiges of former times. On a hill contiguous to the estate of Ty-yn-y-Blaenau, or Llwyn-y-Moylin, are constructed three large tumuli, or barrows, placed not in a straight line, but forming three points of a triangle, the sides of which extend about 300 yards equally. Each of them is surrounded with a deep foss and high vallum, which appendages, together with their number, afford an irrefragable argument that their original formation was done with a military designation, and not to serve merely as watch towers, though their elevated situation, and the extensive prospect which they command on all sides, are favourable to that purpose. They must have been a conspicious and picturesque object to the garrison of the castle of Colwyn.

On the bank of the river Edw, and at a small distance from the parish church, stand the ruins of a small castle, erected, as it is supposed, by Radulphus de Baskerville, Lord of Yerdisley; of which, however, his descendants were deprived by Rhys ab Tewdwr, and by Llewelyn ab Gruffudd, the latter of whom occasionally made this castle his residence. At a short distance from these ruins, and close to the line of the Edw, is a circular mound, or tumulus, supposed by many to have been an appendage of the castle, but which, in the opinion of the author of this work, constituted the residential palace of the British *reguli* of this district long prior to the Norman invasion. There is also, at the distance of a quarter of a mile from the castle, a remarkable cavern, or grotto, cut out of the solid rock, and containing internally a square apartment, measuring six feet every way. The entrance into it is exceedingly narrow, for the purpose of more effectual concealment. Artificial excavations of this description are frequently to be met with in several parts of Wales, and undoubtedly were used as places of refuge and secure retreat in periods of trouble and danger. Perhaps, also, the disciples of druidism resorted thither, in order to contemplate with greater freedom and abstraction, and to treasure up in their memories the mysterious arcana of their order. Tradition reports that, in this cave, Llewelyn, the last Prince of Wales secreted himself from the pursuit of his enemies, and waited with anxious impatience for the arrival of the expected succours from South Wales. Here he was betrayed by the blacksmith, who recognized the horse he was employed to shoe, and who, in addition to his own indelible infamy, had like to have stained the honour of this county with the ignominious assassination of its prince. But that fate was reserved for Brecknockshire, as already related. The parish of Aberedw comprises two lordships, viz., the lordship of Aberedw, and the lordship of Porth Cadwgan. By a fatal but common vicissitude and revolution in human affairs, that which anciently was the least of these two lordships, or rather no lordship at all before the Norman invasion, is now become the greatest; and what was in times past the most considerable in this part of the county is at present reduced to the smallest compass; for the lordship of Porth Cadwgan, now limited to the narrow confines of a single farm named *Ty-yn-y-coed*, in this parish, the site of the old castle, and of the church and church-yard, together with the fisheries of the rivers Wye and Edw, as far as that farm extends on their respective banks, once constituted a portion of that patrimonial inheritance which belonged to *Cadwgan*, the eldest son of Ellistan Glodrudd, Lord of Fferllys, Moelynaidd, and Elfael, in this county, from whom are lineally descended the present noble family of *Cadwgan*. The site of the old castle is upon Ty-yn-y-coed estate, now belonging to Vaughan Pococke, Esq. The still visible remains of this once formidable fortress enable the spectator to form some tolerable idea of its ancient grandeur. It comprized a square, inclosing an area of half an acre of ground, surrounded by a strong wall, and fortified by a deep intrenchment on all sides, excepting that on the south, where the approach is rendered, by the nature of the ground, inaccessible. At each angle of the square stood a round tower, of which the abutments remain to this day, of six feet in thickness.

In this parish are many respectable mansions: 1. The Court of Aberedw, the late residence of the ancient family of Baskerville. The last heiress [1] conveyed this estate by marriage to the Rev. John Powell, late of Clirow Court,

[1] She was grand-daughter of James Baskerville, Esq., who killed in a duel, rather unfairly, Colonel Powell, or Lloyd, in Presteigne, as before related. It has been remarked that the family of Baskerville, from the time of this unfortunate event, never prospered.

and son of Mr. Hugh Powell, of Pen-y-lan, near Gwithel, in the lower township of the parish of Llanfihangel-nant Moylin. The only issue of this marriage was a daughter, who was married to Peter Ricketts, or Minors, Esq., of Evenjobb, in the parish of Old Radnor. Their eldest son, viz., Peter Ricketts, or Minors, Esq., is the present proprietor of Aberedw Court. The second son has lately assumed the name of Baskerville, at the request of a distant relative, who has left him a large fortune. 2. Swyn-y-Moylen, in the vale of Blaen-y-Moylen, the residence of Thomas Pugh, Esq., in whose family this estate has remained more than four centuries. 3. ——, the property of the Rev. Thomas Jones, who resides in the county of Bucks.

Near the ruins of the old castle stands a corn mill driven by the stream of the Edw, the property of the crown of England, leased by Marmaduke Gwynne, Esq., or his representatives, at the gross annual rent of 13s. 4d. In the year 1784 there were sixteen years in arrears. Opposite to this mill, and on the other side of the Edw, are the most magnificent rocks, perhaps, in the kingdom. They stand nearly in a perpendicular direction, and are elevated 500 feet above the bed of the river. They extend along the bank of the river, in diversified forms, at least a mile in length, majestically towering one above another, and resembling on a moonlight night the fragmented turrets and broken columns of a magnificent and tremendous castle.

Ecclesiastical Account.

The church consists of a porch, nave, chancel, and tower. It is dedicated to St. Gewydd.

This benefice is a rectory, in the deanery of Elfael Ismynydd, and diocese of St. David's, remaining in charge, and estimated in *Liber Regis* to be worth £12 13s. 4d. per annum. The yearly tenths are £1 5s. 4d. The Bishop of St. David's is the patron. All the tithes of the parish are impropriated, and amount in value to £200 per annum.

Charitable Donations.

At a time unknown Lewis Lloyd, Esq., bequeathed by will for the use and benefit of decayed housekeepers of this parish not receiving parochial relief, a parcel of land, now vested in Mr. John Gwynne, producing the annual rent of £4 0s. 6d.

In the year 1746 Mrs. Elizabeth Price bequeathed by will the annual interest of £20, for the use and benefit of decayed housekeepers of this parish, not receiving parochial relief. The principal is vested in James Pugh and James Baskerville, Esqrs.

List of Incumbents.

Thomas Williams 1715   John Williams 1770
Joseph Williams 1743

In the year 1649, the Rev. Henry Mellon, rector of this parish, was ejected by the parliamentary commissioners, and his benefice sequestrated.

BETTWS DISERTH.

This parish contains about 2000 acres of land, of which about 1200 are inclosed and cultivated; the remainder consists of wastes. Its resident population, according to the return made in the year 1801, consisted of 103 individuals. The parochial assessments for the service of the year 1803 amounted to the sum of £75 14s., levied at 6s. in the pound.

Ecclesiastical Account.

The chapel of Bettws Diserth is a very humble structure, and situated in a narrow recess on the bank of the river Edw, and dedicated to St. Mary. It contains one small bell.

This benefice is a perpetual curacy, annexed to the rectory of Diserth, and is of the certified yearly value of £18; but the total emoluments at present amount to the sum of £75 per annum.

Charitable Donations.

In a year unknown a rent-charge of £1 per annum, now vested in the Rev. Mr. Jones, was devised by a person whose name is unknown, and whether by will or deed alike unknown, for the benefit of the poor inhabitants of this parish not receiving parochial relief.

In the year 1746 Mrs. Elizabeth Jones bequeathed by will, for the use and benefit of the poor of this parish not receiving parochial relief, the principal sum of £40, the yearly interest arising from which was paid a few times by the executor, but afterwards stopped.

The Rev. Rees Powell, in a year unknown, left by deed the annual rent of lands, sum not ascertained, vested in the Bishop of Hereford, Sir Edward Williams, Bart., Philip Williams, J. Bullock Lloyd, James Hughes, Walter Jefferys, Esqrs., Rev. John Williams, and Walter Wilkins, Esq., M.P., for the purpose of apprenticing poor children, not only of this parish in particular, but of ten others, and for other purposes.

CLASCWM.

This name has been erroneously interpreted to signify the green dingle. If the name expressed that meaning, it would have been written Cwmglâs, the adjective in the Welsh language being generally postponed to the substantive. Clâs is the name of a river that intersects this parish, and therefore Clâscwm signifies the vale or dingle of the Clâs.

This parish contains 4500 acres of land, of which about 3000 are inclosed and cultivated, the remaining 1500 being unenclosed and uncultivated wastes, and consists of two townships, viz., Drewern, or the orl township, and Faenor-glâs, or the summit impending over the rivulet Glâs. The money raised by the parish rates for the service of the year 1803 amounted to the following sums in each township, viz., in Drewern, the sum of £162 10s. 10d., at 7s. 2d. in the pound; in Faenor-glâs, the sum of £150 2s. 10d., at 6s. 8d. in the pound, making an aggregate of £312 13s. 8d. Faenor-glâs is a lordship belonging to the Bishop of St. David's, now holden by Perceval Lewis, Esq., of Downton, in the parish of Radnor.

The celebrated wells of Blaen-Edw are situated in this parish.

There lies in this parish a piece of crown-land, named Allivies, lately tenanted by Richard Austin, Esq., at the gross annual rent of 3s. 8d.

This parish, together with the adjoining territory, was in ancient times the scene of much military action, and consequently abounds in barrows and camps. About a quarter of a mile to the north-east of the village of Clâscwm stand the remains of a very strong camp on a farm named Wern, on a commanding eminence, judiciously selected to overlook the defiles leading to the village, as well as to check the approach of an enemy advancing through the narrow vale of the before-mentioned river Clâs, which discharges itself into the river Arrow, in the neighbouring parish of Colfâ. This intrenchment, which was double, embraced about three-fourths of the circumference of the summit on which it is constructed, being open partly to the south and south-west, the natural difficulties of those points superseding the necessity of fortifying them; and probably the approach of an enemy from that quarter was unexpected. This circumstance indicates this encampment to have been Silurian, and constructed in opposition to the Romans, advancing into this district along the Roman road which communicates with Gwilfach-ar-heol, on the river Arrow, in the parish of Newchurch. This encampment was distinguished by the name of Clâs-gwyr; and the dingle leading to it is now called Cwm-Jwrch, or Jowarch. No appearance of buildings at present exists. At a short distance from hence, viz., about one mile and a half towards the west, is a small tumulus, or barrow, of great antiquity, supposed to have been used as a beacon. Upon a farm named Brynllwyd are several tumuli, or barrows, of which one is conspicuously distinguished from the others by its superior elevation and magnitude, and by being surrounded by a deep trench and high vallum. Partly on the east side of this tumulus, and adjoining to the vallum thereof, is an ancient camp inclosed with embankments, and containing about two acres of land. Contiguous to this is a small portion of land, elevated above the adjoining land, where appear some traces of building. This camp is supposed to be of Roman construction, and the elevated piece of ground the prætorium. About twenty years ago a farmer, by clearing some brush-wood that grew near the above-mentioned tumulus, found several pieces of silver, and coins of various forms and sizes, of which some were circular, others square; none, however, were preserved. And in the year 1806 another quantity of silver coins, of the reign of King William, was discovered by a shepherd's boy in a mole-hill on the hills.

At a short distance from the before-mentioned tumulus is a large stone, placed erect, seven feet broad, two feet thick. About two or three yards from this stone is another of nearly equal dimensions, lying flat upon the ground, and has been apparently undermined, from motives of avarice or curiosity. On a farm named Llwyn-y——, in this parish, an inferior castle has been erected; the foundations of the walls now remain. It is named Brynllys Castle, and the fields adjoining are distinguished by the appellation of the castle meadow, the castle field, &c. About seventeen years ago the Rev. Benjamin Jones sold this estate to Edward Rogers, Esq., of Stanage, in this county, the present proprietor. This was a point extremely well chosen to guard the narrow defile leading from the village of Clâscwm to the river Edw, as well as to transmit intelligence to the other fortified points of this interesting district, of which the most remarkable is Colwyn Castle, described in Llansantfraid parish.

On a farm named Graig-fawr, and on a commanding eminence also called Graig, in this parish, has been a very important fortification, partaking in some degree of the nature of an inferior castle. Under the summit of this military station, on a farm named Caermyrddu, contiguous to the buildings, is a very ancient cromlech, covered with huge coarse stones. This estate is now the property of T. F. Lewis, Esq., of Harpton, M.P. About a quarter of a mile on the opposite side of the river Edw, in a piece of land named Rhôs-y-merch, is a small portion of ground encircled with large coarse stones placed erect in the earth. This had been a carn, constructed for druidical or bardic purposes.

Bryn-llhwyd, an estate in this parish, is the property of —— Price, Esq., who resides in the county of Berks, and served the office of high sheriff for the county of Radnor. This estate is said to have remained in this family more than 1000 years, and will, after the decease of the present owner, devolve upon his sister's heirs, viz., Peter Edwards, of the parish of Cascob, in this county, a gentleman of the persuasion of Friends, or Quakers, who married the daughter of Mr. Price's sister, manages the estate, and has issue two sons.

Ecelesiastical Account.

The church of Clâscwm consists of a nave and chancel, separated by a timber frame.

This benefice is a discharged vicarage, having the chapelries of Colfâ and Rhiwlen annexed, and is valued in *Liber Regis* at the yearly sum of £13 6s. 8d. The yearly tenths are £1 6s. 8d. The total emoluments of the vicar amount at present to the yearly sum of £62 2s. 5d. He has also a vicarage house and glebe land.

Charitable Donations.

In the year 1620 John Evans, Esq., left by will, for the benefit of the poor of this parish not receiving parochial relief, a sum of money; and in the year 1717 David Davies, Esq., left also a sum of money, by will, for the same charitable purpose; which two sums added together make a principal of £100, the annual interest of which, viz., £5, is ordered to be distributed among poor persons not chargeable to the parish.

About thirty years ago Mr. John Davies gave to the poor of this parish a rent-charge of £4, secured on an estate named Cwm-sych. The same was never paid.

Another estate, named Cwm-mawr, in this parish, is charged with 10s. annually, to be paid to the poor of this parish. This estate is the property of Mr. Thomas Lewis, of the Yatt, who has paid it some years ago. He is also the person in whom the principal sum of £100 above-mentioned is vested. It is reported that each of these wills is lodged in the Registrar's office in Brecknock.

List of Incumbents.

Athelstane Williams............ 1733 Jenkin Jenkins 1787
Walter Meyric .... 1741 John Jones 1788
Chambele Davies, A.B. 1744

CRUGINA.

It contains by estimation 1000 acres of land, of which two-thirds are inclosed and cultivated; the remainder consists of hills.

According to the return made in the year 1801, its resident population consisted of 133 individuals. The money raised by the parochial rates for the service of the year 1803 amounted to the sum of £67 1s. 7d., assessed at 4s. 6d. in the pound.

Ecclesiastical Account.

The church consists of a porch, nave, chancel, and low tower. It is dedicated to St. David. The benefice is a discharged rectory, having the chapelry of Llanbadarn-y-garreg annexed, and is estimated in *Liber Regis* to be yearly worth £35. The yearly tenths are 18s. 8d. The total emoluments of this rectory amount at present to the annual sum of £80 14s.

Charitable Donations.

In a year unknown, the Rev. Rees Powell devised a sum of money not specified, secured upon land, and vested in trustees, viz., Bishop of Hereford for the time being, Sir Edward Williams, Bart., John Morgan, Charles Powell, Philip Williams, J. Bullock Lloyd, Walter Wilkins, M.P., James Hughes, Walter Jefferys, Esqrs., and John Williams, for apprenticing poor children, not only of this parish, but of ten others in this county, and for other charitable purposes. Some of the lands so devised are situated in this parish.

In a year unknown the Rev. Thomas Williams bequeathed by will the annual sum of 10s., vested in Mr. Evan Evans, for the use and benefit of decayed housekeepers of this parish.

List of Incumbents.

In the year 1649 the Rev. Rowland Vaughan, rector of Crugina-morion, was ejected by the parliamentary commissioners, and his benefice sequestrated. This pious and learned divine translated the *Practice of Piety*, Archbishop Ussher's *Catechism*, and other religious books, into the Welsh language, for the Christian edification of his parishioners and countrymen. The publication of these excellent treatises excited the hatred, and inflamed the persecution, of the fanatics and enthusiasts of those times.

DISERTH.

This name seems to be compounded of Du and Serth. It extends in length about four miles, and nearly three in breadth. It is divided into two townships, viz., Duserth and Tre 'r Coed, the latter being a woody township, as its name implies. It contains about 4000 acres of land, of which nearly 3000 are inclosed and cultivated; the remainder are commons and hills, uninclosed and uncultivated.

According to the return made in the year 1801, the population of this parish consisted of 517 individuals. The parochial assessments are collected and paid separately, each township having distinct officers. The money raised in each for the service of the year 1803 was as follows:—For the township of Diserth, £117 12s. 5½d., assessed at 8s. 2d. in the pound; for Tre 'r Coed, £131 14s. 1d., at 7s. 8d. in the pound; amounting in the whole to the sum of £249 6s. 6½d.

Relics of antiquity are extremely rare. Neither a tommen, nor a cairn, nor a cromlech, nor a castle, have been discovered. There is, however, a farm-house named Yr-heol, that is, the street, or causeway, through the fold of which the Roman road passed, and of which the course may be traced from the river Wye to the Roman station Magos, or Caerfagu, on the river Ieithon, in the parish of Llanfihangel Helygen. In this parish is situated the village of Howey, so named from the brook which flows through it, on the banks of which its few houses are erected; or, perhaps, it derives this appellation from a chieftain and governor of Fferllys in the year 640 of the name of Hoyw. He was the son of Gloyw, the son of Caw, the son of Cawrda. He was a personage of great celebrity, and is described in the Triads as "one of the seven blessed first cousins of Britain." If Howey was ever dignified by the royal residence of either of these chieftains its present state is a melancholy picture of fallen greatness. And the privilege which it possesses of holding three fairs annually, viz., on Saturday before the 11th of February, on Saturday before the 11th of May, and on Saturday before the 11th of September, for the sale of sheep, cattle, horses, swine, and other produce of the district, may be adduced in proof of the high estimation with which it was regarded in former times. On the common of Howey, a little towards the south-east of the village, is a British encampment, of an elliptical form, and apparently of remote antiquity, of which no authentic information can be obtained. Its present name is Caer-du, that is, the black camp, probably so given from the dark hue of the soil. It is suspected that this was not its original appellation.

Ecclesiastical Account.

The church is dedicated to St. Gwydd, of whom little or nothing is known. The wake is holden annually on the first Sunday after St. Swithin's-day. This benefice is a rectory, having the chapelry of Bettws Diserth annexed, and is estimated in *Liber Regis* at £16 per annum. The yearly tenths are £1 12s. According to the diocesan report, published in the year 1809, the total emoluments of this benefice amount from £280 to £300 per annum. The oldest register of this church and parish commences only in the year 1734.

Charitable Donation.

In the year 1762 Mr. Ezekiel Williams devised by will, for the use and benefit of the poor of this parish not receiving parochial relief, the sum of £2 per annum, being the legal interest of a principal of £40.

List of Incumbents.

In the year 1649 John Philipps was rector of Diserth and Bettws Diserth, and ejected by the parliamentary commissioners, and his benefice sequestrated by the fanatics and enthusiasts of those days.
Philip Lewis, A.M. 1737   John Wilkins, recollated 1786
John Wilkins, A.M............ 1768   Charles Griffith ....

LLANBADARN-Y-GARREG.

On the survey of this parish nothing presented itself worthy of historical record; no tumuli, no cairns, no castles. According to the return made in the year 1801, its resident population consisted of 77 individuals. The money raised by the parochial rates for the service of the year 1803 amounted to the sum of £12 4s. 5d., upon an assessment of 7s. 6d. in the pound.

Ecclesiastical Account.

This benefice is a chapelry, or perpetual curacy, not in charge, annexed to the rectory of Crugrina, stated in *Liber Regis* to be of the certified value of £12 6s. 8d. per annum. The chapel is dedicated to St. Padarn.

Charitable Donations.

Lewis Lloyd, Esq., devised by will, date unknown, a rent-charge of £4, secured upon land, and vested in Mr. John Gwynne, for the relief of decayed housekeepers in this parish.

A person unknown bequeathed the sum of £10, now vested in Mr. Tobe, the yearly interest of which is ordered to be distributed among decayed housekeepers in this parish.

LLANELWEDD.

This name perpetuates the remembrance of a saint called Elwedd. The parish is of small extent, about two miles and a half in length, and the same in breadth, containing 6000 acres of land inclosed and cultivated, together with some commons uninclosed, and rocky hills. The principal landed proprietors are Thomas Thomas, Esq., of Pencerrig, David Thomas, Esq., of Wellfield House, and M. H. T. Gwynne, Esq., of Llanelwedd Hall. The estate of Pencerrig formerly belonged to the ancient family of Powel, who derive their pedigree from Ellistan Glodrudd, Lord of Fferllys and Moelynaidd. The last proprietor of that name left no male issue, but had two daughters, of whom the elder was married to Walter Williams, Esq., of Caebalfa, and secondly to Hugh Morgan, Esq., of Bettws Diserth. She lies buried in the back aisle of the church of Leominster, in the county of Hereford, where an antique monument has been erected to her memory, with the following inscription:—

" M.S.

" Annæ juxta humatæ filiæ Thomæ Powel de Pencerrig in com. Radnor, Gen: ex Mariâ fil. Hoeli Gwynne de Glanbrane in agro Maridun. Armig. ideoque præcipuis de Cambria Silurum et in eo divitum familiis cognatione conjunct. Pridem Gualteri Williams Gen: Dein Hugonis Morgan, Gen: conjugis amantissimæ. Variolarum malefi. valetud. decessit 8vo die Octobris anno Domini 1719. Ætatis suæ 53. H. M. maritus heu superstes uxori bene merenti mærens posuit."

The younger daughter was married to John Jones, Esq., of Trefonnen, in the parish of Llandrindod, who served the office of high sheriff for this county in the year 1737. Their issue was Mary, the relict of the late Thomas Jones, Esq., of Pencerrig. This estate, together with several others in the parishes of Diserth, Llandrindod, &c., were conveyed to Thomas Thomas, Esq., by marriage with the grand-daughter of the above-mentioned Thomas Jones, Esq. The sister and co-heiress of Mrs. Thomas was married to —— Dale, Esq., Captain of the Royal Navy, and took with her several other estates. The mother of these two ladies was a native of Italy, to whom their father, the late Thomas Jones, Esq., eldest son of the above-mentioned Thomas Jones, Esq., was passionately attached, when on his travels thither to improve himself in that fine art in which he excelled; and whom it is reported, after his return to England, he married, according to the prescribed form of our National Church, though unfortunately in a period subsequent to their birth. This circumstance produced a tedious and expensive litigation, commenced at the suit of Middleton Jones, Esq., of Penybont Hall, the eldest surviving son of the grandfather of Mrs. Thomas, on the ground that this lady being born previous to the solemnization of matrimony agreeably to the form of the Church of England, he stood entitled to the estate as heir-at-law. After many trials in a court of judicature, it was decided that the estates which composed his mother's jointure, viz., Trefonnen, &c., should be awarded to that gentleman, who has since laid claim to the whole property as of right devolving to him after the decease of Mrs. Thomas, and has publicly advertised the sale of the reversion. The mansion-house of Pencerrig is built with brick, having in front a very large piece of water well stocked with fish, and situated amid very beautiful scenery.

The resident population of this parish, according to the return made in the year 1801, consisted of 146 individuals. The money raised by the parish rates for the service of the year 1803 was assessed at 5s. in the pound, and amounted to the sum of £74 15s. 10½d.

This parish is further entitled to regard on account of the antiquities it contains, and the national events which have been in former ages transacted in it. On the hill named Caerneddau is an immense quantity of huge but loose stones, in colour vying with alabaster in whiteness, and resembling, though not equalling in number, the Cerrig-gwynion, or white stones, upon Cwystedin-fawr, near the post town of Rhayader. Tradition reports that these stones were conveyed thither by labour in the druidical times, which surely must be an erroneous statement. The labour required for such a purpose must have been immense, and far beyond human means. Their extremely irregular and disorderly disposition militates against the supposition of the existence of a carn, or carns. The most rational account ascribes them to be the contents of a disembowelled mountain. At the distance of about a quarter of a mile is a huge square stone, placed erect in the ground, which now serves as a boundary between the parishes of Llanelwedd and Llanfaredd. Besides these two, the parish of Llansantfraid also has a right of commonage on this hill. As Caerneddau commands a full view of the Roman station upon the Ieithon, and of the line of the Roman road leading to it from the Wye, it is conjectured by some antiquaries that this large heap of stones was the concerted point of rendezvous where the Silurians were to assemble, and from which they darted and attacked the Roman convoys charged with the lead ore extracted from the mines in the parish of Llan-y-drindod.

On the left hand of the road leading to Rhayader, and also at a short distance from the Wye, and about two miles from the village of Llanelwedd up the river, are the remains of a very ancient fortification, or camp, on a farm named Court Llechrhyd, which the historian of Brecknockshire erroneously states to be in the parish of Diserth. It was surrounded by a deep and wide foss, or trench, and high rampart, and it inclosed about ten acres of land. The intrenchment at this time is in many places full of water, and the quality of the soil is marshy. The foss, or trench, was at least twenty feet wide, and six or seven feet high, and could be filled with water, which a small rill supplied. No internal trench appears at present. To the west of this fortification, several circular mounds of earth have been thrown up, on which are no marks of intrenchment, as they appear at present; but these may have been obliterated by the plough, as cultivation has been carried up to their summit. These mounds, or hillocks, seem well calculated to serve as outposts, or stations of observation, commanding a view of the vale of the Wye, both to the east and west of the principal fortification, as far as the winding of the river, and the obstruction of intervening hills will admit. This station seems judiciously selected for the purpose of surprizing an enemy advancing up the line of the river Wye, and indeed appears more fitted to hold an army of reserve than for any other purpose. Ill adapted for defence, or to repel the common enemy, it seems more appropriated to the ill-fated purpose of deciding the intestine quarrels which, unhappily for the independence of Wales, too often prevailed among its chieftains and princes. And accordingly we find that this was the use to which it had once been applied. For in the year 1809 Cadwgan, Riryd, and Madoc, the sons of Bleddyn ab Cynfyn, Prince of North Wales, had with a formidable force overrun and ravaged this part of Radnorshire, which belonged to Rhys ab Tewdwr, Prince of South Wales, and his son-in-law Madoc ab Idnerth, Lord of Moelynaidd and Elfael, and shutting themselves up within the lines of this fortified encampment, defied the united strength of these combined princes. Vain was their confidence; for Rhys ab Tewdwr, and Madoc ab Idnerth, on the first intelligence of this hostile irruption, having effected a junction of their respective forces, marched against the invaders, attacked them in the midst of their intrenchments, and burst into them with irresistible fury. Then a terrible carnage ensued. Riryd and Madoc shared the fate due to their rebellion, together with a great number of their deluded countrymen. Cadwgan saved himself by flight. Thus did Wales waste its strength in civil dissension, and by this weakness forwarded the views of its foreign enemies.

The present farm-house and buildings are erected on a small eminence on or near the spot where the old court or castellated mansion originally stood. This fortress was made use of by Llewelyn, the last Prince of Wales, in his unfortunate expedition into this country, which terminated in his death, for the purpose of securing, in case of a defeat, his return over the Wye into the north.

Cilleg Cadwgan is the almost inaccessible rock to which Cadwgan fled wounded from the battle of Llechrhyd, in this parish, and from which he afterwards had the good fortune to effect his escape.

Ecclesiastical Account.

The church, or rather chapel, is a small edifice, consisting of a porch, nave, chancel, and a low tower containing one bell. The church-yard is a spacious plain, from which is a most beautiful and picturesque view both up and down the river. It is dedicated to St. Matthew, and the wake is holden on the first Sunday in October.

This benefice is a perpetual curacy, not in charge, stated in *Liber Regis* to be of the yearly certified value of £6. The tithes of the parish are occupied by the prebend, with the power of leasing, and annexed to the prebendary. The terrier is as follows:—" Church-yard, and ¼ of an acre of pasture land adjoining the road; ½ of all grain and hay; some of the lands are covered with a modus ½d. for every day's math, payable at Easter; ½ of wool and lambs; ½d. for sheep brought in at May; for summered sheep 1s. per score; tithe of cheese from first day of May to first day of November; composition of 1s. for every cow yearly; smoak 1d.; garden 1d.; colt 1d.; calf ½d.; offerings 2d. from every person 17 years old; from the estate of Trewern 5s.; from non-resident occupiers of land 2s. in the pound; tithe of pigs, geese, fruit, hops, turnips, flax, and hemp, and honey; tithe of coppice wood; ½ of the tithes of all profits and increase growing within this parish; burial 1s.; wedding 4s. 6d. or 5s.; churching 1s." It has received two augmentations from Queen Anne's bounty, which money has been laid out in the purchase of two small estates; one of which lies in the vicinity of Kington, Herefordshire; so that the total emoluments of this benefice at present amount to the sum of £45 18s. per annum. The Rev. John Williams, Archdeacon of Cardigan, is the patron.

The prebend of Llanelwedd, discharged, in the Collegiate Church of Brecknock, is estimated in *Liber Regis* at £6 10s. per annum, the clear yearly value of which is £25. The yearly tenths are 13s. In the year 1649 this prebend was abolished by the parliamentary commissioners, and its revenue sequestrated and applied to the godly purposes of fanaticism and rebellion. The Bishop of St. David's is the patron.

Charitable Donations.

In a year not certified Lady Hartstronge, relict of Sir Standish Hartstronge, Bart., the late proprietor of Drewern, devised by will an estate named Penbedw, together with a small messuage adjoining, situated in the parish of St. Harmon, in this county, the annual rental of which being about £18, for the purpose of establishing and supporting a free school in this parish. A person of the name of Thomas Jones was regularly nominated by Uvedale Price, Esq., of Foxley, in the county of Hereford, and licensed by the Right Rev. Dr. Horsley, Bishop of St. David's, to the said school; which appointment he held more than forty years. He, dying, was succeeded in the school by his son, John Jones, without any regular nomination or licence. Keeping the parishioners in profound ignorance of the amount and situation of the endowment, and accustomed for many years to receive the rents thereof, he proceeded at length to the unparalleled impudence of not only claiming the property as his own patrimonial inheritance, but also of actually selling it to an honest attorney in the town of Presteigne, named Edward Lee James. The compiler of this work, in the course of his researches, happened to obtain information of the nature and situation of the endowment, and laid it before the parishioners, who brought an action against the attorney, and recovered the estate. No benefit, however, has yet resulted to the poor children of the parish from this spirited measure. The funds of the charity are obliged to be mortgaged for some years to defray the expenses of the law suit.

List of Incumbents.

Evan Powell	1736	John Williams, LL.B.	1784
Rice Williams	1768	Thomas Morgan	

LLANFAREDD.

This parish is of small extent, about two square miles, containing not more than 400 acres of land, of which the greatest portion is inclosed and under cultivation. Its resident population, according to the return made in the year 1801, consisted of 194 individuals. The money raised by the parish rates for the service of the year 1803 amounted to the sum of £48 4s. 11½d., at 6s. in the pound.

Ecclesiastical Account.

The church, or rather chapel, of Llanfaredd is a humble edifice, consisting of a porch, nave, chancel, and low tower containing one bell. It is dedicated to St. Mary. In the chancel is a tablet commemorating the family of Phillips, of this parish. This benefice is a perpetual curacy, not in charge, annexed to the rectory of Aberedw, of the certified yearly value of £43 10s. The Rev. John Williams, Archdeacon of Cardigan, is the patron.

LLANSANTFRAID.

This name is derived from the female saint to whom the church is dedicated, and who lived about the middle of the seventh century. According to the return made in the year 1801, its resident population consisted of 293 individuals. The money raised by the parish rates for the service of the year 1803 amounted to the sum of £205 6s., at 9s. in the pound.

To the antiquary this parish presents many interesting relics. The first that deserves to be mentioned is the celebrated castle of Colwyn, so called from a small brook that runs at the foot of it. This fortress was surrounded with a deep and wide trench, or foss, which in certain places at this time contains water. Its external intrenchment incloses an area of ten acres of land. The part towards the west is now converted into a corn-field, containing at least five acres. This castle is situated on the Forest Farm, and was constructed for the purpose of defending the country from hostile incursions advancing from the eastern parts of the kingdom. On a small common, about eighty yards from the exterior intrenchment, a huge coarse stone, about six feet square, and about two feet thick, lies flat upon the ground, differing in quality from all the stones in the neighbourhood, generally supposed to have been conveyed thither for the purpose of covering the remains of a person of distinction, but which, in the judgment of the author of this work, composed the fragment of a cromlech.

Within half a mile of this castle are several tumuli, or barrows, one on a small common near to the river Edw, in which were lately found two earthen jars, of brown ware, curiously embossed, about two feet high, closely covered with plain stones, and capable of containing five gallons of liquid, and inclosing originally, as it is supposed, human bones. These vases, on being exposed to the air, fell in pieces, and the contents became dust and ashes, emitting an offensive smell, which continued for several days. There are two other barrows undisturbed, on a farm named Bryn-llwyd; and also a conspicuous artificial mound on the bank of the Edw, of considerable height and extent, surrounded by a deep trench and high rampart. A little to the south-west of the castle, and on the farm on which that fortress was erected, stands another artificial mound, near to the fork of a dingle, and to the bottom of a very steep piece of wood-land, surrounded by a deep foss and high rampart. This spot is admirably well chosen, not only to give intelligence to the garrison of the castle of the approach of an enemy, having the castle and three out-posts within its view, viz., Brinllwyd, Cwm-Boltwr, and Craig-fawr, but also to conceal in ambush a force which might annoy the besiegers of the castle, and in case of a repulse retire into that fortress, or disperse in the woods, where pursuit would be difficult.

On a common, partly between the church of Llansantfraid and that of Llan-y-drindod, near to an estate named Llwyn-Madoc, now the seat and residence of Hugh Vaughan, Esq., is a high and rocky bank, in some places perpendicular, named the Castle Bank, on which has been a camp or military position of remote antiquity, encompassed by a moderate intrenchment, containing a spacious but uneven area about 800 yards in circumference, commanding an extensive view of the country lying between it and Rhayader, and distant about two miles west from the castle of Colwyn. The sides of this intrenchment are constructed with loose stones, and on the very summit are large heaps of stones of the same kind, viz., from two to six pounds weight each. There exists no appearance of building. This fortification seems to have been a place of refuge when the destructive engines of war were unknown, and when the inhabitants had no other instrument but stones to defend themselves, or to annoy their invaders.

At what period, or by what person, this once formidable and famous castle of Colwyn was constructed is a matter of which neither history nor tradition afford any authentic detail. The author's opinion is, that on this advantageous spot originally stood a Silurian stronghold, coeval and cooperating with all the other Silurian fortifications on the banks of the Edw, as well as on those of the different 'streams which discharge themselves into that river, and which water the adjoining parishes; and that this stronghold was at first employed in repulsing, or at least obstructing the progress of, the Roman invaders, who, it is well known, directed their operations against this part of the Radnorshire district from the Brecknockshire side. This conjecture derives some confirmation from the circumstance of retaining and preserving to this day its ancient and primitive appellation. When the Norman conquerors of Brecknockshire wrested from Cadwgan, son of Ellistan Glodrudd, and Lord of Moelynaidd and Elfael, Cantref Muallt, which his father had impoliticly conquered, and added to his patrimonial possessions, and when they had passed the river Wye, this Silurian fortress was among the first of their acquisitions, and was bestowed on Ralph de Todeni, who bore the standard of William in the battle of Hastings, and who had previously been made governor of the castle of Clifford. It was soon afterwards destroyed by the Welsh; rebuilt and regarrisoned by that powerful baron William de Braos, Lord of Brecknock, Buallt, Gower, and Bramber, who more than once caused King John to tremble on his throne. It was denominated Maud's Castle in honour of his wife, Maud de St. Valeri, a port-town in France, whence Duke William set sail on his English expedition. The Welsh, indignant at this tyrant's numerous cruelties and oppressions, demolished it a second time. It was afterwards rebuilt, in the year 1231, by Henry III., who by this route retreated out of South Wales after an unsuccessful expedition into that country, and by him conferred on a descendant of that family to which it originally belonged; for we find that, in the reign of Edward II., it was possessed by Robert de Todeni, a person of considerable distinction in those days.

Near Llwyn-Madoc, in this parish, was fought a battle between Llewelyn, the last Prince of Wales, and Sir Edmund Mortimer, deputy-lord of Moelynaidd and Elfael. The victory was claimed by both parties. Sir Edmund, however, received a mortal wound, of which he soon after died in the castle of Wigmore.

Ecclesiastical Account.

The church is dedicated to St. Bridget, and consists of a porch, nave, chancel, and tower containing one bell, neither of which contains any

HISTORY OF RADNORSHIRE. 305

article deserving historical record, excepting a tablet in the chancel, dedicated to the memory of John Donne, Esq., of this parish, and decorated with the family arms, viz., a demi-lion upon a globe, a leopard, and a chevron between two bugle horns.

This benefice is a discharged vicarage, estimated in *Liber Regis* at £5 14s. 9½d. per annum. The yearly tenths are 11s. 5¼d. The Bishop of St. David's is the patron. The clear yearly value, as stated in *Liber Regis*, in the reign of Queen Anne, is £40. But as the tithes of this parish are equally divided between the vicar and the trustees of Elwel, or Elfael charity, one moiety to each, the total emoluments of the vicar amount to three times that sum.

The prebend of Llansantfraid, in the Collegiate Church of Brecknock, is estimated in *Liber Regis* so low as £1 6s. 8d. per annum. The yearly tenths are 2s. 8d.

Charitable Donations.

In the year 1710 Mr. Hughes bequeathed a rent-charge secured upon land, and now vested in Mr. Hugh Vaughan, of the amount of £2, to be distributed among the poor of this parish.

In a year unknown a rent-charge of £1 secured upon land, and now vested in Mr. William Bridgwaters, was bequeathed by a person unknown, and whether by will or deed unknown, to be distributed among decayed housekeepers in this parish.

In a year unknown the Rev. Rees Powell bequeathed certain lands and estates, of which the annual rent is to be applied to the apprenticing of poor children of this parish, being one of the sixteen parishes that are entitled to a share of the Colwyn or Boughrood charity.

List of Incumbents.

Rice Williams 1773   John Hughes, A.M. 1796
William Higgs, A.M. 1784   —— Venables, D.D. ....

RULEN, OR RHIWLYN.

This name is derived from a brook of that denomination which flows through the vale of Rulen, and drives a corn-mill near the church of Rulen. It contains 1600 acres of land, of which about 1000 are supposed to be inclosed and cultivated. The remainder is composed of hills and wastes, uninclosed and uncultivated. According to the return made in the year 1801 its resident population consisted of 120 individuals. The money raised by the parish rates for the service of the year 1803 amounted to the sum of £85 14s. 2d., from an assessment of 10s. 3¼d. in the pound.

Ecclesiastical Account.

The church, or rather chapel, is a small edifice, containing no article deserving historical notice. It is dedicated to St. David.

This benefice is a chapelry, the tithes of which are divided between the Bishop of St. David's and the incumbent. Percival Lewis, Esq., of Downton,

2 R

is the bishop's lessee. It is not in charge; it is annexed to the vicarage of Clâscwm, and stated in *Liber Regis* to be of the certified yearly value of £4 13s. 4d. Its present improved value amounts to the annual sum of £16 10s. 6d.

Charitable Donation.

There is now vested in Mr. Thomas Chambers a principal sum of money producing a yearly interest of 10s., bequeathed by a person unknown, in a year unknown, and whether by will or deed unknown, to be distributed among decayed housekeepers of this parish.

ADDITION TO THE ACCOUNT OF CASTLES.

The situation of Pain's Castle, and its connection with the adjoining ones, serve as a clue to unravel the policy and progress of the Norman conquerors. Radnor having previously been made a royal demesne by William the Conqueror, the project of opening a communication between it and the town of Brecknock, which had now fallen into the possession of Bernard de Newmarche, was adopted; and Paganus, or Payne, Ralph de Todeni, *i. e.*, Theodone, or Thionville, in the province of Luxemburg, and Ralph Baskerville, followers of the Norman sovereign of England, were commissioned to carry it into effect. Having taken possession of the adjacent territory, for its preservation and security, Paganus, or Payne, constructed a castle, in which he for some time resided, and at his death left it to his son Thomas. This Paganus was buried in the Cathedral Church of Gloucester, which had been endowed, if not built, by his companion and fellow-warrior, Bernard de Newmarche. The stone over his tomb has this inscription,—" Hic jacet Paganus de Cadurcis," that is, Here lieth Payne of Cahors, now Quercy, in the province of Guienne. This castle afterwards descended among the posterity of Bernard de Newmarche, and, by marriage with a granddaughter of that chieftain, came into the possession of William de Braos, Lord of Brecknock. In the year 1196 it was besieged and taken by Prince Rhys, who restored it to its former possessor. Two years subsequent to this transaction it sustained a second siege of three weeks by Gwenwynwyn, Prince of Powys, who, being himself besieged by a combined force of Normans and Welsh, was compelled to retreat with considerable loss. In 1215 Giles de Braos, a Bishop of Hereford, and a great warrior, who knew how to wield the temporal as well as the spiritual sword, bestowed this castle, together with its dependencies, on Walter

Fychan, the son of Eineon Clyd, the *regulus* of Elfael, from whom is descended the Vaughan family of Clyro.

Aberedw Castle was possessed by a descendant of the family of Baskerville, which came into England with William I., but whether it was constructed in that reign is a matter of uncertainty. In the reign of King Henry II., Sir Ralph Baskerville, of Aberedw, married Drogo, a daughter of Lord Clifford, of Clifford Castle. A violent dispute respecting some property arose between the father and son-in-law, of which the former rudely and unjustly dispossessed the latter. A challenge ensued, and they fought at a place near Hereford, where afterwards a white cross was erected, which stood till Queen Elizabeth's time, and then was pulled down by one Gernons. The event of the battle proved fatal to Lord Clifford, and Sir Ralph Baskerville purchased of the Pope a pardon for killing his father-in-law. Whoever casts his eye upon the map of this county cannot fail to discern the profound policy which directed the construction of this chain of castles. For whilst they secured a contact with Radnor and Huntington in the rear, and in front with Buallt, they completely dissected the district, separating the territory of Elfael from that of Moelynaidd; and, by commanding the adjacent country, preserved a communication with the castle of Hay, and with Brecknockshire.

The advantage that would result from fortifying the line of the river Ieithon with a chain of castles was too obvious to be neglected, even at an early period of the Norman invasion; and consequently, the fortresses of Moelynaidd, Cefn-y-llys, and Duybod, or Tibboedd, were constructed in succession. The fate of the former was various, and the possession of it long and violently contested, sometimes falling into the hands of the invaders, and sometimes into those of the defenders, of the country, till the year 1174, when Cadwallon ab Madoc, making strenuous efforts, succeeded in recovering this lordship and castle, the possession of which was further secured by his submission, and by his doing homage to Henry II. But Roger Mortimer, on whom that sovereign had bestowed this territory, on condition of conquering and garrisoning it with troops which should be at the command of the royal will, having assembled for this purpose a considerable and well-provided army, invaded this district in the year 1194, and after many and bloody battles fought with various success, at length dispossessed Cadwallon of all his lands in the cantref of Moelynaidd, and built and fortified the castle of Cwmavon, where he some time resided.

In the year 1262 Llewelyn ab Gruffudd, Prince of North Wales, with a chosen detachment of troops, surprized and took the castle of Cefnllys, made the governor prisoner, and put the greatest part of the garrison to the sword. It was retaken in the same year by Sir Roger Mortimer, at that time governor of Buallt, who repaired its fortifications, and appointed a garrison for its defence. In the time of Camden it was in a ruinated condition, and the property belonged to the Duke of York.

The castle of Old Radnor, or Pen-y-craig, was destroyed by Rhys ab Gruffudd in the reign of King John. The sieges and destruction of the castles of New Radnor, and Rhayader, have been already detailed.

The Welsh, as Lord Coke justly observes, were always valiant and loyal, and fought for their liege princes. In the bloody contests between the rival houses of York and Lancaster they were divided. Jasper, Earl of Pembroke, and Sir Owen Tudor, espoused the cause of Henry VI.; whilst this district remained attached to its Lord of Moelynaidd, who had been declared by Parliament, and was in reality, the rightful heir of the crown of England. Philip ab Howell, descended from the ancient *reguli* of this district, was at this time proprietor of the castle of Cnwclâs, within the lordship of Moelynaidd; and having offered his services to Richard, Duke of York, which were most graciously received, he carried on continual skirmishes with Roger Corbet, and others of distinction, in the county of Salop, partizans of King Henry, in which he was assisted by the powerful co-operation of Gruffudd ab Nicholas. For this they were both indicted and convicted of felony by justices assigned by the king; but it was found impracticable to apprehend them. In one of these skirmishes was killed at Brampton, on Palm Sunday, Brian, second son of Geoffrey de Harley, of Brampton Castle, in the county of Hereford. When Richard, Duke of York, received that fatal overthrow at the battle of Wakefield, his eldest son, the Earl of Marche and Lord of Moelynaidd, lay at Gloucester, who, having been apprized of his father's death, invited his friends in the Marches of Wales to assist and join him. He soon raised an army of 24,000 men, so much were the inhabitants of the Marches attached to the house and lineage of Mortimer. Among those that crowded to his standard, were Gruffudd ab Nicholas, and Philip ab Howell, followed by 1400 men well armed, of efficient strength, and resolute hearts. The Earl of Marche's plan was to overtake the Queen of King Henry, who was marching to London; but Jasper, Earl of Pembroke, with Sir Owen Tudor, stood as a barrier in his way. They met and fought at Mortimer's Cross, in Herefordshire. (A.D. 1461.) The Earl of Marche obtained a decisive victory, but with the loss of Gruffudd ab Nicholas, and several of his brave men.

APPENDIX.

No. I.

MINISTERS' ACCOUNTS, RADNORSHIRE, IN THE AUGMENTATION OFFICE.

Nuper Monasterium de Comhere infra Dioc' Menevensis.
33 Hen. 8.

Comhere	£ s. D.	£ s. D.
Terr' dominicales - - - - - -		0 10 0
Redd' Tenementi Gollen in tenura Hoell ap Dd Goʒ	0 3 4	
Redd. Ten. voc. Terr Jode - - - - -	0 3 6	
Redd. divers. Terr. &c voc. Esternavanche - -	0 10 0	
Redd. Ten. voc. Brine Rice - - - - -	0 2 0	
Redd. Ten. in Gollen - - - - - -	0 4 0	
Redd. j parcell. ten' infra precinct. Mon. - -	0 3 4	
Redd. Ten. voc. Castell pinnok - - - -	0 3 4	
Redd. Ten. in tenura Joh. ap Phillips - - -	0 5 0	
Redd. Ten. in tenura Hoell ap Price - - -	0 5 0	
Redd. Ten. voc. Byrvebryn - - - - -	0 3 4	
Redd. Ten. intenura Hoell ap Price - - -	0 5 0	
Redd. Ten. in tenura Jevan ap Bedo - - -	0 6 8	
Redd. Ten. voc Ikenen Ipaille - - - -	0 3 4	
Redd. Ten. voc. Paulle Kourbay - - - -	0 3 4	
Redd. Ten. voc. Dinan - - - - - -	0 6 8	
Redd. Ten. voc Borne havod Neweth - - -	0 5 0	
Redd. Ten. voc. Teddyngroftyf Kyon - - -	0 4 0	
Redd. Ten. voc. Igill nat - - - - -	0 6 8	
Redd. Ten. in tenura Dd ap powell ap Dd Lloyd -	0 8 8	
Redd. Ten. voc. Serpin Minor - - - -	0 6 8	
Redd. Ten. voc. Tyddyn Illoyd - - - -	0 3 4	
Redd. Ten. voc. Lechen Wethau - - - -	0 4 0	
Redd. Ten. voc. Cherchelleʒ - - - - -	0 3 4	
Redd. Ten. voc. Tythen Croft - - - -	0 5 0	
Redd. Ten. voc. Mays Inerth - - - -	0 6 8	
Redd. Ten. dimiss Gr. ap Bedo ap Phillippe - -	0 3 4	
Redd. Ten. voc Keven Ipaulle - - - -	0 5 4	
Redd. Ten. voc. Iquarre - - - - -	0 3 4	
Redd. Ten. voc. Tyther - - - - -	0 3 4	
Redd. Ten. voc. Dunhe - - - - -	0 5 0	
Redd. Ten. voc. Crofti parte - - - -	0 2 6	
Redd. Ten. voc. Henvais - - - - -	0 5 0	
Redd. Ten. voc. Condbedo - - - - -	0 3 4	
Redd. Ten. voc. Bewdy - - - - -	0 6 8	
Redd. Ten. voc. Vahigre - - - - -	0 6 8	

310 HISTORY OF RADNORSHIRE.

	£	s.	D.	£	s.	D.
Redd. Ten. voc. Natwrin - - - - -	0	3	4			
Redd. Ten. voc. Esterberwild - - - -	0	6	8			
Redd. Ten. voc. Henarth - - - - -	0	3	4			
Redd. Ten. voc. Limbet - - - - -	0	3	4			
Redd. Ten. voc. Lytle Idarde - - - -	0	2	0			
Redd. Ten. voc. Dolevichian - - - -	0	3	4			
Redd. Ten. voc. Kebeche - - - - -	0	5	8			
Redd. Ten. voc. Cyn'kynned - - - -	0	5	0			
Redd. Ten. voc. Ferth Icaillolym - - - -	0	4	0			
Redd. Molend. voc. Guellanissa - - - -	0	10	0			
Redd. Ten. in tenura Howell Goz Neweth - -	0	1	0			
Redd. Ten. in tenura Lln ap Jevan ap Duoy - -	0	2	0			
Redd. Ten. in man. Gr. ap Dd. - - - -	0	3	4			
Redd. Ten. dimiss. Rice ap Powell Goz - -	0	4	0			
Redd. Ten. in tenura Lewis ap Jevan Goz - -	0	5	4			
Redd. Ten. in man. Jevan ap Bedo ap powell -	0	3	4			
Redd. Ten. dimiss. Bedo ap Dd ap price - -	0	2	0			
Redd. Ten. in man. Dd Benlloid - - - -	0	3	0			
Redd. Ten. voc Gavangle Di - - - -	0	2	0			
Redd. Ten. voc. Ester - - - - -	0	5	0			
Redd. Ten. voc. Abrimawre - - - - -	0	3	4			
Redd. Ten. voc. Bataloid - - - - -	0	3	4			
Redd. Ten. voc. Kennenken - - - -	0	3	4			
Redd. Ten. voc. Dolo - - - - -	0	6	8			
Redd. Ten. voc. Dolth Lluyn - - - -	0	5	0			
Redd. Ten. voc. Saynt Welthian - - - -	0	5	4			
Redd. Ten. voc. Hew Loyvaine - - - -	0	2	0			
Redd. Ten. voc. Brono Denet - - - -	0	5	0			
Redd. Ten. voc. Laneherweith - - - -	0	4	0			
Redd. Ten. voc. Tringor - - - - -	0	5	4			
Redd. Ten. in tenura Rice ap Madock - - -	0	5	0			
Redd. unius Molendini - - - - -	1	0	0			
Redd. Ten. in tenura Owell Bedo ap Lloyd - -	0	3	4			
Redd. Ten. in man. Thome ap price ap Dyo - -	0	1	0			
Redd. Ten. in tenura Rice ap phillippe Meredd -	0	1	0			
Redd. Ten. in tenura Jevan ap Dd ap Powell -	0	1	0			
Redd. Ten. in man. Rice ap Price - - -	0	3	4			
Redd. Ten. in tenura Jenkyn Bydo - - -	0	4	0			
Redd. Ten. in tenura Rice ap Bido ap powell ap phillippe - - - - - - -	0	2	4			
Redd. Ten. voc. Bloyth Wyne - - - -	0	1	0			
Redd. 28. Bussell. de Ottemele prec. le Buss 8ᵈ -	0	18	8			
Summa				18	3	4

Tempseter.

	£	s.	D.
Redd. Ten. voc. Gavell - - - - -	0	10	0
Redd. Ten. voc. Hulgarth - - - - -	0	2	2
Redd. Ten. voc. Iwerde Nowed - - - -	0	5	0
Redd. Ten. voc. Irydwillinge - - - -	0	3	4
Redd. Ten. in Tempseter predict. - - - -	0	2	4
Redd. Ten. voc. Gwyr Iwellen - - - -	0	6	8
Redd. Prat. voc. Ewaglod Day - - - -	0	6	0
Redd. parcell. Ters. dimiss. Lewis ap Dd - -	0	2	2
Redd. Ten. in tenura Howell ap Gr. - - -	0	5	0

APPENDIX.

	£	s.	D.	£	s.	D.
Redd. 3 parcell. terr. in Scovore - - - -	0	13	4			
Redd. Ten. voc. Machnady - - - - -	0	6	0			
Redd. Terr. voc. Mascadolor Monaks - - -	0	5	0			
Redd. Ten. voc. Dole Igillin - - - -	0	6	8			
Redd. Ten. in tenura Hoell ap Dd ap Merike -	0	5	0			
Summa				3	18	8
Grangia de Carnaff						
Redd. nuncupat. Carnaff in parochia de Clero -	1	0	0			
Redd. unius parcell. Terr. & dimid. Gavell infra } Grangiam - - - - - - - -}	0	5	0			
Redd. Prati vocat. Swengloith - - - -	0	2	0			
Summa				1	7	0
Cumbige Arestlye						
Redd. Ten. voc. Buga jacen. inter rivulum voc. Lloyd } & rivulum voc. Bugin - - - - -}	0	6	8			
Redd. Ten. in tenura Lln. Dd ap Jevan Lloyd -	0	6	8			
Summa				0	13	4
Grangia de Gavalva						
Redd. Ten. & Molend. voc. Inis y Gavalva Pull } Imerley - - - - - - - -}	1	6	8			
Redd. Terr. &c. voc Lloyd de Ve Dd - - -	0	4	8			
Redd. unius Domus voc. Graunge House - -	0	10	0			
Redd. Ten. voc. Kaynewood Vayre y eyke - -	0	2	0			
Redd. Terr. Anabil. dimiss. Jenkyn ap Jevan ap } Meredd - - - - - - - -}	0	6	0			
Redd. Ten. voc. Pene Iwerne - - - -	0	5	0			
Redd. Terr. voc. Bronne Llioyrche - - -	0	3	0			
Summa				2	17	4
Breleu in Dominio de Huntingdon						
Redd. Terr & Bosc. in Lloyen Jane - - -	0	2	7			
Redd. divers. terr. in Huntingdon - - -	0	7	0			
Redd. ten. in man' Margerie relict. Dd ap Dd -	0	4	4			
Redd. Ten. dim. p. Rice Goz Taylor - - -	0	4	4			
Redd. Ten. voc. Llete Irmedowe - - - -	0	5	2			
Redd. 30 acr. terr. arab. voc. Kay croys - ' -	0	4	2			
Redd. Ten. voc. Calken - - - - -	0	1	4			
Redd. Terr. voc. Ewellen - - - - -	0	1	4			
Redd. Ten. voc. Benbrill - - - - -	0	1	8			
Redd. Ten. in man. Thome ap Dd - - -	0	1	8			
Redd. Ten. in tenura Lewys ap Jevan Dd ap powell	0	1	0			
Redd. Ten. voc. Baldmard - - - - -	0	3	10			
Summa				1	18	5
Grangia sive Manerium de Manachte Poeth in Melenith						
Redd. Grangie sive Maner' &c - - - - -				1	6	8
Grangia de Gwernogo						
Redd. Grangie in dominio de Key Kerry - - -				8	6	8
Grangia de Nantarian.						
Redd. Grangie - - - - - - - -				1	6	8

No. II.

COMITATUS RADENORE ET BRECKNOCK.

COMPOTA omnium et singulorum dominiorum maneriorum terrarum tenementorum ac aliarum possessionum quarumcunq' tam temporalium quam spiritualium omnibus et singulis nuper Monasterijs Abbathijs sive prioratibus in Comitatibus predictis pertinentium sive spectantium que ad manus Domini Regis nunc devenerunt ac in manibus suis jam existunt et annexantur Corone sue heredum sive successorum suorum Regum Anglie in augmentacione Revencionum ejusdem Corone Anglie virtute cujusdam Actus in parliamento suo tento apud Westmonasterium super prorogationem quarto die Februarij anno regni ipsius Domini Regis 27mo inde edito et proviso prout in eodem Actu inter alia continetur vizt a festo Sancti Michaelis Archangeli anno regni Henrici octavi Dei gratia Anglie Francie et Hibernie Regis fidei defensoris et in terra Anglicane et Hibernice Ecclesie supremi Capitis 37° usque idem festum Sancti Michaelis extunc proximum sequens anno regni ejusdem Domini Regis 38° scilicet per unum annum integrum

COMEHIER nuper Monasterium in Comitatu Radnor predicta authoritate parliamenti suppressum

COMPOTUS Johannis Williams Militis Assignati Willielmi Turner defuncti Firmarij omnium possessionum dicto nuper Monasterio pertinencium vizt per tempus predictum

FIRMA TERRARUM DOMINICALIUM cum omnibus alijs possessionibus dicto nuper Monasterio pertinentibus

Et de £40 18 3 de firma Scitus ejusdem nuper Monasterij cum terris dominicalibus 10s. Redditibus & firmis in villa de Gollen £18 3 4 Heriettis Relevijs & alijs perquisitis Curiarum ibidem communibus annis 23s. 6d. Redditibus in villa de Tempseter in Comitatu Mongomerie 78s. 8d. Grangia de Carnaf in Comitatu Radnor ac in parochia de   27s. Redditu et Firma Grangie de Gabalw in Comitatu Radnor predicta 57s. 4d. Redditibus et Firmis in villa de Breylyn in eodem Comitatu 38s. 5d. Redditu Grangie de Manawghtie poeth in Dominio de Melenyth 26s. 8d. Grangia de Gwyrnogo in parochia de Llanehangell in Kyrrey in Comitatu Mongomerie £8 6 8 Grangia de Nantararion in parochia de Llanbadern Vaur in Comitatu Cardigan 26s. 8d. Que omnia et singula premissa superius expressa & speoificata nuper fuerunt in manibus Johannis Turner Generosi et modo dimissa Johanni Williams Militi per Indenturam sub sigillo Domini Regis Curie augmentationum Revencionum Corone sue datam apud Westmonasterium 4° die Novembris anno regni Regis Henrici octavi 30mo. Habendum sibi et assignatis suis a festo Sancti Michaelis Archangeli ultimo preterito usque ad finem termini 21us annorum tunc proximo sequente & plenarie complendorum Reddendo inde annuatim ac solvendo ad festa annunciationis beate Marie Virginis et Sancti Michaelis Archangeli vel infra unum mensem post utrumque festum festorum illorum per equales portiones Et predictus Dominus Rex vult et per presentes concedit quod ipse heredes et successores sui dictum Johannem et assignatos suos de omnibus redditibus feodis annuitatibus et denariorum summis quibuscumque de premissis seu eorum aliquo exeuntibus seu solvendis preterquam de redditibus superius reservatis versus quascunque personas de tempore in tempus exonerabunt acquietabunt et defendent Ac omnia domos et edificia premissorum que sunt infra et prope Scitum dicti nuper Monasterij tam in Maeremio quam in Coopertura Tegula & Sclate de tempore in tempus tociens quociens necessarie et oportunum fuerit bene et sufficienter reparabunt sustentabunt et manutenere facient durante termino predicto Et predictus Johannes concedit per presentes quod ipse et assignati sui cooperturam straminis ac omnes alias necessarias reparationes premissorum preter reparationes maeremij et cooperture tegule et sclate predicte de tempore in tempus supportabunt et sustentabunt durante termino predicto Et dictus Dominus Rex ulterius vult et per presentes concedit quod bene licebit prefato Johanni et assignatis suis capere percipere et habere de in et super premissis competentem et sufficientem hedgeboote fireboote ploughboote & carteboote ibidem et non alibi annuatim expendendum et occupandum durante termino predicto de 16d. de annuali Decima Domino Regi reservata de redditibus et firmis in Cumbiga Arnscle annui valoris 13s. 4d. concessis per literas Domini Regis patentes Ricardo Andrewes et Nicholao Temple et eorum assignatis imperpetuum minime hic respondet Eo quod oneratur in Compoto Georgij Wall Receptoris in titulo annualis Decime prout ibidem patet

Summa £40 18 3

Summa Oneris cum Arreragijs £250 11 6 de quibus allocatur ei £6 ut pro tantis denarijs per ipsum Computantem expendis in necessarijs Reparationibus factis et appositis in et super firmam predictam vizt in Maeremio Tegula et Sclate in annis 34to 35to & 36to Regis Henrici octavi prout testatur coram Auditore super hunc Compotum sine Billa inde ostensa Et eidm' £4 pro denarijs per ipsum petitis pro feodo Johannis Egerley Clerici Curie omnium possessionum predictorum percipiente 20s. per annum sic per ipsum Computantem admissis ob defectum Senescalli ibidem vizt tam pro anno 36° Regis Henrici octavi q$\bar{m}$ p iij$^{b{\iota}}$ annis p$\bar{x}$ precedentibus quolibet anno ut supra Et eidem 26s. 8d. pro annuali redditu soluto Jacobo Vaughan ad 26s. 8d. per annum sic sibi concessos sub Sigillo Curie Augmentationum Revencionum Corone Regie data 20mo die Junij anno regni ejusdem Domini Regis 37° Habendum sibi et heredibus suis imperpetuum prout per Decretum dicte Curie lacius patet viz in allocatione hujusmodi hoc anno ultra £12 inferius in titulo exonerati arreragiar' virtute ejusdem decreti exoneratos ut supra Et eidem £16 13 pro terris et possessionibus pro Johannem Williams Militem perquisitis ad £11 2 per annum vizt pro toto domo et scitu nuper Monasterij de Comehire predicta cum omnibus Mesuagijs Domibus Edificijs Orreis Stabulis Columbarijs Ortis Pomarijs Gardinis Stagnis Vivarijs terris et solum infra Scitum Septum Ambitum Procinctum et Circuitum ejusdem nuper Monasterij cum terris dominicalibus ibidem 10s. necnon omnibus illis octodecim Modijs ferine Avenarum provenientium et annuatim solvendorum per Tenentem Grangie de Gollen 18s. 8d. necnon Grangie de Manawghty poeth 26s. 8d. et Grangie de Gwyrnogo cum omnibus suis pertinentijs universis £8 6 8 Que omnia et singula premissa superius expressa et specificata Dominus noster Rex Henricus octavus Dei gratia Anglie Francie et Hibernie Rex fidei defensor et in terra Ecclesie Anglicane et Hibernie supremum Caput per literas suas patentes sub magno sigillo suo Anglie datas apud Portesmoth 28° die Julij anno regni sui 37° dedit et concessit prefato Johanni Williams et Waltero Hendley heredibus et assignatis suis imperpetuum Tenendum predictum Scitum dicti nuper Monasterij de Comehyre ac cetera premissa de nobis heredibus et successoribus nostris in capite per servicium quadragesime partis unius feodi militis Ac Reddendum annuatim nobis heredibus et successoribus nostris de et pro predicto Scitu et ceteris premissis 2$\frac{1}{2}$d. ad Curiam augmentac' Revencionum Corone nostre ad festum Sancti Michaelis Archangeli singulis annis solvendos pro omnibus redditibus servicijs et demandis quibuscumque proinde nobis heredibus vel successoribus nostris quoquomodo reddendis solvendis vel faciendis Que quidem Decima oneratur in Compoto Receptoris in titulo annualis Decime infra Summam 44s. 5d. prout ibidem patet Et sic in oneratione hujusmodi virtute literarum patentium predictarum vizt pro uno anno & dimidio finiente ad festum Sancti Michaelis Archangeli infra tempus hujus Compoti accidentem

No. III.

CHARLES by the Grace of God of England Scotland ffrance and Ireland King defender of the ffaith and soforth To all to Whom these present Letters shall Come Greeting Whereas the Tenants of the Manors Lordships Castles Seigniories Burroughs Forests Bailiwics Lands Tenements and hereditaments Called Gladestry Colva Presteign Melenith, Knucklas, Southruraeth, Southugre, Southnethian, Knighton, Gwerthrinian, Ryslin, Uchvid Yschard, Rayder, and Comtoyrer in our County of Radnor and in the same situate which we have lately granted and aliened to Charles Harbord Williams Scrivener and Phillip Eden and their heirs, who together with others (to whom the said Premises) have been assigned by our Grant or of our late Father for our use, for a term of years not yet expired, Have granted the same Premises to (Certain others Particularly to) George Whitmore and William Whitmore, Have brought and given to us of their own free will £741 12 0. of lawful Money of England That we might reassume the same for a royal Patrimony That they themselves might continue Tenants of the Kings of England like as they had been heretofore And for the said sum the same William Whitmore and George Whitmore Have granted the said Lordships Manors Castles and other the Premises to us our heirs and successors and we have required the same from them Know Ye that we graciously accepting the Love and good will of our Tenants aforesaid, of our own special Favor, and by our Certain knowledge, and mere Motion, Have granted to our said tenants, and to each of them, and their heirs, and assigns, All the rights and ancient Customs authorities Liberties and their privilidges in the premises, like as they have held them hitherto well and freely, and we have granted with the said Tenants, and each of them, and their heirs, for ourselves, our heirs, and successors, That they themselves from henceforth may hold the Lands, Tenements, and hereditaments, which are held by us, As touching the Lordships Manors Castles and other the Premises, or touching each of them under us our heirs and successors, for the same rents Customs and services as the same have been heretofore respectively held, altering nothing in future Intending that the said Lordships Castles and other the Premises or any one of them may not be transferred from the Crown of England or aliened or seperated from the same This only excepted that the said Premises may be given or granted by us our heirs and Successors, to our eldest Sons our heirs and Successors and their heirs being Kings of England or to our or their Consort for the time being, Forasmuch as express mention Concerning the yearly real Value in nowise appears made in these Presents either touching the assurance of the said Premises, or any one of them, or touching other Gifts or Grants made by us or by any one of our Progenitors or Predecessors to the said Tenants before this time, Or in any statute act Ordinance Promise Proclamation or Restriction to the Contrary from thenceforth before this had made published ordained or provided or by any other thing cause or matter whatsoever in any wise notwithstanding In witness whereof we have Caused these our Letters to be made patent myself being a witness at Canterbury the sixteenth Day of August in the ninth Year of our reign

WOLSELEY.

P breve De privato Sigillo.

EDITOR'S NOTE.

WE have now completed our task of editing and publishing the "History of Radnorshire," by the late Rev. Jonathan Williams, M.A. In so doing we have adhered to the rule, which we proposed to ourselves at first, of treating his MS. with the scrupulous care and respect that should be shown to the work of a deceased friend, omitting portions irrelevant to the subject, or now of no value from subsequent discoveries, but otherwise giving the text of the MS. just as we found it. This work was not finished by its author—the MS. is full of blanks—and it would have probably received a careful revision from him had his life been prolonged.

As it now stands, it forms a valuable basis of inquiry for future antiquaries; it records the existence of earthworks and other monuments, many of which may, since his time, have disappeared; and the notices of families, houses, churches and charities which it contains, cannot fail to be duly appreciated by our Radnorshire members.

We must express the hope that the examination and illustration of the several classes of antiquities in that county—one of the great fighting-grounds of Wales in early times—will be carried on systematically and energetically, with all the advantages to be derived from the improved condition of archæological science.

ALPHABETICAL INDEX OF CONTENTS.

Abbey Cwmhir, 56, 75, 229, 230, 243.
Aberedw, 34, 285.
Aberedw Castle, 64, 307.
Ariconium, 42, 47, 57.
Arrow River, 40, 55, 111, 218, 226, 290.

Bailiffs of New Radnor, 128.
Barrows, 31, 117, 134, 199, 211, 215, 227, 236, 238, 282, 285, 291, 302.
Battle of Pilleth, 281.
Bedd Garmon, 239.
Bedd y Gre, 199.
Bettws Clyro, 209.
Bettws Diserth, 289.
Birch Forests, 17.
Blaiddfà, 261.
Bloody Field, 40.
Bolitre, 45, 47.
Boughrood, 209.
Boughrhyd Castle, 63.
Braos, William de, 77, 117, 119, 155, 207.
Brilley Mountain, 55, 227.
British Camps, 37, 51, 179, 246, 295, 299.
Broken Cross, 147.
Bryngwin, 217.
Bryn-llwyd, 302.
Brynllys Castle, 291.
Bryn-y-Castell, 179.
Bugaildu, 39, 162.
Bwgey Brook, 256.
Bwlch-y-llys, 245.

Caer Caradoc, 41, 53, 165, 179, 204.
Caer-du, 295.
Cairn, 68, 200, 238, 245, 298.
Cantrefs, 30.
Capel Madoc, 236.
Caractacus, 36, 53, 165, 179.
Carnau, 31.
Carnwen, 245.
Cascob, 14, 104, 106.
Castell Ffaled, 282.
Castell-y-Blaidd, 186.
Castles, 61, 306.
Cefn-y-llys Castle, 65, 75, 307.

Cefn-y-llys Hundred, 260.
Cefn-y-llys Parish, 65, 264.
Cethin, Ellen, 193.
Cilleg Cadwgan, 300.
Civil History, 69.
Clasbury, 211.
Clascwm, 40, 289.
Clàs-gwyr, 41.
Clatterbrook, 104, 146.
Clyro, 214.
Cnwclas Castle and Borough, 41, 65, 75, 164.
Cock-fighting, 152.
Colfa, 110.
Colwyn Castle, 63, 285, 302.
Colwyn Hundred, 284.
Comitatus Radenore et Brecknock, 312.
Council and President of the Marches, 72.
Coxall Knoll, 37, 39, 180.
Craig Dunon, 182.
Croes-Cynon, 194.
Croes-y-Noddfa, 68.
Crown Lands, 90, 102, 149, 237.
Crughallt, 189.
Crugina, 293.
Crug-y-Buddair, 39, 40.
Cwmaron Castle, 66, 196, 198, 270.
Cwmddauddwr, 234.
Cwystudin, 244.

Dedication, 7.
Devereux, Walter, 154.
Discoed, 115.
Diserth, 51, 294.
Domesday Book, extracts from, 104, 134, 144, 204, 281.
Druids, 18, 21, 27.
Dynbod Castle, 66, 115, 189, 307.

Earls of Radnor, 78.
Earthworks, 36, 41, 117, 196, 203, 215, 221, 275.

Farrington, 178.
Ferrars, 115.
Ffer-llys, 28, 50, 140.
Forests, 17, 101.

ALPHABETICAL INDEX OF CONTENTS.

Gaer, 38, 49, 54, 199.
Gladestry, 112.
Graig-fawr, 292.
Grant of Charles I., 314.
Grè, 32, 199.
Gwar-y-beddau, 245.

Helygen, 241.
Hezetre Hundred, 104, 105, 144.
Hu Gadarn, 23.
Humphrey de Bohun, 78.
Hundreds, 30, 85, 104.

Introductory Notice, 1.

Joan Du, 164.

King's Turning, 148.
Knighton Castle, 64, 173.
Knighton Borough, 99, 171.
Knighton Hundred, 161.

Lantardine Hundred, 104.
Litton, 108.
Llanandras, 144.
Llanano, 66, 189.
Llanbadarn-fawr, 56, 268.
Llanbadarn Fynydd, 185.
Llanbadarn-y-Garreg, 295.
Llanbedr, 40, 219.
Llanbister, 192.
Llanddewi-Fach, 220.
Llanddewi-ystrad-Ennau, 32, 38, 54, 195.
Llandegla, 269.
Llandeilo Graban, 221.
Llanelwedd, 296.
Llanfair Llethonow, 112.
Llanfared, 301.
Llanflhangel-Fach, 241.
Llanflhangel-nant-Melin, 32, 115.
Llanflhangel-rhyd-Ieithon, 279.
Llangunllo, 274.
Llanhir, 242,
Llansantfraid, 33, 234, 301.
Llanstephan, 222.
Llan-y-drindod, 31, 33, 51, 271.
Llechrhyd, 52, 298.
Llechrhyd Battle, 298.
Llowes, 223.
Llwyn-Madoc, 303, 304.
Llys-Ifor, 215.
Llys-sin, 280.
Lord-Lieutenants, 115.
Lords Marchers, 30, 61, 69.
Lug River, 13, 34, 275.

Magna Castra, 42, 57.
Manors, 100.
Market Towns, 85.

Maud's Castle, 63, 304.
Members for New Radnor, 130.
Members for the County, 82, 83.
Michaelchurch, 40, 226.
Ministers' Accounts in the Augmentation Office, 309.
Moelynaidd, Cantref of, 87.
Moelynaidd Castle, 66, 307.
Moelynaidd, Lords of, 65, 75, 175, 229, 265.
Monachlog, 230.
Monachtu, 166.
Monach-ty, 261.
Mortimers, 65, 75, 105, 122, 146, 165, 174, 197, 261, 265, 282, 308.
Mortimer's Cross, Battle of, 308.
Mynach Ty, 277.

Nant Castell Gwytherin, 68.
Nantmel, 243.
Newcastle Camp, 38.
Newchurch, 226.
Newmarche, Gilbert de, 100.

Offa's Dyke, 12, 30, 58, 182.
Old Radnor, 48, 138.
Owen Glyndwrdwy, 122, 249, 281.

Pain's Castle, 63, 207, 219, 306.
Pain's Castle Hundred, 206.
Pain's Castle Township, 219.
Parishes, 30, 85, 106, 208, 260.
Payne, Family of, 63, 207, 219, 306.
Pencastle Camp, 40.
Pencraig, 61, 142, 308.
Penybont, 268.
Pilleth, 76, 105, 276, 281.
Population, 86, 108, 272.
Portway, 217.
Preface, 8.
Presteigne, 144.
Prospectus (original one), 4.

Radnor, Earls of, 78.
Radnor Forest, 102.
Radnor Hundred, 106.
Radnor, New, 83, 99, 119.
Radnor, New, Castle, 62, 120.
Radnor, Old, 138, 308.
Radnorshire, Situation, Boundaries and Extent, 11; Name and Etymology, 15; Primitive Inhabitants, 20; Ancient Divisions, 28; Cromlechau, &c., 31; Fortifications and Encampments, 36; Roman Stations and Roads, 41; Offa's Dyke, 58; Castles, 61; Civil History, 69; Titles of Honour, 75; Divisions, 85; Manors, 100; Parochial Antiquities, 106; Appendix, 309.
Rhayader Castle, 67, 251.

Rhayader Hundred, 228.
Rhayader Town, 34, 247.
Rhiwy, 116.
Rhys ab Gruffudd, 259.
Roman Camps, 37, 51, 291.
Roman Stations and Roads, 41, 48, 179, 216, 217, 223, 227, 241, 268, 291.
Rosehill, 45, 47.
Rulen, or Rhiwlyn, 305.

Sheriffs of Radnorshire, 79.
Silures, 20, 26, 31, 36, 117, 196.
Stanage, 39, 104, 202.
Stapleton Castle, 146.

St. Harmon, 237.

Teame, River, 12, 34, 165.
Tibboeth Castle, 66, 190, 307.
Tommenau, 32.
Trewern, 116.
Tumuli, 31, 117, 134, 199, 211, 215, 227, 236, 238, 282, 285, 291, 302.
Ty-yn-y-bwlch, 191.

Wakes, 119, 280.
War-clos Battle, 134.
Whitton, 284.
Wye, River, 12, 55, 60, 64, 214.

LIST OF ILLUSTRATIONS.

Mynachty House	*Frontispiece*
Arms of the Borough of New Radnor	31
Town and Castle of New Radnor	119
Seal Found at Radnor	122
Chancel Screen	135
Coffin Lids, New Radnor Church	136
Arms at Mynachty and Pilleth	262